SCRIPTURAL TRACES: CRITICAL PERSPECTIVES ON
THE RECEPTION AND INFLUENCE OF THE BIBLE

24

Editors
Claudia V. Camp, Texas Christian University
Matthew A. Collins, University of Chester
Andrew Mein, Durham University

Editorial Board
Michael J. Gilmour, David Gunn, James Harding, Jorunn Økland

Published under

LIBRARY OF HEBREW BIBLE/
OLD TESTAMENT STUDIES

693

Formerly Journal for the Study of the Old Testament Supplement Series

Editors
Claudia V. Camp, Texas Christian University
Andrew Mein, Durham University

Founding Editors
David J. A. Clines, Philip R. Davies and David M. Gunn

Editorial Board
Alan Cooper, Susan Gillingham, John Goldingay,
Norman K. Gottwald, James E. Harding, John Jarick, Carol Meyers,
Daniel L. Smith-Christopher, Francesca Stavrakopoulou, James W. Watts

SEARCHING FOR SARAH IN THE SECOND TEMPLE ERA

Images in the Hebrew Bible, the Septuagint, the Genesis Apocryphon, and the *Antiquities*

Joseph McDonald

LONDON • NEW YORK • OXFORD • NEW DELHI • SYDNEY

T&T CLARK
Bloomsbury Publishing Plc
50 Bedford Square, London, WC1B 3DP, UK
1385 Broadway, New York, NY 10018, USA
29 Earlsfort Terrace, Dublin 2, Ireland

BLOOMSBURY, T&T CLARK and the T&T Clark logo
are trademarks of Bloomsbury Publishing Plc

First published in Great Britain 2020
This paperback edition published in 2021

© Joseph McDonald, 2020

Joseph McDonald has asserted his right under the Copyright, Designs and Patents Act, 1988, to be identified as the Author of this work.

Cover design: Charlotte James
Cover image ©: MS. Douce 211, fol. 23r, 'The Bodleian Libraries, The University of Oxford'

All rights reserved. No part of this publication may be reproduced or transmitted in any form or by any means, electronic or mechanical, including photocopying, recording, or any information storage or retrieval system, without prior permission in writing from the publishers.

Bloomsbury Publishing Plc does not have any control over, or responsibility for, any third-party websites referred to or in this book. All internet addresses given in this book were correct at the time of going to press. The author and publisher regret any inconvenience caused if addresses have changed or sites have ceased to exist, but can accept no responsibility for any such changes.

A catalogue record for this book is available from the British Library.
A catalog record for this book is available from the Library of Congress.

ISBN: HB: 978-0-5676-8912-2
       PB: 978-0-5677-0379-8
       ePDF: 978-0-5676-8913-9

Series: Library of Hebrew Bible/Old Testament Studies, ISSN 2513-8758, volume 693
Scriptural Traces, volume 24

Typeset by: Forthcoming Publications Ltd

To find out more about our authors and books visit www.bloomsbury.com and sign up for our newsletters.

Contents

Acknowledgments	ix
Permission Acknowledgments	xi
Abbreviations	xiii

Chapter 1
INTRODUCTION, STUDIES OF SARAH, AND ASPECTS OF MY APPROACH	1
Studies of Sarah in the Bible and Beyond	6
Aspects of My Approach	13

Chapter 2
SARAH IN THE MASORETIC TEXT	32
Introduction	32
To Have and to Have Not: Origins, Family, Power, Possessions, and People (Gen. 11:26–12:9)	35
Egyptian Traffic (Gen. 12:10–13:2)	40
Silence, but Reflected Light (Gen. 13:2–15:21)	46
Sarai, Hagar, Abram—and a Son (Gen. 16:1-16)	51
Years of Silence, More Promises—and a New Name? (Gen. 17:1-27)	60
Sarah Chortles (Gen. 18:1-15)	63
Destructive Interlude (Gen. 18:16–19:38)	71
"Asylum" Redux in Gerar (Gen. 20:1-18)	71
The Arrival of Isaac, and the Departure of Hagar, Ishmael— and Sarah (Gen. 21:1-14)	76
"The Life of Sarah" (Gen. 23:1-20)	82
Conclusion: Sarah in the MT	84

Chapter 3
SARRA IN THE SEPTUAGINT	88
Introduction	88
Sara, Muted (Gen. 11:26–12:9 LXX)	93
Passive and "Pretty-Faced" in Egypt (Gen. 12:10–13:2 LXX)	97
Silence and Stress (Gen. 13:2–15:21 LXX)	103

vi Contents

Broken Inertia, Blurred Gender, and Misused Agency
   (Gen. 16:1-16 LXX)   104
Different Name, Different Prospects? (Gen. 17:1-27 LXX)   116
Volition and Restriction (Gen. 18:1-15 LXX)   117
More Imitative Agency—and Questions of Consistency
   (Gen. 20:1-18 LXX)   125
Who Will "Rejoice with" Sarra? (Gen. 21:1-14 LXX)   129
The Death of Sarra (Gen. 23:1-20 LXX)   133
Conclusion: Sarra in the LXX   134

Chapter 4
SARAI IN THE GENESIS APOCRYPHON   139
Introduction   139
A Fragmentary Beginning (GenAp 19.7-10)   142
Famine and Entry into Egypt (GenAp 19.10-13)   144
Abram's Dream (GenAp 19.14-23)   145
Abram and Sarai's Three Visitors (GenAp 19.23-31)   159
In Praise of Sarai (GenAp 20.2-8)   164
Sarai Uprooted, Abram Spared (GenAp 20.8-11)   171
Abram's Prayer (GenAp 20.12-16)   174
Response to Abram's Prayer (GenAp 20.16-21)   176
Herqanosh's Errand, and the Revelation of the Truth
   (GenAp 20.21-23)   178
Report and Rebuke; Healing, Payment, and Return to the Land
   (GenAp 20.24–21.4)   179
Conclusion: Sarai in the Genesis Apocryphon   182

Chapter 5
SARRA IN THE *JEWISH ANTIQUITIES*   186
Introduction   186
Beginnings (*Ant.* 1.148-160)   189
Egypt (*Ant.* 1.161-168)   193
Separation and War (*Ant.* 1.169-182)   200
Child and Sacrifice (*Ant.* 1.183-185)   201
Sarra, Hagar, Abraham, and Ishmael (*Ant.* 1.186-190)   201
Another Child, and Circumcision (*Ant.* 1.191-193)   208
Angelic Visitation (*Ant.* 1.194-206)   209
"Just Like Before"—but Now in Gerar (*Ant.* 1.207-212)   213
Birth and Banishment (*Ant.* 1.213-221)   219
Isaac's sacrifice (*Ant.* 1.222-236)   228
Sarra's Death (*Ant.* 1.237)   232
Conclusion: Sarra in the *Antiquities*   233

Chapter 6
CONCLUSIONS, CONTRIBUTIONS, AND PROSPECTS 240
    Sarah in the Hebrew Bible, the Septuagint,
        the Genesis Apocryphon, and the *Antiquities* 240
    Some Contributions and Prospects of This Study 247

Bibliography 250
Index of References 261
Index of Authors 270

Acknowledgments

Any lengthy study is a collaboration. What merits this one has, others helped me craft, and it is a pleasure to acknowledge their contributions here. What weaknesses remain are my responsibility alone.

I am happily indebted, first, to Warren Carter, a very fine scholar and reader whose insights helped to shape this project from its earliest stages. More importantly, he is a good, just, and genuine person who has been, in good times and in bad, a teacher, mentor, and friend in the truest senses of those words. He has my affectionate and most sincere appreciation. The life and work of Toni Craven, an אשת חיל who has broken many boundaries in her time, continue to exert a pervasive influence on my approaches to the Bible and related literature. Ariel Feldman, the best kind of friend and scholarly partner, smart, gentle, and genuine, deserves special mention not only for his acumen and erudition, but also for first exposing me to rewritten scriptural compositions. Without the interest, encouragement, and patience of Claudia Camp, this book would likely still be languishing somewhere between thought and page. Of my many other teachers and colleagues, I have space only to name Leo Perdue—may he rest, at last, in peace. My friends at the Graduate Theological Union, Brite Divinity School, and Texas Christian University, too many to mention here, know that they too merit, and have, my gratitude.

Not least, I recognize the contributions of my entire family, particularly my parents, Gerry and Pat; my father-in-law, Bill; my sisters, Rose, Trisha, and Laura; my sister-in-law, Laura; and my splendid children, Fiona and Dylan. In a special way, too, I honor here my mother-in-law, Paula O. Hughes, of blessed memory, who died as I wrote this study.

But I dedicate this work to my wife, Caroline. It is a well-worn scholarly custom to append an apt, learned citation to a dedication to one's spouse. However, conventions are only trite in the absence of real feeling, and in this case, the sentiment is keenly felt (and absent any of the cautions I express in my discussion of this passage in Chapter 4!):

ועם כול שפרא דן חכמא שגיא עמהא

Along with all this beauty, much wisdom is hers.

(Genesis Apocryphon 20.7)

Permission Acknowledgments

Daniel A. Machiela, *The Dead Sea Genesis Apocryphon: A New Text and Translation with Introduction and Special Treatment of Columns 13–17.* STDJ 79. Leiden: Brill, 2009. Reprinted by permission of the copyright holders, Koninklijke Brill N.V.

Louis H. Feldman, *Flavius Josephus: Translation and Commentary, Vol. 3, Judean Antiquities 1–4.* Edited by Steve Mason. FJTC 3. Leiden: Brill, 2000. Reprinted by permission of the copyright holders, Koninklijke Brill N.V.

Quotations marked NETS are taken from *A New English Translation of the Septuagint*, ©2007 by the International Organization for Septuagint and Cognate Studies, Inc. Used by permission of Oxford University Press. All rights reserved.

Revised Standard Version of the Bible, copyright 1952 [2nd edition, 1971] by the Division of Christian Education of the National Council of the Churches of Christ in the United States of America. Used by permission. All rights reserved.

Abbreviations

AB	Anchor Bible
ABR	*Australian Biblical Review*
Abr.	*On the Life of Abraham* (Philo)
Ant.	*Jewish Antiquities* (Josephus)
AS	*Aramaic Studies*
ATTM	Beyer, Klaus. *Die aramäischen Texte vom Toten Meer samt den Inschriften aus Palästina, dem Testament Levis aus der Kairoer Genisa, der Fastenrolle und den alten talmudischen Zitaten.* Göttingen: Vandenhoeck & Ruprecht, 1984
BDAG	Danker, Frederick W., Walter Bauer, William F. Arndt, and F. Wilbur Gingrich. *A Greek–English Lexicon of the New Testament and Other Early Christian Literature.* 3rd ed. Chicago: University of Chicago Press, 2000
BDB	Brown, Francis, S. R. Driver, and Charles A. Briggs. *A Hebrew and English Lexicon of the Old Testament*
BHS	*Biblia Hebraica Stuttgartensia.* Edited by Karl Elliger and Wilhelm Rudolph. Stuttgart: Deutsche Bibelgesellschaft, 1983
BIOSCS	*Bulletin of the International Organization for Septuagint and Cognate Studies*
BJS	Brown Judaic Studies
BLS	Bible and Literature Series
BRLJ	Brill Reference Library of Judaism
BZAW	Beihefte zur Zeitschrift für die alttestamentliche Wissenschaft
CahRB	Cahiers de la Revue biblique
DCH	*Dictionary of Classical Hebrew.* Edited by David J. A. Clines. 9 vols. Sheffield: Sheffield Phoenix Press, 1993–2014
DJD	Discoveries in the Judaean Desert
DJPA	Sokoloff, Michael. *A Dictionary of Jewish Palestinian Aramaic of the Byzantine Period.* 2nd ed. Ramat-Gan, Israel: Bar Ilan University Press, 2002
DSD	*Dead Sea Discoveries*
DSGA	Machiela, Daniel A. *The Dead Sea Genesis Apocryphon: A New Text and Translation with Introduction and Special Treatment of Columns 13–17.* STDJ 79. Leiden: Brill, 2009
EJL	Early Judaism and Its Literature

FAT	Forschungen zum Alten Testament
FJTC	Flavius Josephus: Translation and Commentary
GA	Fitzmyer, Joseph A. *The Genesis Apocryphon of Qumran Cave 1 (1Q20): A Commentary*. 3rd ed. Rome: Pontifical Biblical Institute, 2004
GELS	*A Greek–English Lexicon of the Septuagint*. Takamitsu Muraoka. Leuven: Peeters, 2009
GenAp	Genesis Apocryphon
Gen. Rab.	Genesis Rabbah
HALOT	*The Hebrew and Aramaic Lexicon of the Old Testament*. Ludwig Koehler, Walter Baumgartner, and Johann J. Stamm. Translated and edited under the supervision of Mervyn E. J. Richardson. 4 vols. Leiden: Brill, 1994–99
HTR	*Harvard Theological Review*
HUCA	*Hebrew Union College Annual*
JA 1–4	Feldman, Louis H., translation and commentary. *Judean Antiquities 1–4*. Edited by Steve Mason. FJTC 3. Leiden: Brill, 2000
JAAR	*Journal of the American Academy of Religion*
JAJSup	*Journal of Ancient Judaism Supplements*
JANES	*Journal of the Ancient Near Eastern Society*
JJS	*Journal of Jewish Studies*
JNES	*Journal of Near Eastern Studies*
JQR	*Jewish Quarterly Review*
JSJ	*Journal for the Study of Judaism*
JSJSup	Supplements to the Journal for the Study of Judaism
JSNTSup	Journal for the Study of the New Testament Supplement Series
JSOT	*Journal for the Study of the Old Testament*
JSOTSup	Journal for the Study of the Old Testament Supplement Series
JSP	*Journal for the Study of the Pseudepigrapha*
Jub.	*Jubilees*
J.W.	*Jewish War* (Josephus)
LAB	Liber antiquitatum biblicarum (Pseudo-Philo)
LCL	Loeb Classical Library
LSJ	Liddell, Henry George, Robert Scott, Henry Stuart Jones. *A Greek–English Lexicon*. 9th ed. with revised supplement. Oxford: Clarendon Press, 1996
LSTS	The Library of Second Temple Studies
LXX	Septuagint
MT	Masoretic Text
NABR	New American Bible, Revised Edition
NETS	*A New English Translation of the Septuagint*. Edited by Albert Pietersma and Benjamin G. Wright. New York: Oxford University Press, 2007

NJPS	*Tanakh: The Holy Scriptures: The New JPS Translation according to the Traditional Hebrew Text*
NRSV	New Revised Standard Version
OG	Old Greek
OTL	Old Testament Library
RevQ	*Revue de Qumran*
RSV	Revised Standard Version
RTL	*Revue théologique de Louvain*
SBLDS	Society of Biblical Literature Dissertation Series
SBLSPS	Society of Biblical Literature Seminar Papers Series
SCS	Septuagint and Cognate Studies
SJ	Studia Judaica
Smyth	Smyth, Herbert Weir. *Greek Grammar*. Cambridge: Harvard University Press, 1920
SP	Samaritan Pentateuch
SSEJC	Studies in Scripture in Early Judaism and Christianity
SSN	Studia Semitica Neerlandica
SSS	Semitic Study Series
STDJ	Studies on the Texts of the Desert of Judah
StPB	Studia Post-biblica
StSam	Studia Samaritana
T. Abr.	*Testament of Abraham*
TAPA	*Transactions of the American Philological Association*
Text	*Textus*
VTSup	Supplements to Vetus Testamentum
WGRW	Writings from the Greco-Roman World
ZAW	*Zeitschrift für die alttestamentliche Wissenschaft*

Chapter 1

Introduction, Studies of Sarah, and Aspects of My Approach

Sherlock Holmes sleuths on, despite the death of his creator, in the literary efforts of "Sherlockians" devoted to repairing the "gaps, contradictions, and inconsistencies" in the "canon" of Arthur Conan Doyle. In its generative "theorizing about the undisclosed backstories of characters and events," this exegetical and creative activity presages the rise of modern "fan fiction."[1] But it also echoes the ancient interpretive ventures that produced much of the captivating literature often called "rewritten Bible."[2]

Just like Holmes, many of the biblical characters whose stories were retold in antiquity are men, and until relatively recently scholars showed little interest in asking "questions about women's roles" in the Bible or related literature.[3] The work of Phyllis Trible, Phyllis Bird, and others signaled the beginning of a shift in the early 1970s, and the intervening decades have seen a dramatic proliferation of scholarly studies that focus

---

1. Laura Miller, "A Study in Sherlock: How the Detective Escaped His Creator," *Harper's Magazine*, May 2014: 91.
2. The scope, aptness, and utility of "rewritten Bible" and related terms are matters of fractious debate. For one treatment, see Jonathan G. Campbell, "Rewritten Bible: A Terminological Reassessment," in *Rewritten Bible after Fifty Years: Texts, Terms, or Techniques? A Last Dialogue with Géza Vermès*, ed. József Zsengellér, JSJSup 166 (Leiden: Brill, 2014), 49–81. In my work here, I employ the appellation as a pragmatic, umbrella term that says more about scholarly reception than ancient generic categories.
3. Alice Ogden Bellis, "Feminist Biblical Scholarship," in *Women in Scripture: A Dictionary of Named and Unnamed Women in the Hebrew Bible, the Apocryphal/Deuterocanonical Books, and the New Testament*, ed. Carol Meyers, Toni Craven, and Ross S. Kraemer (Grand Rapids: Eerdmans, 2000), 28.

on women in biblical texts and contexts.[4] Yet female characters still draw less attention than their male counterparts in mainstream biblical studies, a disparity that is far more marked in research on retellings of biblical stories.[5] The figure of Abraham alone, inside and outside the Bible, has been the subject of an enormous number of investigations, including the study in which the term "rewritten Bible" was coined.[6]

So this study looks at Sarah instead. I perform readings of the narratives that feature her in the Hebrew Bible, the Septuagint, the Genesis Apocryphon, and the *Jewish Antiquities* of Josephus, employing a narrative-critical methodology centered on characterization that both incorporates and reacts to aspects of rewritten Bible approaches. I detail Sarah's depiction as a woman who has and has not in the Masoretic Text (MT) of Genesis, Sarra's faded portrait in the Septuagint (LXX) version of Genesis, the intriguing but ultimately disappointing trajectory of the wise Sarai in the Genesis Apocryphon (GenAp), and the complicated presentation of Sarra in the *Antiquities* (*Ant.*), where narratorial efforts to polish her character's image often end in obfuscation and moral hazard. In the end, I suggest that one of Sarah's trans-narrative or "deep traits" is a recurring resemblance to the character of Abraham, though I argue that she cannot be reduced to this role. Instead, Sarah is a complex and sometimes contradictory character whose individuality still occasionally escapes the various pressures—human, divine, and narratorial—that are ranged against her in an androcentric tradition.

---

4. Phyllis Trible, "Depatriarchalizing in Biblical Interpretation," *JAAR* 41 (1973): 30–48; Phyllis Bird, "Images of Women in the Old Testament," in *Religion and Sexism: Images of Woman in the Jewish and Christian Traditions*, ed. Rosemary Radford Ruether (New York: Simon & Schuster, 1974), 41–88.

5. The extent of scholarly absorption with male characters in scriptural rewritings can be seen in a glance at Michael E. Stone and Theodore A. Bergren, eds., *Biblical Figures Outside the Bible* (Harrisburg, PA: Trinity Press International, 1998), or Lorenzo DiTommaso, "Pseudepigrapha Notes I: 1. *Lunationes Danielis*; 2. Biblical Figures Outside the Bible," *JSP* 15 (2006): 116–44. Examples of studies that do focus on female characters in the Hebrew Bible and retellings or versions include Linda Day, *Three Faces of a Queen: Characterization in the Books of Esther*, JSOTSup 186 (Sheffield: Sheffield Academic Press, 1995); Joan E. Cook, *Hannah's Desire, God's Design: Early Interpretations of the Story of Hannah*, JSOTSup 282 (Sheffield: Sheffield Academic Press, 1999); Sara M. Koenig, *Isn't This Bathsheba? A Study in Characterization*, Princeton Theological Monograph Series (Eugene, OR: Pickwick, 2011); and Hanna Tervanotko, *Denying Her Voice: The Figure of Miriam in Ancient Jewish Literature*, JAJSup 23 (Göttingen: Vandenhoeck & Ruprecht, 2016).

6. Géza Vermès, *Scripture and Tradition in Judaism*, StPB 4 (Leiden: Brill, 1961), 67–126.

I have three primary, interrelated ambitions here. First, allying my work with the efforts of those who have focused on women in biblical and cognate literature, I wish to contribute to the recognition and rediscovery of a female character who has been relatively neglected, especially in her extrabiblical incarnations. This is the most extensive investigation of Sarah across these texts to date.

Second, I want to pursue this search in a particular way, employing the theoretically informed, character-driven, narrative-critical approach that I outline below to perform my readings in each text. Sarah's image in the MT has drawn a fair amount of attention, but most studies do not attempt a comprehensive reading. In the other three texts, Sarah has received little scrutiny, and has not been approached with narrative-critical concerns in mind. No less than my decision to look for Sarah in the first place, my adoption of narrative criticism is an ideological choice. Given an approach that reads characters as human analogues and treats narrators as fallible witnesses whose testimony may be suspect, narrative criticism has the capacity to draw marginal or previously ignored figures out of the shadows.[7] Readerly suspicion of the narrators of these tales—and I will note ample grounds for suspicion in the chapters that follow—lends a reader license to "glance around the fictive landscape to pick up clues about the story that didn't tempt the narrator."[8] This latitude is especially relevant to a project that reads a female character, such as Sarah, in androcentric literature.[9] In an extension of this second aim, I hope that my readings may provoke other readers to examine other neglected characters, particularly female characters, and especially in extrabiblical, Second Temple texts, from similar narrative-critical perspectives.[10]

---

7. These are postures or tools available to the narrative critic, not qualities intrinsic to narrative criticism, which can also read characters as "paper people" (Mieke Bal, *Narratology: Introduction to the Theory of Narrative*, 3rd ed. [Toronto: University of Toronto Press, 2009], 113–14) and often grants narrators "an unearned confidence and credibility" (Gina Hens-Piazza, *Nameless, Blameless, and Without Shame: Two Cannibal Mothers Before a King*, Interfaces [Collegeville, MN: Liturgical Press, 2003], 15).

8. Alice Bach, "Signs of the Flesh: Observations on Characterization in the Bible," in *Women in the Hebrew Bible: A Reader*, ed. Alice Bach (New York: Routledge, 1999), 362; compare Alice Bach, *Women, Seduction, and Betrayal in Biblical Narrative* (Cambridge: Cambridge University Press, 1997), 17, 21.

9. Bach, *Women, Seduction, and Betrayal*, 14, 16.

10. While Josephus completed the *Antiquities* in about 93 CE (*Ant.* 20.267), I define the "Second Temple period" broadly, as in Louis H. Feldman, James L. Kugel, and Lawrence H. Schiffman, eds., *Outside the Bible: Ancient Jewish Writings Related to Scripture* (Philadelphia: Jewish Publication Society of America, 2013),

Third, in performing my readings of these four texts under one cover, I would like not only to offer a broad and representative, if not fully comprehensive, look at the character of Sarah in the literature of the Second Temple period, but also to illustrate a profitable way to approach rewritten biblical material.[11] Most scholarship that examines characters in these works takes an explicitly "comparative" approach, comparing descendant texts point-by-point with the Bible. "Contrastive" might be a more apt term, however, as the goal of this work is the discovery of a text's distinctive features, usually with a view to revealing characteristics of its author or original audience. This contrast and its attendant conclusions are often achieved by mechanical juxtaposition, sometimes to the point of synoptic, tabular apposition of verses, cola, and even individual words.[12]

This kind of contrastive juxtaposition has patently paid dividends in the biblical disciplines. But such an appositional approach, especially when used as the point of departure in a reading, can predispose a reader to overlook the interaction of elements in a narrative that may be critical to its operation. An emphasis on disparities may lead a reader to ignore the ways in which parts of narratives that are not thrown into high relief by the contrast of versions may still vitally contribute to the overall picture of each version considered in itself; how elements intrinsic to a narrative might inform one another risks being lost in the glare of the spotlight of another text. Undue concentration on the differences between related narratives can even lead to neglect of the narratives in themselves, and to their replacement by a hybrid metanarrative constructed mostly from the disparities between the narratives concerned, which is then the subject of a reader's analysis. This may be especially likely in the investigation

---

xv, which speaks of "the period between the end of the Babylonian exile (538 BCE) and the transmission of the Mishnah (200 CE)." Moreover, I acknowledge that at least the theoretical "final form" of consonantal MT Genesis is also a "Second Temple" work.

11. I do not suggest this is completely uncharted territory. Others such as Mark Roncace have reacted against the dominance of the "comparative" model in rewritten Bible studies, as I discuss below. Moshe J. Bernstein, "Is the Genesis Apocryphon a Unity? What Sort of Unity Were You Looking For?" *AS* 8 (2010): 133–4, has repeatedly stressed the need to move beyond a focus on the Apocryphon's "sources or relationship to the Bible" in favor of considering "the work itself."

12. See, for example, Erkki Koskenniemi and Pekka Lindqvist, "Rewritten Bible, Rewritten Stories: Methodological Aspects," in *Rewritten Bible Reconsidered*, ed. Antti Laato and Jacques T. A. G. M. van Ruiten, Studies in Rewritten Bible 1 (Winona Lake, IN: Eisenbrauns, 2008), 27.

of a descendant version of a parent text with attributed authority such as the Bible, a standard from which deviation is easily measured; the descendant text may never be fully read in itself, but only considered in its differences from its norm. In this way, paradoxically, a predilection for isolating contrasting elements can prevent a reader from forming a complete picture of one of the objects to be compared, thus potentially flawing a tradition's description. In my readings of Sarah in the MT, the LXX, the Apocryphon, and the *Antiquities*, I practice and advocate a more conscious consideration of these texts as texts, in keeping with the canons of narrative criticism, and not just as deviations from something else. Perhaps this, too, could suggest an alternative or complementary way forward for others interested in the ancient reception and transformation of biblical stories and characters.

Many narratives retell Sarah's story. Some of these are of great intrinsic interest, such as the *Testament of Abraham*, a darkly comic work in which Sarah outlives her spouse.[13] Other narratives that would repay work on Sarah include the targumim and later rabbinic, Islamic, and Samaritan treatments.[14] Among other Second Temple literature, *Jubilees* and the works of Philo also rework her story. Practical constraints have forced me to make choices, and I have deliberately if reluctantly left these last two aside. In the case of *Jubilees*, I agree with Maren Niehoff that its composer "took no interest at all in the figure of Sarah, but was overwhelmingly concerned with Abraham's image."[15] Philo presents an

---

13. Sarah is still alive at the end of Recension A of the *Testament of Abraham*; the less colorful Recension B (ch. 12) preserves the traditional order of events.

14. Many haggadic stories involving Abraham and Sarah are collected in Louis Ginzberg, *Legends of the Jews*, 2nd ed., trans. Henrietta Szold and Paul Radin (1909–38; repr., Philadelphia: Johns Hopkins University Press, 2003), especially 167–250. For Sarah specifically, David J. Zucker, "Sarah: The View of the Classical Rabbis," in *Perspectives on Our Father Abraham: Essays in Honor of Marvin R. Wilson*, ed. Stephen A. Hunt (Grand Rapids: Eerdmans, 2010), 221–52, provides an overview of her treatment in the Talmud and midrash. Riffat Hassan, "Islamic Hagar and Her Family," in *Hagar, Sarah, and Their Children: Jewish, Christian, and Muslim Perspectives*, ed. Phyllis Trible and Letty M. Russell (Louisville: Westminster John Knox Press, 2006), 149–67, discusses traditions about Hagar, Sarah, and Abraham in both the Qur'an and the *ḥadīth*. The Samaritan *Asatir* contains a few retellings of stories of Sarah and Abraham.

15. Maren Niehoff, "Mother and Maiden, Sister and Spouse: Sarah in Philonic Midrash," *HTR* 97 (2004): 415. Contrast Betsy Halpern-Amaru, "The Portrait of Sarah in Jubilees," in *Jewish Studies in a New Europe*, ed. Ulf Haxen, Hanne Traudner-Kromann, and Karen Lisa Goldschmidt Salamon (Copenhagen: C. A. Reitzel, 1998), 336–48, and compare Betsy Halpern-Amaru, *The Empowerment of*

inverse problem, employing "Sarah," sometimes at considerable length, in a dozen or more treatises. Almost all of these discussions, though, reduce her to an analogue of "virtue," "wisdom," or "philosophy," among other abstractions, and subsequently deploy this analogue in allegorical schemes virtually devoid of plot. This complicates analysis of the only truly narrative material concerning Sarah in Philo, in *On the Life of Abraham*, which also alternates "literal" retelling with allegorical exposition.[16] Striking a balance between comprehensiveness and practicality, I leave all of these works and others for future investigations.[17]

In this opening chapter, I set the stage for my readings by briefly surveying relevant work on Sarah in the MT, the LXX, the Apocryphon, the *Antiquities*, and Second Temple literature more broadly.[18] After this, I detail my approach to these narratives.

Studies of Sarah in the Bible and Beyond

Sarah in the Masoretic Text

The secondary literature on Gen. 11:27–25:10, which concerns the founding of the family line that will give rise to the Israelites, is overwhelming in extent. And while the female characters of these chapters

Women in the Book of Jubilees (Leiden: Brill, 1999) and Betsy Halpern-Amaru, "Portraits of Women in Pseudo-Philo's Biblical Antiquities," in *"Women Like This": New Perspectives on Jewish Women in the Greco-Roman World*, ed. Amy-Jill Levine, EJL 1 (Atlanta: Scholars Press, 1991), 83–106.

16. Scholars who reflect, at least in part, on Sarah's "literal" representation here include Judith Romney Wegner, "The Image of Woman in Philo," in *Society of Biblical Literature 1982 Seminar Papers*, SBLSPS 21 (Chico, CA: Scholars Press, 1982), 551–63; Dorothy Sly, *Philo's Perception of Women*, BJS 209 (Atlanta: Scholars Press, 1990); Niehoff, "Mother and Maiden"; and Atar Livneh, "Jewish Traditions and Familial Roman Values in Philo's *De Abrahamo* 245–254," *HTR* 109 (2016): 536–49.

17. Other texts of roughly the same period feature only relatively brief mentions of Sarah. *LAB* mostly reworks her traditions by omitting them. Of the New Testament passages that refer to Sarah (Rom. 4:19; 9:9; Gal. 4:21–5:1; Heb. 11:11; 1 Pet. 3:6), Galatians has probably received the most scrutiny, but there is little to be gleaned from a narrative perspective here. Other minor references can be found in the *Testament of Levi*, the *Joseph and Aseneth* novella, and a fragment of Pseudo-Eupolemus.

18. I have limited this overview to work that concerns Sarah directly. For more detail and further bibliography, including important studies of other female characters in the Bible and related literature, see Joseph McDonald, "Searching for Sarah in the Second Temple Era: Portraits in the Hebrew Bible and Second Temple Narratives" (PhD diss., Brite Divinity School, 2015), 5–47.

have been relatively neglected, Sarah's depiction here in the MT of Genesis, of all her varied representations in antiquity, has received by far the most scholarly attention.[19] However, most of this work folds neatly into a few distinct categories. The first consists of studies that focus their analysis on a single episode or a pair of closely related episodes; work here clusters around the "sister-wife" scenes,[20] the relationship of Sarah and Hagar,[21] and, interestingly, the binding of Isaac.[22] A second category is comprised of investigations that employ data from Sarah's story in the service of a thematic, often typological approach to the biblical

19. Throughout this section, I refer to "Sarah" when speaking in general terms of the character whose change of name, from Sarai to Sarah, is announced to Abraham by God in Gen. 17:15.

20. Fokkelien van Dijk-Hemmes, "Sarai in Exile: A Gender-Specific Reading of Genesis 12:10–13:2," in *The Double Voice of Her Desire*, trans. David E. Orton, ed. J. Bekkenkamp and F. Dröes (Leiden: Deo, 2004), 137, 143, 145, was the first to "place Sarai at the center of attention" in the Egyptian episode (Gen. 12:10-20), finding that she is oppressed and silent, embodying "the lot of all those who are the victims of the trade in women." The most influential treatment is that of J. Cheryl Exum, "Who's Afraid of 'The Endangered Ancestress'?" in *The New Literary Criticism and the Hebrew Bible*, ed. J. Cheryl Exum and David J. A. Clines (Valley Forge, PA: Trinity Press International, 1993), 100, who takes a "psychoanalytic-literary" approach to the three versions of the tale (Gen. 12:10-20; 20:1-18; 26:1-16), reading through the categories of Freud and Girard to uncover a series of stories driven by a male, unconscious fantasy "that the wife have sex with another man."

21. Phyllis Trible, "Hagar: The Desolation of Rejection," in *Texts of Terror: Literary-Feminist Readings of Biblical Narratives* (Philadelphia: Fortress Press, 1984), 13, 28, a liberationist close reading in which Sarah is depicted as an abuser backed by God's authority, has had the greatest impact in terms of both approach and conclusions. Compare Renita J. Weems, "A Mistress, a Maid, and No Mercy," in *Just a Sister Away: A Womanist Vision of Women's Relationships in the Bible* (San Diego: LuraMedia, 1988), 1–21, and Susanne Scholz, *Sacred Witness: Rape in the Hebrew Bible* (Minneapolis: Fortress Press, 2010), 59–60.

22. The most influential study is again that of Phyllis Trible, "Genesis 22: The Sacrifice of Sarah," in *"Not in Heaven": Coherence and Complexity in Biblical Narrative*, ed. Jason P. Rosenblatt and Joseph C. Sitterson Jr. (Bloomington: Indiana University Press, 1991), 182–91, esp. 182, 188–9. The title refers to patriarchy's "sacrificing" Sarah by "eliminating" her from this story (190), which, Trible argues, also denies her a chance at "redemption" from the "attachment" that mars her character and leads to her ill-treatment of Hagar. Wendy Zierler, "In Search of a Feminist Reading of the Akedah," *Nashim* 9 (2005): 17–19, is in part a response to Trible's effort, critiquing in particular the latter's "wholesale acceptance of the high spiritual merit of the *Akedah* exercise," and disputing her evaluation of Sarah's "attachment" as a negative quality.

text.²³ A third group, the largest but most homogeneous, is made up of efforts that look at Sarah as part of a broader survey of women in the Bible.²⁴

All of these approaches face challenges when it comes to providing a reading of Sarah that is both comprehensive and clear. Those in the first, episodic group treat only a portion of Sarah's story in the MT, while those in the third, survey group subordinate their readings to a broader thesis on biblical women. Those in the second, thematic or typological group occupy a middle place, both focusing narrowly on parts of Sarah's story and using her narrative data as evidence in larger arguments.

Only two extended scholarly investigations adopt the larger trajectory of Sarah in Genesis as their organizing principle. Savina Teubal's *Sarah the Priestess* takes an idiosyncratic, sometimes speculative approach founded in ancient Near Eastern contexts. Building on various textual silences, and elements of the narrative such as Sarah's childlessness and Abraham's claim that Sarah is his sister in Gen. 20:12, Teubal paints Sarah as a (mostly) celibate Mesopotamian priestess who dwells in a sacred precinct at Mamre.²⁵ Teubal's contentions have not garnered broad support. More importantly, her aim, which is the reconstruction of traditions buried deeply behind the text, is very different from mine here.

Tammi Schneider's monograph *Sarah: Mother of Nations* adopts a literary and feminist approach that is also informed by ancient Near

---

23. Esther Fuchs, "The Literary Characterization of Mothers and Sexual Politics in the Hebrew Bible," in *Feminist Perspectives on Biblical Scholarship*, ed. Adela Yarbro Collins (Chico, CA: Scholars Press, 1985), 117–36, has set much of the agenda here, arguing in a discussion of "annunciation type-scenes" that biblical mothers such as Sarah are generally flat, colorless, secondary characters whose roles are completely circumscribed by a patriarchal text. For a more optimistic view, see Lori Hope Lefkovitz, *In Scripture: The First Stories of Jewish Sexual Identities* (Lanham, MD: Rowman & Littlefield, 2010), 31–46.

24. Among many examples, see Irmtraud Fischer, *Women Who Wrestled with God: Biblical Stories of Israel's Beginnings*, trans. Linda M. Maloney (Collegeville, MN: Liturgical Press, 2005); Sharon Pace Jeansonne, *The Women of Genesis: From Sarah to Potiphar's Wife* (Minneapolis: Fortress Press, 1990); Tammi J. Schneider, *Mothers of Promise: Women in the Book of Genesis* (Grand Rapids: Baker Academic, 2008).

25. Savina J. Teubal, *Sarah the Priestess: The First Matriarch of Genesis* (Athens, OH: Swallow Press, 1984), 96–106. Teubal casts Sarah's interactions with Pharaoh and Abimelech, as well as her reception of the visitors in Gen. 18, as performances of the *hieros gamos* in which the Queen of Heaven, with Sarah as conduit or avatar, joins sexually with earthly rulers (110–28, esp. 121).

Eastern contexts.[26] Schneider argues that "Sarah is as much chosen by the Deity as is Abraham," and that she, more than her husband, fulfills God's demands and helps realize God's promises in the narrative.[27] Schneider's work offers the most detailed study of Sarah in the MT to date, but her approach leaves room for constructive expansion. One difficulty is an apologetic agenda that seeks to protect the image of God, as well as that of Sarah, in the narrative. Schneider justifies actions of Sarah that commentators often find morally dubious, such as her treatment of Hagar, by identifying her conduct with the will of God, which is left unquestioned; both God and Sarah are thus summarily let off the hook.[28] Methodological issues also emerge. While Schneider adopts a literary approach, she only hints at her methodology here and is almost completely innocent of interaction with narrative-critical theory, although such studies, especially those focusing on characterization, would seem to be natural resources in a project that "evaluates the character of Sarah and her role in the text."[29] Finally, in further distinction from my broader study, Schneider does not discuss later transformations of Sarah at any length.

Sarah in the Septuagint

Susan Ann Brayford provides the only sustained discussion of the depiction of Sarah—here eventually called Sarra—in LXX Genesis.[30] Brayford foregrounds the influence of the Mediterranean code of honor and shame on the translators of Genesis, a process she contends resulted in a Septuagint Sarah recast as a "model, i.e., shameful, Hellenistic wife."[31] After arguing on historical and philological grounds that divergences between LXX Genesis and its *Vorlage* are interpretive, Brayford tries to show that these disparities amount to an effacement in the LXX of what she argues is the MT's more frankly sexual portrayal of women, including Sarah.[32]

---

26. Tammi J. Schneider, *Sarah: Mother of Nations* (New York: Continuum, 2004), 2–5.
27. Ibid., 3, 5, 129.
28. Ibid., 53.
29. Ibid., 2.
30. Especially Susan Ann Brayford, "The Taming and Shaming of Sarah in the Septuagint of Genesis" (PhD diss., Iliff School of Theology; The University of Denver / Colorado Seminary, 1998).
31. Ibid., 51, 153. "Shameful" in this context is not pejorative, denoting rather a woman possessed of positive "shame," meaning "modesty, virginity, seclusion" (130).
32. Ibid., 17, 48–50, 96–7, 146–50, 155, 178–9, 185–7, 211–12.

Brayford also briefly considers Sarah's "postbiblical literary afterlife" in a number of other narratives.[33] Brayford's approach and concerns, however, diverge markedly from mine. Foremost for Brayford is the lens of honor and shame, which informs her entire presentation and results in a selective reading of the LXX and the other narratives. Only parts of Sarah's story contribute to an examination of this code, and so only certain pericopes—especially that containing Gen. 18:12, which is the linchpin of Brayford's larger argument—are considered at length. In addition, Brayford approaches Sarah primarily as a representative of a category, that of "shameful" Hellenistic matron, within her sociological scheme. In contrast, I employ narrative-critical approaches that foreground characterization to pursue a portrait of Sarah as an individual actor in the LXX, in addition to the other narratives, in each instance considering the full arc of her story and declining to subordinate my reading to thematic concerns.

Finally, Brayford's procedure, which is characteristic of most work on rewritten Bible, depends on consistent juxtaposition and contrast of the MT and the LXX.[34] A narrative-critical reading such as that pursued here, however, emphasizes the necessity of considering the full and linear rhetorical sweep of a narrative in its interpretation. The plain dependence of the LXX on something close to what became the MT does generate theoretical obstacles for my project, as I note later. Yet my primary aim is not to isolate and discuss the differences between these traditions, but to perform a reading of Sarra that respects the integrity of the LXX as a narrative in its own right, with its own idiom and internal coherence.

Sarah in the Genesis Apocryphon

A significant amount of research in the area of rewritten Bible concerns the retelling of the antediluvian and "Abramic" sections of Genesis in

---

33. Ibid., 215. Brayford looks at the treatment of Sarah, at least in the context of Gen. 18:12 and occasionally in the broader narrative, in Aquila and Symmachus (217–18), the targumim (218–20), *Jubilees* (224–8), the Genesis Apocryphon (229–31, 33), *LAB* (235–7), Philo (241–5), and Josephus (251–5), and cites her mentions in the New Testament (257–8).

34. Translations such as the Septuagint are usually excluded from all but the broadest definitions of rewritten Bible, though Géza Vermès included the "Palestinian Targum" (a group of targumim such as *Neofiti* and *Pseudo-Jonathan*) in his initial description of the term: Vermès, *Scripture and Tradition*, 95. See the critique of Vermès on this matter in Moshe J. Bernstein, "'Rewritten Bible': A Generic Category Which Has Outlived Its Usefulness?" *Text* 22 (2005): 174–5, and Vermès's pointed response in Géza Vermès, "The Genesis of the Concept of 'Rewritten Bible'," in Zsengellér, ed., *Rewritten Bible*, 8.

the Genesis Apocryphon. However, the character of Sarah, here called Sarai, is mostly passed over in the literature. She features prominently only in work on the description poem of GenAp 20.2-8, which details her physical and mental charms, but even here her characterization is not usually the primary object of analysis.[35] Indeed, sustained study of any female characters in the Apocryphon—from any perspective, let alone from a narrative or literary approach—is not easy to find.[36] This neglect leaves a broad opening for a narrative inquiry into the image of Sarai here.

Sarah in the Antiquities

Studies of Josephus's *Antiquities* also display a lack of interest in Sarah, or Sarra, as she is named here. The few that offer more than cursory remarks, moreover, subordinate their analyses to broader arguments: Sarah is a representative "matriarch" for James Bailey, and a type of Josephan biblical heroine for Betsy Halpern-Amaru, while Niehoff uses Josephus's portrayal primarily to illuminate that of Philo.[37] Bailey contends that her depiction is "softened," while Halpern-Amaru and Niehoff see Josephus's Sarah as a hollow character, transparent in her passivity. All three, however, reveal a deeper affinity in their basic approach, which echoes that of

---

35. See especially Shaye J. D. Cohen, "The Beauty of Flora and the Beauty of Sarai," *Helios* 8 (1981): 41–53; Sebastian P. Brock and Simon Hopkins, "A Verse Homily on Abraham and Sarah in Egypt: Syriac Original with Early Arabic Translation," *Le Muséon* 105 (1992): 87–145; and J. F. van Rensburg, "Intellect and/or Beauty: A Portrait of Women in the Old Testament and Extra Biblical Literature," *Journal for Semitics* 11 (2002): 112–25.

36. Eileen Schuller, "Response to 'Patriarchs Who Worry About Their Wives: A Haggadic Tendency in the Genesis Apocryphon'," in *George W. E. Nickelsburg in Perspective: An Ongoing Dialogue of Learning*, ed. Jacob Neusner and Alan J. Avery-Peck (Leiden: Brill, 2003), 201, wrote that George W. E. Nickelsburg, "Patriarchs Who Worry About Their Wives: A Haggadic Tendency in the Genesis Apocryphon," in Neusner and Avery-Peck, eds., *George W. E. Nickelsburg in Perspective*, 177–99, was "the most comprehensive study that I know of the women in the Genesis Apocryphon." However, as she notes, Nickelsburg's article is a wide-ranging treatment of many themes in this narrative, only some of which have relevance to the characterization of the women in the text. In the years since the appearance of these essays, exegetes have not displayed any concentrated interest in the stories of the women of the Apocryphon.

37. James L. Bailey, "Josephus' Portrayal of the Matriarchs," in *Josephus, Judaism, and Christianity*, ed. Louis H. Feldman and Gohei Hata (Detroit: Wayne State University Press, 1987), 154–79; Betsy Halpern-Amaru, "Portraits of Biblical Women in Josephus' Antiquities," *JJS* 39 (1988): 143–70; Niehoff, "Mother and Maiden."

most studies of Josephan characters: nearly all of the relevant secondary literature adheres at root to the kind of synoptic comparative program associated with the foundational work of Louis Feldman.[38]

Even efforts that directly challenge this dominant paradigm seem to find its centripetal pull irresistible. Mark Roncace, treating the story of Deborah in Josephus, argues that Feldman's consistent application of a "redactional and comparative approach…is of limited value for character analysis." In its place, Roncace advocates a "literary/narrative" methodology that better takes into consideration "basic literary (surface) features" often ignored in analyses concerned only with the disparities between the accounts of Josephus and his biblical source material.[39] Yet Roncace fails to realize the promise of his proposal, focusing instead on the "distinctive features" of Josephus's retelling of Deborah's story, and maintaining, with a consistency that rivals that of Feldman himself, a fundamentally comparative posture.

My work here keeps a steady focus on Sarah in Josephus and adopts a narrative-critical approach that takes the literary integrity of Josephus's composition seriously. In this it takes up the unmet challenge of Roncace, whose argument, despite a failure in execution, is well-taken: focusing solely on differences between the Bible and its literary offspring risks leaving basic elements of the descendant texts unexamined.

Sarah throughout Second Temple Literature

Treatments of Sarah in extrabiblical narratives, even considered as a group, are substantially fewer than those that discuss her in the context of the MT. Efforts that examine her in more than one of these texts, even briefly, are yet more rare. Nearly all of the relevant investigations track one episode or theme from Sarah's presentation in the Bible through later retellings. Irmtraud Fischer and a few others survey the "sister-wife" episodes through several subsequent interpretations.[40] Adele Reinhartz

---

38. Sarah herself is the focus of little extended comment in Feldman's work, though she is considered as a matter of course in Louis H. Feldman, translation and commentary, *Judean Antiquities 1–4*, ed. Steve Mason, FJTC 3 (Leiden: Brill, 2000)—hereafter *JA 1–4*—71 n. 589, 81 n. 654, 82 n. 661, 83 n. 666. In general, Feldman says, Josephus casts Sarah in a "more favorable light" as compared to her portrayal in Genesis, depicting her as both less harsh in her dealings with Hagar and more faithful in her response to the divine promise of offspring.

39. Mark Roncace, "Josephus' (Real) Portraits of Deborah and Gideon: A Reading of *Antiquities* 5.198–232," *JSJ* 31 (2000): 247.

40. Irmtraud Fischer, *Die Erzeltern Israels: Feministisch-theologische Studien zu Genesis 12–36*, BZAW 222 (Berlin: de Gruyter, 1994), 247–9, 252–5; Barry L.

and Miriam-Simma Walfish trace the retellings of the Sarah and Hagar episodes, briefly surveying treatments in *Jubilees*, *LAB*, Josephus, and the allegorical readings of Philo.[41] Elaine Phillips examines "post-biblical" interpretations of the reactions of Sarah and Abraham to the prediction that they will have a son.[42] Brayford, too, focuses on Gen. 18:12 and its retellings in her reading of Sarah in the LXX.[43]

Aside from these works, barring the occasional incidental reference, there is very little indeed beyond short items such as the summary of Josephus's Sarah used as a foil in Niehoff's analysis of Philo.[44] Every treatment is relatively brief, and most are ancillary to the primary aim of the study in question. Finally, none of these works adopts a narrative-critical perspective.

Aspects of My Approach

My approach to reading Sarah in these works, on the other hand, flows directly from my understanding of what characters are and how they are formed. I first outline here my conception of the nature of literary characters, and examine the related issues of story and discourse, character and plot, and the role and identity of the reader, treating the concepts of audience, reception, and rewriting along the way. Subsequently, I consider

---

Eichler, "On Reading Genesis 12:10-20," in *Tehillah le-Moshe: Biblical and Judaic Studies in Honor of Moshe Greenberg*, ed. Mordechai Cogan, Barry L. Eichler, and Jeffrey H. Tigay (Winona Lake, IN: Eisenbrauns, 1997), 23–38; Jan Joosten, "Abram et Saraï en Égypte: Composition et message de Genèse 12, 10-20," in *La sœur-épouse (Genèse 12, 10-20)*, ed. Matthieu Arnold, Gilbert Dahan, and Annie Noblesse-Rocher (Paris: Cerf, 2010), 11–25; Yair Zakovitch and Avigdor Shinan, *Abram and Sarai in Egypt: Gen 12:10-20 in the Bible, the Old Versions and the Ancient Jewish Literature* [in Hebrew], Research Projects of the Institute of Jewish Studies Monograph Series 2 (Jerusalem: Hebrew University, 1983).

41. Adele Reinhartz and Miriam-Simma Walfish, "Conflict and Coexistence in Jewish Interpretation," in Trible and Russell, eds., *Hagar, Sarah, and Their Children*, 101–25. See also Elaine James, "Sarah, Hagar, and Their Interpreters," in *Women's Bible Commentary*, 3rd ed., ed. Carol A. Newsom, Sharon H. Ringe, and Jacqueline E. Lapsley (Louisville: Westminster John Knox Press, 2012), 51–5.

42. Elaine A. Phillips, "Incredulity, Faith, and Textual Purposes: Post-Biblical Responses to the Laughter of Abraham and Sarah," in *The Function of Scripture in Early Jewish and Christian Tradition*, ed. Craig A. Evans and James A. Sanders, JSNTSup 154, SSEJC 6 (Sheffield: Sheffield Academic Press, 1998), 22–33.

43. Brayford, "Taming and Shaming."

44. Niehoff, "Mother and Maiden," 416–18.

how the traits that are the building blocks of character construction are realized, examining the relative weight of different kinds of narrative information, discussing means of characterization, and offering an integrated view of character based on the notion of relationality.

Theory: Character and the Reader

"People or words"?

What is a "character"? Something real, or a figment of textuality? Baruch Hochman speaks of the "paradox" at the center of any fictional character, who is "at once an extremely vivid entity…and a highly delusive one," something that can seem more real than people we know while remaining existentially absent.[45] In the early 1960s, these two poles were described by Marvin Mudrick as the "realistic" and "purist" conceptions of character, respectively, and this basic distinction has endured for several generations of literary critics.[46] I found my conception of character on the realistic, or "mimetic" view, which emphasizes the constructed reality of literary characters as human analogues with whom we may become acquainted. The case for this approach has been convincingly laid out by William Harvey, Seymour Chatman, and, most forcefully, by Hochman, who argues for a "profound congruity" in our apprehension of literary characters, historical figures, and real embodied people "of whom we have what we think of as direct knowledge."[47] Crucially, Hochman's argument is about perception, not abstract identity:

---

45. Baruch Hochman, *Character in Literature* (Ithaca, NY: Cornell University Press, 1985), 32–3, discussing Rawdon Wilson, "The Bright Chimera: Character as a Literary Term," *Critical Inquiry* 5 (1979): 725–49. I follow the contention of Robert Alter, *The Art of Biblical Narrative*, rev. ed. (New York: Basic Books, 2011), 27–30, that "prose fiction is the best general rubric for describing biblical narrative," and expand it to include the other narratives considered. Here Sarah and the other characters, human and divine, are fictional constructs, no different than Tolkien's Frodo or Tolstoy's Napoleon.

46. Marvin Mudrick, "Character and Event in Fiction," in *On Culture and Literature* (New York: Horizon, 1970), 150–1. The distillation of these two positions into "people or words," the title of this section, is adopted from Shlomith Rimmon-Kenan, *Narrative Fiction: Contemporary Poetics* (London: Methuen, 1983), 31, issued in a (substantially identical, but containing a new retrospective final chapter) second edition by Routledge in 2002.

47. Hochman, *Character*, 36; see also W. J. Harvey, *Character and the Novel* (Ithaca, NY: Cornell University Press, 1965), 200–205; Seymour Chatman, *Story and Discourse: Narrative Structure in Fiction and Film* (Ithaca, NY: Cornell University Press, 1978), 116–19.

fictional characters and flesh-and-blood people are not the same, but the methods and tools we use to get to know characters are largely built and honed in our experience with human beings.[48] In the mimetic view "life" itself is the "source of the whole spectrum of characters in literature," and it is this human–character analogy that lends meaning to our reading of fictional characters.[49]

Story and discourse. Two important subsidiary points of theory support and clarify my mimetic conception of character. The first is the distinction between "story" and "discourse," which Chatman terms the only two "necessary components" of a narrative. Story is the "what," "the content or chain of events (actions, happenings), plus what may be called the existents (characters, items of setting)," while discourse is the "how," "the expression, the means by which the content is communicated."[50] These two elements are interdependent in practice, because access to a story, which is an abstraction constructed in the mind of the reader, can only be gained by means of a discourse. However, these components are conceptually separable. The plainest evidence of this is the "transposability" of a story, which may be communicated in any number of media—a play, a film, a novel, a verbal report—while remaining recognizably "the same" story.[51]

The recognition and maintenance of the story/discourse distinction is vital to a mimetic conception of character, for it shows that the question "people or words?" confuses these two "necessary components." Characters "live" in a metonymy of the text, within the "story-space" of a narrative.[52] And just as a story is transposable, so are its constituents, such as character: as Chatman asks, if characters are "mere words," how can it be that we frequently "recall fictional characters vividly, yet not a single word of the text in which they came alive"?[53] Characters, curiously, often outlive their media, an observation of pointed relevance to an investigation that reads Sarah through a number of discursive refractions.

Character and plot. The second subsidiary point is also a distinction, this time between character and plot. The relationship and relative primacy of these story-level narrative elements have exercised critics at

---

48. Hochman, *Character*, 36; see also Chatman, *Story and Discourse*, 137–8.
49. Hochman, *Character*, 58.
50. Chatman, *Story and Discourse*, 19. A full discussion of these and their many partially cognate terms is too complex to attempt here.
51. Ibid., 20, 101; see also Rimmon-Kenan, *Narrative Fiction*, 4.
52. Chatman, *Story and Discourse*, 107, 116–18.
53. Ibid., 118.

least since Aristotle, who seems to subordinate character to the exigencies of plot, at least in the context of tragedy.[54] In the modern era, this debate became another thread in the broader dispute between "purists" and "realists" over the nature of character, with formalists and some structuralists going further than Aristotle in arguing that characters are purely functional and at the service of a narrative's action.[55]

But what is important to my mimetic understanding of character is not the relative dominance of either plot or character over the other. Rather, as with the story/discourse distinction, what matters is that these elements are, while interdependent, conceptually separable.[56] Chatman's enduring idea of a character as a "paradigm of traits" is helpful here. For Chatman a "trait" is simply an adjective in ordinary language—"callous," "timid," or the like—that describes a relatively persistent aspect of a character. Since traits endure outside the linear temporal progression to which events must submit, characters, which are sets, or paradigms, of traits, are not bound to the chronological sequence of happenings that comprise a plot.[57] Thus character illustrates, and is illustrated by, event, but may be discussed in abstraction.

As I understand it, then, my interest in characters is a facet of my human interest in other people, and the methods I employ to "get to know" characters—usefully if loosely defined as "concrete semblances of real men and women"—are genetically related to those I use in social interaction.[58] This means that in my readings of Sarah I make inferences, form and reform hypotheses, try to reconcile incongruous actions or speech, empathize, and wonder about motive, among other mental and emotional moves, just as I do with people I know. This process, however, is not uncontrolled, any more than my suppositions about an acquaintance are uncontrolled: "there are limits.... [S]omehow we know when to stop speculating."[59] In fact, a mimetic approach, no less than any "purist"

---

54. *Poetics* chapter 6 (§§1450a–b).

55. Chatman, *Story and Discourse*, 111–13; Rimmon-Kenan, *Narrative Fiction*, 34–6.

56. Chatman, *Story and Discourse*, 113; Rimmon-Kenan, *Narrative Fiction*, 35; compare Henry James, "The Art of Fiction," in *The Art of Fiction and Other Essays*; with an introduction by Morris Roberts (New York: Oxford University Press, 1948), 13 (originally published in 1888).

57. Chatman, *Story and Discourse*, 119–31.

58. "Concrete semblances" is the language of Ronald Crane, quoted in ibid., 137. I understand "concrete" to evoke something substantial, not fixed or immobile.

59. Ibid., 119–20. Compare Robert Alter, *The Pleasures of Reading in an Ideological Age* (New York: Simon & Schuster, 1989), 47: "as readers we will sometimes

method, must remain deeply committed to wrestling with the discourse, the text in its expression, for it is only through these signs that the story, and the characters such as Sarah who live there, may be known.

The role of the reader

These notions of character were formed largely in readings of European novels and are vulnerable to charges of anachronism when brought to bear on ancient narratives.[60] These are acknowledged and answered, however, by the psychological implications of Hochman's broader mimetic theory. While he does not dispute the necessity of learning what we can about the language and world in which a work was produced, Hochman argues strongly that we can only "retrieve figures from older literatures in terms of our own perception of character and of our perception of motives operative within character."[61] The fact that "the modern conception of character," speaking broadly, is only a few centuries old, is ultimately not relevant to the task of reading ancient characters because we have no other—no authentic way to adopt, say, a Homeric understanding of personhood, even if this could be reliably defined. While it would be a mistake to fail to "acknowledge the otherness" of such conceptions, in the end we can only read through ourselves: there is literally "no alternative but to construct our images of character in terms of our own knowledge and experience."[62] Because our reading of character can only be governed by our ideas of "what people are and how people work," Hochman maintains that "the patterns of behavior projected in earlier texts, all the way back to Homer and Bible, lend themselves to interpretation along lines congenial to us."[63]

---

run the risk of inventing a connection in the text where there is only a gap. For the most part, however, the dangers of overreading are far outweighed by the dangers of underreading."

60. Hochman, *Character*, 54. For a variety of views on the legitimacy of reading biblical narrative with the tools of modern literary study, see Alter, *Art*, 15–19, 25–6; Shimon Bar-Efrat, *Narrative Art in the Bible*, BLS 17 (Sheffield: Almond Press, 1989), 7–11; Adele Berlin, *Poetics and Interpretation of Biblical Narrative*, BLS 9 (Sheffield: Almond Press, 1983), 19–21; Yairah Amit, *Reading Biblical Narratives: Literary Criticism and the Hebrew Bible*, trans. Yael Lotan (Minneapolis: Fortress Press, 2001).

61. Hochman, *Character*, 54.

62. Ibid., 55–6. Compare Alter, *Pleasures of Reading*, 73–4, who argues, in some contrast, for the essential continuity of human experience.

63. Hochman, *Character*, 56–9.

So the role of the individual reader—in this case, me—is implicit in and inseparable from the mimetic view I have outlined here. My readings of Sarah are based upon my readings of people, and I have no personality-reading knowledge divisible from myself.

The work of Wolfgang Iser still provides one of the most persuasive accounts of the role of the reader in the construction of meaning. In an early article, Iser contests the modern notion that meaning hides within a text, awaiting discovery. Rather, "meanings in literary texts are mainly generated in the act of reading."[64] The fact that literary things are neither real objects nor within the lived experience of the reader creates an "indeterminacy" that can only be resolved in the reader's mental action. Thus a literary text occupies a liminal place, a "peculiar halfway position between the world of real objects and the reader's own world of experience. The act of reading is therefore a process of seeking to pin down the oscillating structure of the text to some specific meaning."[65]

Iser details the formal means that create conditions for this indeterminacy and its resolution by the reader. Underlying all of these means is the idea that literary objects can only be shown or constituted in a series of "schematized views" that necessarily leave intervening "gaps," or "blanks."[66] A simple example of this might be the presentation of two successive discourse-level scenes that evoke temporally disparate events in the story. It is impossible for the discourse to bridge the gap that remains; only the reader can fill it, and this by "a free play of meaning-projection" that "repairs the unformulated connections between the particular views."[67] In Iser's scheme, these gaps are basic to the act of reading—the indeterminacy that they generate is in fact "the fundamental precondition for

---

64. Wolfgang Iser, "Indeterminacy and the Reader's Response in Prose Fiction," in *Aspects of Narrative: Selected Papers from the English Institute*, ed. J. Harris Miller (New York: Columbia University Press, 1971), 4. If it were true that meaning need only be "found" by readers, Iser says, "one cannot help wondering why texts should indulge in such a 'hide-and-seek' with their interpreters; and even more puzzling, why the meaning, once it has been found, should then change again, even though the letters, words, and sentences of the text remain the same."

65. Ibid., 9–10.

66. "Schematized views," defined as "views which constitute the 'object' in stages and at the same time give a concrete form for the reader to contemplate," is based upon a concept of philosopher Roman Ingarden (ibid., 10; see also Wolfgang Iser, *The Act of Reading: A Theory of Aesthetic Response* [Baltimore: Johns Hopkins University Press, 1978], 170–3, and elsewhere). Rimmon-Kenan has a summary of some relevant aspects of Ingarden's work that is characteristically brief and clear (*Narrative Fiction*, 118).

67. Iser, "Indeterminacy," 12.

reader participation"—and they are unavoidably present in a literary text. Indeed, as Iser points out, the more determined or "precise" such a text may be, that is, the more "schematized views" that are presented, the more gaps necessarily open between the views.[68]

What is especially attractive about Iser's presentation is that it itself bridges a gap between text and reader, striking a balance that avoids overburdening either extreme. For as much as "a text can only come to life when it is read," there is yet a structure that inheres in the text, as the key term itself reveals: these "views" are "schematized," each presenting its object "not in an incidental or even accidental way, but in a representative manner."[69] Thus it remains justified to speak of "techniques," as Iser goes on to do.[70] Moreover, texts vary in terms of the "performance" required of the reader—that is, texts are not all equally indeterminate.[71] Meaning, then, arises out of a symbiosis that develops between a particular literary text and a particular reader, and is a construct "conditioned by the text itself, but only in a form that allows the reader" to realize it.[72] A literary character such as Sarah, too, as a "concrete semblance" of a human being, is constructed at just such a junction of discourse structure and readerly consciousness.

The question of audience. However, the fact that Sarah, a character in narratives composed two millennia and more ago, is the person of interest in this investigation—and not, say, Robert Jordan of *For Whom the Bell Tolls*, or even Don Quixote—presents a special set of problems regarding the role and identity of the reader. It is plain that these narratives were created by and for real human beings whose cultures differ greatly from mine. Questions of orality, literacy, and performance, semantic concerns and the comprehension of idiom, and uncertainties about a host of other cultural assumptions that may never be fully reconstructible are only some of the quandaries that arise from this divide.

Biblical narrative critics have responded to this situation in two primary ways. The first, which may be described as ahistorical, is that adopted in much "classical" biblical narrative work.[73] This movement was prompted

---

68. Ibid., 11–14.
69. Ibid., 2–3, 10.
70. Ibid., 14–17.
71. Ibid., 21–2.
72. Ibid., 43. Compare Iser, *Act of Reading*, 169.
73. The term "ahistorical" is here descriptive, not pejorative, and describes a tendency rather than a strict ideology of reading. For a variety of perspectives, see David M. Gunn and Danna Nolan Fewell, *Narrative in the Hebrew Bible* (Oxford

not only by biblical narrative critique's New-Critical and structuralist roots, which emphasized the "text-in-itself," but also by a deliberate revolt against the unrelenting historical focus of traditional biblical criticism.[74] Roughly put, this first kind of reading asks what a narrative *means*, in the present tense: "in itself," perhaps, but often implicitly "to me," or "to a reader like me," or "to my reading community."[75] The second, which might be broadly termed historical-contextual, was, in turn, partly a reaction against this ahistorical posture, and emphasizes the reconstruction of an audience or reader loosely contemporaneous to a work's composition.[76] Roughly put, again, this second kind of reading asks what a narrative *meant*, in the past tense, to its original auditors or readers.[77]

As a number of critics have recognized, neither of these extremes is fully sustainable. The chief weakness of an attempt to take a strictly ahistorical approach to ancient narratives is that these are exclusively manifest in written texts whose culturally bound means of expression are alien to our own. To learn the meaning of ancient words in their syntax, to puzzle out their idioms, euphemisms, and figures, which is not to mention higher-level phenomena such as type-scenes or generic conventions—this is already historically focused cultural investigation of a profound sort. On the other hand, reconstructions of an "original reader" or audience frequently stumble on a dearth of evidence and end in speculative proposals that vary from critic to critic.[78]

Bible Series (Oxford: Oxford University Press, 1993), 7–12; J. P. Fokkelman, *Reading Biblical Narrative: An Introductory Guide*, trans. Ineke Smit (Louisville: Westminster John Knox Press, 1999), 206–7; W. Lee Humphreys, *The Character of God in the Book of Genesis: A Narrative Appraisal* (Louisville: Westminster John Knox Press, 2001), 19.

74. John A. Darr, *On Character Building: The Reader and the Rhetoric of Characterization in Luke-Acts* (Louisville: Westminster John Knox Press, 1992), 13; compare Gunn and Fewell, *Narrative in the Hebrew Bible*, 7–12.

75. This does not imply that ahistorical criticism must be a postmodern free-for-all—indeed, Alter, whose approach is largely ahistorical in the terms of my discussion here, assumes that a competent reader can be persuaded of the validity of his generally author-centered readings. The distinction I am making here is conceptually separate from, if necessarily related to, the question of the locus of meaning in literature.

76. Darr, *Character Building*, 13–14, 23–9.

77. Of course, historical-contextual readings do not strictly or even primarily serve antiquarian ends, as audience reconstructions contribute to arguments meant to inform how we read ancient narratives today.

78. See Darr, *Character Building*, 23–5, for examples from work on Luke-Acts.

Reception and rewriting. I locate my own work in this study at a little-visited intersection of approaches, where character-driven narrative critique meets the ancient reception and rewriting of the tradition surrounding Sarah. My primary questions are literary, not historical, though I make some basic assumptions regarding history and influence. The Septuagint, the Apocryphon, and the *Antiquities* all rework narratives from something close to what became MT Genesis, alongside other elements of tradition and composition, and all in sharply varying proportions.[79] MT Genesis too is not an aboriginal spring of tradition but the result of a tortuous process of production, reception, and reworking that may well have overlapped temporally with the reception and composition processes of some of these other texts. Even if some elements of the MT as it stands are later than parts of the LXX, however, I am convinced that the Sarah traditions that underlie MT Genesis were generative for those in LXX Genesis.[80] The Apocryphon also draws on something similar to what became the MT, but much more freely, in addition to traditions that also appear in *1 Enoch* and *Jubilees*.[81] The *Antiquities* may draw on Genesis "in varying text-forms" and several languages, in addition to a number of other named and unnamed written or unwritten sources, including traditions also adopted and adapted by other extrabiblical texts.[82]

---

79. Genesis circulated in at least two text-types in the Second Temple period, and the Septuagint and the Apocryphon are more closely affiliated with the pre-Samaritan type than the proto-MT: Sidnie White Crawford, *Rewriting Scripture in Second Temple Times* (Grand Rapids: Eerdmans, 2008), 20–1, 107; Emanuel Tov, "Textual Harmonization in the Five Books of the Torah: A Summary," in *The Bible, Qumran, and the Samaritans*, ed. Magnar Kartveit and Gary N. Knoppers, SJ 104, StSam 10 (Berlin: de Gruyter, 2018), 51. However, the disparities between these types do not merit the distinction of different literary editions (Crawford, *Rewriting Scripture*, 21).

80. John William Wevers, *Notes on the Greek Text of Genesis*, SCS 35 (Atlanta: Scholars Press, 1993), xiii. Tervanotko, *Denying Her Voice*, 209–10, discusses evidence that suggests that the Greek witnesses preserve earlier, more positive traditions involving Miriam (and Hannah, in the work of Anneli Aejmelaeus) than are reflected in the MT. As Tervanotko notes, it is difficult to make generalizations across the variety of translations that comprise "the Septuagint," and my analysis of Sarah in LXX Genesis shows the opposite trend.

81. Joseph A. Fitzmyer, *The Genesis Apocryphon of Qumran Cave 1 (1Q20): A Commentary*, 3rd ed. (Rome: Pontifical Biblical Institute, 2004), 20.

82. Christopher T. Begg, "Genesis in Josephus," in *The Book of Genesis: Composition, Reception, and Interpretation*, ed. Craig A. Evans, Joel N. Lohr, and David L. Petersen, VTSup 152 (Leiden: Brill, 2014), 303–8. Étienne Nodet, *The Hebrew Bible of Josephus: Main Features*, CahRB 92 (Leuven: Peeters, 2018), 12, 19, 23, 26, 28,

But in my thinking about reception for this project, I am also influenced by a "rhizomorphous" model developed by Caroline Vander Stichele from the work of Gilles Deleuze and Félix Guattari.[83] In distinction from "arborescent" systems comprised of roots and a single trunk feeding spreading branches, rhizomorphous systems such as bamboo are interconnected throughout and have no center or hierarchy, no firm beginning or end. Vander Stichele argues for a reevaluation of "'reception history' as a dynamic and open-ended process, with multiple entries and exits, rather than linear trajectories," so that "'the Bible' is no longer conceived as origin or centre, but as a node from which its history unfolds in multiple directions."[84] This metaphor itself might unfold further, as parts of a rhizome, cut off from the rest, can often generate "new" rhizomorphous systems. My arrangement of the following chapters in the likely order of the basic composition of their subject texts, then, is not intended to emphasize issues of linear descent and derivation—though I do not avoid these when they may bear on the reading at hand. What is most important to me, however, is to read each of these narratives as a work with its own integrity and generative ability, and not only as a source of points of comparison for another, privileged narrative.

Questions of reception, reader, and audience blur, moreover, when I admit that this study of the ancient reception of the Sarah traditions is also, inescapably, a performance of my own reception of these traditions. "Reception" is even too passive a concept. Vander Stichele, drawing on the work of Mieke Bal, complicates the idea of cultural transmission and reception as a one-way process through time, positing that a retelling (in whatever medium) is nothing short of an "active intervention" into its inspiration.[85] Perhaps as the Apocryphon, for example, actively intervenes into its antecedents, my reading of Sarah in the Apocryphon intervenes into it. "Reading," finally, is probably too weak a word for this kind of intervention. What I am doing in performing my readings—what all

---

40–2, 260–1, argues that Josephus used only a Hebrew source of the Pentateuch that had close affinities with the *Vorlage* of the OG (in addition to extrabiblical Jewish traditions and other Greek authors). The material involving Abraham in particular may also draw on other literary sources, however (263).

83. Caroline Vander Stichele, "The Head of John and Its Reception or How to Conceptualize 'Reception History'," in *Reception History and Biblical Studies: Theory and Practice*, ed. Emma England and William John Lyons, LHBOTS 615, Scriptural Traces 6 (London: Bloomsbury T&T Clark, 2015), 84–5.

84. Ibid., 85.

85. Ibid., 83–4.

literary analyses are doing, as the critic Gary Weissman argues—is itself, quite literally, "rewriting" these ancient narratives.[86]

I readily own a complicated, hybrid identity as the reader, receiver, and rewriter of these narratives.[87] I consider close work with original languages and means of expression to be indispensable to quality narrative-critical readings; for this and other reasons, which include a deep respect for the real human beings who created them, I would never claim that the historical context of the composition of these narratives is irrelevant. However, the highly mediated fashion in which I comprehend these languages impels me at once to recognize the cultural distance that separates me from these narratives' original composers and consumers, and to confess the difficulty that lies in their reconstruction. Nor do I see a satisfactory solution in the detection or assembly of an "implied reader," which, as its name indicates, is a function of a text.[88] I respectfully decline to identify with a text-function, and I assert my freedom to ask questions of these narratives, prompted by my social location and personal concerns, that may never have occurred to their ancient writers, auditors, or readers. At the same time, I contend that my task of reading character is not separable from my reading of human beings, and I believe that there is an irreducible humanness expressed in these ancient stories that I am able to comprehend.

With Hochman, then, I "acknowledge the otherness" of these ancient narratives' cultures and ideas of personhood, and affirm the necessity of historical and cultural investigation into the meanings of the words that depict the worlds of their stories. However, my construction of character, though "guided by the signs" of a given text, is finally actualized in its gaps, which I can only fill by drawing on my own experience and perception

---

86. Gary Weissman, *The Writer in the Well: On Misreading and Rewriting Literature*, Theory and Interpretation of Narrative Series (Columbus: The Ohio State University Press, 2016), 7.

87. See the formulation of Darr, *Character Building*, 26, who "images" a "*hybrid reader, part ancient, part modern, part reader, part critic*" (emphasis in the original). However, Darr still attempts a reconstruction of an original audience member, albeit with significant "gaps" plugged by his own identity and context (25, 27).

88. See Rimmon-Kenan, *Narrative Fiction*, 118–19, on the welter of terms used to define "the reader." David Herman et al., *Narrative Theory: Core Concepts and Critical Debates* (Columbus: The Ohio State University Press, 2012), 151–4, argues that the use of "reader constructs" risks "losing sight of the heuristic status of these models and reifying or hypostatizing the entities they encompass"; in fact, an "implied" reader can never be anything but an interpretation of an actual reader.

of what a person is. I, at last, am "the reader" here—the receiver, even the rewriter—a man, fortyish, a practicing if critical Roman Catholic with a justice orientation, of northern European descent and North American origin with, however, significant cross-cultural experience and a love for old languages and stories, straight, able-bodied, married, a father.

Practice: Characterization and Its Means

A fluid paradigm

In speaking practically of the formation of one of these "concrete semblances" of a human being, it is useful to reprise Chatman's conception of character as a "paradigm of traits." A "trait" here, again, is an adjective in ordinary language that describes a relatively enduring, individuating quality of a character: brave, shy, unfeeling, cruel, and so on. These adjectives are story-level elements that may, but often do not, appear directly in the discourse. A character's traits may conflict with one another, and they may arise, transform, or pass away during the course of a story. Considered as a set or "paradigm," usually distilled into a proper name, traits are constitutive of a character, a story-level entity that, while obviously fictive, transcends a story's plot and can endure indefinitely in a reader's memory.[89]

The process of assembling traits is not a mechanical or specifically literary enterprise. The concept of "trait" itself directly ties the reading of literary characters to the experience of real-life human intercourse: what Chatman calls the "transaction between narrative and audience" depends upon the audience's familiarity with the "enormous" thesaurus of traits culturally available to social human beings. As readers of literary characters we evaluate traits we infer against trait "paradigms" we have established through earlier inferences, integrating, adding, revising, and puzzling out conflicts as we go—a process that Chatman argues does not meaningfully "differ in kind from our ordinary evaluations of human beings."[90]

Yet both Shlomith Rimmon-Kenan and Hochman regard Chatman's concept of character as "paradigm" as too "static," and Chatman does not discourage an impression of fixity when he speaks metaphorically of a trait-set, and thus a character, as a "vertical assemblage" intersecting the plot.[91] In my mimetic scheme, I emphasize with Rimmon-Kenan that

---

89. Chatman, *Story and Discourse*, 121–31.
90. Ibid., 125, 127–8.
91. Rimmon-Kenan, *Narrative Fiction*, 39; Hochman, *Character*, 50; Chatman, *Story and Discourse*, 127.

"discussion of the 'directional' dimension of character (development, 'biography')" must be an integral part of character reading, and I stress with Hochman that conflict, both "intrapsychic" and social, is a vital catalyst for character development.[92] I soften the edges of Chatman's metaphor, then, allowing for conflict and growth while allowing that a mimetic understanding of character demands some structure and coherence: a "paradigm" that is yet progressively fluid, organic, and relational.

Means or clues to generating a fluid paradigm

The "weighing of claims" in characterization. Many biblical narrative critics generate detailed rubrics of "means" of characterization.[93] By far the most influential has been the weighted scale of Robert Alter, which is adopted or adapted by a majority of scholars engaged in critique of characters in the Bible. The elements of this scale, in "ascending order of explicitness and certainty," are actions, appearance, comments of another character, direct speech, thought, and narratorial remarks about motivation. Alter argues that actions and appearance leave a reader "substantially in the realm of inference"; that speech about and by a character "lead us from inference to the weighing of claims"; that thought or "inward speech" enters "the realm of relative certainty about character"; and, finally, that "we are accorded certainty" in statements made by the reliable narrator.[94]

Alter's "scale of means" possesses simplicity and utility, but its enormous influence owes most to the sheer verve and perspicacity of Alter's readings. His performances demonstrate that the distillation and employment of lists of means need not lead to lifeless criticism: if others have applied his rubric mechanically, this is not owing to close observation of Alter's practice. Still, the scale's distinctions and hierarchy raise questions: isn't "speech" also an "action"? Or if the distinction is between verbal and nonverbal acts, why should the former be intrinsically more reliable as an indicator of character? Common wisdom, of course, would have it the other way around. A more basic issue, however, and the

---

92. Rimmon-Kenan, *Narrative Fiction*, 39; Hochman, *Character*, 50–4.

93. The fifteen-point "spectrum" of Meir Sternberg, *The Poetics of Biblical Narrative: Ideological Literature and the Drama of Reading* (Bloomington: Indiana University Press, 1985), 475–81, represents the extreme of a tendency toward a taxonomy of means reflected generally in biblical narrative work. My own understanding of "means" is not text-centric but emphasizes instrumentality, as nothing is finally formed apart from the agency of the reader.

94. Alter, *Art*, 146–7.

reason that simple rearrangements of Alter's categories fail to satisfy, is the spectrum's ordering principle of narratorial authority.

Several critics have challenged the absolute authority and omniscience of Alter's narrator.[95] For my purposes here, the most significant is Alice Bach, who in her rereading of the Bathsheba narratives takes the role of a reader or "narratee" who is "irritable" and "suspicious" of the narrator's projected transparency and honesty.[96] This casts the narrator not as a disinterested entity floating above the story world but as another kind of character, a "storyteller with whom the reader must contend," and one who is often "telling it slant" in tones of patriarchy.[97] When the narrator is recognized as a "figure possessing various attitudes" and traits much like a character, the reader is freed to break from the narrator's "fixed gaze" and to question what may have been obscured or left out of the account, whether due to an inability to see, disinterest, or active motives of concealment.[98] As mentioned earlier, these contentions are of signal value to a project that performs readings of a female character in androcentric narratives such as Genesis and its related texts. Taking up the language of Gayatri Spivak, Bach argues forcefully that when a reader "challenges the notion of the omnipotent voice of an impassive narrator, female biblical characters will not be in so much danger of oozing away."[99]

So I am convinced that a reader cannot escape the "weighing of claims" at any point; even the evaluations of a narrator, on the extreme upper end of Alter's scale of reliability, must be delicately weighed with other narrative features. If this is true in readings of the Bible, it is even surer in this study, which sounds the tales of several patently distinct narrators. Practical hierarchies are often established, but all claims bear weighing, in prospect and retrospect, and as a reader I calibrate this process by my own experience with people, the world, and other literature, if always as cued by the text to hand.

Weighing kinds of means. Rimmon-Kenan joins many critics in dividing means of characterization or "textual indicators of character" into two basic kinds: "direct definition" and "indirect presentation." Direct or "told" indicators in this scheme name a character trait in the discourse,

---

95. Among others, Gunn and Fewell, *Narrative in the Hebrew Bible*, 53–6.

96. Bach, "Signs," 352, 362; compare Bach, *Women, Seduction, and Betrayal*, 21.

97. Bach, "Signs," 351, 353, 356; compare Bach, *Women, Seduction, and Betrayal*, 14. See also Gunn and Fewell, *Narrative in the Hebrew Bible*, 52–3.

98. Bach, "Signs," 356, 362.

99. Bach, *Women, Seduction, and Betrayal*, 14.

usually taking the form of adjectives or nouns in the text, though other parts of speech may also serve: Esau is "hairy" (Gen. 27:11); David is a "youth" when he faces Goliath (1 Sam. 17:42); Job "avoids evil" (Job 1:1).[100] Physical attributes, social locations, moral predilections, emotions, mental states, or any other human phenomenon amenable to direct description may be specified in this way. Conversely, indirect or "shown" indicators prompt a process of inference that shapes a trait in the mind of the reader. These include depicted actions or speech, as well as plainly literary artifacts such as access to the thoughts of others or trait-reinforcing personal names.[101]

These divisions can be heuristically profitable, but their borders blur under inspection, and critics do not always agree on whether a certain means of characterization is direct or indirect.[102] Internal distinctions and hierarchies can also be fuzzy. Direct indicators are words in a discourse, which implies a speaker; but whose words count, and for how much?[103] Characters and narrators may be or become more or less reliable, and their testimony may agree or clash.[104] Among indirect indicators, the distinction between "action" and "speech" is not always clear. "Thought," too, as it can only be bound in a linear sequence of words in a text, can be hard to meaningfully distinguish from speech in a literary context.

Direct indicators are sometimes privileged over indirect as defining aspects of a character that are "supra-temporal" or "static," but their "domains," to use the language of Chatman, can and do end: David does not remain a youth forever.[105] Moreover, the varying focalization—often called "point of view"—of direct indicators reveals subjectivities that complicate these claims. Although David is noted to be young elsewhere in the near context of his fight with Goliath (1 Sam. 17:14, 33), in this event he is a "youth" who is "flushed and handsome" specifically in the eyes of the Philistine who "looks at" and "sees" him (v. 42).[106]

---

100. Rimmon-Kenan, *Narrative Fiction*, 59–60; Bar-Efrat, *Narrative Art*, 48, 51, 53.
101. Rimmon-Kenan, *Narrative Fiction*, 59–60, 67–70.
102. Ibid., 63–6; Bar-Efrat, *Narrative Art*, 48–53, 63–77; Berlin, *Poetics*, 34–9.
103. For differing views, see Rimmon-Kenan, *Narrative Fiction*, 60; Bar-Efrat, *Narrative Art*, 54, 64; Berlin, *Poetics*, 34, 38.
104. Gunn and Fewell, *Narrative in the Hebrew Bible*, 51–3.
105. Rimmon-Kenan, *Narrative Fiction*, 60; Bar-Efrat, *Narrative Art*, 89–90; Chatman, *Story and Discourse*, 126.
106. Rimmon-Kenan, *Narrative Fiction*, 72, succinctly summarizes the distinction between focalizer and narrator as "'who sees?' v. 'who speaks?'"

On the other hand, critics such as Shimon Bar-Efrat lay the "burden of characterization" on indirect indicators, as these predominate even in ancient fiction, which does not display the late-modern and postmodern aesthetic preference for "showing" over "telling."[107] Yet this matter is highly variable. Josephus's narrator displays a positive predilection for direct definition, and the detailed physical description of Sarai in column 20 of the Genesis Apocryphon is foreign to the economy of expression that marks Genesis.

Nor, finally, do the differing modes of operation of direct and indirect indicators point to hierarchies of reliability or clarity. It is true that direct indicators usually appear in the discourse as adjectives, while indirect indicators manifest most often as verbs of action. As a trait in Chatman's scheme is a narrative adjective, indirect indicators may thus require a formally higher degree of inference to resolve a trait. Yet the proportion of readerly involvement and liberty in the recognition or construction of traits indicated cannot be determined in advance in any case. A narrator's direct definition may stand in flat contradiction to other narrative elements, as shown repeatedly in my reading of the *Antiquities* in this study. Indirect means can also afford a reader more or less freedom in inferring a trait. When Ezra tears his clothes and pulls his hair out at the news of the people's marriage practices, it is difficult not to infer a trait such as a strong regard for the letter of the law, or, less charitably, xenophobia (Ezra 9:3). But the opacity of an action such as Yahweh's disdain for Cain's offering demands a higher degree of inference, shading into speculation (Gen. 4:5). In short, the manner of character construction and the degree of readerly freedom may vary between direct and indirect categories, and also within each category. There is no mechanical way to assess these literary situations; as in life, they may only be evaluated by an informed weighing of claims in the light of experience.

All of this supports a fluid conception of means of characterization; these categories are mutually informing and ultimately not separable. A character, especially in a mimetic scheme, is no bundle of fragments but a potentially evolving, personal unity. Provisional demarcation may be heuristically profitable, but what is found is weighed and shaped, by the reading process and in the consciousness of the reader, into a character who, as an organic whole, is more than the sum of her parts.

---

107. Bar-Efrat, *Narrative Art*, 64, 89–90.

Relationality, development, and linearity in character construction. Therefore, in my readings of Sarah, I explore the ways in which she relates—to other characters and narrative elements, including the narrator, but also to herself—as a kind of holistic rubric. Relationality as an organizing concept dovetails with my mimetic understanding of character construction, and is helpful in a reading that both admits the potential of a character to develop and regards gender as a significant aspect of character construction.

The plainest way that relationality affects characterization is in a character's connections with other characters. For Harvey the "web of human relationships" is "by far the most important of contexts" in characterization: "characters do not develop along single and linear roads of destiny but are, so to speak, human cross-roads."[108] Conflict, in particular, is key to readings of Sarah, whose story is marked by strife with Hagar, Ishmael, Abraham, foreign rulers, and the deity.[109] Gender, too, a kind of relationality that includes but transcends personal relationships to encompass social assumptions and norms, affects all of Sarah's interactions—not only with Abraham, Pharaoh, or Abimelech, but also with Hagar, their sons, God, and Sarah's absent family of origin and wider social structures as depicted in the narrative.[110]

With Bach, I do not exempt the narrator from consideration in discussion of these aspects of relationality. A narrator is a character-like element in a narrative, a storytelling voice who exhibits perspectives and so possesses an identity. This is significant when evaluating issues of conflict and gender: narratorial information and perspectives can clash with those of a character, and a narrator may, under questioning, reveal values about gender that are relevant to the reading of gendered characters in relationship.[111]

In addition to her relationships with other characters and the narrator, a character also relates to herself in what Rimmon-Kenan calls the

---

108. Harvey, *Character*, 52, 69.

109. Compare Hochman, *Character*, 50–4; Berlin, *Poetics*, 40; Colleen M. Conway, *Men and Women in the Fourth Gospel: Gender and Johannine Characterization*, SBLDS 167 (Atlanta: Society of Biblical Literature, 1999), 62.

110. Conway, *Men and Women*, 65–8, foregrounds the issue of gender as it pertains to Hochman's ideas of relationality. See also Mignon R. Jacobs, *Gender, Power, and Persuasion: The Genesis Narratives and Contemporary Portraits* (Grand Rapids: Baker Academic, 2007), 15–16, 73–102, 129–55; Koenig, *Isn't This Bathsheba?* 22.

111. Bach, "Signs," 351–3; Gunn and Fewell, *Narrative in the Hebrew Bible*, 51–3.

"'directional' dimension of character."[112] Speech may clash with deeds, or later actions conflict with earlier ones, leading to dissonances that the reader may struggle to resolve.[113] "Intrapsychic" conflict, conscious or otherwise, may motivate characters in a mimetic scheme just as it does human beings.[114]

This notion of development, finally, emphasizes the concept of linearity, which binds this entire discussion. In the reading of narratives, a linear orientation is inescapable, simply because "language prescribes a linear figuration of signs and hence a linear presentation of information about things."[115] *Process* is thus the heart of the fluid model of character outlined here with the help of Chatman, Iser, Hochman, Rimmon-Kenan, and others: the construction of a character such as Sarah is effected by an organic accretion of traits, cued by the discourse but sorted, weighed, assembled, taken apart, and put back together again in the mind of the reader.[116]

The reading process itself, then, is key to the central question raised in this section: what gives shape and proportion to a character under construction, if claims cannot be weighed automatically? Certain artifacts of the linear process of reading can have a marked effect on the task of weighing. Trait information appearing first in a narrative tends to endure and color later impressions, a phenomenon Rimmon-Kenan, after Menakhem Perry, calls a "primacy effect." This, in turn, can clash with a "recency effect," as information just absorbed often requires a reconciliation or balancing of prior data.[117] So the structure of a text is not without power to shape character construction; but neither is the reader bound to follow its directions slavishly, for unfilled gaps or blanks always remain. The process of reading is a "continuous process of forming hypotheses," of making and acting upon "hunches" while attempting to integrate earlier

---

112. Rimmon-Kenan, *Narrative Fiction*, 38–9.
113. Berlin, *Poetics*, 40; see also David W. Cotter, *Genesis*, Berit Olam (Collegeville, MN: Liturgical Press, 2003), xxxv–xxxvi.
114. Hochman, *Character*, 50–3.
115. Rimmon-Kenan, *Narrative Fiction*, 119.
116. Chatman, *Story and Discourse*, 127–8; Wolfgang Iser, "The Reading Process: A Phenomenological Approach," in *New Directions in Literary History*, ed. Ralph Cohen (Baltimore: Johns Hopkins University Press, 1974), 127–33; Hochman, *Character*, 49–50; Rimmon-Kenan, *Narrative Fiction*, 36–9.
117. Rimmon-Kenan, *Narrative Fiction*, 119–21; Menakhem Perry, "Literary Dynamics: How the Order of a Text Creates Its Meanings (with an Analysis of Faulkner's 'A Rose for Emily')," *Poetics Today* 1 (1979): 53–8.

testimony and present evidence, of examining a character's past and guessing about her future.[118]

Rooted in a mimetic conception of character, and thus admitting my key role in Sarah's construction, I now move to weigh the claims of these four narratives, seeking a relational character paradigm in each case that is substantial yet fluid and open to development. Throughout, I admit with Iser that in these, as in "all literary texts," "the potential text is infinitely richer than any of its individual realizations."[119]

---

118. Rimmon-Kenan, *Narrative Fiction*, 37–9, 121–2.
119. Iser, "Reading Process," 131.

Chapter 2

SARAH IN THE MASORETIC TEXT

Introduction

Sarah emerges from my reading of the Masoretic Text of Genesis as a complex but ultimately coherent figure whose development over the course of the narrative is most clearly revealed in her relationships with others. In distinction to interpretations that emphasize Sarah's divine election—such as that of Tammi Schneider, who maintains that God's enduring "support" of Sarah shows that she is "chosen by the Deity"—I argue that Sarah is "chosen" just as a tool is selected: she is used, by Abraham and by God, then discarded when her utility is exhausted.[1] While there are notes of "blessing" for Sarah in Gen. 17:16, I contend that she is blessed merely as an instrument or vessel for the fulfillment of God's covenant with Abraham and his son, Isaac—a point supported by the context of this blessing, which is a colloquy between Abraham and God alone. Abraham's use and abuse of Sarah, which is only abetted by the deity, plays a catalytic role in her own use and abuse of her slave Hagar. This abuse, which is also not only countenanced but encouraged by God, represents a stage in Sarah's emotional evolution that features a progressive hardening in her character, which, in turn, finds curious expression in Sarah's increasing resemblance to Abraham.

Many readers of Sarah in the MT seek to defend or damn her. Often the decision turns on the episode chosen for analysis: Sarah is an oppressed and silent victim in Egypt for Fokkelien van Dijk-Hemmes, but in Phyllis Trible's influential reading in *Texts of Terror*, the suffering of the "tortured" and "exploited" Hagar only underlines Sarah's relative "privilege and

---

1. Schneider, *Mothers of Promise*, 40; Schneider, *Sarah*, 5, 129, and throughout. Compare Fischer, *Women Who Wrestled*, 7, 27, 46.

power," albeit "within the confines of patriarchal structures."[2] I do not disagree in either case. However, I seek a broader view that strives to integrate such polarities, contending that Sarah is characterized throughout the narrative by a pattern of possession and lack, or gain and loss, most notably in her connections with other characters. This motif of Sarah as a woman who both has and has not finds its climactic expression at the birth of Isaac, where the reversal of Sarah's most enduring significant trait—her childlessness—is overshadowed by an acute sensitivity to her appearance in the eyes of others. Sarah, in my reading, does not ultimately evoke condemnation for her misdeeds, but sympathy—even pity.

Practical Preliminaries

My reading grows out of the poetics of character and characterization that I outlined in Chapter 1. While interpreters such as Esther Fuchs emphasize Sarah's functions in conventional patterns in the text, I read Sarah as a "concrete semblance" of a human being, in keeping with my mimetic understanding of fictional character.[3] Thus I do not avoid inferring Sarah's traits and motives—prompted by clues in the discourse, but always supplemented by and filtered through my own experiences trying to understand other human beings—any more than I avoid drawing such conclusions about people I know. My discoveries have sometimes surprised me, and I have rarely found occasion to agree with those, such as Martin Noth, who dismiss Sarah in the MT as "colorless," a mere "construct created for the purpose of the Abraham narratives."[4] But this too is a testament to the power of perspective and the vital role of the reader.

Although the effects of primacy and recency inform the construction of character, and linearity is intrinsic to narrative, I do not restrict myself to narrative data already presented, or adopt the posture of a "first-time" reader. I am not a first-time reader of this narrative, and I am not convinced that such a pose confers a substantive advantage, even if I believed it possible to achieve in an authentic way. In performing my reading here,

---

2. Van Dijk-Hemmes, "Sarai in Exile"; Trible, "Desolation," 9, 13, 28; compare Phyllis Trible, "Ominous Beginnings for a Promise of Blessing," in Trible and Russell, eds., *Hagar, Sarah, and Their Children*, 33–69, and Weems, "A Mistress, a Maid, and No Mercy," 10.

3. Fuchs, "Literary Characterization."

4. Martin Noth, *A History of Pentateuchal Traditions*, Scholars Press Reprint Series, trans. Bernhard W. Anderson (Atlanta: Scholars Press, 1981), 151. Fuchs, "Literary Characterization," also characterizes Sarah as flat and colorless.

among other strategies, I assemble Sarah's traits—in the language of Seymour Chatman—as I find them revealed in the narrative.[5] A catalogue of traits is a list, not a reading; but the collection, revision, and integration of traits provides a focusing lens to attach to the spotlight my work seeks to shine on Sarah (to adopt the fine metaphor of Sara Koenig in her work on Bathsheba).[6] This narrative is practically inexhaustible, due to the partnering of the text and its gaps and the consciousness that strives to fill them. More could always be said, about other characters, about the narrator, about the plot, setting, focalization, and so on; but Sarah draws the light here.

For my analysis I rely upon the MT of Genesis as represented in *Biblia Hebraica Stuttgartensia* (*BHS*).[7] The episodes or sections that I examine most closely are Gen. 11:26–12:9; 12:10–13:2; 16:1-16; 18:1-15; 20:1-18; and 21:1-14, though I also treat intervening material at a level of detail in keeping with my estimation of each portion's contribution to Sarah's characterization. Other minor mentions in Genesis, such as 24:36; 25:10, 12; and 49:31, do not materially affect Sarah's image here, so I leave these to the side. The interesting reference to Sarah in Isa. 51:2 (and see vv. 1, 3) is, to my reading, part of a homiletic, analogical illustration, and thus not of direct relevance to my work here.

For ease of reference, I reprint, in block format, the text of the Revised Standard Version (RSV) for the longer, more significant episodes listed above. The literal quality of the RSV, which often extends even to wooden replication of word order, recommends it over the syntactically smoother New Revised Standard Version (NRSV) for its limited function here.[8] The renderings in the body of the discussion are my own, unless otherwise noted.

---

5. Chatman, *Story and Discourse*, 119–31.
6. Koenig, *Isn't This Bathsheba?* 26.
7. I do not give much weight to versional evidence, which is primarily a methodological consideration given my subsequent analysis of Genesis in the LXX. Though I acknowledge that MT Genesis is likely comprised of originally disparate sources or traditions woven together, I am interested in the character of Sarai or Sarah as she appears in the first book of the Pentateuch as it stands. This is consistent with the canons of narrative criticism, and it would be hard to justify treating the MT as a pastiche while examining the other narratives under consideration as coherent wholes.
8. This is no endorsement of the RSV's lack of gender-inclusive language for human beings, which makes it unfit for many other contexts.

To Have and to Have Not:
Origins, Family, Power, Possessions, and People (Gen. 11:26–12:9)

Gen. 11:26 When Terah had lived seventy years, he became the father of Abram, Nahor, and Haran. 27 Now these are the descendants of Terah. Terah was the father of Abram, Nahor, and Haran; and Haran was the father of Lot. 28 Haran died before his father Terah in the land of his birth, in Ur of the Chaldeans. 29 And Abram and Nahor took wives; the name of Abram's wife was Sarai, and the name of Nahor's wife, Milcah, the daughter of Haran the father of Milcah and Iscah. 30 Now Sarai was barren; she had no child. 31 Terah took Abram his son and Lot the son of Haran, his grandson, and Sarai his daughter-in-law, his son Abram's wife, and they went forth together from Ur of the Chaldeans to go into the land of Canaan; but when they came to Haran, they settled there. 32 The days of Terah were two hundred and five years; and Terah died in Haran. 12:1 Now the LORD said to Abram, "Go from your country and your kindred and your father's house to the land that I will show you. 2 And I will make of you a great nation, and I will bless you, and make your name great, so that you will be a blessing. 3 I will bless those who bless you, and him who curses you I will curse; and by you all the families of the earth shall bless themselves." 4 So Abram went, as the LORD had told him; and Lot went with him. Abram was seventy-five years old when he departed from Haran. 5 And Abram took Sarai his wife, and Lot his brother's son, and all their possessions which they had gathered, and the persons that they had gotten in Haran; and they set forth to go to the land of Canaan. When they had come to the land of Canaan, 6 Abram passed through the land to the place at Shechem, to the oak of Moreh. At that time the Canaanites were in the land. 7 Then the LORD appeared to Abram, and said, "To your descendants I will give this land." So he built there an altar to the LORD, who had appeared to him. 8 Thence he removed to the mountain on the east of Bethel, and pitched his tent, with Bethel on the west and Ai on the east; and there he built an altar to the LORD and called on the name of the LORD. 9 And Abram journeyed on, still going toward the Negeb. (RSV)

Few readers of Sarai's story devote much analysis to her life before her descent into Egypt.[9] But even the introduction to the narrative complex centering on Sarai, Abram, and Lot in the MT (Gen. 11:26-32) sheds a surprisingly strong light on Sarai: her definition here arguably exceeds that of Abram, and she is far better formed than Lot. Sarai, first, is female, a woman, a wife. Abram's first act "takes" (לקח) her as its object, and she

---

9. As is conventional, I refer to Sarah as Sarai until God clarifies her name to Abraham in Gen. 17:15. Schneider, *Sarah*, 8–30, represents a significant exception to the usual neglect of this material.

is immediately a "woman of" (אשת־), possessed in her earliest mention (v. 29). That Abram takes her shows that he is the more powerful; he is also more connected in relationship. The narrator professes much precise genealogical knowledge about the descent of Abram's family, noting, for example, the paternity of Milcah, the sister-in-law of Sarai and Abram, who barely figures in the narrative to come (but see 22:20-23). Even Iscah, Milcah's sister, has a lineage, though she remains a name only in the text as it stands. But Sarai, neither daughter nor sister, is descended from no one worth mentioning. Abram represents her only human tie, though it is a significant one, with implications of cohabitation and sexual involvement. From the verse in which she appears, then, Sarai is defined: female, married, likely sexually mature and active; not as well connected to others as those in her near context, and less powerful than the one to whom she is most closely bound (11:29).

She also has a name: שם אשת־אברם שרי—"the name of the woman of Abram was Sarai." שרי is connected to the root שרר, which denotes dominion and mastery and so carries connotations of ownership; a near synonym is מלך, to be "king" or chief.[10] Other relatives of שרר in classical Hebrew include שר and שרה, male and female nobles or rulers, and משורה, which describes government, or power over people and resources.[11] Sarai's name thus reinforces an image of her as isolated, without peers. However, its implication of mastery and ownership beats against the fact that she is "taken" from the first, a "woman of." Sarai appears fixed in a minor contradiction, set apart, in her apparent lack of family ties, but not, clearly, therefore more free.

In 11:29, Sarai was contrasted with Milcah, whose family of origin is at least partly specified; in v. 30, Sarai continues to be defined by her lack with emphatic and mutually reinforcing direct textual indicators: Sarai is עקרה, "infertile"; "she has no child" (אין לה ולד). That she is of childbearing age and sexually active is confirmed here, as a state of "infertility" demands a sexual relationship from which one could otherwise expect a child.[12] The narrator explicitly attributes this lack to Sarai; nothing is mentioned about Abram's ability to engender a child, and his ancestors' proven potency underlines his presumed virility (vv. 10-26). This prominent mention of

---

10. BDB 979a–b; *DCH* 8:192b, 8:199a. I resist the common rendering of שרי as "princess" for the same reason I prefer to call Sarai "master," not "mistress," in her role as slaveowner. The diminution of the English feminine form "princess" gives a female role a benign veneer that is not justified by any intrinsic difference in the way that women and men exercise power over others.

11. *DCH* 5:501b, 5:505b; *HALOT* 641a–b, 1354b.

12. Contrast Teubal, *Sarah the Priestess*, 128; see also 37, 98.

Sarai's infertility and childlessness in such a laconic narrative defines an implicit conflict with unmet social expectations in the story world, and it may be justified to consider whether Sarai's perceived lack thus leads to conflict with Abram. That a signal goal of Abram's "taking a woman" in v. 29 is offspring and the continuation of a lineage seems clear from the detailed list of fathers and children that immediately precedes this notice (vv. 10-28). Without ancestor or descendant, then, this "Sarai," whose name, in a mild irony, suggests the exercise of power and ownership, is possessed but does not possess.

Sarai is again "taken" in 11:31, by Abram's father Terah, but with a different force, as she shares her identity as object here with Abram and Lot. She is also depicted as somewhat more connected in relationship, for in addition to being Abram's "woman," she is, by implication, Lot's aunt, and she is explicitly the כלה or daughter-in-law of Terah. Sarai's initial lack of stated ancestry is, perhaps, partly remedied here, albeit through the agency of Abram. This sense of slowly increasing connection is bolstered by Sarai's presence as part of the collective subject of the following verbs. Sarai, Terah, Abram, and Lot "went out together…in order to go to the land of Canaan," and as a group "they went as far as Haran and settled there."[13] Sarai is a part of a collective whose members seem, at this point, to possess nothing but each other; she is a wife and daughter-in-law, a migrant who settles with those to whom she is connected. After an uncertain amount of story time, but straightaway in the discourse, however, one of these relational strands is cut, as her father-in-law Terah dies at their new home in Haran (v. 32). Sarai's circle becomes smaller by one, and her tenuous connection to the previous generation is severed. What is more, the modest sense of increasing belonging that is initially evident here is further undercut by a consideration of other, possible relationships that are passed over in silence in the discourse. If Sarai had an unmentioned family of origin, back in "Ur of the Chaldeans," then she has been separated from them, forever, by her migration. This pattern of possession and lack, or gain and loss, will persist as the narrative progresses.

A new chapter in the life of Sarai and her small family begins in the narrator's unadorned description of the first instance of Yahweh's personal communication with Abram (12:1-3). It is almost impossible to draw conclusions about the story context of this message; it is not clearly a visitation, a dream, or a vision, unlike events to be described later, but simply a reported direct address out of the void. This brief speech, which is a curious amalgam of command and pledge—with the pledge not

---

13. ויצאו אתם...ללכת ארצה כנען ויבאו עד־חרן וישבו שם.

explicitly contingent upon fulfillment of the command—is emphatically in the singular, directed to Abram alone. It is Abram's land, Abram's relatives, and Abram's father's house that Abram must leave behind to "Go!" (לך־לך) to another land that Yahweh will show Abram (v. 1). Yahweh promises to turn Abram "into a numerous people" (לגוי גדול), to bless Abram, and, in what reads like a small jest, to "enlarge" Abram's name, to "cause it to grow" (ואגדלה שמך, v. 2; compare 17:5). Yahweh further orders Abram to "be a blessing!" and pledges to "bless" Abram's "blessers" and to "curse" the "one who calls [Abram] damned," while predicting that "all the clans of the soil" will "bless themselves"—again, "by" Abram alone (12:2-3). The simple occurrence of this speech directed to Abram, not to mention its content, marks Abram, again, as more significant and powerful than "his woman" Sarai. When Abram complies with Yahweh's first command to "Go!" it is not even initially clear on the discourse level that Sarai accompanies him, though after a narratorial remark on Abram's age she is again "taken" along (vv. 4-5). Despite Sarai's consignment to the murky background behind Abram's epiphany, however, there is a barely submerged tension between the second person singular form of Yahweh's address and one of Yahweh's pledges in particular. The multiplication of Abram into a "numerous people" or "great nation" carries an implicit biological demand that Abram cannot fulfill alone, yet Abram's apparently sole sexual partner is not privy to Yahweh's address. What is more, she has been indelibly marked by a flat narratorial assertion as unable to give birth (11:30).

The remainder of 12:5 contains a small series of surprises that are little remarked in readings of Sarai: Abram "takes" not only "Sarai, his woman, and Lot, his brother's son," but also "all their acquisitions that they had acquired" (כל־רכושם אשר רכשו). This is the first hint that this itinerant group possesses portable assets; more interesting, however, is the fact that they own them in common. These are not Abram's possessions, but theirs, and they are not only held by all but obtained by all (רכשו). Sarai, possessed from the first, has become a possessor, at least of things: רכוש refers to durable goods and, often, property on the hoof. But this is not all that is brought along to the land of Canaan: in addition, the group brings הנפש אשר־עשו בחרן, literally, "the people that they had 'made' in Haran." As in the English idiom "to make money," Sarai and the others have acquired slaves, which they transport to their new home along with their other possessions.[14]

---

14. BDB 795a (עשׂה *qal* II 7): "*acquire* property of various kinds (cf. 'make money')"; *DCH* 5:732a (נפש 8d); G. R. Driver, "Hebrew mothers (Exodus i 19)," *ZAW* 67 (1955): 248.

When Sarai first appeared, her name, which evokes images of mastery and ownership, seemed little more than a sad joke. Here, although she emphatically remains and is directly defined as a "woman of," repeatedly "taken" and clearly of lesser power in her relationship with Abram, Sarai is also an "owner of," master of the human beings that she and Abram and Lot "made," by means that can only be guessed at, during their time in Haran. The question of Sarai's relationality broadly construed becomes much more complicated here, and conflict between owner and owned, though not yet specified in the discourse, lies just below the surface. Sarai occupies a medial position: clearly lower in status than Abram, who takes her; she is quite literally "his woman"—but these נפש are hers, too, suggesting a status differential perhaps even more profound.

As with their move to Haran (itself a journey apparently intended to end in the land of Canaan, 11:31), Abram, Sarai, and Lot are all subjects of the verbs that detail their departure from Haran and their entrance into Canaan (12:5). Then, curiously, Abram appears to be utterly alone, except for a second communication from Yahweh, as he proceeds through the land visiting or establishing cultic centers (vv. 6-8). Even as he travels toward Egypt, where Sarai, at least as a physical object, will figure prominently in the narrative, the verbs continue in the masculine singular (vv. 9-11a). However, this is not a reliable indicator of Sarah's absence from the events and places detailed, and I generally assume her presence.[15] As with the earlier speech from Yahweh (vv. 1-3), though, it is not clear that Sarai is aware of the occurrence or content of this divine appearance in which "this land" is pledged to Abram's offspring (v. 7). But Abram's religious observances—the construction of altars and execution of the cult of Yahweh (vv. 7-8)—are unlikely to have escaped Sarai's notice.

As early as this, a surprisingly complex image of Sarai in the MT begins to emerge. She is defined from the first by what she does not have: a family of origin, complex social ties, fertility, a child, and power in comparison with Abraham. That she is taken and possessed while possessing so little seems to give the lie to her regal name; but straightaway Sarai makes gains, acquiring both goods and the power of a slaveowner. Many of these characteristics, and the themes they help to outline, including those of want, acquisition, and possession or ownership, are only emphasized in the following episode—where, however, Sarai's recent advancement in the hierarchy of power will suffer a total reverse.

---

15. Abram, for instance, is the only character explicitly said to enter Egypt in Gen. 12:14, though he has just spoken extensively to Sarai, and she attracts the notice of the Egyptian men immediately.

Egyptian Traffic (Gen. 12:10–13:2)

> Gen. 12:10 Now there was a famine in the land. So Abram went down to Egypt to sojourn there, for the famine was severe in the land. 11 When he was about to enter Egypt, he said to Sarai his wife, "I know that you are a woman beautiful to behold; 12 and when the Egyptians see you, they will say, 'This is his wife'; then they will kill me, but they will let you live. 13 Say you are my sister, that it may go well with me because of you, and that my life may be spared on your account." 14 When Abram entered Egypt the Egyptians saw that the woman was very beautiful. 15 And when the princes of Pharaoh saw her, they praised her to Pharaoh. And the woman was taken into Pharaoh's house. 16 And for her sake he dealt well with Abram; and he had sheep, oxen, he-asses, menservants, maidservants, she-asses, and camels. 17 But the LORD afflicted Pharaoh and his house with great plagues because of Sarai, Abram's wife. 18 So Pharaoh called Abram, and said, "What is this you have done to me? Why did you not tell me that she was your wife? 19 Why did you say, 'She is my sister,' so that I took her for my wife? Now then, here is your wife, take her, and be gone." 20 And Pharaoh gave men orders concerning him; and they set him on the way, with his wife and all that he had. 13:1 So Abram went up from Egypt, he and his wife, and all that he had, and Lot with him, into the Negeb. 2 Now Abram was very rich in cattle, in silver, and in gold. (RSV)

The established theme of lack is immediately reinforced here, as a scarcity of food leads Sarai's household to seek refuge in Egypt. לגור (12:10), often rendered by the archaic "to sojourn," as in the RSV, seems better understood here as "to seek asylum." This is especially apt given its immediate context, which notes twice in the space of a few words that there is a "famine" and that it is "severe" (כבד הרעב), and also considering the close of this episode, where Abram and Sarai are "deported" or, at the least, "escorted out" (וישלחו) as *personae non gratae* after angering Pharaoh (v. 20). Later notes on the fertile abundance of the Jordan valley, however, the "entirety" of which is said to be "saturated with water… like the garden of Yahweh—like the land of Egypt" (כלה משקה...כגן־יהוה בארץ מצרים, 13:10), prompt retrospective questions about the combination of motives driving this move. Calculation and deception mark this tale from the start, as Abram, in his first direct speech in the narrative, tries to persuade Sarai to lie about their relationship (12:11-13). Abram's supposed fear of violent death at the hands of his hosts, moreover, would also have been more credible in the Jordan basin, as the later narrative shows (v. 12; 13:13; 19:1-11). The result of his scheme here—that Abram becomes "positively rich" (כבד מאד, 13:2)—provides not only a neat *inclusio* with the episode's inception (כבד הרעב), but also raises further suspicions that a supply of food, which may have been available closer to home, is not the only advantage Egypt offers.

The brief scene between Abram, who speaks, and Sarai, whose reply, if any, is left unreported, reveals something about Sarai even as it contributes to significant ambiguity in her characterization (12:11-13). Abram's wheedling and flattering tone here, mostly lost in the RSV, leaves some initial doubt as to the sincerity of his direct description of Sarai as "lovely to look at" (יפת־מראה). However, his evaluation is soon emphatically reinforced by narratorial assertion (v. 14) and further underlined by the reported estimations of other, bit characters (v. 15). What is more, the stated motive and eventual success of Abram's rather sketchy plan turns precisely on Sarai's ability to attract. This dramatic "loveliness" is the only direct physical description of any kind, of any character, in the entire narrative about Sarai's family. That it is repeatedly emphasized early in the narrative, and particularly here, in such a laconic tale, lends it considerable characterizing force, with a primacy similar to her condition of infertility. Though intangible, Sarai's bodily beauty is something that she possesses, a physical state that markedly affects other characters. Such a singular quality, it is not too much to surmise, may also affect Sarai's self-conception, a possibility which may, in turn, help to elucidate her feelings and deeds later in the narrative.

For Sarai's beauty contributes to an element of her characterization that will grow in significance as her story proceeds: in the eyes of the other characters, Sarai, in Egypt, is *worthy of notice*. I say this simply as a statement of what seems to me to be a narrative fact, without lending any moral weight to the reason why she is notable, which, after all, appears to be unconnected to her intrinsic worth as a human being. In the wake of Abram's declaration that Sarai is "lovely to look at" (12:11), she is "noticed" by the Egyptian men in v. 14, a good translation here of ראה due to the כי that explains why this is so: they "noticed"—not just "saw"— "the woman *because* she was very lovely" (ויראו המצרים את־האשה כי־יפה הוא מאד). These men take note of Sarai, as do Pharaoh's nobles in the following verse, where it is likewise clear that a special kind of approving and covetous "seeing" is going on: "they noticed her...and they sang her praises to Pharaoh" (ויראו אתה...ויהללו אתה אל־פרעה). Again, for Sarai to be noticed in these ways is not a simple positive, or an advantage that she holds; it is an objectification that sits seamlessly in a narrative that sees her bought and sold as a valuable item.[16] But it may help to explain her

---

16. Contrast Howard Wallace, "On Account of Sarai: Gen 12:10–13:1," *ABR* 44 (1996): 36–7.

reaction to the chain of events recounted in 16:4-5, where Hagar "sees" or notices that she is pregnant and, as a result, "overlooks" her master, Sarai; it may aid, too, in unpacking Sarah's cryptic pronouncement in 21:6, with its concern over the reaction of others to her delivery of Isaac.

The initial revelation of Sarai's beauty on the threshold of Egypt, however, is tempered by the ambiguity that lies in the utter silence of the discourse on Sarai's response to Abram's persuasive speech. Nothing is recorded here: no physical reaction or shift in posture, no vocal reply, no interior view. As some of the goals expressed in his address are realized—Sarai is thought, at first, to be Abram's sister, and things certainly do "go well" for Abram due to this deception—it seems unlikely that she actively works to thwart his plan from the start. But as a reader I am left to speculate as to Sarai's attitude here, and the range of possibilities is complex. Is she fully persuaded, a willing participant, a "trickster" who cynically enjoys a lucrative profit for her family by misrepresenting her relationship with Abram and renting out her body?[17] Or does she reluctantly agree, driven by fear brought on by Abram's threat that she will be deprived of him but "kept alive" for purposes left ominously unexpressed (12:12)? Or, finally, is Sarai simply tractable, understandably cowed by a man whose power over her, indeed ownership of her, is shortly confirmed by his ability to bargain her away in exchange for security and prosperity?[18]

Though their firm resolution remains permanently elusive, this evolving sketch of Sarai cannot proceed without worrying these questions. For their answers deeply affect the reader's ongoing construction of Sarai's character and her development, or lack thereof, as the narrative progresses: if Sarai is here merely calculating, a full even if silent partner in Abram's deceit, then her bitter, ungenerous behavior toward Hagar and Ishmael is simply in line with what would seem to be her covetous, utilitarian—and unchanging—nature. But if Sarai is a pawn here, browbeaten, tricked, or simply physically forced into Pharaoh's harem, then this episode may instead be read as a catalyst for some of her features that emerge later in the narrative: used and abused as a possession for gain here, she becomes hardened, a user and an abuser herself, suspicious, grasping, and protective of what she has gained.

---

17. Susan Niditch, *Underdogs and Tricksters: A Prelude to Biblical Folklore* (San Francisco: Harper & Row, 1987), 45, 59; Susan Niditch, "Genesis," in Newsom, Ringe, and Lapsley, eds., *Women's Bible Commentary*, 36; compare André Wénin, "Abram et Saraï en Égypte (Gn 12, 10-20) ou la place de Saraï dans l'élection," *RTL* 29 (1998): 447–8.

18. Compare Jeansonne, *Women of Genesis*, 17.

The measure of sympathy granted to Sarai by the reader certainly influences his or her responses to these questions. But the narrative also features strong indicators that Sarai, while valuable, is almost entirely lacking in power here: a costly article. Concepts of possession, ownership, and trade bind this entire episode and further emphasize the importance of these themes to the broader narrative. Sarai, despite appearances, remains a "woman of" Abram (12:11-12, 17-20, especially v. 17), "taken" from Abram, who in turn "takes" her back (vv. 15, 19); and when they are sent away she appears alongside his baggage: "his woman and all that he owned" (ואת־אשתו ואת־כל־אשר־לו, v. 20; compare 13:1). Moreover, the assumption that Sarai, as a woman, is the rightful, valuable possession of only one man is integral to the plot. Some of the evidence for this claim is peripheral in that it only confirms this convention as a social norm in the story world. Abram's concern for his safety, whether real or feigned, depends for its justification on this principle (12:12), and it is implied that the belief that Sarai is unmarried is the reason that Pharaoh and his courtiers do not scruple to covet and take "the woman." In the account of her abduction, אשה is notably lacking its customary possessive suffix (vv. 14-15), and Pharaoh's implicit claim is that he never would have acted the way he did if he had known the truth: "Why did you say, 'She is my sister,' so that I took her for myself as a wife?" (vv. 18-19). Neither Abram nor Pharaoh inspires confidence in this regard, however: the boundaries of his marriage, both here and later, are obviously negotiable for Abram, while Pharaoh's indignation follows suspiciously hard upon his being "diseased...with severe diseases" (וינגע יהוה את־פרעה נגעים גדלים, v. 17) in apparent punishment for his act.

But it is this pivotal event, in which Yahweh intervenes "because of Sarai the woman of Abram" (על־דבר שרי אשת אברם, v. 17), that most clearly highlights not only that Sarai is powerless here, but also that she belongs to Abram and that this is the reason for Yahweh's action. The plain fact of the intervention emphasizes that Sarai lacks the power to alter her situation.[19] And while the narrative is laconic in the extreme,

---

19. The suggestion of van Dijk-Hemmes, "Sarai in Exile," 143, among other critics (and partly following the rabbis, as in *Gen. Rab.* 41.2), that על־דבר שרי refers to a plea voiced to Yahweh ("on" or "because of the word" or, by extension, "prayer of Sarai"), thus attributing some agency to the captive and burnishing the image of the deity somewhat, is a creative but strained reading of a common idiom. The simplest reading here corresponds with that of the only other occurrences of על־דבר in the narrative of Sarah, in Gen. 20:11, 18. In v. 11, a rendering of והרגוני על־דבר אשתי as "they will kill me on the word of my wife" makes little sense; v. 18, which is topically and lexically very similar to 12:17 (Yahweh has afflicted Abimelech's

it is shown by the resolution of the matter that Yahweh's punishment is aimed at restoring Sarai to Abram, and the only clue in the discourse as to Yahweh's motive references Abram's possession of her: "because," again, she is "the woman of Abram."[20] This cannot be simply "because of Sarai." If Yahweh's move were prompted by an abstract, humane indignation at her plight, it is hard to see why Abram, as the architect of this sordid situation, escapes all censure. And despite the insistence of a range of commentators—such as Schneider, David Cotter, and van Dijk-Hemmes—that Sarai is somehow "liberated" by Yahweh here, it is even harder to see how she is benefitted by being restored to the man who traded her away.[21]

The notion of Sarai as a durable good suitable for trade may be further underlined by Abram's language in 12:13, where he urges her to say she is his sister "so that it will go well for me בעבורך." This word, here used as a preposition, is employed with a nuanced range of meanings in biblical texts, often with a basic force of "because of."[22] This can shade into a meaning of "for the price of" in a context of barter or sale, as in Amos 2:6, where the Israelites are condemned "because of their sale" of "the poor for [the price of] a pair of sandals" (על־מכרם...אביון בעבור נעלים; compare 8:6). The possibility that this could be part of the sense of the phrase in Gen. 12:13 is strengthened by its appearance in what is clearly a transaction in v. 16, where בעבורה could be rendered "for the price of her," or "in exchange for her," without strain: "And [Pharaoh] treated Abram well in exchange for her: [Abram] got flocks and herds and jacks and male slaves and female slaves and jennies and camels."[23]

---

household אשת אברהם (על־דבר שרה אשת אברהם), seems contextually even less likely to hint at a submerged, story-level petition, as the episode of Genesis 20 is much more explicit about a variety of communications between the characters—including prayers.

20. Compare Trible, "Ominous Beginnings," 37.

21. For Schneider, *Sarah*, 35, this is the "first of many situations where the Deity comes to Sarai's aid"; Cotter, *Genesis*, 92–3, sees this as part of "an important biblical motif" where God frees women "trapped" in a relationship; van Dijk-Hemmes, "Sarai in Exile," 143, 145, uses language of liberation and the redress of "injustice" to describe Yahweh's action here. Even Fewell and Gunn, *Gender, Power, and Promise*, 43–4, who reliably raise issues of justice in their readings, characterize Yahweh's action here as a "rescue." They also posit that Abram is in fact *not* expecting to see Sarai returned, which only shows Yahweh's restoration of their relationship in a bleaker light.

22. *DCH* 2:234b–235a; *HALOT* 778a; BDB 721a.

23. See van Dijk-Hemmes, "Sarai in Exile," 141, for a similar reading; compare Shula Keshet, *"Say You Are My Sister": Danger, Seduction and the Foreign in Biblical Literature and Beyond*, trans. Anthony Berris, The Bible in the Modern World 53 (Sheffield: Sheffield Phoenix Press, 2013), 35.

There seems to be little hint here in Egypt, then—unlike, perhaps, in the similar episode to follow in Gerar in Genesis 20—that Sarai possesses the capacity for self-determination, let alone that she is a collaborator in Abram's plan. The absence of any justification for his ostensibly motivating fears suggests that his scheme is cynical; indeed, all that the narrative confirms is that it does "go well" for Abram "for the price of" Sarai. Rather, she is here a victim, virtually without agency, degraded into a costly object swapped for other property. Among the many details of this story that remain hidden in gaps is the matter of how the truth of the couple's relationship becomes known to Pharaoh (12:17-18); it is just possible that Sarai reveals this, which could indicate the exercise of some initiative.[24] But this is a blank whose profundity resembles that of the gap of the scene between Sarai and Abram (vv. 11-13): whether Sarai ever follows Abram's cajoling instructions to lie, even by omission of the truth, also continues to be obscure. It is dehumanizing to be sold, however, whatever the circumstances, and when Sarai reifies Hagar later, it is, perhaps, partly because she was turned into chattel here.

By the time Sarai and her family are deported from Egypt, a number of elements of her characterization have been reinforced and deepened. She continues to be possessed, becoming an object of acquisition in a trade that resembles nothing so much as what is now called trafficking in persons, in its crossing of borders, deceptive and coercive methods, and sexual context.[25] In being possessed, traded, and repeatedly "taken," Sarai proves to be of great value—worth herds of domestic animals and a number of enslaved humans—but only, again, in an entirely objectified capacity, and as the "woman" or "wife" of a man. Here, in fact, she is serially the wife of two different men, with the strong implication of sexual activity, willing or not, with both (especially 12:19).[26] Tied in complex ways to all of this is Sarai's striking beauty, a trait that makes her the object of the "noticing" gaze of the men who covet her.

Sarai also continues to be defined by a state of lack. First, a dearth of food threatens her family's security; soon thereafter she is taken, bodily, and stripped of her personal security. In her abduction and captivity—even in her release, which only results in her return to the man who sold

---

24. Compare *Ant.* 1.165.
25. Compare van Dijk-Hemmes, "Sarai in Exile," 136–7, 143.
26. Compare 12:19 (ואקח אתה לי לאשה, "so that I took her for myself as a wife") and 16:3 (ותקח שרי...את־הגר...ותתן אתה לאברם...לו לאשה, "Sarai took...Hagar... and gave her to Abram...as a wife for him"). In 16:4, Hagar and Abram's union is explicitly consummated.

her—Sarai is powerless, seemingly without volition; the discourse, in which she is voiceless, lacks even a hint of any exercise of her will. And despite her alternating spouses Sarai remains, as she was in the beginning, childless.

However, Sarai is also incrementally, if implicitly, developing, especially from the perspective of the narrative's evolving theme of gain and loss. While she "made" slaves in Haran, she is sold in Egypt; but this wild swing in status, in turn, paradoxically leads to tremendous financial gain for her family. While the wealth resulting from this sordid trade is specified as Abram's (12:16, 20; 13:1-2), in contrast to the earlier, more inclusive note in 12:5, the standard of living for his entire household has likely increased. As is clarified by later events, then, Sarai, so lately powerless and owned, here regains a certain level of power and ownership, albeit always as relative to the power of Abram. These contradictions and conflicts, both social and personal, may also lay the ground for Sarai's later development as a character. Interpersonal conflict with men, and with Abram in particular, bubbles just beneath the surface of the discourse, while social contact with women, suggested only obliquely in Sarai's stay in בית פרעה (v. 15), is consigned to the deep background. But it is her treatment by those who have power over her that is most suggestive here. Callously abused and traded for gain, Sarai, perhaps, begins to take steps toward the use and abuse of those in her power.

Silence, but Reflected Light (Gen. 13:2–15:21)

Sarai, having been unceremoniously dumped back with Abram in Gen. 12:19, sets out for Canaan again as part of his retinue (12:20–13:1). Somewhere in the Negeb desert, however, she disappears from the discourse until 16:1-6, where she proposes what proves to be a disastrous liaison between Hagar and Abram. This intervening silence serves to strengthen the link between Sarai's actions there and her treatment in Egypt, as nothing in the discourse interferes with the narrative recency of her Egyptian experiences. The several episodes in between are not therefore without value for Sarai's characterization, however, as characters are "human cross-roads," necessarily affecting each other, and there are a few elements here that still shed light on the process of her character's construction.[27]

27. Harvey, *Character*, 69; compare 52. Schneider, *Sarah*, 42–6, also recognizes the importance of considering this intervening material (and compare 3–4), though she focuses on Abram's development as a character here.

The Loss of Lot (Gen. 13:2-13)

This episode is closely bound to the family's stay in Egypt, with the possessions and people obtained there serving as a catalyst for a conflict that results in Lot's household breaking from that of Abram and Sarai. In fact, 13:2, with its note of Abram's great riches, serves the two tales as a hinge, both reporting the outcome of the Egyptian deception and setting up a comparison with Lot's wealth in v. 5. Acquisition and possession continue to be dominant themes in the life of Sarai's family, and the social conflict that this engenders leads directly to another personal loss for Sarai, this time of her nephew, Lot: "the land could not bear them living together, because their acquisitions were many.... And they parted, each from his brother" (ולא־נשׂא אתם הארץ לשבת יחדו כי־היה רכושם רב...ויפרדו איש מעל אחיו, vv. 6, 11). Gain is again answered by loss.

Although the discourse is reticent on the ties between Sarai and Lot, a poetics of characterization that emphasizes mimesis and human relationships invites responsible speculation.[28] The two seem to have lived and traveled in close proximity for years, at least since their departure from Ur, when they were both "taken" by Terah, then Abram, to foreign lands (11:31; 12:5). Moreover, neither appears to possess any other family connections, apart from a common link to Abram. Sarai is "without child," and introduced absent any reference to a family of origin, while Lot, whose mother is never mentioned, is apparently orphaned at the death of his father Haran in Ur, where his sisters are also left behind (11:27-31). Lot's wife and daughters, further, do not appear in the narrative for what may be as long as two decades or more in story time.[29] Given this relational vacuum, and Sarai and Lot's enforced togetherness in unfamiliar contexts, it is not too much to surmise that this fissure between Abram and Lot's groups may have a negative emotional impact on Sarai. It may, indeed, be worth considering whether Sarai's feelings toward Lot might verge on the maternal.[30] I do not think that this line of inquiry is

---

28. Alter, *Pleasures of Reading*, 47; compare Chatman, *Story and Discourse*, 119–20; Hochman, *Character*, 41–2.

29. The chronology, as often, is not entirely clear. However, Abraham is almost one hundred years old by the time of the events of Genesis 19, where Lot's wife and daughters appear (17:1; 21:5); here, Abram is probably closer to eighty, on the evidence of 12:4; 16:3, 16.

30. Compare *Ant.* 1.151, 154, where Abraham formally adopts Lot, making Sarra, as she is called there, not only Lot's sister, but also his stepmother. The relative ages of Sarai and Lot in the MT are no clearer than the broader chronology, but it seems likely that she is a generation older than he. Haran, Lot's father, appears to be the youngest brother of Abram, and Sarai, as shown later, is only about ten years younger than Abram (Gen. 11:26-27; 17:17).

idle, given the narrative centrality of Sarai's lack of a child and this trait's eventual reversal. Moreover, Sarai is repeatedly shown to be ambivalent toward motherhood as her story proceeds; if an infertile Sarai is wounded here by the loss of someone she regards as a son, this could help to explain her later equivocation. Following the trauma of Egypt, this loss of Lot, which is similarly partly prompted by acquisitiveness, may also add to a hardening of Sarai's personality, increase her protectiveness of what is hers, and contribute to the development of a jaundiced attitude toward possessions, relationships, and their mutual effects.

Unfulfilled Promises and a Nighttime Raid (Gen. 13:14–14:24)

Emphasis on possession and possessions continues throughout the remainder of Genesis 13 and all of Genesis 14. Yahweh, having promised Abram "the whole land" along with "offspring" to occupy it, urges him to survey this future gift (13:14-17); Abram, however, settles down instead, pitching his tent at "the terebinths of Mamre" and erecting another altar (v. 18). The incongruity noted above in Yahweh's first communication (12:1-3)—just how Abram will turn into a "great nation" with an infertile wife who is not privy to these revelations—not only remains unresolved but is exacerbated here by the passage of time in the story world. Yahweh, speaking again out of the void, continues to address Abram alone, even repeating the phrase "your [sg.] offspring" (זרעך) three times (13:15-16). Yet this presumes a biological process that Abram simply cannot complete in isolation; one, moreover, whose prospects seem ever dimmer, as the repetition of these pledges in the absence of discernible intervening action does not contribute to their credibility. Sarai, meanwhile, remains offstage, perhaps unaware of Abram's recurring epiphanies but watching him conduct Yahweh's cult, possibly occupied by the kind of domestic tasks that are suggested as her province later (18:6), likely visited at night, fruitlessly, by Abram. Of her other relationships, especially with women, there is only frail, mostly retrospective evidence, limited to the implied presence of Hagar and other slaves and household retainers—which are, however, incredibly numerous by now, to judge by the 318 vassals Abram leads forth in 14:14—and, just possibly, the wives and retainers of Abram's Amorite allies (vv. 13, 24).

Abram's swashbuckling expedition in Genesis 14 casts only a faint reflected light on Sarai, who continues to wait in the wings. Sarai is the wife of a man who is increasingly rich and powerful, able and willing to defend members of his extended family and, importantly, their "acquisitions" (רכש). The possession, theft, restoration, and exchange of these acquisitions constitute a major theme in this section—the word רכש itself appears five times in vv. 11-21—which further reinforces the importance of this motif to the wider narrative. This martial episode may be read as evidence that Abram places little value on Sarai: as David Gunn and Danna Nolan Fewell note, Abram's concern for a captive family member and proud refusal to be further enriched by a foreign potentate provide a disquieting contrast with his earlier conduct in Egypt.[31] Given his profit there, however, and his tidy gains to come, in Gerar and Machpelah (20:14-16; 23:4-20), it might be more precise to say that Abram knows Sarai has some value—but only as an instrument, not as a person.

Still Only Promises (Gen. 15:1-21)

Somewhat later, Abram receives yet another communication from Yahweh, this time in a series of revelations in which דבר־יהוה initially comes in a kind of ecstatic "vision" (מחזה, 15:1).[32] Themes of acquisition and possession, now familiar from earlier epiphanies, continue to define the content of Yahweh's pronouncements, and pecuniary language is sprinkled throughout.[33]

A new note emerges here as well, though, as the tensions implicit in the contexts of Yahweh's former oracles come at least partly into the open. Abram's sequential responses to Yahweh's pledges and commands, in fact, suggest a waning enthusiasm for the deity's plans. From Haran, Abram "went as Yahweh told him" (12:4), but in Canaan, perhaps "between Bethel and Ai," he quietly ignores Yahweh's order to survey the land, settling instead at the "terebinths of Mamre" (13:3-4, 12, 17-18). Here, Abram's reply is, at least initially, almost derisive, as he talks back to Yahweh for the first time: Yahweh says, "'Do not be afraid, Abram—I am your shield; I will make your wages great!' But Abram said, 'My lord Yahweh, *what* will you give me, with me dying childless?'... 'Look—you have not given me offspring!'" (15:1b-2a, 3a).[34] For reasons that remain

---

31. Gunn and Fewell, *Narrative in the Hebrew Bible*, 93.

32. As this uncanny, multi-part encounter wears on, however, there is some suggestion of Yahweh's physical manifestation, foreshadowing what is apparently a bodily visitation to Sarah and Abraham in Genesis 18.

33. This begins already at the end of Gen. 15:1, where Yahweh refers to Abram's שכר, or "wages." Concern with inheritance binds the entire chapter (Gen. 15:2-4, 7-8, 18), while the predicted outcome of Abram's offspring's service in a foreign land is that "they will emerge with great acquisitions" (יצאו ברכש גדול, v. 14).

34. אל־תירא אברם אנכי מגן לך שכרך הרבה מאד ויאמר אברם אדני יהוה מה־תתן־לי ואנכי הולך ערירי...הן לי לא נתתה זרע; הרבה is apparently an infinitive absolute; I have taken the suggestion of the *BHS* apparatus and read ארבה, which is the reading of the SP.

obscure, Abram is soon said to regain confidence in Yahweh's predictions (v. 6); but, just as quickly, he seems to retreat into skepticism, employing the same honorific as in his first statement of doubt: "My lord Yahweh, *how* will I know?" (אדני יהוה במה אדע, v. 8). Promises of inheritance, and the offspring required to make this concept concrete, provide a ground note sounded over and over in this series of rituals and proclamations (vv. 2-5, 7-8, 13-14, 16, 18-21); but the emotional stress over their lack of fulfillment, only intensified here by a pledge that emphasizes Abram's genetic, sexual connection to his eventual heir (v. 4), seems to have reached an unsustainable pitch.[35]

This stress, founded in a biological conundrum, could partly anticipate Sarai's feelings in Genesis 16. Perhaps Abram's newly revealed disquiet about "dying childless" contributes to or even prompts Sarai's anxiety, which may be implied there. There has been no explicit indication in the discourse that Sarai is aware of the content of Yahweh's by-now numerous pledges of offspring, and this gap endures here.[36] However, Abram's performance of Yahweh's cult would likely have been plain to her, for the simple reason that such ritual observance—or, at a minimum, certain components of it, such as the construction of altars—has a public element. Similar considerations imply that Sarai would at least have had knowledge of the turmoil created by this most recent series of revelations. For the events of Genesis 15, and the sacrifices in particular, when taken seriously as a narrative and not regarded merely as a collection of similar oracular episodes, push far beyond private, interior illumination.

If Sarai's physical proximity to Abram can usually be assumed on the story level, at least to this point in the narrative, even when only he is mentioned in the discourse—leaving aside, probably, the nighttime raid on the hostile kings' camp—it does not seem too much to infer that this sequence of events would have attracted Sarai's notice and interest. While the reader's knowledge gap about what she knows remains, the possibility that she may have heard or sensed something of Abram's newly voiced angst over the lack of an heir might be strengthened by the scene that immediately follows, where Sarai may make this worry her own. Many familiar themes—possession and lack, ownership, abuse, disposal

---

35. Gen 15:4 is bowdlerized in the RSV, rendering "your own son shall be your heir" for כי־אם אשר יצא ממעיך הוא יירשך. But ממעיך, referring to Abram's lower belly, is already a euphemism; our archaic "loins" might serve. The NRSV's "your very own issue" may make the point in a sly manner: Abram's heir is predicted to "come out" of his own sexual equipment.

36. Contrast *Jub.* 14:21, where Abram tells Sarai about the promises and the covenant.

of another's sexual resources for personal gain, and a variety of desires, including a simple hunger for acknowledgment—now mix together, with explosive results.

Sarai, Hagar, Abram—and a Son (Gen. 16:1-16)

Gen. 16:1 Now Sarai, Abram's wife, bore him no children. She had an Egyptian maid whose name was Hagar; 2 and Sarai said to Abram, "Behold now, the LORD has prevented me from bearing children; go in to my maid; it may be that I shall obtain children by her." And Abram hearkened to the voice of Sarai. 3 So, after Abram had dwelt ten years in the land of Canaan, Sarai, Abram's wife, took Hagar the Egyptian, her maid, and gave her to Abram her husband as a wife. 4 And he went in to Hagar, and she conceived; and when she saw that she had conceived, she looked with contempt on her mistress. 5 And Sarai said to Abram, "May the wrong done to me be on you! I gave my maid to your embrace, and when she saw that she had conceived, she looked on me with contempt. May the LORD judge between you and me!" 6 But Abram said to Sarai, "Behold, your maid is in your power; do to her as you please." Then Sarai dealt harshly with her, and she fled from her. 7 The angel of the LORD found her by a spring of water in the wilderness, the spring on the way to Shur. 8 And he said, "Hagar, maid of Sarai, where have you come from and where are you going?" She said, "I am fleeing from my mistress Sarai." 9 The angel of the LORD said to her, "Return to your mistress, and submit to her."... 15 And Hagar bore Abram a son; and Abram called the name of his son, whom Hagar bore, Ishmael. 16 Abram was eighty-six years old when Hagar bore Ishmael to Abram. (RSV)

Following the relentless talk of offspring in Genesis 15, the initial *vav* of this episode is likely better rendered as an adversative that sharpens the quandary of the plot: "Yahweh cut a deal with Abram: 'To your offspring I give this land.'... *But* Sarai the woman of Abram did not bear a child to him" (15:18; 16:1).[37] Another nuance lost in the translation and punctuation of the RSV is the partial mirroring of the two halves of this first verse, which not only establishes the poles of the narrative's conflict, but also neatly encapsulates one of Sarai's central characteristics:[38]

ושרי אשת אברם לא ילדה לו / ולה שפחה מצרית ושמה הגר

---

37. כרת יהוה את־אברם ברית לאמר לזרעך נתתי את־הארץ הזאת...ושרי אשת אברם לא ילדה לו.

38. See Trible, "Desolation," 10, for another reading that emphasizes the architecture of this verse; compare Trible, "Ominous Beginnings," 38.

Sarai, still the "woman of" Abram, has yet to bear a child "to him" (לו); however, "to her" (לה) belongs an "Egyptian slave" named Hagar. The names of the episode's principal antagonists bookend the verse, and Sarai's quality as one who both lacks and possesses finds succinct expression here even as it defines the germ of the plot: Sarai has no child, but she does have a slave. Her lack is here made more pronounced by the grammar, which frames Sarai's childlessness in terms of her failure to produce for Abram. Sarai's possession of Hagar, however, is thus the more emphasized, a fact only further cemented as the story develops. What was revealed in 12:5, that Sarai is a slaveowner, is now reconfirmed. Whether or not שפחה is limited to a meaning of "slave" in the broader lexicon, the immediate context here shows that the RSV's "maid" is far too weak.[39] The repeated possessives of the narrator and every character bar the infant Ishmael strongly suggest that Sarai owns Hagar, and the role in counterpoint to Hagar as שפחה is Sarai as גבירה, or "master." Word-studies, moreover, are superfluous in the face of the plot here, which shows Sarai possessed of sweeping authority over Hagar, whose sexuality and fertility are Sarai's to allocate (16:2-3, 5). When her scheme produces unforeseen results, Sarai abuses Hagar with impunity, regarded as within her rights here not only by Abram (v. 6), but by Yahweh's messenger, who urges Hagar: "submit yourself to abuse under her hand" (התעני תחת ידיה, v. 9). Sarai, then, is the owner, Hagar the owned.

Sarai's address to Abram in Gen. 16:2, which is her first recorded direct speech, is interesting in content but even more intriguing in tone. Nothing explicit about Sarai intervenes in the discourse between this episode and that of Egypt. This silence is only emphasized by a striking formal resemblance, not reflected in the RSV or the NRSV, between Abram's speech there—also his first direct utterance—and Sarai's here.[40] She adopts Abram's very syntax, opening her persuasive address by drawing attention to a perceived problem with the particle pair הנה־נא, then moving to propose a solution with an imperative followed by ־נא. Finally, as Abram did, she closes with a mention of the desired result, which involves personal acquisition. Where Abram had previously said, "Look...*I* know[, if anyone does,] that you are a woman who is lovely to look at.... Just say you are my sister! That way it will go well for me" (הנה־נא ידעתי כי אשה יפת־מראה את...אמרי־נא אחתי את למען ייטב־לי, 12:11, 13), Sarai urges, "Look...Yahweh [not you, Abram!] has stopped

---

39. The NRSV (1989) updates this language to "slave-girl."
40. Compare André Wénin, "Saraï, Hagar et Abram: Une approche narrative et contextuelle de Gn 16, 1-6," *RTL* 32 (2001): 33–5.

me from giving birth. Just 'go into' my slave! Perhaps I will be built up out of her" (הנה־נא עצרני יהוה מלדת בא־נא אל־שפחתי אולי אבנה ממנה, 16:2). Sarai, it seems, has learned from Abram how to wheedle and scheme.

These parallels, which represent only a portion of the ties between these episodes, immediately prompt questions about Sarai's sincerity and motives. Abram's speech at the edge of Egypt was a murky mix of seeming-truths and duplicitous, self-serving exaggeration. The formal likeness of Sarai's persuasive talk here suggests that it, too, be read with caution. Is she wholly ingenuous in her emphatic attribution of her childlessness to Yahweh? Or could her seemingly artless suggestion—"why don't you just 'enter' my slave?"—be prompted by something more complex? If Sarai's stratagem were a ruse designed to expose Abram's impotence, for instance, her coming rage, thus partly prompted by the plan's failure, might be more easily understood.[41] Or perhaps she has tired of Abram's amorous visits—again, these notes of lack of reproductive success make little sense if their sexual activity has ceased—and uses her power over Hagar to provide him with a surrogate partner. Either of these hypotheses, further, might illuminate Sarai's chortle and aside in 18:12, where she thinks or mutters, "After my being worn out, there is pleasure for me, huh? With my husband as old as he is!"

Moreover, inquiries into Sarai's candor in her final statement in this first speech end inconclusively. "Perhaps," she says, "I will be built up out of her"—a punning use of בנה that seems to refer to Sarai's establishment as a mother of a son through Hagar. But does Sarai want to be a mother, by her own body or otherwise? Her desire is not strong enough to keep her from abusing the pregnant Hagar until she flees, and she certainly shows no affection for Ishmael later (16:6; 21:10). Her response to the eventual birth of her own son (21:6) is also deeply ambiguous. Sarai's proposition and statement here, though, could also reflect a real anxiety over her lack of offspring, similar to that exhibited by Abram in 15:2-3. Essentializing appeals to Sarai's "biological clock," or to a supposedly natural desire for women to have babies, do not satisfy here. But the narrative primacy of her childlessness has prepared the reader from the start for just such a conflict (11:30); indeed, the immediate recency of the similar note in 16:1 recalls and underlines this fundamental datum, emphasizing its complicating role in the plot. The drumbeat of promises of offspring to Abram, moreover, coupled with their lack of fulfillment, implies a level of stress

---

41. A similar hypothesis is developed by Burton L. Visotzky, *The Genesis of Ethics* (New York: Three Rivers Press, 1996), 44–5.

over this disjunction that could easily, it seems, have spilled over into Sarai's consciousness after a decade in the land (v. 3). The centrality of the themes of acquisition and possession to this narrative, too, makes it difficult to dismiss the possibility that Sarai wants to obtain offspring, and this by any means available.

These means, unlike their ultimate motives, lie open for inspection—and they are clearly abusive, despite the efforts of interpreters such as Schneider to justify them.[42] Disturbing echoes with the Egyptian episode multiply here, and this scene comes to resemble nothing so much as an arranged rape.[43] Sarai, as the party in power, casually disposes of a voiceless subordinate's sexual resources—just enter my slave!—and uses her as an instrument for personal gain (16:2). Sarai's proposal may even be more troubling than Abram's, as it does not include the object of the scheme as an interlocutor. Further startling is Sarai's adoption of a role formerly played by those with power over her own body: "Sarai, woman of Abram, took Hagar the Egyptian, her slave…and she gave her to Abram" (v. 3).[44] Taken so often in the past (11:29, 31; 12:5, 15, and twice in v. 19), Sarai evokes the meaning of her powerful name by becoming a taker here, giving Hagar to Abram "as a wife" (לאשה, 16:3; compare Pharaoh's statement in 12:19).

This does not mean that Sarai has emerged from Abram's power over her, which was so clearly depicted in Egypt. Indeed, her imitation of him here merely underlines the profound and lasting effects of his domination there. To the narrator, moreover, she is still the "woman of" Abram, evaluated by her failure to produce "for him" (16:1). The note in v. 2, that "Abram listened to the voice of Sarai" (וישמע אברם לקול שרי), does not imply that his is the inferior position, which a consideration of

---

42. The interpretation of Schneider, *Sarah*, 48, is characteristic of her penchant to defend Sarai's actions by showing that God approves of them. Rejecting the influential contention of Trible, "Desolation," that Sarai is abusive, Schneider asks: "are Sarai's actions really so bad?" She goes on to excuse Sarai's disposal of Hagar by noting that Abram did something similar in Egypt, and, after all, there is "nothing in Sarai's plan that counters anything promised by the Deity"—therefore, apparently, all is well. Contrast the readings of Fewell and Gunn, *Gender, Power, and Promise*, 43–5, and Trible, "Ominous Beginnings," 38, who also comment on the similarities between Sarai and Abram here.

43. Compare Scholz, *Sacred Witness*, 58–9, who does not hesitate to identify Genesis 16 as a rape narrative.

44. ותקח שרי אשת־אברם את־הגר המצרית שפחתה...ותתן אתה לאברם. This play with לקח is frequently noted; see, among others, Jacobs, *Gender, Power, and Persuasion*, 138.

the parallel scene in Genesis 12 shows. To mention that Abram agrees is to assume that he has a choice in the matter; to raise the concept of his response at all suggests that he has an agency that Sarai was not afforded on the threshold of Egypt. However, the language of 16:3 might hint at the beginning of a subtle realignment in power between Sarai and Abram. Here, Sarai is referred to by the familiar epithet אשת־אברם at the opening of the verse; but Abram, after receiving Hagar from Sarai, is also so qualified near the end of the verse, for the first time in the narrative: he is "her man" or "husband" (אישה). From here on, Sarai will act before and speak to Abram in considerable freedom, and never as one cowed (v. 5; compare 21:10).

Abram's scheme in Egypt may have had some unintended consequences; but Sarai's plan here seems to unravel almost totally. Whether Sarai's true motive is to get Hagar with child or not, her slave conceives with no intervening detail in the discourse: "[Abram] 'went into' Hagar, and she conceived" (ויבא אל־הגר ותהר, 16:4). Just as rapidly, Hagar is said to notice her condition (ותרא כי הרתה). Here there may be some play with the concept of "noticing" that helps to tie Sarai's reaction here to her treatment in Egypt. The usually inconspicuous word ראה, radically "to see," serves to link Sarai's reception in Genesis 12 with Hagar's apparent motive here, and notes of "seeing" and "eyes" are rapidly forming motifs that grow in importance as the narrative progresses. The seeing of Sarai in Egypt was something of great power: it was the predicted trigger for the purported, covetous homicidal impulses of the Egyptians in 12:12, and the actual catalyst for the praise of the courtiers that resulted in Sarai's being "taken" by the ruler of that land (vv. 14-15). Again, this "noticing" was no boost to Sarai's self-esteem. Rather, in a manner wholly congruent with the rest of that tale, it was predatory and objectifying, and it culminated in her abuse. But any attention can sometimes be preferable to none at all; and here, after Hagar "sees" or "notices" her pregnancy, Sarai—so "lovely to look at"—is "insignificant in her eyes" (ותקל...בעיניה, 16:4): simply "overlooked." The verbal root קלל most often appears in the *piel*, where it carries the strongly negative meaning "to curse." In the *qal*, however, as in Gen. 16:4-5, קלל never means "curse," but rather something milder: to be "trifling," "of little account"—simply not worthy of notice or thought.[45] Sarai has not been overtly outraged or abused, but ignored.

---

45. See BDB 886b. Contrast Schneider, *Sarah*, 49–50, who glosses over the varied meanings of the *binyanim* in order to argue that Hagar's action is extremely serious. See also *HALOT* 1103b; *DCH* 7:256b, 7:600b.

Experience tells me that it is wounding to be treated as unworthy of notice. And Hagar's attitude inverts the customary hierarchy in the story world, as is emphasized by the subject situated in the center of the phrase: not merely the character Sarai, but "her *master* became insignificant in her eyes" (ותקל גברתה בעיניה). Hagar, the Egyptian slave, is clearly the one who should be invisible, overlooked. But Sarai explodes into hyperbole and rage out of all proportion to this slight. In fact, she first responds with something that itself reads like a curse. Sarai, who, in an act of reciprocal overlooking, never speaks to Hagar in the discourse—here or later—tells Abram, in a highly compressed phrase suggestive of strangling anger: חמסי עליך (Gen. 16:5). The RSV's "May the wrong done to me be on you!" communicates the curse-like feeling well; but חמס, which literally means "violence," demands something stronger. Even the NABR's "outrage" may fall short: another context featuring חמס plus על is Jer. 51:35, where amid images of martial brutality the curse "the חמס done me…be upon Babylon" is paired with "my blood be upon those who live in Chaldea." The only other occurrences of the noun in the broader narrative of Genesis, furthermore, are in the exposition to the flood, where God is led by the חמס of humanity to put an "end to all flesh" (6:13; compare v. 11), and in Jacob's curse of Simeon and Levi, where the phrase כלי חמס is tied to their vicious slaughter of the Shechemites (49:5; compare 34:25-26). "Savagery," then, may come closer to the mark.

This cry of "savagery!" may lead a reader to wonder what the narrator has left out. But Sarai offers no new evidence, instead underlining her own disposal of Hagar's sexuality before recounting the provocative events in language that resembles the preceding narration very closely. "*I* gave *my* slave into your lap," Sarai begins, employing a transparent euphemism for Abram's genitals, "and when she noticed that she had conceived I became insignificant in her eyes" (אנכי נתתי שפחתי בחיקך ותרא כי הרתה ואקל בעיניה, 16:5; compare vv. 3-4).[46] Sarai's report both confirms the narrator's account and emphasizes her own outsize reaction. The slave—Sarai never refers to her by name, now or later—is *hers* to give, a note that highlights Sarai's identity as a possessor, and Sarai's evaluation of her slave's offense of indifference corresponds in every particular with what has been described. That Hagar became pregnant, which was, after

---

46. "Lap" is the evocative offering of *HALOT* 312b. Compare E. A. Speiser, *Genesis: A New Translation with Introduction and Commentary*, 3rd ed., AB 1 (Garden City, NY: Doubleday, 1982), 116, 118; Robert Alter, *Genesis: Translation and Commentary* (New York: Norton, 1996), 68.

all, Sarai's stated plan (v. 2), and as a result overlooked her master—this Sarai calls "savagery," invoking Yahweh to support her claim: "Yahweh find for me or you!" (ישפט יהוה ביני וביניך, v. 5).

But the only obvious savagery in this scene is that of Sarai herself. This is foreshadowed in literal fashion in Abram's reply to Sarai's curses: "Here—your slave is in your hand" (הנה שפחתך בידך, 16:6). יד is a frequent biblical metonym for power, and this is plainly a context of transfer of "power over" a subordinate that echoes that of 12:19, where Pharaoh returns Sarai with a similar implied gesture: "Here—your woman! Take her and go!" (הנה אשתך קח ולך). But Sarai's "hand" here is also, it seems, a weapon. After Abram caps his abdication of responsibility with a closely packed phrase that both continues to play on the episode's absorption with seeing and anticipates Lot's cowardice in Sodom—"do to her what is good in your eyes" (עשׂי־לה הטוב בעיניך, 16:6; compare 19:8)—Sarai acts: ותענה שׂרי. If her description of being ignored as חמס was hyperbolic, her response here is completely unmeasured. ענה, especially in the *piel*, as here, is a strong word often employed in contexts of tremendous suffering and violation: it is what Egyptian slavemasters do to the captive Israelites (Exod. 1:11-12; compare Yahweh's prediction to Abram in Gen. 15:13); it is what the Israelites are warned never to do to the powerless widow or orphan (Exod. 22:21-22); and often, when women are the object of this verb, it denotes sexual humiliation and rape. The rapes of Dinah (Gen. 34:2), Tamar (2 Sam. 13:12, 14, 22, 32), the nameless "concubine" (פילגשׁ) of a Levite (Judg. 19:24; 20:5), and the women of Zion (Lam. 5:11) are all described with ענה. Sarai, then, having characterized Hagar's indifference as "savagery," herself responds with brutal, humiliating abuse of her slave who, it should not be forgotten, carries an unborn child.[47] That this abuse may even contain an element of sexual violence cannot, it seems, be easily dismissed, and the list of citations just mentioned offers only one consideration here.[48] Even more important is the immediate context of the episode at hand, which has already shown that Sarai can do whatever she wants with the sexuality of "her slave": "I put my slave in your lap!" And the verbal link between Lot's attempted sacrifice of his daughters to the men of Sodom and Abram's surrender of Hagar to Sarai may do more than

---

47. Schneider, *Sarah*, 53, while admitting that Sarai's action is "harsh," and "may not seem 'nice,'" excuses it as "consistent with ancient Near Eastern and biblical tradition." Again, Schneider points out, without qualm, that Sarai's abuse of Hagar is "not out of line" with "the Deity."

48. See Scholz, *Sacred Witness*, 59–60, for a reading that characterizes Sarai's action as rape.

show Abram in a bad light: Lot's neighbors, after all, are bent on sexual violence (Gen. 19:4-11, especially v. 5). The troubling possibility remains, then, that "Sarai violated her" so that "[Hagar] fled from her" (ותענה שרי ותברח מפניה, 16:6; compare v. 8).

Hagar's flight and epiphany in the desert have many interesting and puzzling features, such as a continuation of the motif of seeing (16:13-14; and note the play with עין in v. 7) and a divine promise that a first-time reader might well identify with those already given to Abram (v. 10)—thus giving rise to the assumption that Sarai has no part in the pledges of offspring at all. Most startling, however, is that Yahweh, by way of a character, מלאך יהוה, whose identity seems to waver between a divine messenger and the immanent deity, does "find for" Sarai here (compare v. 5). This is not despite Sarai's violent mistreatment of Hagar; instead, it is an endorsement of their abusive relationship: "Return to your master and submit yourself to abuse under her hand" (שובי אל־גברתך והתעני תחת ידיה, v. 9).[49] This does more than emphasize, by the reappearance of ענה and יד, the brutal edge to Sarai's conduct. It is also revealing of Sarai's relationship with the deity, which is taking shape as a kind of strange, utilitarian alliance where any means are acceptable but the ends remain unclear. For it is also the second time in this narrative where divine direction or influence has restored an abusive relationship. Liberative interpretations such as that of Cotter fail to recognize the paradox inherent in their readings here: Yahweh rescues a woman from her distress in harem or desert—but only to return her to a situation potentially as dangerous.[50] Both times, Sarai has been a party to the arrangement, but in opposite roles: in Egypt, she was given back to the man whose scheme had placed her in harm's way (12:17-19), where here she is poised to receive back the slave whose sorry state is a direct result of her own scheme. These restorations of rightful possessions only emphasize the contribution of the narrative's underlying rhythm of loss and gain to Sarai's characterization.

Sarai's proffer of Hagar and its aftermath have shined a light on a character of increasing complexity. Some of Sarai's traits and qualities have been

---

49. Compare the reading of Trible, "Desolation," 16, who calls 16:9 a "divine word of terror"; see also Trible, "Ominous Beginnings," 40–1, and Scholz, *Sacred Witness*, 60–1; compare 57. Contrast, however, Weems, "A Mistress, a Maid, and No Mercy," 13, who attributes the command of the "angel" to Hagar's failure to alter her self-conception.

50. Cotter, *Genesis*, 104, contends that God "frees" Hagar in this episode, contributing to a theme in which God saves "trapped" women (92).

reinforced. She is still seemingly infertile, lacking a child despite effort, which deepens an ongoing conflict with the divine promises, and thus, perhaps, with Abram, and even herself—all of which may account for some of her motives in this dark episode. Have the passage of years, accompanied by the accumulation of dissonant pledges, built up to a breaking point? Sarai is still a slaveowner, too, and the depths of what that means have been illuminated to a disturbing degree here.

Sarai also remains a "woman of" Abram, though holes seem to have begun to wear in his authority. This is partly shown, moreover, by Sarai's transformation into a "woman of" Abram in another sense entirely: she has become like him, following his example in scheming, taking, and abusing. This, in turn, throws much into doubt. Does she really believe that she has been the faulty link in the couple's failure to produce? Does she even want a child, even if "built up" by a surrogate? The progression of this episode does not return certain answers to these questions, but it does depict Sarai—so "lovely to look at"—as someone who is highly sensitive to her appearance in the eyes of others, someone who repays a slight with rage and unrestrained violence.

Much of this further defines Sarai's relationships with Abram, with Hagar, with Yahweh, and with herself in her development as a character. In Sarai's imitation of Abram she shifts the balance of power between them. Sarai's relationship with Hagar may be a sad commentary in microcosm on her broader ties with women. While much of the story content of these connections remains in the deep background, it seems that Sarai's relationships with women are of two primary kinds: some she owns (12:5, for example), and some she shares a sexual partner with (if בית פרעה of 12:15 implies, as most conclude, the king's harem). These categories are united in Hagar, and it is unsurprising when this arrangement erupts so spectacularly. Yahweh proves to be an ally to Sarai's worst impulses, and is again complicit in the restoration of an abusive relationship. As for Sarai's own development, the many similarities and echoes between this episode and that of Egypt cement, for me, the notion of a direct tie between her treatment there and her actions here: in a sad evolution, the abused becomes the abuser.[51] Dehumanized

---

51. This reading depends on the narrative data of Genesis, not on psychological generalizations about cycles of abuse. Such dynamics are possible, however: Elizabeth Mayfield Arnold, J. Chris Stewart, and C. Aaron McNeece, "Perpetrators as Victims: Understanding Violence by Female Street-Walking Prostitutes," *Violence and Victims* 16 (2001): 154, concludes that for its subjects, "the best predictor of… later violence," among other negative factors, is "a history of physical abuse"; "Blood, Sweat and Tears," *The Economist*, 27 September 2014: 42 (no byline),

in Egypt, Sarai dehumanizes Hagar here; and when Hagar's response channels this degradation by demeaning Sarai, Sarai snaps, responding even more basely in violence.

All this shows Sarai ever more clearly as someone "with" and "without," characterized by gain and loss. Without a child, Sarai gives away the slave she has, ostensibly to gain a child; given back the slave who is with child, she brutally drives her away. Here, at last, Sarai may lose slave and child alike. For although Hagar comes back, it remains ambiguous whether she follows Yahweh's messenger's directive to "submit" to "abuse" under Sarai's hand. After Hagar's implied return in 16:15, she is never called the "slave of" Sarai while Sarai is alive; and Ishmael is never Sarai's son.

Years of Silence, More Promises—and a New Name?
(Gen. 17:1-27)

A yawning gap in story time now opens up in the space of fewer than twenty words in the discourse: in the final verse of Genesis 16, at the birth of Ishmael, Abram is said to be eighty-six years old; he is noted to be ninety-nine when he receives yet another communication from Yahweh in the first verse of Genesis 17. So much is passed over in silence here; and while the narrative has never pretended to be a complete chronicle of events, this chronological gap is more profound than any that has come before. It is wider, that is, it spans more time, than any except the primary blanks in Ur, and possibly Haran, at the very beginning; indeed, it is longer than the story time of the entire narrative arc from the family's emigration from Haran to Ishmael's birth, as Abram is said to be seventy-five at their departure (12:4). But this gap also feels deeper than any other thus far, for the end of Genesis 16 draws many relational tensions together and leaves most of them unresolved. How does Sarai receive Hagar when she returns? For whom does Hagar slave? Are these years of uneasy détente between Sarai and the others, perhaps made easier by the small shifts in power implied in 16:5-6, or are they marked by further open, even violent confrontation?[52] Or has Hagar simply been cowed and broken by her master's abuse and its subsequent divine endorsement? How does Sarai engage, if at all, with Ishmael, the son she once felt was possible for her to have, as he grows from infancy to adolescence?

---

details the self-perpetuating cycle of bullying in the South Korean military, where a case of death by abuse was linked to the perpetrators' own abuse at the hands of their superior.

52. Compare Jeansonne, *Women of Genesis*, 47.

These and other questions remain open—some, at least, for good. While these narrative elements go into suspension, thirteen years of silence ends with Abram in a familiar situation, as God speaks of the man's role as "father of a crowd of nations" who will possess the "whole land of Canaan" (17:5, 8).[53] One significant factor, however, is different this time: "Abraham," his name now "enlarged" (compare 12:2), actually has a son on the cusp of adulthood. This may still fall short of the grandiosity of some of God's promises—such as "I will make you fruitful beyond measure" (17:6)—but it is a start. The discursive recency of Ishmael's birth suggests that he is the "seed" of Abraham's offspring with whom Yahweh's covenant will be established (v. 7); indeed, Abraham's laugh at God's prediction that he will become a father once again implies that he shares this assumption (v. 17). Ishmael, for Abraham, is enough: "Would that Ishmael live in your presence!" (v. 18).

It is a surprise, then, when God, having spoken at some length about the removal of the male foreskin as a "sign" of the covenant (17:10-14), abruptly begins to talk to Abraham about his "woman"—and not, oddly, referring to Ishmael's mother.[54] "Sarah," rather, is the object of a divine pronouncement where she is prospectively characterized in ways that partly recall earlier forecasts about Abraham: God will "bless" Sarah, who will "turn into nations; kings of peoples will come from her" (וברכתיה והיתה לגוים מלכי עמים ממנה יהיו, v. 16; compare 12:2-3, and especially the similar language in 17:6). The announcement of her name, שרה, also partly evokes the message of v. 5, where Abram is told "your name will not be 'Abram' any longer, but your name will be 'Abraham'" (ולא־יקרא עוד את־שמך אברם והיה שמך אברהם). There is a strange divergence between the two pronouncements, however, for while Abram's is clearly a name change, this reads like simple revelation: "don't call her

---

53. The noun אלהים first appears in the narrative of Sarai/Sarah and Abram/Abraham here in 17:3. For my narrative purposes I read this as another name for the character called Yahweh. Yahweh has just self-referred using yet another epithet (אני־אל שדי, "I am El-Shaddai") in v. 1. Other names for what I read as the same character have been "El-Elyon" (אל עליון, 14:18-20, 22), "Lord Yahweh" (אדני יהוה, 15:2, 8), and "El-Roï" (אל ראי, 16:13).

54. All this talk of circumcision makes the exhortation of Yahweh in 17:1 read like another little jest: Abram is told there to be תמים, literally, "intact." This was marked already in the Mishnah, which, however, gives the pun a pious spin: Abraham is "whole only when he had circumcised himself" (*m. Ned.* 3:11; Jacob Neusner, trans., *The Mishnah: A New Translation* [New Haven: Yale University Press, 1988], 412). Other notes, such as the pronouncement that one uncircumcised will be "cut off" (כרת, v. 14) from the people, add to the mildly ribald tone here.

Sarai—for her name is Sarah" (לא־תקרא את־שמה שרי כי שרה שמה, v. 15). The significance of this clarification is not immediately plain.[55] Lexically, there seems to be no distinction of importance between שׂרי and שׂרה: both are related to שׂרר, "to rule" or "to dominate."[56] However, the revision or revelation of Sarah's name marks a momentous shift that reverberates in the plot and in her characterization. The primacy of her infertility, so often reinforced throughout the narrative, is here predictively reversed by simple fiat, and in a way that places a bold line under the basic meaning of her name: "kings of peoples will come from her" (v. 16). Sarai "had no child," but Sarah will "turn into nations" (11:30; 17:16).

The genuine magnitude of this change is tempered at once, however, by a consideration of what remains the same. It is not necessary to reject the text of the MT in Gen. 17:16b, as Sarah Shectman does, in order to conclude that the character Sarah is not the focus of God's promises here.[57] "Sarah" doesn't even know her name—because God's revelation is not to Sarah. It is about Sarah; and it is about her only in a very narrow way that primarily emphasizes her function as a vessel for Abraham's offspring. God's first declaration in 17:16 saws back and forth a bit, hinting first at a blessing that might be truly hers: "I will bless her; *and what is more*, I will give you a son through her" (וברכתי אתה וגם נתתי ממנה לך בן). What directly follows, however, clarifies that her "blessing" and her birthing are one in the same, in a line that could with justice be rendered, "I will bless her *so that* she will turn into nations" (וברכתיה והיתה לגוים).[58] After Abraham punctures the solemnity of the scene, falling on his face and laughing as he soliloquizes about the absurdity of "a man of one hundred" fathering a child—"or 'Sarah!' As if a woman of ninety could give birth!"—God reiterates not only that Sarah is Abraham's, but also that the child, with whom God will establish a "perpetual covenant," will be Abraham's, too: "Sarah your woman will give birth to a son for you" (שרה אשתך ילדת לך בן, v. 19; compare v. 21). Isaac is the true focus of these oracles, and thus "Sarah" emerges from a blank of thirteen years only to be shown again as one who has and has not: at last, she will give birth, but not to be "built up" herself. Rather, her blessing is to be an instrument that will "bear for" Abraham, and for God's promised covenant.

---

55. This disparity is also noted by Schneider, *Sarah*, 57–8, who similarly struggles to make much of it.

56. *DCH* 8:191–2, 199.

57. Sarah Shectman, *Women in the Pentateuch: A Feminist and Source-Critical Analysis* (Sheffield: Sheffield Phoenix Press, 2009), 138–9; compare 178.

58. Compare the rendering of Shectman, ibid., 138.

Sarah Chortles (Gen. 18:1-15)

Gen. 18:1 And the LORD appeared to him by the oaks of Mamre, as he sat at the door of his tent in the heat of the day. 2 He lifted up his eyes and looked, and behold, three men stood in front of him. When he saw them, he ran from the tent door to meet them, and bowed himself to the earth, 3 and said, "My lord, if I have found favor in your sight, do not pass by your servant. 4 Let a little water be brought, and wash your feet, and rest yourselves under the tree, 5 while I fetch a morsel of bread, that you may refresh yourselves, and after that you may pass on—since you have come to your servant." So they said, "Do as you have said." 6 And Abraham hastened into the tent to Sarah, and said, "Make ready quickly three measures of fine meal, knead it, and make cakes." 7 And Abraham ran to the herd, and took a calf, tender and good, and gave it to the servant, who hastened to prepare it. 8 Then he took curds, and milk, and the calf which he had prepared, and set it before them; and he stood by them under the tree while they ate. 9 They said to him, "Where is Sarah your wife?" And he said, "She is in the tent." 10 The LORD said, "I will surely return to you in the spring, and Sarah your wife shall have a son." And Sarah was listening at the tent door behind him. 11 Now Abraham and Sarah were old, advanced in age; it had ceased to be with Sarah after the manner of women. 12 So Sarah laughed to herself, saying, "After I have grown old, and my husband is old, shall I have pleasure?" 13 The LORD said to Abraham, "Why did Sarah laugh, and say, 'Shall I indeed bear a child, now that I am old?' 14 Is anything too hard for the LORD? At the appointed time I will return to you, in the spring, and Sarah shall have a son." 15 But Sarah denied, saying, "I did not laugh"; for she was afraid. He said, "No, but you did laugh." (RSV)

This episode begins in a manner wholly familiar: "Yahweh appeared to him" (וירא אליו יהוה, 18:1; compare 12:7; 17:1). Vital differences immediately distinguish this encounter from earlier epiphanies, however. Where most of those contained only bare hints about the bodily dispositions of the characters, here the sequence of scenes is ceaselessly physical, almost blocked as for a drama: "sitting in the opening of the tent at the time of the heat of the day," Abraham glances up—"look! Three men standing near him" (ישב פתח־האהל כחם היום...והנה שלשה אנשים נצבים עליו, 18:1-2). He then scrambles about in an almost comic manner, running to and prostrating himself before the visitors, hurrying back toward the tent to urge Sarah to haste, running out again to the herd, and hovering over their guests while they eat (vv. 2-8).[59] Physical presence and the needs of the

---

59. For a reading that emphasizes the comic in this pericope generally, see Gina Hens-Piazza, "New Historicism," in *New Meanings for Ancient Texts: Recent Approaches to Biblical Criticisms and Their Applications*, ed. Steven L. McKenzie and John Kaltner (Louisville: Westminster John Knox Press, 2013), 64–72.

body—refreshment, rest, food and drink—dominate the narrative matter. Sarah's central part in this play, too, depends on her senses and her bodily presence, precisely recalling Abraham's position in the "opening of the tent" (פתח האהל, v. 10; compare v. 1) as she listens to one of the visitors make predictions about her reproductive biology.

And it is the presence of Sarah, albeit somewhat obscured by the tent, that most distinguishes this visit from the others. Sarah has never been a direct party to any of Yahweh's communications, and whether she has subsequently become aware of their content has been a matter of hypothesis and guesswork. Here, too, the evidence is mixed, but tends to support the notion that Sarah is generally ignorant, even now, a quarter century after the first divine address to Abraham, of most of what has been revealed. In fact, her lack of confusion at being called "Sarah" is the only clear indication that any part of God's promises and revelations have trickled down to her. Sarah's response to what she hears does not suggest that she is aware even of God's recent prediction of her pregnancy to Abraham, and much of the most important content of the earlier pledges is notably absent here. Sarah hears that she will have a son—and that is all. Other information, such as the fecundity of Abraham's descendants, their possession of the land, and their involvement in a special covenant with the deity, so often repeated, is omitted here. This is true even though Sarah herself has been implicated, if only as a vehicle, in at least the fertility and covenant aspects of the promises (17:16, 19, 21). All this, further, is particularly odd if the proximate motive for this visit is to let Sarah in on the secret of her coming child.[60] The other characters, human and divine, seem agreed that Sarah ought to know only the bare minimum, even where her body and offspring are concerned.

However, much interesting if sometimes ambiguous information about Sarah may be gleaned from this episode. She is first mentioned in 18:6, in a novel context: "Abraham hurried toward the tent, to Sarah; and he said, 'Hurry! Three *seahs* of flour, the good stuff—knead and make loaves!'" (וימהר אברהם האהלה אל־שרה ויאמר מהרי שלש סאים קמח סלת לושי ועשי עגות). Sarah's sphere, it seems, is domestic, her position subordinate and

---

60. Gunn and Fewell, *Narrative in the Hebrew Bible*, 95, argue that the visit is "God's move to include Sarah" in knowledge of the promise after Abraham fails to relay her role in it, but it is hard for me to detect much divine solicitude for Sarah in the broader narrative. The account of 18:1–16a in Hens-Piazza, "New Historicism," 68–9, which highlights structural issues, is more convincing on the matter of the narrative's focus on Sarah. But any claim that Yahweh is including Sarah here should acknowledge that this inclusion is partial at best.

akin to that of the "boy" (נער) who helps Abraham with the main course (v. 7). But reflection on just how little is shown here leads to much uncertainty. This is Sarah and Abraham's first discourse-level communication since the disaster involving Hagar, many years ago, and it partly evokes their very first explicit verbal encounter on the border of Egypt. There, too, Abraham does all the talking, urging a course of action—but does Sarah comply, or even reply? Abraham does not clearly enter the tent here, and there is no indication that Sarah acknowledges or even hears his order, which in any event is comically overblown: "Hurry! make 'several hundred pita breads'!"[61] It is difficult to imagine the Sarah of thirteen years ago, who curses Abraham and attacks Hagar (16:5-6), assiduously obeying Abraham's passing cry to bake for an army—and "several hundred pita breads" are notably absent from the menu in 18:8.

When the visitors ask Abraham, "Where is Sarah your woman?" (איה שרה אשתך, 18:9), the thrust of the question is opaque. Have they been saving room for the promised "bit of bread" (פת־לחם, v. 5)? And after Abraham indicates that she is "there, in the tent" (הנה באהל, v. 9), one of the guests—apparently Yahweh in human form, to judge by vv. 13-14—takes the opportunity to inform Abraham, in the singular, of what he already knows: "Watch: your woman Sarah will have a son" (והנה־בן לשרה אשתך, v. 10; compare 17:16, 19, 21). Is this prediction, then, still not intended for Sarah's ears? On the one hand, the language suggests an audience that is subtly different from that of the revelations in Genesis 17. There, the "son" is emphatically for Abraham (לך in all three verses: 16, 19, and 21); here, he belongs to Sarah (לשרה, 18:10, 14).[62] And the visitors seem to have no agenda beyond relaying this information, which is no news to Abraham and might be expected to be easily heard through the tent's impermanent structure. But on the other—why not summon Sarah outside if the object is to inform her? Why address Abraham alone, here and even after Sarah's chuckle (vv. 10, 13-14)—at least until the rebuke of v. 15?

Whether it is obliquely aimed at her or not, Sarah does hear the guest's prediction, as she is "listening in the opening of the tent" (שמעת פתח האהל, 18:10). While she is clearly out of sight of the visitors, who are unsure where she is (v. 9), there seems to be no need to conceive of Sarah

---

61. This rendering is from the amusing summary of Stephen Mitchell, *Genesis: A New Translation of the Classic Biblical Stories* (New York: HarperCollins, 1996), xxv. Estimates of the size of a *seah* vary; BDB's guess would make Abraham's suggested recipe call for about eight pounds of flour (684a).

62. Compare Hens-Piazza, "New Historicism," 70.

as hiding, eavesdropping, or even showing undue curiosity here.[63] Her posture in the tent door may be prompted by the same desire for cool that seems to have motivated Abraham's identical position earlier, and she is presumably no less visible than he was then, with a clear line of sight to the outside (compare v. 1). The speaker of v. 10 is merely behind the tent, or is seated with back turned to it.[64] After hearing her new (or clarified) name spoken in v. 9, perhaps, Sarah's attention to the following prediction is simply to be expected.

Just now, the narrator retreats slightly from the scene to offer a key bit of exposition that raises the stakes for the predicted event. After noting that "Abraham and Sarah were elderly, far along in days" (ואברהם ושרה זקנים באים בימים, 18:11), this complication receives a concrete illustration: "the way of women had stopped for Sarah" (חדל להיות לשרה ארח כנשים, v. 11). This note, which is almost universally taken as referring to menopause, reemphasizes the narrator's conception of Sarah's role as the broken link in the family's chain of descent, and seems to render permanent her well-established trait of infertility.

Sarah's reaction to the visitor's prediction is sensible, and entirely in line with the hardening arc of her character to this point: she scoffs at such a ridiculous notion. "Sarah chortled," or "laughed in her chest" (ותצחק שרה בקרבה), "thinking, 'After my being worn out, there's pleasure for me! And 'my lord' as old as he is!'" (לאמר אחרי בלתי היתה־לי עדנה ואדני זקן, 18:12). I have trouble reading this as a note of hope, or wonder, as Schneider would have it; to me the tone is one of sarcastic mirth, a skeptical remark delivered with rolling eyes.[65] The RSV obscures Sarah's metaphor by rendering בלתי as "I have grown old," meanwhile associating Sarah's evaluations of her and Abraham's physical conditions more closely than her language justifies. Abraham, Sarah says, confirming the judgment of the narrator in v. 11, is "old" (זקן); but she characterizes herself as "worn out," using a verb most often associated

---

63. Lori Hope Lefkovitz, "Eavesdropping on Angels and Laughing at God: Theorizing a Subversive Matriarchy," in *Gender and Judaism: The Transformation of Tradition*, ed. Tamar Rudavsky (New York: New York University Press, 1995), 160, characterizes what she calls Sarah's "eavesdropping" positively, as a "survival strategy" undertaken by a woman to navigate a world dominated by gods and men.

64. The MT's והוא אחריו is ambiguous here: "and it/he was behind him/it," apparently referring to the guest and the masculine noun אהל, "tent," but in uncertain order.

65. Schneider, *Sarah*, 72, contends that Sarah's "response contains no explicit questioning of the Deity's plans; to the contrary, her laugh expresses joy"; compare 69.

with tattered clothing and other fabrics.[66] It is possible that this refers to being post-menopausal, and thus that בלתי means "after my wearing out," in a simple, intransitive process of entropy. But this robs the image of something essential: clothes, after all, do not wear themselves out. What is more, Sarah's most closely associated thought here is not about infertility, which might, given its narrative primacy, be expected to be the most salient fact of her menopause, but of the unlikely prospect of her achieving sexual pleasure (עדנה) with Abraham. Sarah scoffs here, then, to my reading, having been "worn out" by Abraham's fruitless and unsatisfying attentions, and incredulous at the thought that Abraham could even perform—"With 'my lord' as old as he is!"

It is worth underlining what is absent from Sarah's aside, which is any explicit mention of a child. Sarah hears that she will have a son, but her incredulity does not even arrive at the potential product of a sexual encounter; the absurdity of Abraham rising to this occasion is object of mirth enough. This contributes to the question, raised in the discussion of Sarah's taking and giving of Hagar, of whether Sarah demonstrates any actual desire to bear children—a matter further complicated by the ambiguity of her reaction to Isaac's birth in 21:6.

This absence of concern is only highlighted by Yahweh's erroneous, if politic, report of Sarah's soliloquy (18:13). Still, remarkably, speaking only to Abraham, which underlines Sarah's conceptual, if not literal, invisibility in this scene, Yahweh says, "Why on earth did Sarah laugh? 'How could it possibly be true that I will give birth? But I'm old!' she says. As if it were too hard for Yahweh!" (vv. 13-14a).[67] Being too hard was scarcely the issue, however, as Sarah's cynical amusement turned on Abraham's sexual incapacity and advanced age; she made no plain remark about either giving birth or her own age.

After Yahweh reiterates the prediction in 18:14b—again, addressing Abraham alone—in language that recalls both v. 10 and the previous private revelation to Abraham in 17:21, there follows a cryptic exchange, seemingly cast by the narrator as a nervous attempt at deception followed by a rebuke: "But Sarah denied it: 'I didn't laugh!'—because she was afraid. But he said, 'No, you did laugh'" (ותכחש שרה לאמר לא צחקתי כי יראה ויאמר לא כי צחקת, 18:15). There seems to be little grammatical or lexical obscurity here, and the lack of a more explicit subject for ויאמר does not generate significant ambiguity. Contrary to Schneider's unusual

---

66. Deut. 8:4 (compare Neh. 9:21); 29:4; Josh. 9:4-5, 13; Isa. 50:9; 51:6; Ps. 102:27; Job 13:28.

67. למה זה צחקה שרה לאמר האף אמנם אלד ואני זקנתי היפלא מיהוה דבר.

reading here, Yahweh, not Abraham, as the one who first mentioned Sarah's laugh in v. 13, is the most natural speaker of this rather childish comeback: "Did too!"[68] But the meaning of the exchange, and thus its function in the larger web of plotting and characterization, is unclear, and this verse provides an odd and somehow unsatisfying close to this episode. Yahweh has spoken to Abraham so many times, and often about significant future geopolitical developments; Sarah is directly addressed only this once, and about an issue that struggles to deserve to be termed tangential. The justice of Yahweh's pique—if that is what this is—is another issue, and often remarked: Abraham, of course, had the same reaction to a very similar prediction, but God's reply was nothing harsher than "on the contrary" (אבל, 17:19; compare vv. 16-17). Gender bias provides one explanation for both: Sarah, as a woman, is not worthy of receiving revelation beyond what she strictly needs to know, and her subordinate station makes her disbelief sting the proud deity more: "Is anything too hard for Yahweh?" At first, this may seem to sit uneasily in the broader context of the narrative, where Sarah's abuse of her slave receives divine warrant, and where God backs Sarah, against Abraham, in her desire to banish Hagar and Ishmael (16:9; 21:12). But events to come may not exhibit divine favor for Sarah as much as they show her utility to the execution of God's purposes.

What, though, leads Sarah to "dissemble" (כחש, 18:15) and deny her laughter, which, after all, is the only part of her response that Yahweh described accurately in v. 13? And if the answer is as the narrator says— "because she was afraid"—why is she afraid? If she were merely said to be afraid, her fear might be most easily attributed to the dramatic uncertainty surrounding the thought of giving birth, for the first time, in a tent, at age ninety—certainly a life-threatening proposition. Equally, if Sarah were simply to lie about her laughter, other motives might be mooted. But the narrator ties her fear to her disavowal of her laughter most clearly: "Sarah denied it: 'I didn't laugh!' (This was because she was afraid.)"[69] This is the first and last explicit narratorial remark reflecting on Sarah's motive for any action. Elsewhere, her motives must be inferred, whether from

---

68. That Yahweh is the subject of ויאמר in 18:15 is the traditional consensus. Schneider, *Sarah*, 73, contends that Abraham is the speaker here, partly on the grounds that Sarah would not be afraid of "the Deity" given that character's deliverance of her in Egypt. But there is no indication in the narrative that Sarah is aware of Yahweh's role there, as Schneider acknowledges elsewhere (50). Compare Ramban's third comment on Gen. 18:15.

69. ותכחש שרה לאמר לא צחקתי כי יראה.

her inaction or action, silence or speech: perhaps she passively complies with Abraham's scheme in Egypt because he completely dominates her at that point in her life; perhaps she suggests Hagar's surrogacy to show that Abraham is himself impotent. Even when Sarah ventures to explain her own rage in 16:5, much must still be inferred, as shown earlier. Here, though, the reader seems to be faced with a thorny, either/or choice—one denied completely by some biblical narrative theorists—to accept or reject the motive ascribed to Sarah by the narrator.[70]

I confess that I find this choice very difficult to make. If Sarah is afraid, it seems that she is alarmed by the uncanny psychic penetration of the visitor, whom she may or may not recognize as Yahweh. Again, however, Yahweh's insight is limited and inaccurate, at least as relayed in 18:13. Alternatively, some action or nonverbal communication might be postulated in the gaps of the discourse: a turn of the head, an intimidating stare, a tone of voice that conveys the supernatural power of what had seemed like a human guest venturing a ridiculous and presumptuous prediction. If Sarah intuits something of Yahweh's violent power, so soon to be on display down in Sodom, then a response of fear and attendant confusion makes good sense—better sense, in fact, than Abraham's largely futile haggling over the fate of the valley's residents in the remainder of Genesis 18. All the same, the motive of fear seems anomalous in a character who shows none, for instance, in her dramatic confrontations with Abraham (16:5; 21:10); and if Sarah's "dissembling" carries connotations of "feigning obedience," as in some other occurrences of this root, the clash may be highlighted further.[71] Perhaps it is possible to split the difference here, and to postulate Sarah's fear as yet another step in the hardening of her character. Made afraid by intimations of supernatural power and a growing dread of her own ability to survive an unnatural and unlooked-for

---

70. The theoretical difficulties in such a choice—how can anything a narrator says be trusted, if aspects of her or his presentation come into question, for example—are ameliorated by adopting a view of the narrator as a special kind of character. That the narrator in this case has a unique kind of insight is clear in this episode, where Sarah's thoughts are exposed to view (18:12). However, this is a kind of speech, even so marked in the discourse (לאמר), and the observation and reporting of even internal speech is arguably of a different order of penetration than specifying the motives that prompt it. In other words, the narrator's discernment is a privilege that may not extend to omniscience, and his or her evaluations, which emanate from a perspective that the reader may not share, may be challenged. This entire debate operates outside the poetics of major figures such as Alter and Sternberg.

71. See BDB 471a; *HALOT* 469b–470a; *DCH* 4:382a–383b.

pregnancy that so recently seemed impossible, Sarah makes a show of acquiescence, denying her initial reaction in the hope of avoiding something even worse. This practice in dissembling may even serve Sarah in her next major episode, where she and Abraham collaborate in re-staging the Egyptian transaction, this time in a new venue.

When Sarah last occupied the stage, in 16:6, she was a childless but sexually active woman, a slaveowner whose own abuse seemed to have contributed to her adoption of the role of abuser. This was a transformation that made Sarah more like Abraham, and its operation in the plot helped point to shifts in their relationship and in its balance of power. Here, as partly prefigured in Genesis 17, some of these traits change, even to the point of reversal, and in unexpected ways. Sarah's infertility, most strikingly, is somehow deepened here, as she has entered menopause and herself alludes to a cessation of sexual activity (18:11-12); but at the same time all this is lifted, at least in divine pledge, and what seemed most sure about Sarah is thrown into doubt. Other aspects of this issue, such as the question of whether Sarah desires a child at all, remain as opaque as before. Her relationships with slaves, and particularly Hagar, also hang suspended in the background. Sarah's curious resemblance to Abraham, however, is reinforced here, as she adopts his position in the opening of the tent (vv. 1, 10) and rehearses his incredulous response to the news of her son (v. 12; 17:17). Sarah's reactions in this episode may further underscore a modest realignment in power: Abraham's bizarre request for a bushel of bread goes unheeded, and Sarah privately complains of being "worn out" while doubting Abraham's sexual potency (18:6, 12). These power shifts should not be overstated, however, for Sarah remains inside the tent and, at least in the main, outside the promises, made aware—and this as a third party—only of the prediction of her birth of a son.

Sarah's relationship with Yahweh, just now made personal, whether she fully knows it or not, has also grown in its dark complexity. In the Hagar episode, where Sarah invoked Yahweh's judgment, Yahweh abetted Sarah's violent abuse, thus contributing to the process of her hardening. This evolution seems illustrated by Sarah's cynicism here, which, however, is also—strangely—the pretext of Yahweh's indignation and rebuke (18:13-14). If Sarah is indeed made afraid here, feigning submission for self-preservation, then this, too, may help cement this process of hardening, and in a way that oddly recalls Abraham's catalytic role earlier. After being abused in Egypt by Abraham, and now intimidated into stammering fear in her own home by Yahweh, Sarah will betray no further vulnerability.

Destructive Interlude (Gen. 18:16–19:38)

Although the episodes of Abraham's bargaining on behalf of the residents of Sodom (18:16-33), the city's subsequent destruction (19:1-29), and the sorry struggles of what remains of Lot's family (19:30-38) are not without a number of interesting links to the broader narrative in which Sarah appears, none of these reflects much light on her as a character.[72] The ruin of the Jordan valley may, however, prompt Abraham and Sarah's journey to Gerar, where the couple reenacts the transaction of Egypt—but with even greater and more lasting success.

"Asylum" Redux in Gerar (Gen. 20:1-18)

Gen. 20:1 From there Abraham journeyed toward the territory of the Negeb, and dwelt between Kadesh and Shur; and he sojourned in Gerar. 2 And Abraham said of Sarah his wife, "She is my sister." And Abimelech king of Gerar sent and took Sarah. 3 But God came to Abimelech in a dream by night, and said to him, "Behold, you are a dead man, because of the woman whom you have taken; for she is a man's wife." 4 Now Abimelech had not approached her; so he said, "Lord, wilt thou slay an innocent people? 5 Did he not himself say to me, 'She is my sister'? And she herself said, 'He is my brother.' In the integrity of my heart and the innocence of my hands I have done this." 6 Then God said to him in the dream, "Yes, I know that you have done this in the integrity of your heart, and it was I who kept you from sinning against me; therefore I did not let you touch her. 7 Now then restore the man's wife; for he is a prophet, and he will pray for you, and you shall live. But if you do not restore her, know that you shall surely die, you, and all that are yours." 8 So Abimelech rose early in the morning, and called all his servants, and told them all these things; and the men were very much afraid. 9 Then Abimelech called Abraham, and said to him, "What have you done to us? And how have I sinned against you, that you have brought on me and my kingdom a great sin? You have done to me things that ought not to be done." 10 And Abimelech said to Abraham, "What were you thinking of, that you did this thing?" 11 Abraham said, "I did it because I thought, There is no fear of God at all in this place, and they will kill me because of my wife. 12 Besides she is indeed my sister, the daughter of my father but not the daughter of my mother; and she became my wife. 13 And when God caused me to wander from my father's house, I said to her, 'This is the

---

72. Just a few of the rich connections include similarities between the depictions of Lot and Abraham (compare, for example, 19:1-3 with 18:1-8; 19:19 with 18:3 and 12:3; or 19:22 with 18:6-7). For one example that may obliquely illuminate Sarah, see the ties between 19:8 and 16:6.

kindness you must do me: at every place to which we come, say of me, He is my brother.'" 14 Then Abimelech took sheep and oxen, and male and female slaves, and gave them to Abraham, and restored Sarah his wife to him. 15 And Abimelech said, "Behold, my land is before you; dwell where it pleases you." 16 To Sarah he said, "Behold, I have given your brother a thousand pieces of silver; it is your vindication in the eyes of all who are with you; and before every one you are righted." 17 Then Abraham prayed to God; and God healed Abimelech, and also healed his wife and female slaves so that they bore children. 18 For the LORD had closed all the wombs of the house of Abimelech because of Sarah, Abraham's wife. (RSV)

If the outcome of Abraham's taking refuge in Egypt raised retrospective doubts about the gravity of the famine that reportedly drove him there, the verbal echoes displayed here prompt similar questions immediately. Once again, Abraham, spoken of in the singular, "travels on" (נסע) to the Negeb (נגב) and "seeks asylum" (גור) in the territory of a foreign potentate, this time Gerar of King Abimelech (20:1; compare 12:9-10). The marked density of this set of key words, each elsewhere connected with Abraham only in the near context of his sale of Sarah in Egypt, provides a trigger to recollection. This episode, it seems, will closely parallel that, in motive, process, and outcome—a hint that is partly confirmed as the action proceeds. There is, however, a serious counterweight to this apparent predictability: contrary to readings that emphasize the characters' stasis here, Sarah herself now bears only a passing resemblance to the powerless pawn of Egypt.[73]

This is so despite a number of patent similarities between these episodes. Here, as in Egypt, Sarah is given no opportunity for direct speech; she is once again "taken" (לקח) by a foreign ruler (20:2-3; compare 12:15); and the root complication here, as there, is not any attendant danger to Sarah—or, indeed, to her potential offspring—but that she is the rightful property of another man (20:3; compare 12:17).[74] Further, basic injustice, abetted in part by the deity, similarly forms the foundation

---

73. Compare Fewell and Gunn, *Gender, Power, and Promise*, 49.

74. The notion of stolen property is clearest here, where God visits Abimelech in a dream and says, "Look at you! A dead man on account of the woman whom you've taken! For she is a wife of a husband," or "one owned by an owner" (הנך מת על־האשה אשר־לקחת והוא בעלת בעל, 20:3). Compare Keshet, *"Say You Are My Sister,"* 37 n. 33, who names "property" as one of the connotations of בעלה here; see BDB 127a. The element of transaction is only emphasized in this episode by the absence of any noted motive of attraction, which more firmly suggests that the interests of the parties to the exchange are financial or dynastic.

of this tale in Gerar: those actually responsible for this "great sin" (חטאה גדלה, 20:9) are greatly rewarded, while the deceived and innocent, perhaps even those unborn, suffer (vv. 3-10, 14-18).[75] But there are also key differences that go beyond what is often regarded as the main disparity between these episodes, which is that Sarah is apparently not forced into a sexual relationship with Abimelech. No persuasive colloquy between Sarah and Abraham is detailed here, which may suggest a greater unanimity of purpose between them from the beginning. The king's transfer of human slaves and wealth on the hoof to Abraham, further, is not given in exchange for Sarah's conjugal services, as Pharaoh's similar payment was (20:14; 12:16). There, the closest analogy was prostitution, with Abraham serving as pimp; here, with the truth already known and the situation's remedy in the hands of one who set the trap in the first place, extortion is a better model.[76] And while the content of the king's address to Sarah is steeped in patriarchy, the bare fact that he speaks to her directly about rehabilitating her reputation—interestingly, given the motif of Sarah's sensitivity to the regard of others, partly expressed as "a covering of eyes" (כסות עינים)—may indicate that she is more than a pure object here (v. 16).[77]

The most significant difference, however, is indicated by the reported speech of Sarah in Abimelech's attempted self-exoneration in v. 5. After rhetorically asking God whether Abraham hadn't misrepresented the facts in declaring Sarah to be his sister, Abimelech plaintively notes: "And she, even *she* said, 'He is my brother'" (והיא־גם־הוא אמרה אחי הוא). Abimelech's transcripts are implicitly confirmed by God, who concurs with the king's self-evaluation of his "integrity of heart" (תם־לבב, vv. 5-6). Here, then, in potent distinction to the Egyptian episode, where the question of Sarah's active connivance remained open, there is an explicit claim that Sarah herself helped perpetrate a deception for gain

---

75. It may be implied that pregnancies in the house of Abimelech were held in suspension by Yahweh's action—not merely that the women were temporarily infertile. "God healed Abimelech"—of what?—"and his woman and his slaves, and they gave birth, because Yahweh had completely sealed up every womb" (וירפא אלהים את־אבימלך ואת־אשתו ואמהתיו וילדו כי־עצר עצר יהוה בעד כל־רחם, 20:17-18). Compare 16:2.

76. Compare Trible, "Ominous Beginnings," 59.

77. Sarah is not an equal party to the transaction. Abimelech's speech, rather, shows that Sarah is "justified" (יכח) under a system that assigns her worth in terms of her being appropriately possessed by one man. But addressing her directly is a step further than Sarah herself ventures in her trading and disposition of Hagar.

that results in emotional and physical suffering for the couple's hosts. Revelation, as the flip side of deception, may also mark an important difference between these tales. How Pharaoh learned the truth was lost in a gap that was never subsequently filled, but it is possible that Sarah somehow revealed the reality of her relationship with Abraham in the wake of the afflictions visited on Pharaoh and his household, which could suggest a humane motive aimed at alleviating suffering. Here, God tells Abimelech the truth, which both Abraham and Sarah had deliberately concealed all the while.

More than simply hinting at the similarities between the tales, then, the key words at the outset of Genesis 20 invite a reading of this episode in the light of the earlier one. Even if the narrative data featuring Sarah in Genesis were limited to these two episodes in immediate sequence, relatively detailed hypotheses about her character's trajectory might still be offered: Sarah, a victim of Abraham's abusive sex trafficking in Egypt, becomes inured to her degradation and joins her oppressor, with God's complicity, in a cynical reenactment of a deception that harms the innocent while it enriches her family. As it is, however, these clues to Sarah's development found within the episode in Gerar only supplement and underline the evolution that she has displayed in the roughly twenty-five years of story time that have elapsed since the deportation from Egypt.[78] Sarah has already channeled her abuse and loss into a scheme that disposed of a powerless subordinate's sexuality, already cursed Abraham to his face and scoffed at his potency behind his back, already erupted in violence that threatened the life of a slave and her unborn child—and it is not credible that this figure reprise the role of voiceless victim in Gerar. This older, harder Sarah, rather, only further displays her growing resemblance to Abraham by acting as his junior collaborator here in a deal that brings, in precious metal and land for settling, even more profit than that of Egypt.[79]

But do the similarities between Abraham and Sarah stem from a blood tie? A reading that takes note of Sarah's traits, finally, must deal with Abraham's stammering claim in 20:12: "…and anyway, actually, she *is* my sister, the daughter of my father—only not the daughter of my mother;

---

78. Abraham is about eighty-five at the opening of the action in Genesis 16, as v. 16 implies, which is about ten years after the Egyptian episode (v. 3); shortly after these events in Gerar, Abraham is noted to be one hundred (21:5).

79. Abraham and Sarah are not equal partners here. Jacobs, *Gender, Power, and Persuasion*, 96, notes that while Sarah is "an active participant in the ruse," as confirmed by Abimelech's report to God in 20:5, Abimelech's public blame is reserved for Abraham.

and she became my wife" (וגם־אמנה אחתי בת־אבי הוא אך לא בת־אמי ותהי־לי לאשה). If this were true, it would constitute a startling twist that might force a reexamination of a number of conclusions drawn to this point, especially in a reading that foregrounds relationships in characterization. While such a revelation might thus display some aesthetic appeal from a narrative perspective, however, Abraham's claim here has nothing to recommend it. The primacy of Sarah as Abraham's אשה was established at her very first mention at the outset of this narrative (11:29), and this concept has been repeatedly reinforced since.[80] But the idea that Sarah is truly Abraham's non-uterine sibling never receives any credible support.[81] Indeed, when the concept first arises in the discourse, in 12:11-13, it is clearly proposed as part of a deceptive ploy—"they will say, 'this is his woman.' …Just say you are my sister!"—as the remainder of that episode only confirms (vv. 18-19). That this exhortation is Abraham's first direct speech establishes him as a deceiver, a characterization that his halting reply to Abimelech does nothing to dispel. After seeming at a loss for words, as the king must demand an answer twice (20:9-10), Abraham's avowal in v. 11 that he feared for his life rings hollow, given how unjustified this same supposed concern proved in Egypt, and Abraham's account of his initial persuasion of Sarah in v. 13 does not track with other narrative data.[82] His declaration of blood kinship with Sarah in v. 12, then, embedded in lies and lacking corroboration elsewhere, is incredible.

The outward resemblances between this episode and that of Egypt cannot obscure Sarah's own transformations over the nearly quarter-century that has elapsed since her captivity in the house of Pharaoh.

---

80. This only continues in this episode. At the crucial point of the initial deception here, the narrator defines Sarah as Abraham's wife: "Abraham said about Sarah his woman, 'She is my sister'" (ויאמר אברהם אל־שרה אשתו אחתי הוא, 20:2; compare vv. 14, 18). The marital relationship is also the only one referenced here by God, who calls her אשה and בעלה (vv. 3, 7). Even Abraham's own explanation of his reasoning turns on his marriage: "they will kill me on account of my wife" (והרגוני על־דבר אשתי, v. 11).

81. Compare Jeansonne, *Women of Genesis*, 26.

82. There is more than one difficulty here. In 20:13, Abraham's account seems to refer to the story time represented in 12:1-4, which is prior to his recorded exhortation, clearly a first-time pitch, at the edge of Egypt in vv. 11-13. Furthermore, his reference to "every place to which we come" (אל כל־המקום אשר נבוא שמה, 20:13) implies a trick pulled more often than once every twenty-five years. But nothing of the sort is suggested elsewhere, and Abraham is depicted as able to form alliances with other foreigners by different means (13:18; 14:13, 24).

Moreover, surface similarities fail to mask significant differences between these tales—most importantly Sarah's own implication here in a deception that trades suffering for gain. These considerations preclude reading her as a victim in quite the same way here. This is not to deny that Sarah, as compared with Abraham, bears the brunt of the risk in this episode, or that Abraham is not the prime human mover in this extortionary scheme, as even he admits (20:13). On the contrary, Sarah, even in her collaboration, is used here, and she remains possessed, a "woman of," in the final words of the episode (v. 18). But the real victims are her erstwhile fellow-wives and their unborn (vv. 17-18). Sarah is related to Abraham here, not by blood, but by imitation of his lack of care for the lives of others.

The Arrival of Isaac, and the Departure of Hagar, Ishmael—and Sarah (Gen. 21:1-14)

Gen. 21:1 The LORD visited Sarah as he had said, and the LORD did to Sarah as he had promised. 2 And Sarah conceived, and bore Abraham a son in his old age at the time of which God had spoken to him. 3 Abraham called the name of his son who was born to him, whom Sarah bore him, Isaac. 4 And Abraham circumcised his son Isaac when he was eight days old, as God had commanded him. 5 Abraham was a hundred years old when his son Isaac was born to him. 6 And Sarah said, "God has made laughter for me; every one who hears will laugh over me." 7 And she said, "Who would have said to Abraham that Sarah would suckle children? Yet I have borne him a son in his old age." 8 And the child grew, and was weaned; and Abraham made a great feast on the day that Isaac was weaned. 9 But Sarah saw the son of Hagar the Egyptian, whom she had borne to Abraham, playing with her son Isaac. 10 So she said to Abraham, "Cast out this slave woman with her son; for the son of this slave woman shall not be heir with my son Isaac." 11 And the thing was very displeasing to Abraham on account of his son. 12 But God said to Abraham, "Be not displeased because of the lad and because of your slave woman; whatever Sarah says to you, do as she tells you, for through Isaac shall your descendants be named. 13 And I will make a nation of the son of the slave woman also, because he is your offspring." 14 So Abraham rose early in the morning, and took bread and a skin of water, and gave it to Hagar, putting it on her shoulder, along with the child, and sent her away. And she departed, and wandered in the wilderness of Beer-sheba. (RSV)

This episode, the last in which a living Sarah explicitly figures in the MT, is remarkable for its revision of what has been a trait of great primacy and endurance: her childlessness. Yet perhaps more significant is what remains unchanged, even deepened, as Sarah's hardening character is here cemented with cruelty. Her final actions in the discourse, however, do not end by evoking aversion in me, but something closer to pity.

A relatively lengthy exposition that sets up the decisive scene at Isaac's weaning party reinforces Sarah's ambivalent feelings about motherhood. Her conception and birth of a son are apparently at least partly the result of a follow-up divine visitation that merits only the barest description: "Yahweh visited Sarah" (ויהוה פקד את־שׂרה), and "Yahweh did to Sarah" (ויעשׂ יהוה לשׂרה), as Yahweh had said (21:1)—seemingly a reference to declarations made during the stopover of the three men at Mamre (18:10, 14). The details of this subsequent visit are left almost entirely to the reader's imagination, in some distinction to the narrations of Abraham's numerous theophanies. However, despite the hypotheses of Savina Teubal and others, there is no convincing evidence, at least in the narrative as it stands, that Sarah is somehow impregnated by the deity.[83] That Sarah's conception has a supernatural element is plain, but Isaac is emphatically Abraham's son, here and elsewhere; and Isaac as a character evinces only divine favor, not descent. Yahweh's visit does underline Yahweh's direction of events, however, and thus foreshadows a continuing divine complicity in the disturbing action to come.

The developments in Sarah's relationships here appear at first profound: she receives what seems to be a solo divine audience, and—having revived what had been a moribund sexual relationship with Abraham—conceives, experiences a full-term pregnancy, labors, and gives birth to a son (21:1-2). She shares with this son, Isaac, the deep bond of nursing (vv. 7-8), and, presumably, a host of other small intimacies that accompany the care of a helpless infant. What a shift, it seems, from the childless victim-turned-abuser portrayed earlier. But Sarah's own evaluation of these developments is thoroughly ambiguous, and any thought that her relationship with Isaac has mellowed her is soon dismissed.

What Sarah says or thinks in reaction to her pregnancy and delivery is of uncertain context. It could be a soliloquy, rehearsed alone, or perhaps spoken over a cradled, nursing Isaac; there is no explicit addressee. What is certain is that her expression admits of conflicting interpretations. צחק עשׂה לי אלהים כל־השׁמע יצחק־לי (21:6) could be a statement of joy, as Irmtraud Fischer takes it: "God made laughter for me; everyone who hears will laugh with me!"[84] Equally plausible, however, is a bleaker reading:

---

83. Teubal, *Sarah the Priestess*, 126–31.

84. See Fischer, *Women Who Wrestled*, 34; compare Schneider, *Sarah*, 92–3, who concludes that Sarah is "thrilled with the joyous news"; Jeansonne, *Women of Genesis*, 27, also describes Sarah's response as "one of joy and personal triumph."

"God turned me into a joke; everyone who hears will laugh at me!"[85] Appeal to Sarah's following utterance does not make matters easier, as E. A. Speiser claims, for if v. 6 reveals embarrassment, v. 7 could be a rueful comment highlighting the absurdity of the situation: "Who would have declared to Abraham that Sarah would nurse children? And here I bore a son in his old age!"[86] The whole may, indeed, as Robert Alter says, be construed as a finely ambiguous pronouncement that captures the thrill of first-time motherhood while admitting that the accompanying circumstances are ridiculous.[87] It is difficult, however, to forget the lack of clarity that attended the idea of Sarah becoming a mother earlier. Her apparent desire to be "sonned" through Hagar did not result in concern for an unborn Ishmael, and her response to the prediction of her own pregnancy made no mention of a child (16:2; 18:12). Neither of these elements finds meaningful resolution in Sarah's ambiguous aside here. Moreover, Sarah has proved to be sensitive to slights and to her position in the eyes of others (16:4-5); her last appearance on the stage of the narrative, in fact, regarded the safeguarding of her reputation in the wake of the deception of Abimelech (20:16). Perhaps here, then, Sarah is shown most starkly as a woman who has, but has not: even the birth of her son, whom she nurses and cares for, is clouded by worry over appearing absurd before others.

A number of narrative threads are pulled together in the climactic encounter at Isaac's weaning party: themes of acquisition and possession, abuse of the powerless and the young perpetrated with divine complicity and abetted by human cowardice, and the sad cruelty of a woman who seems warped by her own suffering. The scene is set with economy, but

---

85. צחק is an uncommon noun, appearing only here and in Ezek. 23:32, where it is paralleled by לעג, an object of mocking or derision. Compare *DCH* 7:112b: "God has brought me laughter" or "God has made me into an object of laughter." The verb יצחק here is less ambiguous, and seems most simply read, especially with the preposition ל, as "laugh at." See BDB 850a; *HALOT* 1019a; compare *DCH* 7:112a, whose initial references undermine its first suggestion with the preposition: "laugh (mockingly) in disbelief (Gn 17:17[;] 18:12, 13, 15, 15); with ל, laugh (joyfully) with, or perh. laugh at someone (Gn 21:6)."

86. מי מלל לאברהם היניקה בנים שרה כי־ילדתי בן לזקניו. Speiser, *Genesis*, 155, argues that the "derisive 'laugh at'" in 21:6 is "ruled out by the tenor of vs. 7." But why the tonal influence can only be read backwards is not clear.

87. Alter, *Genesis*, 97. Compare Gerhard von Rad, *Genesis: A Commentary*, rev. ed., OTL (Philadelphia: Westminster Press, 1972), 231, and Catherine Conybeare, *The Laughter of Sarah: Biblical Exegesis, Feminist Theory, and the Concept of Delight* (New York: Palgrave Macmillan, 2013), x, 14, 41.

much may be inferred about its social context in the story world, which is one of celebration and revelry centered on the happy fact that a child has thrived and negotiated a significant rite of passage: "the child grew up and was weaned; and Abraham staged a great drinking-bout on the day of Isaac's weaning" (21:8).[88] Amid abundant feasting and drinking, in the crowd and noise, something arrests Sarah's tipsy attention: she notices "the son of Hagar the Egyptian, whom Hagar bore to Abraham, מצחק" (v. 9). While this final participle is clearly a play on צחק, "to laugh," which has been so prominent in this narrative, its precise meaning is obscure and has invited several proposals. The provocative idea that some kind of sexual abuse is meant, which takes its cue from Isaac's own "toying" (מצחק) with Rebekah in 26:8, is difficult to sustain in the MT as it stands: מצחק in 21:9 is unaccompanied by any clarifying prepositional phrase, the RSV's "with her son Isaac" being supplied by the LXX.[89] But several other renderings are plausible and offer solid readings. The simplest is also perhaps the most disturbing: that Ishmael, still a young man here, is just "playing," joking around in the festal atmosphere, and that the sight

---

88. ויגדל הילד ויגמל ויעש אברהם משתה גדול ביום הגמל את־יצחק. I render משתה—derived, after all, from שתה, "to drink"—as "drinking-bout" to press a point that is usually submerged in English translations. Only Everett Fox, *Genesis and Exodus: A New English Rendition* (New York: Schocken Books, 1991), 83, translates "drinking-feast." But the drunkenness of the characters has legitimate explanatory power as regards motive here. The only other occurrence of משתה in the narrative complex featuring Sarah is found in Lot's welcome of the two strangers in 19:3; Lot, of course, is associated with intemperate imbibing elsewhere (vv. 30-38). Examples further afield include 1 Sam. 25:36, where Nabal is "dead drunk" (שכר עד־מאד) at his משתה; compare Job's concern for his children's morals after their days-long debauches (Job 1:4-5). See also Isa. 5:12, Jer. 51:39, Est. 7:2, and others. For another interpretation that emphasizes drunkenness in this scene, see Pamela Tamarkin Reis, "Hagar Requited," *JSOT* 87 (2000): 95–7, who, however, hypothesizes that Ishmael is drunk and thus angers Sarah.

89. This idea of Ishmael "fondling" Isaac is not, as might be suspected, of recent vintage; nor is it "simply too hot for most scholars to handle," as claimed in the lurid article of Jonathan Kirsch, "What Did Sarah See?" in *Abraham and Family: New Insights into the Patriarchal Narratives*, ed. Hershel Shanks (Washington, DC: Biblical Archaeology Society, 2000), 109. In fact, von Rad, *Genesis*, 232, and Speiser, *Genesis*, 155, both refer to the hypothesis, albeit decorously, and Alter, *Genesis*, 98, associates the theory with "some medieval Hebrew exegetes." In any event, the proposal turns on an assumption of the loss of a prepositional phrase that appeared in the *Vorlage* of the LXX; a simpler explanation might be that the translators of Genesis found the text confusing and supplied μετὰ Ἰσαὰκ τοῦ υἱοῦ αὐτῆς on the strength of the following verse.

of his innocent fun reignites in a drunken Sarah a hate that had smoldered since the humiliating events detailed in Genesis 16.[90] Other interpretations, however, may demonstrate closer ties to the context. If, for instance, Ishmael is "mocking" or "ridiculing" someone or something here, this could be read in the light of Sarah's demonstrated sensitivity to slights and concern for public appearance.[91] Her dread of being laughed at (21:6) is perhaps realized here, and intolerably so, given Ishmael's status as the son of "this slave" (האמה הזאת, v. 10). Then, too, the obvious derivation of מצחק strongly suggests a connection with the proper noun יצחק, which fits well with Sarah's stated concern that Ishmael not inherit with Isaac (v. 10). Ishmael is thus spotted "Isaac-ing," as Alter has it, playing the heir, at least in the eyes of Sarah.[92] The nature of such punning, finally, may recommend holding multiple meanings in tension here: Sarah's sensitivity is inflamed by Ishmael's mockery, while his perceived usurpation of what is hers and her son's multiplies the insult.[93] Fueled by drink and old resentments, Sarah adds a last, callous deed to her sad repertoire, urging Abraham: "Expel this slave and her son!" (גרש האמה הזאת ואת־בנה, v. 10).

What follows raises once again the issue of the relative power of Sarah, Abraham, and God. Has Sarah, in part by imitating and collaborating with Abraham, completed a trajectory begun in powerlessness in Egypt to arrive, finally, at ascendancy over Abraham? After all, Sarah's command is "abominable in the eyes of Abraham" (וירע הדבר מאד בעיני אברהם, 21:11), yet God tells him to "obey" Sarah in "everything she says" (כל אשר תאמר אליך שרה שמע בקלה, v. 12). But Sarah clearly demonstrates here only her power over Hagar and Ishmael, which endures mostly unchanged from Genesis 16, and, as there, is refracted and channeled through the potencies of Abraham and God. Contrary to Trible's characterization of Abraham as "dominated," his reluctance and need for a second opinion shows that he is able to refuse to comply with Sarah's order; indeed, his reaction suggests that he actively considers alternatives (21:11-12).[94] That he is initially disturbed, however, hardly absolves Abraham of his cowardice

---

90. See, for example, BDB 850a, which simply suggests "sport, play" for Gen. 21:9, a meaning close to that of 19:14, where Lot is regarded "as a jester" (כמצחק) by his sons-in-law after his predictions of destruction.

91. See *DCH* 7:112a, "mock, ridicule, make fun of, make sport of"; *HALOT* 1019a, "make fun of."

92. Alter, *Genesis*, 98.

93. See, again, the reading of Alter, *Genesis*, 98, which is difficult to improve.

94. Trible, "Ominous Beginnings," 60.

here, which echoes his washing of his hands in the matter of Hagar and the unborn Ishmael in 16:6. Abraham can argue at length for the lives of the residents of Sodom—"shouldn't the judge of the whole earth do what is right?" (18:25; see vv. 22-33)—but his son, and his son's mother, do not merit a word here.⁹⁵ Abraham's dismissal of Hagar and Ishmael with a snack for the road in 21:14 is another surrender of an opportunity to do the right thing, not an indication of powerlessness; and there is no indication that his "obedience" to Sarah lasts beyond the immediate event. But God is strongest here. What Sarah urges Abraham to do, to "expel" or "banish" (גרש) Ishmael and his mother, is a divine prerogative elsewhere in Genesis, describing both the ejection of humanity from Eden and Cain's sentence to wander the earth (3:24; 4:14). And it is God who orchestrates the task here, too, which merely confirms the deity's direction of the entire sequence of events (compare 21:1-2, 4, 6). Abraham's acceptance of God's casuistry in v. 13 leads him to implement the plan: he sends his slave Hagar away, along with their son, Ishmael (v. 14).

Hagar and Ishmael's stories continue, even in exile. Oddly, however, their departure marks the end of Sarah as a living and active force in the narrative. The reader was left to guess at Sarah's response to Hagar's flight and eventual return in Genesis 16; here, too, the discourse maintains a permanent silence over Sarah's reaction to Hagar and Ishmael's expulsion. Is she grimly triumphant, watching from the opening of the tent as a hungover Abraham sends the pair away with inadequate provisions (21:14)? Or does she come to regret her drunken haste, perhaps not the morning after, but sometime, over the more than three decades of life that remain to her? The uncertainties of the earlier gap compound those here, but the duration of story time between the narrated explosions of conflict between Sarah and Hagar—perhaps as much as eighteen years— suggests that they had found some way of living alongside each other in the interim.⁹⁶ And while the narrative is utterly quiet on the relationship of Sarah and Ishmael, it remains possible that Sarah's attitude toward the

---

95. Ishmael's survival was, however, the subject of Abraham's petition in 17:18. Compare with all these scenes Abraham's wordless acquiescence in the matter of the ritual slaughter of Isaac (22:2-3).

96. Sarah, who is said to live to be one hundred and twenty-seven (23:1), is presumably here a few years older, perhaps ninety-three, than her approximate age of ninety at Isaac's birth (17:1, 17; 21:5): a difference of thirty-four years. Given that Abraham is eighty-six when Ishmael is born (16:16), the initial conflict between Sarah and Hagar seems to have occurred when Sarah was seventy-five or so: a difference of eighteen years.

son she once may have desired, and now has helped send away, was not one of unremitting enmity for all of his formative years.[97]

Final resolution of these aspects of Sarah's character remains somewhere out of reach. But it is clear that Sarah, soon after she gains Isaac, loses Ishmael and Hagar. These losses are permanent, just as her separation from Lot proved to be; this time, however, it is Sarah's own covetousness and rash actions that are partly to blame. Nor does the narrative give the impression that Sarah and Abraham are brought together in mutual affection by these events. Even Sarah's possession of her son proves to be temporary: as Genesis 22 shows, Isaac is really Abraham's—and God's—to control.

At the close of Sarah's last appearance as a living character, she is a mother, a caregiver to a small boy; but she demonstrates a continuing ambivalence toward this role, and is preoccupied with her appearance in the eyes of others. On the surface, Sarah seems favored by God, receiving both divine visitation and vindication for her urged course of action; but God's support here is for an undertaking that is morally suspect, and of God's favor to Sarah there is not even a whisper more in this narrative. Sarah appears jealous and defensive of what is hers, through the agency of her son; but this grasping only leads to a last act that is intemperate, cruel, and weak. As a reader I am, finally, moved to a kind of pity for Sarah. Used by her husband, debased in bondage, a hard and violent master whose insecure and retributive acts only leave her more alone—even her crimes do not, in the end, elicit outrage in me. Rather, Sarah, at the close of her time onstage in the MT, strikes me as pathetic and sad. If this is divine election, as some such as Schneider would have it, count me out.[98]

"The Life of Sarah" (Gen. 23:1-20)[99]

Ancient and modern readers alike have wondered about Sarah's disappearance from the discourse of the MT following Hagar and Ishmael's departure. What happens to Sarah in the more than thirty years that remain to her—a span greater than that between her Egyptian abduction and her weaning of Isaac? What does she think as Abraham further

---

97. Compare the narratorial claim (of uncertain credibility) in Josephus that Sarah "was accustomed to show affection for Ishmael" as he was growing up (*Ant.* 1.215).

98. See Schneider, *Sarah*, 5, and throughout; Schneider, *Mothers of Promise*, 40, 219.

99. חיי שרה is the traditional, ironic name for the *parashah* running from Gen. 23:1–25:18.

consolidates his political and financial positions with Abimelech (21:22-34)? How does God's perverse "assay" (נסה) of Abraham, in which he is asked to murder his son (22:1-19), affect the woman who bore and nursed the boy?[100]

One answer can serve all of these questions, I think, and it is simple and grim. Sarah has been used up—by Abraham, certainly, but also by the deity, whose covenantal promises required her body—and she is discarded as soon as her utility is exhausted. After Isaac is born and nursed through his vulnerable first years, after Sarah sets the elimination of a rival heir in motion, her fellow characters—Abraham, God, and the narrator, too—lose all interest in her. Having been hardened and schooled in cruelty by abuse, perhaps the better to do a dirty job, Sarah completes the tasks set and is abandoned. She may, indeed, suffer a final loss here, of the relationship that has dominated most of her narrative life, as it is not clear that she even continues to stay in Abraham's camp: while he lives at Beer-sheba (21:31-34; 22:19; compare 21:14), she dies in Kiriath-arba, apparently another name for Hebron or Mamre (23:2; see 13:18), to which Abraham must "come" (בוא) to mark her mourning rites.[101] So it is plausible that Sarah dies in ignorance of Isaac's mortal peril at the hands of Abraham and God; but her story life is all but irretrievable after Hagar and Ishmael are expelled.

This reading of Sarah as expedient instrument is only supported by her final appearance, as a corpse, where she is used once more as a mechanism for acquisition. Having lived out her 127 years, she dies, and Abraham arrives "to ululate for Sarah and to bewail her" (לספד לשרה ולבכתה, 23:2). Whether these rites are perfunctory or heartfelt is hard to say; if the latter, this could serve as a final reminder of how Sarah came to be molded in Abraham's image as the narrative drew on. But Abraham wastes no time or tenderness in turning the event to his advantage.[102] After rising "from alongside his dead" (מעל פני מתו, v. 3)—Sarah's body, of course, still "his"—and citing his legal status as an "alien" (תושב), Abraham urges the local inhabitants: "give me real estate from what is yours for a tomb, so I can entomb my dead away from my presence" (תנו לי אחזת־קבר עמכם ואקברה מתי מלפני, v. 4). When the residents urge him to use "the most

---

100. The willingness of Abraham to sacrifice Isaac partly recalls Sarah's own willingness to put Ishmael at risk, both in and out of the womb (16:6; 21:10), though Abraham was also complicit in those situations. This particular similarity between Sarah and Abraham becomes more explicit in the *Antiquities*.

101. Compare Schneider, *Sarah*, 115.

102. See ibid., 127, who notes that Sarah's death is largely a "bracket for an extended account of Abraham buying land"; compare 117.

exclusive of our tombs" (מבחר קברינו, v. 6) free of charge, it emerges that Abraham has his eye on a particular plot—and that he wants to own it, free and clear (vv. 8-9). After further haggling, Abraham gets his wish; and he entombs Sarah, "his woman" to the end, on his new property near Mamre (v. 19). In her death, then, Sarah's body is used to acquire a holding (אחזה) in the land of Canaan, the first concrete step toward fulfillment of the deity's promise to make over the entire land to Abraham and his descendants "as a perpetual possession" (לאחזת עולם, 17:8; compare 23:4, 9, 20). This may, as some such as Sharon Pace Jeansonne have suggested, underline the importance of Sarah to the realization of God's plans; but it is Sarah as instrument, not agent, that is used here.[103]

Conclusion: Sarah in the MT

Sarah in the MT is a figure of considerable complexity. Despite the occasional ambiguities that my reading has exposed, however, she does not devolve into incoherence, but traces an arc within her story world that is as plausible as it is sad. As mentioned at the outset of this chapter, a list of traits does not constitute a reading, and I will not merely enumerate Sarah's many and varied qualities here. Rather, in keeping with my discussion in Chapter 1, which described character in terms of a softened "paradigm" that is relational and fluid, I will consider how Sarah is revealed through her relationships, broadly conceived: with Abraham, with God, with Hagar and Ishmael, and with herself as she develops over the course of her story.

Sarah's most important relationship is with Abraham. She is first and last defined as his—not his sister, but "his woman"—and nearly everything that happens to her, nearly all that she does, leaves a trail that leads back to him. This connection is marked throughout by acquisition, use, abandonment, and a grim sort of mimicry. Sarah, in her first mention, is "taken" and possessed by Abraham (11:29), and he exploits her lack of power to trade her away for valuable animals and slaves in Egypt, only to take her back when his bargain is successful (12:10-20). This trauma contributes to Sarah's own use and abuse of Hagar (16:1-6), which is Sarah's first step in a curious process, continued in the couple's reactions to predictions of Isaac's birth and their reception of the visitors (17:15-22; 18:1-15), where she grows to resemble Abraham. This evolution, and the

---

103. Jeansonne, *Women of Genesis*, 29. Compare Fischer, *Women Who Wrestled*, 46: "Sarah, by her death, becomes the first heir of the promise of the land." But an heir, surely, is a living beneficiary of the dead.

subtle gains in power that it suggests, culminates in Sarah's collaboration in a restaging of the Egyptian deception in Gerar (20:1-18). However, the similarities of this scheme generate echoes of Sarah as object of use and abuse in Egypt, which help to expose the true balance of power between her and Abraham. This is bolstered at the banishment of Hagar and Ishmael (21:8-14), where Sarah's power is more apparent than real—a fact only underlined by Abraham's subsequent desertion of Sarah in her waning years. The bleak tenor of their relationship is emphatically confirmed, finally, when Abraham uses Sarah's body, one more time, as an object in pursuit of gain (23:1-20).

Sarah's relationship with the deity—Yahweh, or God—displays several depressingly similar themes. Most significantly, God uses Sarah for God's own ends, and as a corollary actively cultivates the worst in her. Though the end of Sarah's captivity in Egypt is hastened by divine intervention, Yahweh's motive is not to protect or rescue Sarah herself, but to give her back to Abraham, who had traded her for profit (12:17-20). In converse fashion, Yahweh abets Sarah's transformation into an abuser by restoring, by proxy, the escaped object of her violence (16:9). That Sarah is most important to God as an instrument of the divine promises is shown when God reveals her role in the plan—to Abraham alone (17:15-22). This is confirmed when Yahweh communicates only the bare minimum, and that indirectly, to Sarah in the tent, and closes their encounter with blustering intimidation (18:9-15). In Gerar, two established themes combine as the deity restores Sarah to Abraham for the sake of their relationship and aids the couple in a scheme that enriches them while bringing suffering to the innocent (20:3-7, 14-18). Yahweh finally visits Sarah to achieve Yahweh's purposes, and explicitly supports her—but again, in a cause that is unjust and ultimately degrading to Sarah's humanity (21:1-14). In the end, too, Abraham's employment of Sarah's body in acquiring land is only part of the fulfillment of the divine promises (23:1-20).

Sarah's relationship with Hagar resembles her tie with Abraham, marked by possession, use, loss, and desertion, but in the negative. Sarah's acquisition of slaves in 12:5 provides a counterweight to her possession by Abraham and foreshadows her brutal conduct later, when Sarah reinscribes her own employment as instrument in her disposition of Hagar's sexuality. Sarah uses Hagar's body for her purposes, and abuses her violently when slighted; in the process, Sarah loses, in prospect, both "her slave" Hagar and the son she once said might be hers (16:1-15). This loss is completed when Sarah contributes to the callous banishment of Hagar and Ishmael, which, in a small paradox, marks not their but her own final effacement from the narrative (21:8-21; 25:7-18). However, this note only strengthens the sense that Sarah's possession of Hagar is a derivative and relative power: both of the key incidents between the pair are countenanced and catalyzed by Abraham and by God.

Each one of these relationships plays a significant role in Sarah's "'directional' dimension," or development over story time.[104] Much of her evolution can be usefully considered under the general rubric of gain and loss, or possession and lack. Sarah is often a woman who has, but has not: possessed of a powerful name but possessed by Abraham, owning a slave but herself traded as an object, lacking a family of origin but repeatedly gaining and losing human connections. Her childlessness is a parade example of this motif. This lack, underscored from the beginning, seems to provide part of the motive for Sarah's scheme with Hagar, but just as she is "built up" in potential by the plan's success, she violently abuses her pregnant surrogate, and Ishmael is never Sarah's son (16:1-6, 15-16; 17:18-21; 21:8-10). When Sarah does give birth, her gain is undercut by her ambiguous attitude toward motherhood (21:6-7); and Isaac, despite Sarah's labor and care, is, from his first predictive advent in Sarah's absence, "for Abraham," and for the fulfillment of God's promises to Abraham (17:16-21; 21:1-2).

Each of these relationships—even, perhaps, that with Isaac—also contributes in its own way to the gradual hardening of Sarah's character that can be observed over her narrative arc in Genesis. In the cases of Abraham and God, this hardening is sanctioned, even promoted, as an aid to their own ends. Related in various ways to these themes, finally, is the curious and sad recurring note of Sarah's increasing sensitivity to her position in the eyes of others. So "lovely to look at," worthy of notice as an object, Sarah is prompted to violence by being overlooked, and is perhaps goaded into her final urging of banishment by a boy's ridicule (12:11, 14-15; 16:4-6; 21:9-10). Even the reversal of her childlessness, her most fundamental and enduring trait, is overshadowed by the suspicion that others will find her new state absurd: "everyone who hears will laugh at me!" (11:30; 21:6).

For me, at last, this morbidly sensitive Sarah evokes sympathy, even pity. A good face cannot be put on her use and abuse of her slave, Hagar; but this is part of a sorry cycle of use and cruelty where Sarah is sometimes the victim, sometimes the perpetrator. In her first and last major appearances in the narrative, in Egypt and in death, Sarah is an object used to gain wealth and advantage for Abraham in a foreign land (12:10-20; 23:1-20). In between, both her body and her developing

---

104. Rimmon-Kenan, *Narrative Fiction*, 39.

capacity for cruelty prove their utility to the prosecution of the deity's plans. I cannot agree with the central contention of Schneider, that Sarah is "as much chosen" as Abraham.[105] Sarah's "election," rather, calls to mind the selection of a tool, and Mignon Jacobs's evaluation of Sarah's worth in the eyes of the narrator could, in my reading, stand for her value to Abraham, and to God: "intermittently useful but clearly dispensable."[106]

I said earlier that Sarah's story life after the banishing of Hagar and Ishmael is nearly irretrievable. There is, however, one further significant note on Sarah in Genesis, one that might contain a small seed of hope. Although Genesis 22 suggests that Isaac is Abraham's, and God's, to do with as they will, Isaac's actions as an adult may imply that Sarah was able to forge a meaningful relationship with her son after the narrator and the other characters lost interest in her. When Isaac weds Rebekah, he brings her "into the tent of Sarah, his mother" (האהלה שרה אמו, 24:67).[107] In this tent, and in his love for Rebekah, Isaac is "consoled" (נחם) "after his mother" (אחרי אמו). Perhaps, then, in the end, Sarah in the MT is characterized not by something she lacked, but by someone she had.

---

105. Schneider, *Sarah*, 5.
106. Jacobs, *Gender, Power, and Persuasion*, 102.
107. האהלה שרה is grammatically irregular, but it is difficult to see how it could be rendered differently without emending the text.

Chapter 3

SARRA IN THE SEPTUAGINT

Introduction

Sarra (as she is eventually called) in the Septuagint of Genesis is, to my reading, a complex, sometimes erratic figure who faces a variety of narrative pressures that persistently work to limit her individuation. In the narrative's early stages, Sarra is portrayed as passive, inert, and powerless, even inanimate, if occasionally of use to the attainment of the divinely supported aims of Abraam (as he is ultimately named here). When she does break free of this inertia, in the first episode involving Hagar, Sarra's agency comes at a steep price. Here, in what is only the first instance of a major theme, Sarra's initiative is undermined before she can exercise it, as her actions prove to be largely derivative of those of Abraam. As the narrative moves on, other elements accumulate that also oppose Sarra's volition and contribute to an impression of a narratorial strategy that aims at her restriction.

While Sarra is intermittently useful to Abraam throughout the narrative, her programmatic role as an instrument in the fulfillment of the deity's promises to Abraam and his descendants emerges most clearly after 17:15-21, where God informs Abraam—in Sarra's absence—that she will bear him a son to be favored with a divine covenant. Sarra's utility is underlined in a variety of ways, as she catalyzes the banishment of a competing heir, or as her corpse provides a pretext for Abraam's first permanent acquisition of territory in the land pledged to him. Equally, however, Sarra's value as a tool in God's broader scheme is emphasized the more her individuation is curbed. When Sarra isn't passive and inert, she is portrayed as imitating Abraam; and when she finally acts in a way that doesn't recall the actions of Abraam, it is only to express delight at the accomplishment of God's plan in the birth of Isaac. What is left of Sarra in the LXX is a washed out, faded figure whose occasionally erratic activity is explained best not by any exercise of her will, but by this myopic focus on her utility to the establishment of the relationship between the deity and the men in her family.

Practical Preliminaries

My basic approach and concerns here remain as defined by the poetics of character and characterization outlined earlier. Just as in my reading of Sarah in the MT, I focus a spotlight on Sarra in the LXX by gathering and integrating her traits, always with an eye on other narrative data such as the trajectory of the plot, thematic elements, and the construction of other characters. I do not pretend to be a first-time reader of this LXX narrative, and I freely anticipate later narrative developments in aid of my discussion.

A few matters need clarification here. First, I acknowledge some obstacles to the performance and presentation of a reading of Sarra in the LXX. After noting the paucity of other readings of Sarra with which to engage, I treat several related issues that arise from the origin of the LXX as a translation, considering the quantity and quality of the agreement between the LXX of Genesis and the proto-MT; the effect of narrative continuities across the tradition on my production of this chapter, particularly as regards its place in my broader investigation; and the influence of the uneven distribution of such narrative continuities on my approaches to various episodes. Finally, I mention the critical text that underlies my reading and the English translation that I have provided as an aid to the reader.

Other readings of Sarra in the LXX

The contextualization of my reading of Sarra in the LXX is both eased and complicated by the scarcity of scholarly works that address her character in depth. My findings pose a clear challenge to the conclusions of some studies that neglect to consider the full scope of Sarra's story. Stefan Schorch, for example, employs a small piece of Sarra's narrative data in the LXX as part of his argument that "LXX Genesis tends to present women as more active" than their counterparts in the MT.[1] Jennifer Dines similarly bases her claim that "by and large, LXX maintains, and even enhances, Sarah's independent spirit" on brief analyses of a few verses.[2]

---

1. Stefan Schorch, "Hellenizing Women in the Biblical Tradition: The Case of LXX Genesis," *BIOSCS* 41 (2008): 16.
2. Jennifer M. Dines, "What If the Reader Is a She? Biblical Women and Their Translators," in *The Reception of the Hebrew Bible in the Septuagint and the New Testament: Essays in Memory of Aileen Guilding*, ed. David J. A. Clines and J. Cheryl

Whether the description of Sarra as συνῳκηκυῖα ἀνδρί in 20:3 really "avoids…the association of marriage with the relation between an owner and his property" implicit in the MT's בעלת בעל, as Schorch contends, may be a legitimate topic of debate.[3] Likewise, the assertion of Dines that the pronoun switch in 21:7 (לזקניו, "his old age," as opposed to ἐν τῷ γήρει μου, "my old age") makes Sarra "the centre of attention" may be correct, as far as it goes, within its very near context.[4] But my reading, which examines Sarra in detail throughout the narrative, shows that Sarra's passivity is in fact more pronounced in the LXX, and that her actions, when they do occur, are actually more often derivative of those of Abraam. This is partly a commentary on methodology, and I contend that "comparative study that proceeds from a collection of differences between the MT and the text of the LXX," as Schorch describes his approach, may founder on its lack of attention to the horizontal interplay of elements within each strand of the tradition.[5] Schorch and Dines not only isolate small trees for comparison, but draw conclusions about their respective forests without examining their ecosystems in detail.

Although Susan Ann Brayford's evaluation of Sarra has more in common with my own, her work exhibits some of the same problems found in that of Schorch and Dines. Brayford's dissertation, completed in the late 1990s, represents the most concentrated engagement with the figure of Sarra in the LXX to date.[6] Yet Brayford, too, argues that Sarra is "recharacterized" in the LXX primarily on the basis of narrative data contained in two verses (Gen. 18:12 and, to a lesser extent, 16:2).[7] This

---

Exum (Sheffield: Sheffield Phoenix Press, 2013), 61. Dines notes that "there are also moments where her interests are subordinated to Abraham's or her speech is toned down."

3. Schorch, "Hellenizing Women," 11–12.
4. Dines, "What If the Reader Is a She?" 62.
5. Schorch, "Hellenizing Women," 3. The method of Dines, "What If the Reader Is a She?" 58, is the same, founded on "examining differences between LXX and MT…and asking what these differences reveal."
6. Brayford, "Taming and Shaming." Some of her conclusions are abstracted and summarized in Susan Ann Brayford, "To Shame or not to Shame: Sexuality in the Mediterranean Diaspora," *Semeia* 87 (1999): 169–72, and Susan Ann Brayford, "Feminist Criticism: Sarah Laughs Last," in *Method Matters: Essays on the Interpretation of the Hebrew Bible in Honor of David L. Petersen*, ed. Joel M. LeMon and Kent Harold Richards (Atlanta: Society of Biblical Literature, 2009), 317–28.
7. Brayford, "Taming and Shaming," 155–8, 163–8, 176–9, and especially 182–7 for 18:12; 187–96 for 16:2. Other episodes, such as those of Genesis 12 and 20, come under discussion at times (196–200), but not with a view to illuminating Sarra.

is a corollary of Brayford's central contention that women in the LXX of Genesis, and especially Sarra, are transformed in translation into Hellenistic matrons who exhibit a degree of positive, sexual "shame" that is appropriate to the translators' social milieu: Sarra's treatment of Hagar and Ishmael, or her victimization in Egypt, or her collaboration in Gerar, or her reaction to Isaac's birth, to cite only a few examples, have less to offer this thesis. Brayford's conclusion that Sarra in the LXX was "domesticated, her sexuality was suppressed, and her significance in the family diminished" is, as a thumbnail sketch, not incompatible with my reading of Sarra as a muted figure whose individuation is stymied by the consistent portrayal of her actions as derivative.[8] However, my investigation of Sarra offers substantially more breadth, depth, and nuance. This is not a claim to special literary acumen, but a result of an approach that pursues Sarra as she develops through her entire trajectory in the LXX. Moreover, my reading is not restricted to the sociological axis of sex and shame; rather, as elsewhere, I seek Sarra as a "concrete semblance" of a human being—even when narrative forces seem ranged against this aim.

Aside from Brayford's dissertation, there is a decided lack of studies that treat Sarra in the LXX at meaningful length.

Narrative continuities and their effects

In the context of my larger project, my reading of Sarra in the LXX is complicated by the origin of the text. The narratives of Genesis in the MT and the LXX often display substantial agreement, which is unsurprising given that the latter is patently an attempt to render into Greek the content of something close to a precursor of the former.[9] At points this agreement may approach identity, or as close as this may be in very different language systems, where the lexical range of translated words is very close to that of the original, and the syntax, mutatis mutandis, communicates much the same idea. Such seems to me to be the case—to take a small example more or less at random—in Gen. 16:15, where the LXX reads Καὶ ἔτεκεν Ἁγὰρ τῷ Ἀβρὰμ υἱόν, καὶ ἐκάλεσεν Ἀβρὰμ τὸ ὄνομα τοῦ υἱοῦ αὐτοῦ, ὃν ἔτεκεν αὐτῷ Ἁγάρ, Ἰσμαήλ for the MT ותלד הגר לאברם בן ויקרא אברם שם־בנו אשר־ילדה הגר ישמעאל. Composition Greek might have sought a different connector than the initial καί, employed a greater

---

8. Brayford, "Taming and Shaming," 9.
9. Wevers, *Notes*, xiii; J. A. L. Lee, "A Note on Septuagint Material in the Supplement to Liddell and Scott," *Glotta* 47 (1969): 238 n. 9. See Susan Ann Brayford, *Genesis*, Septuagint Commentary Series (Leiden: Brill, 2007), 12–16, for a summary of dissenting views.

degree of subordination, and deployed the words in a different order, but none of these issues amounts to a violation of idiom. The meanings of the common nouns overlap almost perfectly, and the semantic ranges of τίκτω and καλέω are very similar, respectively, to ילד and קרא, especially when their objects are considered. The αὐτῷ, then, represents the only real textual disparity, and it is difficult to make too much of this. Just possibly, the LXX goes a bit further here in its insistence that Ishmael is Abram's; but this is hardly a novel element if the MT represents the essentials of the Greek's *Vorlage* (בנו, לאברם).[10] In short, the LXX offers a literate if not elegant rendering of (proto-)MT's Gen. 16:15 that communicates a close approximation of its content.

One effect of these kinds of similarities, which are found throughout the narrative, is that a number of themes, motifs, and character traits in the LXX resemble their analogues in the MT. Where these continuities are plain, I feel that to rehearse them in full would unduly try the patience of my reader, as I assume her familiarity with my earlier analysis of the MT. This does not mean that I adopt an exclusively synoptic view of the traditions, or that I make an effort to catalogue the disparities between them. On the contrary, I strive to develop a reading of Sarra in the LXX that possesses an integrity grounded in internal criteria. But the extent of the material, and its qualities as a translation, leave me with two choices that are honest. The first is to fully draw out all of my observations on Sarra's character, even when these correspond very closely with those made in the preceding chapter; the second is simply to evoke these versional continuities, in a somewhat compressed form, whenever they are relevant. For the sake of readerly interest, I opt for the second strategy. This is a practical concession; but I emphasize that discontinuities, considered across the tradition, do not carry any special intrinsic weight in their native narrative contexts.

A connected issue that affects the presentation of my reading is that developments in the tradition that reflect on Sarra are unevenly distributed throughout the narrative: one episode or scene may be somewhat divergent, another nearly identical, to its presumed *Vorlage*. An observation of this phenomenon in practice convinces me that an attempt to apply a schematic and uniform approach to each episode in turn would be a disservice to the narrative. So at times my discussion of a particular section begins with a consideration of significant versional continuities or discrepancies; in other cases, the narrative at hand demands substantial engagement before

---

10. Contrast Brayford, "To Shame or not to Shame," 171; see also Wevers, *Notes*, 227.

disparities or similarities can be named. But I believe that what is vital to an understanding of Sarra in the LXX is found, first, within the LXX, and I try to respect the narrative's integrity without pretending that it is a wholly independent entity. This is a fine line, however, and difficult to tread adroitly at all times.

Notes on texts

My reading depends on Wevers's Göttingen edition of LXX Genesis, supplemented by its first apparatus and Wevers's own subsequent *Notes*, where he occasionally advocates a revision of the critical text.[11] For the more significant, extended episodes treated below (Gen. 11:26–12:9; 12:10–13:2; 16:1-16; 18:1-15; 20:1-18; 21:1-14), I preface my discussion with the text of *A New English Translation of the Septuagint* (NETS). Other renderings are my own, unless otherwise noted.

Sara, Muted (Gen. 11:26–12:9 LXX)

> Gen. 11:26 And Thara...became the father of Abram and Nachor and Harran. 27 ...And Harran was the father of Lot.... 29 And Abram and Nachor took wives for themselves; Abram's wife's name was Sara, and Nachor's wife's name was Melcha, the daughter of Harran, the father of Melcha and the father of Iescha. 30 And Sara was barren, and she was not bearing children. 31 And Thara took his son Abram and his son's son, Lot son of Harran, and his daughter-in-law Sara, his son Abram's wife, and he brought them out of the country of the Chaldeans to go into the land of Chanaan, and he came as far as Charran and settled there.... 12:1 And the Lord said to Abram, "Go forth from your country and from your kindred and from your father's house to the land that I will show you. 2 And I will make you into a great nation, and I will bless you and make your name great, and you shall be one blessed. 3 And I will bless those who bless you, and those who curse you I will curse, and in you all the tribes of the earth shall be blessed." 4 And Abram went, as the Lord had told him to, and Lot left with him.... 5 And Abram took his wife Sara and his brother's son Lot and all their possessions that they had acquired and every person whom they had acquired in Charran, and they departed to go to the land of Chanaan, and they came to the land of Chanaan. 6 And Abram passed through the land in its length as far as the place Sychem, at the high oak.... 7 And the

---

11. John William Wevers, *Genesis*, Septuaginta: Vetus Testamentum Graecum auctoritate Academiae Scientiarum Gottingensis editum 1 (Göttingen: Vandenhoeck & Ruprecht, 1974); Wevers, *Notes*. For references to LXX and OG texts other than Genesis, I consult the edition of Alfred Rahlfs, *Septuaginta* (Stuttgart: Deutsche Bibelgesellschaft, 1935).

Lord appeared to Abram and said to him, "To your offspring I will give this land." And Abram built there an altar to the Lord who had appeared to him. 8 And from there he withdrew to the mountain to the east of Baithel and set up his tent there...and there he built an altar to the Lord and called on the name of the Lord. 9 And Abram set out, and as he traveled he encamped in the wilderness. (NETS)

The opening of the narrative featuring Sara and her family in the LXX depicts her as a largely passive figure who is primarily defined in the negative.[12] Oddly, however, what is revealed here about her biology has greater impact on the broader plot of the story, and more enduring thematic significance, than the narrative data of any other character in these introductory verses (11:26-32). Sara first appears as one constituent of a collective object: "And Abram and Nahor took women for themselves; the name of Abram's woman was Sara, and the name of Nahor's woman was Milcah, daughter of Haran, father of Milcah and father of Iscah" (v. 29).[13] In parallel with Milcah, Sara is a woman, taken in marriage, and necessarily less powerful than the man who takes her. But an important personal deficit is also highlighted by Sara's juxtaposition with Milcah. In distinction from everyone else in vv. 10-29, Sara lacks a father and thus, by implication, a family of origin; she possesses only her sexual-social marriage connection with Abram.

Sara's absence of ancestors quickly finds an analogue in her lack of descendants: "And Sara was sterile and was not bearing children" (καὶ ἦν Σάρα στεῖρα καὶ οὐκ ἐτεκνοποίει, 11:30). Sara's subjectivity here, a grammatical privilege she will not again exercise alone in a meaningful way until her conflict with Hagar in Genesis 16, is almost purely negative: she is "sterile," wanting and empty by definition, while the only dynamic verb of which she is subject paradoxically describes merely what she has never done and continues not to do.[14] However, this particular want and lack of action will undergird, and at times dominate, the narrative matter of several episodes to come.

---

12. I follow Wevers's edition in referring to her as Sara (Σάρα) until 17:15, Sarra (Σάρρα) thereafter; I apply the same principle to Abra(a)m. I retain "Sarah" or "Sarai" as appropriate in references to the MT, to help clarify the version under discussion, but I consider all of these names to refer to one recognizable human analogue.

13. καὶ ἔλαβον Ἀβρὰμ καὶ Ναχὼρ ἑαυτοῖς γυναῖκας· ὄνομα τῇ γυναικὶ Ἀβρὰμ Σάρα, καὶ ὄνομα τῇ γυναικὶ Ναχὼρ Μελχά, θυγάτηρ Ἀρράν, πατὴρ Μελχὰ καὶ πατὴρ Ἰεσχά.

14. Sara serves as the grammatical subject of several verbs in Genesis 12, but the only one that is not a form of εἰμί is the imperative εἶπον in v. 13—hardly an expression of agency. Two of the three instances of εἰμί are spoken by Abram (vv. 11, 13); the other is narratorial (v. 14).

It is plain at a casual reading that the LXX of 11:26–12:9 is, in general, strikingly similar to the text of the MT. Even at this early point, though, minor distinctions can be felt. Already, Sara's childless state has been described by the narrator in terms that may convey a feeling of permanence. That Sara "was not bearing children," "could not bear children," or even "kept on not bearing children" (οὐκ ἐτεκνοποίει, 11:30), as the imperfect verb might be variously rendered, augments the force of the flat adjective "sterile" to emphasize her enduring condition.[15] This may be less obvious in the MT's corresponding, matter-of-fact noun phrase, "she had no child" (אין לה ולד), which likewise reinforces the Hebrew term for "infertile" or "sterile" (עקרה), but, perhaps, without a similar implication of continuation or story-time futurity. The Greek's verbal formulation, too, necessarily personalizes the concept in a way that may add moral heft: "she had no child" in potential contrast with "she continued to fail to give birth." These are small contentions, operating within the realm of possibility; οὐκ ἐτεκνοποίει could also simply mean "she had not borne a child." But the latitude I explore here is granted by the grammar and idiom of the medium of the narrative.

Another small versional crack opens up in Sara's name itself. The MT's שרי evokes dominion and mastery. At times, juxtaposed with Sarai's powerlessness, this regal name provokes only a sad irony; at others, its connotation of domineering ownership proves especially apt. But this entire interplay is more than absent here: it is not even a thought. Sara's name in the LXX is a small agglutination of syllables with no meaning beyond its immediate referent: Σά-ρα.

Sara's passivity, too, while not lacking in the MT's presentation, is just slightly more thorough here. Her enduring failure to give birth gives an impression of inertia from the start. Then, instead of exercising subjectivity alongside her family members at their departure from "Chaldean" territory, as in the MT—"they went out together...and they went as far as Haran and settled there" (ויצאו אתם...ויבאו עד־חרן וישבו שם)—Sara in the LXX forms part of a collective object "led out" by Terah, Abram's father, who is also the sole subject of the following verbs: "he led them out... and he went as far as Haran, and he settled there" (ἐξήγαγεν αὐτούς...καὶ ἦλθεν ἕως Χαρράν, καὶ κατῴκησεν ἐκεῖ, 11:31). Abram is thus depicted as more passive, as well; but very soon in the discourse Abram's importance is underlined, as he is favored with the first of a series of direct divine revelations (12:1-3).[16] In response to the Lord's command and pledge

---

15. Compare Brayford, *Genesis*, 289. See Smyth §§1889–1909.
16. In story time, the situation is quite different, as Terah's time in Haran before his death is given as 205 years (11:32). In the MT this figure is Terah's entire lifespan.

here, Abram adopts the role formerly played by his father, journeying on and taking Sara along (vv. 4-5). While Sara may still be plausibly postulated as a constituent of the plural subjects in the verbs that follow (ἐκτήσαντο twice; ἐξῆλθοσαν; ἦλθον), her complete lack of subjectivity in the family's travels up to this point—as distinguished from Abram and Lot, who both feature as solo subjects of finite verbs of movement in v. 4—suggests, to my reading, that she is less convincing as a key, active agent in this corporate acquiring, departing, and arriving. As in the MT, too, the discourse goes on to feature Abram as the singular subject of a relative flurry of verbs, as he travels through the land, builds altars, settles here and there, and invokes the Lord's name (vv. 6-9).

In the introduction to Sara's story in the LXX, then, there is indisputably much that is familiar from her characterization in the MT. She is a "woman of," a wife taken and lacking in power and family connections. Though sexually possessed she is apparently infertile; she is defined from the start by what she does not have and what she has failed to do. These deficits are answered to some degree by Sara's gains in 12:5, where she seems to be accorded possessions (τὰ ὑπάρχοντα) and slaves (ψυχήν) alongside Abram and Lot.[17] This ownership of humans and its attendant implied conflicts anticipates Sara's treatment of Hagar later.

But certain discontinuities also begin to emerge. The suggestion that Sara's reproductive dysfunction is an indefinitely enduring state heightens the drama of this element going forward, and raises the issue of her utility to God's plans, a theme that will come to greater prominence later; immediately, though, this note ratchets up the tension between the Lord's promises of descendants to Abram (12:2, 7) and the seemingly limited biological potential of his and Sara's sexual relationship. Sara's responsibility for this shortcoming is likewise underlined by her role as personal subject of the failure: "she kept on not bearing children" (11:30). In general, however, what disparities exist seem rooted in a kind of subtle muting of Sara's character. Her agency is virtually nonexistent, at least until 12:5, and her portrait is the poorer for lacking entirely the delicate and multivalent play with her name that is possible in the Hebrew.

Two points, both touching on narrative primacy and recency, are worth mentioning here. First, it is notable how thoroughly Sara's initial character indicators are bound to those of other characters. Even the

17. It is not wholly clear whether the Hebrew נפש should be taken as a collective; the Greek, however, with its repetition of πᾶς, seems to make this explicit: "all their possessions…and every person" (πάντα τὰ ὑπάρχοντα αὐτῶν…καὶ πᾶσαν ψυχήν). While disputing that a "new sense" of ψυχή as "slave" is established by its usage here, J. A. L. Lee, "Note," 234–5, concedes that "household slaves" is what is meant.

direct narratorial assertions of infertility and ongoing failure to give birth can only be comprehended with reference to her social ties. As the narrative moves on, however, these notes, which might be taken for signs of connectedness, begin to look more like early intimations of Sara's lack of individuation.

Second, all these early elements—continuities no less than discontinuities—matter, to reiterate a larger point about narrative meaning, because they initiate the reader into contact with a character and thus prepare the ground for later interaction. When considered together, these elements suggest traits that subtly shift the burden of proof in the detection or construction of traits later. Sara is a "woman of," in the power of Abram, which helps to explain her powerlessness in Egypt. Again, this is not less central to Sara's characterization in the LXX because it precisely echoes the MT; however, it is hardly news. But Sara's slightly increased passivity in the LXX combines with this lack of power to make it just a little less likely that she exercise any agency in the gaps of the Egyptian tale. Later gaps, in turn, are just that much less likely, to my mind, to be plausibly filled with resolute action; on the flip side, however, a discourse-cued break in this inertia, such as appears in Sara's first conflict with Hagar in Genesis 16, is all the more startling. Thus discontinuities that are tiny within themselves—and especially those that open in the beginning of the linear course of a narrative—may have exponential, rather than simple arithmetic, effects.

Passive and "Pretty-Faced" in Egypt
(Gen. 12:10–13:2 LXX)

Gen. 12:10 And a famine occurred upon the land, and Abram went down to Egypt to reside there as an alien, for the famine prevailed upon the land. 11 And it came about when Abram drew near to enter into Egypt that Abram said to his wife Sara, "I do know that you are a woman beautiful in countenance; 12 it will be, therefore, that should the Egyptians see you, they will say 'This is his wife,' and they will kill me, but you they will keep for themselves. 13 Say, therefore, 'I am his sister,' so that it may go well with me because of you, and my soul will live on your account." 14 And it came about when Abram entered into Egypt—as the Egyptians saw the woman, that she was very beautiful— 15 that then the rulers of Pharao saw her and praised her to Pharao and brought her into Pharao's house. 16 And for her sake they dealt well with Abram, and he had sheep and calves and donkeys, male and female slaves, mules and camels. 17 And God tried Pharao and his house with great and grievous trials because of Sara, Abram's wife. 18 Now when Pharao had called Abram he said, "What is this you have done to me, that you did not tell me that she is your wife? 19 Why did you say, 'She is my sister'? And I took her to myself for a wife. And now here is your wife before you; take her; hurry off." 20 And Pharao commanded men concerning Abram to join in escorting him and his wife and all that he had and Lot with him. 13:1 Then Abram went up from Egypt, he and his wife and all that was his and Lot with him, into the wilderness. 2 Now Abram was very rich in livestock and in silver and in gold. (NETS)

The decision of Abram to go down to Egypt "in order to take refuge" or "seek asylum" (παροικῆσαι) may not have been hastily taken. Although matters are perhaps not improved by his earlier choice to camp "in the desert" (ἐν τῇ ἐρήμῳ, 12:9), a "famine" (λιμός) that had developed "held fast," or "only grew in strength" (ἐνίσχυσεν), apparently forcing a move for Abram—and, by natural extension, for "Sara his woman," who continues to display almost no agency in this episode (v. 10; compare v. 11).[18] However, it becomes clear that Abram's mind is not idle during this journey, and that hunger, even if the proximate cause for the family's descent, is far from Abram's central concern; in fact, want of food merits no mention in the rest of the tale. When he is "just about to enter" (ἤγγισεν...εἰσελθεῖν) this place of refuge, Abram pulls aside Sara, "his woman," and addresses her in a brusque, businesslike manner:

> *I* know that you are a pretty-faced woman. This fact means that as soon as the Egyptian men catch sight of you, they will say "This is his woman," and they will kill me; but you they will save—for later. Accordingly, say "I am his sister," in order that it accrue to my advantage because of you, and I will go on living in return for you.[19]

Abram's speech does not aim to persuade. It is ruthlessly if only formally logical and delivered in the expectation of compliance: a superior relaying to his subordinate a decision that has already been taken. That this pronouncement receives no reply is unsurprising, as it anticipates none. Sara's part in this deception is already scripted, and delivered as an order, not a suggestion or a request: "Say 'I am his sister.'" Even the implied expectation of derivative action here—that Sara will parrot the line Abram gives her—is not fulfilled, however, as Sara remains silent throughout the episode.

---

18. On the evidence of 12:20, Lot also accompanies Abram to Egypt. See *GELS* 239a for ἐνισχύω as "to grow in intensity and severity, gain strength."

19. Γινώσκω ἐγὼ ὅτι γυνὴ εὐπρόσωπος εἶ· ἔσται οὖν ὡς ἂν ἴδωσίν σε οἱ Αἰγύπτιοι, ἐροῦσιν ὅτι Γυνὴ αὐτοῦ αὕτη, καὶ ἀποκτενοῦσίν με, σὲ δὲ περιποιήσονται. εἰπὸν [should read εἶπον, see Wevers, *Notes*, 170] οὖν ὅτι Ἀδελφὴ αὐτοῦ εἰμι, ὅπως ἂν εὖ μοι γένηται διὰ σέ, καὶ ζήσεται ἡ ψυχή μου ἕνεκεν σοῦ (12:11-13).

In keeping with the practical tone of his address, Abram's direct assertion that Sara is "pretty-faced" (εὐπρόσωπος) reads less as flattery than as an admission of an initial operational hurdle. This is underlined by his inferential connection of this evaluation to the events that he forecasts: "You are pretty-faced; therefore (οὖν)..." The deceptive context is subtly filled out by Abram's employment of this adjective, which occurs just this once in the whole of the LXX and the OG. Εὐπρόσωπος or "pretty-faced" can mean just that—an outward, surface charm that may hide something false within—and the word is employed elsewhere as a metaphor for specious display.[20] The subsequent evaluations and actions of other characters in this scene, however, tend to confirm only the aesthetic component of Abram's description. The Egyptian men are soon said to note that "the woman" is "exceedingly beautiful" (καλή...σφόδρα, 12:14), and the praise of Pharaoh's retainers, as well as their implied motive for abducting her, likewise follows directly upon their setting eyes on her (v. 15). Indeed, καλός frequently extends to virtues of personality, emphasizing, in direct contrast to εὐπρόσωπος, the identity of outward form and inward excellence.[21] This could anticipate the poem in praise of Sarai in the Genesis Apocryphon (20.2-8), where she is lauded not only for her beauty, but also for her wisdom and fine handiwork. In any case, again, there is no evidence here that Sara voices the false script that Abram writes for her. Pharaoh, significantly, mentions only Abram's deception in his later interrogation: "What is this you did to me—namely, you did not inform me that she is your woman? Why did you say, 'She is my sister'?" (vv. 18-19).[22] Abram's characterization of Sara as "outwardly fair," then, seems to speak only to his estimation of her worth in his plan here, and need not imply any overt collaboration on her part.

The remainder of Abram's short speech is marked, first, by coercion, which combines a veiled threat with an implied benefit to Sara. This element is curiously undercut by a second, however, in which Abram

---

20. Compare Herodotus, *Hist.* 7.168: "While [the Corcyraeans] replied in this way, with outward charm" (ὑπεκρίναντο μὲν οὕτω εὐπρόσωπα), when their help was needed they betrayed their promise. See LSJ 728b. Zakovitch and Shinan, *Abram and Sarai in Egypt*, 22, suggest that the rendering of יפת־מראה as εὐπρόσωπος may reflect a concern for Sara's modesty: Abram remarks on Sara's "face" because that is her only exposed feature.

21. Although καλός can be employed ironically to indicate its opposite, this is a sarcastic rhetorical trope, not the metaphorical extension that marks the use of εὐπρόσωπος. See LSJ 870a.

22. Τί τοῦτο ἐποίησάς μοι, ὅτι οὐκ ἀπήγγειλάς μοι ὅτι γυνή σού ἐστιν; ἵνα τί εἶπας ὅτι Ἀδελφή μού ἐστιν; The first ὅτι is epexegetical; compare Smyth §2577.

admits, with startling candor, that only he stands to gain from his proposed scheme. If their true relationship is known, Abram claims, Sara's pretty face will prompt the Egyptians to "murder" (ἀποκτείνω) him; "but you," he says, "they will keep alive" (σὲ δὲ περιποιήσονται, 12:12). That "to let live" is part of the meaning of περιποιέω here is confirmed by its contrast with ἀποκτείνω, as in some other LXX instances of the word, such as Exod. 1:16: "if it is male, kill it; if female, preserve it alive."[23] In the circumstances, according to Abram, even Sara's putative survival implies hazard. This tacit message is further underlined, however, by the semantic range of περιποιέω, which, especially in the middle voice, as here, often means "to acquire," or "preserve for oneself"; the other two occurrences of the word in Genesis refer to the acquisition and possession of movable property.[24] Abram's attempt at coercing Sara's lie thus suggests that the alternative is to invite abduction; in a bald irony, this is precisely the outcome of his machinations.

That Abram's proposition is no miscalculation, but rather cynical from the start, however, is shown by its stated desired results. Abram neatly turns the supposed complication, Sara's pretty face, into a strategic advantage by advocating an outward revision of their relationship: "Say 'I am his sister.'" This script is urged "in order that" (ὅπως) two related outcomes occur. Dropping any pretense of benefit to Sara, Abram's hopes are that events "turn out" to his "advantage," "because of" her (εὖ... γένηται διά), and that he continue to live "in return for" her (ἕνεκεν, 12:13). This last preposition may help to underline the transactional nature of Abram's proposal. In what seems to be a semantic extension dating from about the time of the translation of the Hebrew scriptures into Greek, ἕνεκεν, radically "on account of," or "for," comes to be used in contexts of frank exchange, such as Isa. 5:23, where a "woe" is spoken to "those who vindicate the impious in return for gifts" (οἱ δικαιοῦντες τὸν ἀσηβῆ ἕνεκεν δώρων).[25]

---

23. ἐὰν μὲν ἄρσεν ᾖ, ἀποκτείνατε αὐτό, ἐὰν δὲ θῆλυ, περιποιεῖσθε αὐτό. Compare Num. 22:33. Brayford, *Genesis*, 67, 291, pushes too hard here for an exclusive meaning of "you they will keep for themselves" (compare NETS); Brayford, "Taming and Shaming," 198–9, is more balanced.

24. See Gen. 31:18, where its objects are τὰ ὑπάρχοντα, "possessions," and τὴν ἀποσκευήν, "gear"; compare 36:6.

25. See also Amos 2:6; the usage of ἕνεκεν in Mk 10:29-30 and parallels (Mt. 19:29; Lk. 18:29-30) also suggests reciprocity. According to *GELS* 237a, this extension of meaning is not attested before the OG/LXX materials; compare xiii; LSJ 563a.

What is Sara's reaction to Abram's order, so replete with efficient selfishness? Does she reply? Does she offer silent consent, or quietly resist? The outcome makes it unlikely that she voices opposition from the start, and her passivity to this point in the broader narrative does not encourage the supposition of decisive action; but the discourse here offers no clues whatsoever. And what motives may be operative for Sara, whether she acts or does not? To consider only the coercive arguments Abram adduces for her compliance, Sara may tacitly agree, in the hopes of saving Abram's life, or that "an advantage accrue" to his account; or perhaps she goes along out of fear of being "kept," alive and in the possession of the Egyptians. The possibility of the first may be strengthened by Sara's demonstrated interest in advancing Abram's prospects later, in her disposal of Hagar (16:2). If, on the other hand, fear for her safety induces her to voice or assent to the lie, this can only add to the rude shock of being treated exactly as Abram predicted she would be in the absence of such deception. For after the Egyptian men notice this apparently unattached woman, due to her remarkable attractiveness, Pharaoh's courtiers praise her to their superior and summarily bring her "into Pharaoh's house" (12:14-15). These actions are likewise presumably tied to Sara's beauty, and undertaken with the aim of making her sexually available to Pharaoh. That this plan succeeds is later confirmed when Pharaoh declares, "I took her for myself as a woman" or "wife" (ἔλαβον αὐτὴν ἐμαυτῷ εἰς γυναῖκα, v. 19).[26] The discourse is, again, permanently silent on Sara's reaction to being used in this way. Easy to surmise, however, are Abram's feelings subsequent to being "well used" (εὖ χράομαι) by the Egyptian rulers "because of her" (δι' αὐτήν), as he comes into a lengthy list of valuable domestic animals and slaves (12:16). After all, such an outcome was part of the projected result of his ploy: "Say 'I am his sister,' in order that it accrue to my advantage because of you" (v. 13).

Others are not so fortunate, however: "in connection with Sara the woman of Abram" (περὶ Σάρας τῆς γυναικὸς Ἀβράμ), "God tested Pharaoh with serious and painful tests, along with his household" (ἤτασεν ὁ θεὸς τὸν Φαραὼ ἐτασμοῖς μεγάλοις καὶ πονηροῖς καὶ τὸν οἶκον αὐτοῦ, 12:17).[27] How Pharaoh comes to the conclusion that these divine "tests" are the result of his being taken in by Abram's deception, and thus that the restoration of Sara to Abram is the necessary remedy, is completely submerged; in fact, that Pharaoh's action rectifies the situation, from his perspective and that

---

26. εἰς here seems to indicate the purpose for which the action was taken; see LSJ 492a (A.V.2).

27. *GELS* 545b, 576a; LSJ 700a–b (compare Supplement 135a), 1447b.

of his dependents, is only implied. But Sara, having been taken, physically and sexually, by Pharaoh, is taken back by Abram, and is suitably counted among Abram's assets when Pharaoh's men escort him out "along with his woman and everything that was his" (καὶ τὴν γυναῖκα αὐτοῦ καὶ πάντα, ὅσα ἦν αὐτῷ, v. 20). Sara's passivity and subordination are only emphasized by Lot's relative agency here: "and Lot was with him" (καὶ Λὼτ μετ' αὐτοῦ). Abram's state at his ascent from Egypt (13:1) provides a stark contrast to the want that prompted his descent: as a direct result of the trade of Sara's person, so "exceedingly beautiful" (καλή...σφόδρα, v. 14), Abram has become "exceedingly wealthy" (πλούσιος σφόδρα, 13:2; compare 12:16).

There are a number of versional continuities between Sara's characterization here and that of Sarai in the relevant portion of the MT. As I have emphasized, these elements are not therefore less important to the construction of Sara in the LXX, but their relative familiarity means that they need not be rehearsed at length here. Sara in Egypt continues to be a "woman of," here further defined as a valuable object taken and possessed physically and sexually by two men in turn. She is notable for her beauty, though in the event this is nearly all to her detriment. There is no indication that Sara collaborates in Abram's deception; rather, her role is that of a trafficked and traded victim, and she lacks both security and freedom, along with power, volition—and a child. Having acquired slaves previously (12:5), Sara is sold here; but her family, at least in the person of Abram, makes huge gains as a result. Used and abused in Egypt, Sara may find that the use and abuse of her own subordinates come more easily.

But the tradition also features what seem to be developments. Sara here is brusquely ordered about, her passive compliance assumed; she is not the object of persuasion, however deceptive, as in the MT, but the focus of blunt, imperative coercion. That she is not portrayed as needing to be persuaded points to a figure with a very low degree of agency. This reinforces an image of Sara first built in the introductory section of the narrative, where, except for 12:5, Sara is almost entirely passive. God's intervention in Egypt underlines this further. Here, as in the MT, the deity's action cannot be described simply as a rescue of Sara. Again, these "tests" (v. 17) must be a response to Pharaoh's objective violation of Abram's rightful ownership of Sara; that this is not a story of liberation is proved by the outcome, which sees Sara restored to the man who originally traded her for gain under false pretenses (v. 19). Likewise, the bare fact of divine intervention suggests, with the MT, that matters are out of Sara's control. But the lexical content and syntax of the LXX also preclude, at least at the discourse level, even the remote possibility of Sara's agency in the house of Pharaoh, which some maintain may be hinted at by the MT's עַל־דְּבַר שָׂרַי אֵשֶׁת אַבְרָם.[28] God's tests here are περὶ Σάρας τῆς γυναικὸς Ἀβράμ, "in connection with Sara the woman of Abram": her relationship to Abram is the significant datum, and she could just as easily be an inanimate object as a sentient actor. Proposals for any kind of agency on the part of Sara in Egypt in the LXX would have to float, ex nihilo, purely in the narrative's gaps. Without even a hint of her volition in the discourse to this point, however, this seems a dubious enterprise. The passivity of Sara in the LXX indicates not only that she is less likely to be a collaborator with Abram in his scheme, but also that she is less likely to be in any way instrumental in her release from Pharaoh's house.

Two related aspects of Sara's characterization in the LXX achieve, in prospect, what might be called inverse traction as compared to the MT narrative. Although the element of Sara being "worthy of notice" in Egypt remains salient here, the broader motif of her sensitivity to the opinions of others has lower valency in the narrative to come. Notably, her reaction to Isaac's birth lacks the focus on this matter that is suggested in the MT. However, Abram's description of Sara as "pretty-faced" may lay the foundation for another minor motif going forward. In distinction to the MT, Abram's remark here anticipates later notes about Sara's "face," and its implication of deception may help to illuminate the outwardly similar episode in the court of Abimelech.

Silence and Stress (Gen. 13:2–15:21 LXX)

Sara vanishes from the discourse of the LXX after the ascent from Egypt in 13:1, only reappearing in 16:1, in the first episode featuring Hagar. As in the MT, this suspension and resumption of a discourse-level role for Sara underlines connections between her treatment in Egypt and her subsequent disposition of her slave. A number of details in the intervening narrative are also best described as versional continuities, and can be briefly summarized here. The departure of Lot and his dependents, whose presence is suggested by σκηναί (13:5), is precipitated by the kind of acquisitions highlighted in the Egyptian episode: "their possessions were numerous, and they could not live together" (ἦν τὰ ὑπάρχοντα αὐτῶν πολλά, καὶ οὐκ ἐδύναντο κατοικεῖν ἅμα, v. 6). The narrative data and

---

28. See, among others, van Dijk-Hemmes, "Sarai in Exile," 143. To my reading, the simplest rendering of this Hebrew phrase is "because of Sarai the woman of Abram," which is, of course, supported by the LXX here. But the suggestion that עַל־דְּבַר refers to an act of speech or prayer is at least a possible reading.

gaps that permitted restrained speculation on Sarai's potential surrogate maternal feelings for Lot in the MT may obtain, to some degree, for Sara in the LXX. However, her pronounced inertia to this point makes it difficult to conceive of significant story-level activity for Sara here. In any event, the trajectory of this note would be rather different, as Sara's reaction to giving birth to Isaac is markedly less ambiguous in the LXX.

Acquisition, whether of land, possessions, or offspring, remains a significant motif throughout a second divine pledge to Abram (13:14-18) and Abram's military expedition (14:1-24), as in the MT. In Genesis 15, Abram's complaints and demands for assurance finally give voice to the enduring tension between the content of the pledges and the biological conditions essential to their realization: "Master, what will you give me? *I* am dying childless!" (Δέσποτα, τί μοι δώσεις; ἐγὼ δὲ ἀπολύομαι ἄτεκνος, v. 2; see also 3, 8). For Sara, who continues "not bearing children" (οὐκ ἐτεκνοποίει, 11:30), a point to be taken up again immediately upon her return to the discourse (16:1), this emotional stress may spill over into her consciousness. While Sara's awareness of the content of the promises remains a matter of speculation, the open and public nature of Abram's responses to divine revelation (12:4-5, 7-8; 13:18; 15:5, 10-11, and perhaps 17) may suggest that her ignorance is not total.

Broken Inertia, Blurred Gender, and Misused Agency (Gen. 16:1-16 LXX)

> Gen. 16:1 Now Sara, Abram's wife, was not giving birth for him. She, however, had an Egyptian slave-girl whose name was Hagar. 2 And Sara said to Abram, "See, the Lord has shut me off from giving birth; so go in to my slave-girl in order that you may beget children by her." And Abram listened to the voice of Sara. 3 And after ten years of Abram's living in the land of Chanaan, Sara, Abram's wife, took Hagar the Egyptian, her own slave-girl, and gave her to her husband Abram as a wife for him. 4 And he went in to Hagar, and she conceived. And she saw that she was pregnant, and her mistress was dishonored before her. 5 Then Sara said to Abram, "I am being wronged due to you! I have given my slave-girl into your bosom, but when she saw that she was pregnant, I was dishonored before her. May God judge between you and me!" 6 But Abram said to Sara, "See, your slave-girl is in your hands; treat her as it may please you." And Sara maltreated her, and she ran from her presence. 7 But the Lord God's angel found her by the spring of water in the wilderness, by the spring on the way to Sour. 8 And the angel of the Lord said to her, "Hagar, slave-girl of Sara, where are you coming from, and where are you going?" And she said, "I am running from the presence of my mistress Sara." 9 But the angel of the Lord said to her, "Return to your mistress, and humble yourself under her

hands.'... 15 And Hagar bore Abram a son, and Abram called the name of his son, whom Hagar bore him, Ismael. 16 And Abram was eighty-six years of age when Hagar bore Abram Ismael. (NETS)

This episode marks a significant transition for Sara in the LXX, as she appears to shed the torpor that has previously held her suspended. In the presentation of her seemingly abrupt and resolute actions, moreover, themes quietly emerge that grow in prominence as the narrative moves on. These themes, however, will actually work to limit Sara's definition. Here, for the first time, Sara demonstrates what looks like agency—but, as will be seen repeatedly, the price of Sara's agency is that it be primarily exercised in imitation of Abram. Sara's individuation is also stymied here, and not for the last time, by a related motif that sees her potential for initiative undermined.

To explore these and other elements of these laconic but dense scenes, I will first look back to discuss a note from Genesis 15, unique to the LXX among the narratives considered in this study, that suggests that Sara's idea of obtaining an heir for Abram from a slave is in fact derivative of an earlier impulse of Abram himself. Subsequently I consider the quality of other connections between this episode and prior narrative data, concluding that a number of these ties also point to Sara's growing resemblance to Abram. This note of restriction to Sara's individuation is underscored further in the following section, where I treat several instances of gender ambiguity in the characters' speech, suggesting that this also serves to blur the distinctions between Sara and Abram. Finally, I examine Sara's relationship with Hagar in these scenes; once again, a central theme is Sara's adoption of a role previously associated with Abram, as she reinscribes her own treatment at his hands in Egypt.

An Heir from a Slave?

The friction between the repeated pledges of Genesis 15 and the initial complication of the episode in Genesis 16 is plain. The Lord may promise the land from Egypt to Mesopotamia to Abram's offspring (15:18)—"but Sara, Abram's woman, kept on not giving birth for him" (Σάρα δὲ ἡ γυνὴ Ἀβρὰμ οὐκ ἔτικτεν αὐτῷ, 16:1a). The imperfect here reinforces the enduring nature of Sara's infertility, first established in 11:30.[29] Now,

---

29. These imperfects help to illustrate one of my basic contentions, which is that the complexion of a derivative or rewritten narrative is revealed not only by comparison or contrast with its inspiration, but also by what might be called the horizontal play of elements within the derivative narrative itself. The imperfect here is not less significant to an analysis of the character of the LXX because it represents

though, Sara's ongoing deficit is balanced by a significant possession: "However, she had an Egyptian slave, whose name was Hagar" (ἦν δὲ αὐτῇ παιδίσκη Αἰγυπτία, ᾗ ὄνομα Ἀγάρ, v. 1b). The implication that the fertility of her female slave might be thought to constitute part of the solution to Sara's problem is confirmed soon enough, as Sara urges Abram to "enter" Hagar in order to obtain the offspring that the Lord has prevented Sara from bearing (v. 2). However, even before Sara speaks here, for the first time in the discourse, this notion may generate a small tug of familiarity—for Hagar, in the LXX, is not the first slave proposed as a surrogate mother to Abram's heir.

Some time after Abram's military raid, the deity communicates verbally with Abram yet again—this time, somehow, in a "vision" (ὅραμα, 15:1). In this instance, however, Abram talks back for the first time:

> But Abram said, "Master, what will you give me? *I* am dying childless; but the son of Masek, my houseborn female slave—he is Damascus Eliezer." And Abram said, "Since you didn't give me offspring, my houseborn male slave will be my heir." (15:2-3)[30]

What is interesting here is the abrupt birth in translation of the minor character Masek, a woman among the household's οἰκογενεῖς, or "houseborn slaves."[31] Faced with the perplexing בן־משק ביתי, the translator has apparently taken משק as a proper noun, then construed ביתי as descriptive of this person's role, probably under the influence of בן־ביתי in the following verse. As Wevers notes, however, the "use of the feminine term [τῆς οἰκογενοῦς] is striking," and may cast this little bit of dialogue as a prospective "analogue" to Sara's offer of Hagar.[32] The fraught theme of the offspring of a slave potentially serving as a son and heir to Abram

---

a verbal construction in the MT that may be also best rendered in a durative sense; rather, it is more significant due to its recollection of the imperfect in 11:30. Compare Brayford, *Genesis*, 289, 301; Wevers, *Notes*, 159, 217.

30. λέγει δὲ Ἀβράμ Δέσποτα, τί μοι δώσεις; ἐγὼ δὲ ἀπολύομαι ἄτεκνος· ὁ δὲ υἱὸς Μάσεκ τῆς οἰκογενοῦς μου, οὗτος Δαμασκὸς Ἐλιέζερ. καὶ εἶπεν Ἀβράμ Ἐπειδὴ ἐμοὶ οὐκ ἔδωκας σπέρμα, ὁ δὲ οἰκογενής μου κληρονομήσει με.

31. The same individual is also mentioned, in the same context, in at least the Ge'ez tradition of *Jubilees* (14:2), which is thought to have been rendered from a Greek translation of the original Hebrew. Unfortunately this passage is not extant in Hebrew, and questions of the influence of the LXX tradition on the *Vorlage* of the Ethiopic here remain open. "The sons of Masek" are mentioned in *T. Abr.* 2, Recension A.

32. Wevers, *Notes*, 203. The correspondence may be noted, I would contend, whether or not it were "intended," as Wevers suggests.

is thus anticipated by Abram himself, in the first of a series of interconnected stair-steps: Abram's idea is that his heir will be the son of his slave Masek, not his own; but God denies this, proclaiming that Abram's heir "will come out of" Abram himself (ἐξελεύσεται ἐκ σοῦ, 15:2-4).[33] Subsequently, Sara's idea is that Abram can obtain children—his own, but not hers—from her slave Hagar (16:2); again, the deity will reject this, at least in terms of inheritance, later predicting that the heir to the covenant will come "out of" Sara, too (ἐξ αὐτῆς, 17:15-21). When Sara herself conceives, she places an exclamation point on the entire, halting process, in language that partly recalls 15:2-4: "the son of this slave will not inherit with my son Isaac!" (οὐ...κληρονομήσει ὁ υἱὸς τῆς παιδίσκης ταύτης μετὰ τοῦ υἱοῦ μου Ἰσαάκ, 21:10). Finally, God confirms this arrangement, and the succession is cemented (v. 12).

The emergence of this theme may be an aesthetic gain for the LXX narrative. For Sara, however, and for her character's definition against her story context, the foreshadowing contained in the mention of Masek represents a loss. The conceptual content of Sara's first discourse-level utterance, where she notes the deity's role in her reproductive quandary and suggests that a female slave's offspring might remedy the situation, is strongly reminiscent of Abram's remarks in 15:2-3. This simultaneously casts Sara in Abram's mold and robs her of an opportunity to demonstrate initiative. These connected phenomena, which will recur with frequency in coming episodes, work to erode Sara's individuation just as she begins to exercise some agency in the story.

Questions of Connections

If the device of a slave woman as surrogate casts Sara in the image of Abram, however, the ties between her speech here and that of Abram on the cusp of Egypt are somewhat less pronounced. While the MT features tonal echoes triggered by formal similarities here, the correspondences are less plain in the LXX, especially as it does not uniformly render the MT's initial particle pair הנה־נא, found in both 12:11 and 16:2. Instead, where Abram began without preamble (Γινώσκω ἐγὼ ὅτι, "*I know that...*"), Sara first calls for Abram's attention: Ἰδοὺ συνέκλεισέν με κύριος, "Look," or "Listen: the Lord closed me up..." While both addresses are more direct than their MT counterparts, and share, for

---

33. See, however, the interesting variants noted in Wevers's apparatus: instead of Μάσεκ in v. 2, several late manuscripts give μου εκ or μου ο εκ, hence ὁ δὲ υἱός μου [ὁ] ἐκ τῆς οἰκογενοῦς or "my son by the female slave," a reading that anticipates later narrative developments even more explicitly.

example, an inferential οὖν with an imperative (12:13; 16:2), the absence of formal agreement in their opening phrases means that the reader is not cued to the speeches' similarities in quite the same way. Moreover, minor details of the surrounding syntax, such as the narrator's introduction of each character's direct speech, differ between the episodes.

These formal differences could indicate a less overt connection in the LXX between Sara's disposition of Hagar and Sara's own experience of ill-treatment in Egypt. The establishment of this link in the MT doesn't depend entirely upon psychological factors, though these play a role, as in any mimetic conception of character. Rather, the tie is first cued by lexical and syntactical sympathies between the initial discourse-level utterances of Abram and Sara. The intervening mention of Masek in the LXX, which anticipates Sara's proposal to a degree, could also be construed as making the connection to Egypt just a bit more tenuous: the concept of utilizing the sexuality or reproductive capacity of a subordinate is thus not solely confined to, first, Abram's scheme in Egypt and, second, Sara's plans here.

But this is a complicated set of problems. Small suggestive connections, such as Sara's use of συγκλείω, which hints at imprisonment, retain their force, and the thematic echoes remain distinct.[34] There may even be lexical play between the episodes that is peculiar to the Greek, as I propose below. Moreover, Sara's strange resemblance to, or imitation of Abram, familiar from the MT, begins to be suggested here through avenues that do not exist in the Hebrew. Sara's idea of obtaining an heir through a female slave in 16:2 recalls Abram's thought in 15:2-3; her description of Abram's generative potential uses the same word, τεκνοποιέω, as was first used to describe her lack of such potential (16:2; compare 11:30); and this note, as well as others to be treated shortly, participates in a curious minor motif of gender indeterminacy that may blur the lines between Sara and Abram's expected roles.

It seems, indeed, at least at first, that Sara's resemblance to Abram in the LXX may be just another aspect of her subtle but persistent effacement from the narrative. The most obvious disparity between the

---

34. κλείω, naturally related to κλείς, "bar," or, later, "key," means to "shut," "close in," or "confine"; συγκλείω, too, can mean to "coop up" or "enclose," even "imprison"; its cognate noun refers to the concept of locking something away. As such it is a fine rendering of עצר. The absence of another object, such as μήτρα, or "uterus," which appears in the similar 20:18 (συνέκλεισεν κύριος...πᾶσαν μήτραν), leaves some interesting ambiguity in 16:2. See LSJ 957a–b, 1665a; compare BDAG 546b, 952a.

Hebrew and Greek traditions in this episode illustrates this tie in more than one way. Whereas Sarai speculates that she herself may be, in a pun, "built up" or "sonned" out of Hagar's body (אולי אבנה ממנה), Sara's proposal in the LXX is explicitly aimed at producing children for Abram alone (εἴσελθε...πρὸς τὴν παιδίσκην μου, ἵνα τεκνοποιήσῃς ἐξ αὐτῆς, 16:2).[35] Not only, then, is Sara's initiative softened by the derivative flavor of her idea; not only does she decline to advocate for her own dynastic interests; but Sara also imitates Abram here, not in self-concern, as in the MT, but precisely in concern for Abram. Sara's first discourse-level utterance thus aims at Abram's benefit, just as his did (12:11-13). Even if the relative lack of formal agreement between these speeches in the LXX suggests, for example, that Sara's proposal does not aim to deceive, as Abram's did, this too somehow points to a character with less volition, and thus more limited individuation. In the MT, one may question the candor of Sarai's stated desire for a child; but this at least implies an active if concealed self-interest. Here, Sara's tone evokes resignation and self-abnegation, and a first-time reader might well wonder whether her role in this story will dwindle even further.

Gender Ambiguities

But all this, coupled with Sara's decided inertia to this point in the narrative, makes it just that much harder to understand her sudden, resolute action here. That her plan will benefit Abram doesn't soften her summary disposal of Hagar's sexuality, as Sara reinscribes her own treatment at the hands of Abram and other men, "taking...her own slave" (λαβοῦσα... τὴν ἑαυτῆς παιδίσκην) and giving her to Abram (16:3; compare 11:29, 31; 12:5, 19). This abrupt adoption of what has been a male role, too, prompts consideration of this episode's unusual motif of indeterminacy in matters of biology and gender. This motif is especially prominent in characters' speech to or about others. After Sara tells Abram that the Lord has kept her from giving birth, for example, she urges Abram to "enter" her slave, assigning him a penetrative, male role; but her stated reason—ἵνα τεκνοποιήσῃς—would, in most extant Greek, mean "so that you can bear children" (16:2). When employed in the active, as here, τεκνοποιέω typically refers to the generative power of women; the middle

---

35. The reading τεκνοποιήσῃς (-σεις in Alexandrinus and elsewhere) is not the majority reading, which is first singular; first plural also appears in the tradition. But the later preponderance of minuscule witnesses to the first singular likely reflects a recension back toward the Hebrew (Wevers, *Notes*, 218; see also apparatus in Wevers, *Genesis*).

is usually reserved for male subjects.³⁶ The evidence from the LXX and OG is mixed, but when Sara herself was the subject of this verb, in 11:30, the narrator's form was also active (οὐκ ἐτεκνοποίει, "she was not bearing children").³⁷

This would be easy to discount were there not other spoken biological ambiguities in the near context, as when Sara says to Abram, "*I gave my slave into your 'lap'*" (ἐγὼ δέδωκα τὴν παιδίσκην μου εἰς τὸν κόλπον σου, 16:5). This not only reemphasizes Sara's new, startlingly active role as "taker" and "giver" of a woman's sexuality, first seen in v. 3, but also associates Abram with a term evocative of female anatomy. For while κόλπος can mean a person's "lap," it is also suggestive of other concavities and hollows.³⁸ In poetry, κόλπος can refer to the uterus, as in the *Helen* of Euripides, which speaks of the title character's origin "in Leda's womb" (ἐν κόλποις...Λήδας, 1145-46); in later medical literature, κόλπος is simply a term for "vagina."³⁹ Aristophanes, too, puns on the semantic possibilities of κόλπος in a section of the *Lysistrata* that is replete with bawdy double entendre. In their meditated negotiation of peace, the Athenians and Spartans settle their territorial disputes with winking, lascivious references to the anatomy of a nude female "map" that stands before them; an Athenian lays claim to her "Maliac Gulf" (τὸν Μηλιᾶ κόλπον, 1169-70).⁴⁰

---

36. LSJ 1768a–b. Note that LSJ's text of LXX Genesis reads, with the majority text, a first-person middle here. Strabo's employment of the verb is typical: τὸν δ' Ἰκάριον...τεκνοποιήσασθαι τήν τε Πηνελόπην ἐκ Πολυκάστης ("Icarius fathered Penelope by Polycasta"; *Geogr.* 10.2). As LSJ notes, however, Diodorus Siculus reverses the usual arrangement; see *Bibliotheca Historica* 1.73 for the active with male subjects, 4.29 for the middle with female subjects.

37. In its only other occurrence in the Pentateuch, Rachel is the subject of what reads like a true middle usage of the verb (τεκνοποιήσομαι κἀγὼ ἐξ αὐτῆς, Gen. 30:3; see LSJ 1768b). Isa. 65:23 and Jer. 12:2 feature the active verb with grammatically masculine subjects, but both seem to be collectives; in Jer. 36:6, the subjects of the active verb are more clearly biologically male. The verb in Jer. 38:8 (τεκνοποιήσῃ) is morphologically ambiguous.

38. LSJ 974a.

39. In the *Gynecology* of Soranus, ὁ κόλπος is distinguished from ἡ μήτρα, or "uterus," and is used interchangeably with τὸ αἰδοῖον (1.16-18 and elsewhere). This is a technical usage, not slang: τὸ δὲ γυναικεῖον αἰδοῖον καὶ κόλπος ὠνόμασται γυναικεῖος (1.16).

40. *Lysistrata* 1162-74. The Maliac or Malian Gulf is a gulf of the Aegean. See LSJ 974a, 1126b; see also Aristophanes, *Four Comedies*, trans. Douglass Parker (Ann Arbor: University of Michigan Press, 1969), 94 n. 80; compare 80; and Aristophanes, *Birds; Lysistrata; Assembly-Women; Wealth*, trans. Stephen Halliwell (Oxford: Clarendon Press, 1997), 137.

The notion of Sara claiming to "give" or "put" something "into" Abram's κόλπον, and the immediate obstetrical context of Sara's accusation here (ἐν γαστρὶ ἔχει, v. 5), only heighten the lexical ambiguity.[41]

Sara, too, is associated by other characters in this episode with terms that seem to clash with her gender. When Abram surrenders Hagar back into Sara's power (ἐν ταῖς χερσίν), he says, in what reads like an attempt at mollification, "use her however you like" (χρῶ αὐτῇ, ὡς ἄν σοι ἀρεστὸν ᾖ, 16:6). Χράω is a lexeme of very broad application, its employment extending from contexts of oracular proclamation to service as a kind of auxiliary verb.[42] In the middle, as here, its meanings generally orbit around the theme of "use"; when its object is a human being, χράομαι means "to treat" in a certain way.[43] By extension, the verb is often indicative of intimacy, and in particular of sexual intercourse, regarded from a penetrative, male perspective, as in Demosthenes's *Against Neaera* (59.67): καὶ ὡμολόγει μὲν χρῆσθαι τῇ ἀνθρώπῳ, "he confessed to having sex with the woman."[44] This sense also appears occasionally in the LXX and OG materials, though with a darker, more violent cast. In Gen. 19:8, for example, Lot urges the men of Sodom to "use" his daughters however they like; in 34:31, Simeon and Levi rhetorically ask whether the indigenous inhabitants of the land "should use our sister like a prostitute."[45] Similarly, Sir. 26:22, employing an odd metaphor that may reflect a mistranslation, opines that "a married woman will be reckoned as a tower of death to the men who use her" (τοῖς χρωμένοις)—that is, to those who have extramarital sex with her.[46]

When the Lord's messenger urges Hagar to return to her master, Sara is again tied in speech to a word that can indicate a man's sexual violation of a woman: ταπεινώθητι ὑπὸ τὰς χεῖρας αὐτῆς (16:9). Ταπεινόω could often, throughout the LXX and OG, be fairly rendered "rape," as in the narratives featuring Dinah (Gen. 34:2), the host's daughter and the Levite's concubine (Judg. 19:24; 20:5), and Tamar (2 Kgdms [2 Sam.] 13:12, 14, 22, 32); in legal material, such as Deut. 22:24, 29 (compare 21:14); and in

---

41. δίδωμι for נתן in the sense of "put" may be a "Hebraism" (J. A. L. Lee, "Note," 238), but it seems to me to reflect only a modest extension of the verb's meaning; compare LSJ 422b–423a; *GELS* 165a–167a, esp. 166b.

42. LSJ 2001a–2002b.

43. LSJ 2002a–b.

44. Compare Herodotus, *Hist.* 2.181, and LSJ 2002b (IV.2, "esp. of sexual intercourse") for other examples.

45. χρήσασθε αὐταῖς, καθὰ ἂν ἀρέσκῃ ὑμῖν (Gen. 19:8); ὡσεὶ πόρνῃ χρήσονται τῇ ἀδελφῇ ἡμῶν; (34:31). See *GELS* 735a.

46. ὕπανδρος δὲ πύργος θανάτου τοῖς χρωμένοις λογισθήσεται.

prophetic contexts, where the surrounding imagery is particularly horrific (Lam. 5:11; Ezek. 22:10-11), even implicating the deity in acts of sexual violence against the women of Jerusalem (Isa. 3:17; Lam. 2:5).[47] "Submit yourself," the deity's intermediary tells Hagar, "to violation by [your master's] hands."

Other narrative data, however, beat steadily against these gender ambiguities. As the reader has known from the beginning, Sara remains a "woman of Abram" who continues to "fail to give birth" (16:1). She herself explicitly underlines this biological evaluation, albeit with a significant disclaimer of responsibility: "the Lord has closed me up in order to prevent me from giving birth" (v. 2).[48] Moreover, in the narrated action Sara does not "use" or "violate" her slave, even if she "hurts" or "abuses" her (ἐκάκωσεν αὐτὴν Σάρα, v. 6). Hagar's flight in the immediate context shows that this is a serious, likely violent action, and the employment of κακόω elsewhere, such as in Lot's conflict with the men of Sodom (19:9) and the enslavement of the children of Israel in Egypt (Exod. 1:11; compare Gen. 15:13), supports this reading. But κακόω does not appear in the contexts of male sexual violence against women where ענה occurs in the MT (again, Gen. 34:2; Judg. 19:24; 2 Kgdms [2 Sam.] 13:12; and so on); thus the unsettling image of Sarai in the MT as an active rapist or violator (ותענה שרי) is somewhat muted here. In fact, in this scene in the LXX Sara describes herself as being "wronged" by Abram, employing a word, ἀδικοῦμαι, that can refer to a woman's sexual "ruin" by a man (Gen. 16:5).[49] Abram, too, is hardly depicted solely in terms that evoke gender ambiguity, as he amply demonstrates his virility by entering and impregnating Hagar (v. 4).

Some of this complex of uncertainties may be profitably channeled into a discussion of the construction of Sara's character in the LXX, I think, by relating it to the subtle realignment of the balance of power between Sarai and Abram noted in the treatment of this episode in the MT. As there, Sara has by no means shaken Abram's basic power over her. She is and will remain the "woman of Abram" (16:1, 3), and Abram's assent to her plan, reception of her complaint, and return of her property (vv. 2, 5-6) are plot points that presume his authority. Yet Sara, partly by mimicking Abram's taking and giving of the sexual services of an underling, also

---

47. *GELS* 670b; LSJ 1757a. On Gen. 34:2, see Wevers, *Notes*, 558.
48. συνέκλεισέν με κύριος τοῦ μὴ τίκτειν. See Smyth §§1408, 2032 e.
49. Compare *The Farmer* of Menander (*Georg.* 29-30): "Should this scumbag marry [another woman] after wronging our girl?" (γαμεῖ // ὁ μιαρὸς οὗτος ἠδικηκὼς τὴν κόρην;).

exercises considerable power here, and some kind of shift seems to be marked at this very point: when Sara, as ever ἡ γυνὴ Ἀβράμ, takes Hagar and gives her to Abram, he, too, is branded, and this for the first time, as "her man" or "husband" (τῷ ἀνδρὶ αὐτῆς, v. 3). As in the MT, Sara demonstrates little deference, especially in speech, after this moment. Her next utterance, in fact, is a direct accusation: "I am being wronged by you!" (Ἀδικοῦμαι ἐκ σοῦ, v. 5; compare her preemptory speech in 21:10). The gender ambiguities in the LXX version of this episode, to my reading, also contribute to a blurring of the roles of Sara and Abram that helps to soften the otherwise sharp contrast between the inert, agency-free Sara of the preceding narrative and the resolute but volatile woman who emerges here. Once again, though, Sara's resemblance to Abram suggests that she must cede individuation in exchange for volition.

The Disposition of Hagar

Sara's relationship with Abram, of course, is only one thread of this tale. The broad outlines of her conflict with Hagar are familiar from a reading of the MT. Sara's lack of fertility, underlined by the narrator and by herself (16:1-2), is answered by her firm possession of "her own slave," whom Sara dominates to the extent that she can allocate Hagar's body, sexuality, and reproductive potential as she sees fit—and this precisely in response to her own childlessness (vv. 1-3). That Sara's infertility is cast as an enduring, perhaps permanent condition (v. 1), caused by God (v. 2), or that Sara's motive is not explicitly self-interested (v. 2), cannot soften the brutal and abusive means by which she attempts a resolution: in effect, Sara proposes and arranges Abram's rape of her slave (vv. 2-4).

With Hagar's conception, Sara's stated goal for Abram moves toward its fulfillment (16:4). But an unintended consequence also occurs: Hagar "saw that she was pregnant" (εἶδεν ὅτι ἐν γαστρὶ ἔχει), and, apparently as a result, ἠτιμάσθη ἡ κυρία ἐναντίον αὐτῆς. The corresponding expression in the MT (ותקל גברתה בעיניה) is best understood as "her master became insignificant in her eyes": Sarai is simply "overlooked" or "ignored" by her slave. Here, the specific force of the phrase, which is echoed quite precisely in Sara's own reportage in v. 5, depends on the strength of the word ἀτιμάζω and the implications of ἐναντίον in the story context. Wevers is probably correct in claiming that ἀτιμάζω is a "stronger term" than the MT's קלל, though rendering "dishonor" may lend an unjustified, implicitly public flavor to this narrative development.[50] Such an understanding is explicit in translations such as Brayford's "was shamed,"

---

50. Wevers, *Notes*, 220.

or, even more plainly, Takamitsu Muraoka's "lost face," which suggests humiliation before others.⁵¹ But ἐναντίον plus the genitive is probably best understood radically as "in the presence of"; thus, even if the passive of ἀτιμάζω indicates "suffering dishonor," or "being insulted," the forum seems to be private, not public.⁵² Hagar, then, does not somehow subject her master to widespread social opprobrium; rather, Sara loses status "in the estimation of," or in the opinion of, Hagar alone.⁵³

In the story world, however, this private insult is more than enough to provoke Sara, who is explicitly and by common consent Hagar's κυρία, "master," or "owner," a title cognate to that of the deity—a fact hard to miss especially in the close juxtaposition of these titles in 16:7-9.⁵⁴ Contrary to Brayford's assertion that the Greek "slightly improves Hagar's status vis-à-vis Sarai" by neglecting to attach a superfluous possessive pronoun to κυρία in v. 4, Hagar remains, at a basic level, the property of Sara.⁵⁵ This is only underlined by the fact that Sara does not bother to exaggerate the charge against Hagar, as she does in her claim of "savagery" (חמס) in the MT, but merely echoes the narrator's assessment of the offense (v. 5). Such is nonetheless enough for Abram to return Hagar—now pregnant with his child—to Sara, in order that she be free to "use" her slave as she likes; enough for Sara to abuse Hagar, probably violently; and enough that no one, including God, finds fault with Sara's conduct (vv. 6, 9).

In fact, the deity proves to be an active collaborator in Sara's abusive relationship with Hagar. Though Brayford claims that this narrative casts God as a "benefactor of the marginal and oppressed," this is hard to square with the Lord's messenger's words to this runaway slave: "Return to your master and submit yourself to violation by her hands" (16:9). Again,

---

51. Brayford, *Genesis*, 75; *GELS* 101a.
52. See LSJ 555a; Smyth §1700; compare J. A. L. Lee, *A Lexical Study of the Septuagint Version of the Pentateuch*, SCS 14 (Chico, CA: Scholars Press, 1983), 152, which indicates that ἐναντίον plus the genitive meaning "in the presence of" is also attested in contemporaneous (third-century BCE) papyri.
53. Compare *GELS* 233b (but note Muraoka's rendering of Gen. 16:5).
54. For κύριος as "owner," compare J. A. L. Lee, *Lexical Study*, 83. "Mistress" is not a suitable rendering of κυρία here primarily because it implies that a slaveholder's power differs somehow when a woman exercises it.
55. Sara's ownership of Hagar is explicitly stated in 16:1-3, 5-6; twice in v. 8; and again in v. 9. Brayford, *Genesis*, 303, contends that the LXX's simple ἡ κυρία lacks the possessive force of the pronominal suffix on גברתה (v. 4). However, the Greek article often serves as a possessive (Smyth §1121).

ταπεινόω in the context of the LXX and OG is a word that is even a few degrees worse, in its implications of sexual violence, than κακόω, used to describe Sara's conduct in v. 6. Far from an illustration of the saving action of Brayford's "God-in-the-margins," then, this resolution recalls nothing so much as God's restoration of Sara to Abram, who sold her, in Egypt.[56]

The relative stasis of Sara prior to this episode emphasizes her startling development here. Though partly introduced with notes that exhibit continuity with her demonstrated passivity and lack of volition—her infertility, the derivative nature of her proposed solution to this problem, and the fact that she initially advocates only for Abram, not for herself—other elements show that Sara's inertia is at an end. Her enduring infertility is balanced by her enduring control of her slave, Hagar, and Sara's allocation of her underling's sexual resources is only one of several details in which she begins to exhibit an odd resemblance to Abram. Indeed, unusual ambiguities in traits of biology and gender contribute to a kind of blurring of the roles of Sara and Abram; this indeterminacy, in turn, helps to explain and illustrate subtle shifts in the balance of power between the two characters. Most important for an evaluation of Sara is what all these factors reveal about her apparent newfound agency and openness in speech—freedoms that she uses, however, only to dominate and to abuse her slave, in a divinely sanctioned restaging of her own ill-treatment in Egypt. Once again, when Sara acts, her conduct often echoes Abram's.

One detail here may provide further evidence of Sara's abrupt change in these scenes, even as it furnishes another tie, unique to the LXX among the narratives considered in this study, to the Egyptian episode. Abram characterized Sara there as "pretty-faced" (εὐπρόσωπος, 12:11), an adjective that can imply a disparity between outer appearance and inner motive. His evaluation seemed confirmed, at least on an aesthetic level, when the Egyptians subsequently took notice of Sara's beauty (vv. 14-15). While her face once inspired attraction, however, now it prompts flight: in the wake of Sara's abuse, Hagar ἀπέδρα ἀπὸ προσώπου αὐτῆς— literally, "ran away from her face," an account explicitly supported by Hagar herself in her response to the messenger in the desert (16:6, 8). This modest motif centered on Sara's πρόσωπον may find further traction in an interesting note in the speech of Abimelech later.

---

56. Brayford, *Genesis*, 303.

Different Name, Different Prospects? (Gen. 17:1-27 LXX)

The disparities between Genesis 17 in the LXX and the MT that are relevant to the characterization of Sara are few, so a summary of the continuities will largely suffice. There is a huge gap in story time, as about thirteen years pass in total silence (16:16; 17:1), which raises a number of mostly unanswerable questions about the development of the characters' relationships during the interim. When the tale resumes, Abram is presented as receiving yet another extended revelation from God in which the fate of his descendants plays a prominent part (17:2, 4-15); this time, however, the promises would seem to find focus in the son whom Hagar, in accordance with Sara's plan, bore to Abram at the close of the last episode (16:2, 15-16). This is a presumption shared by "Abraam," as he will now be known (17:5), which his reaction in vv. 17-18 makes plain.

All the stranger, then, when God speaks not of Hagar's offspring, but of Sara's:

> Gen. 17:15 And God said to Abraam, "As for Sara your wife, her name shall not be called Sara, but Sarra shall be her name. 16 And I will bless her, and I will give you a child by her. And I will bless her, and she shall become nations, and kings of nations shall be from her." 17 And Abraam fell face down and laughed and spoke in his mind, saying, "Shall a son be born to a hundred-year-old, and shall Sarra who is ninety years of age give birth?" 18 And Abraam said to God, "As for Ismael, let him live before you!" 19 But God said to Abraam, "Indeed; see, your wife Sarra shall bear you a son, and you shall call his name Isaak, and I will establish my covenant with him as an everlasting covenant and for his offspring after him. 20 Now concerning Ismael, see, I heard you.... 21 But my covenant I will establish with Isaak, whom Sarra shall bear to you." (NETS)

Sara's name, too, is here "amplified" (compare 12:2), meaninglessly in a Greek context, into "Sarra" (Σάρρα). This is another note that emphasizes her resemblance to Abraam, a theme which at first also seems to be highlighted in the promises, partly reminiscent of those given to Abraam earlier, that are spoken about her here (compare, for example, 17:16 with 12:2 and 17:6, or 17:19 with 17:7). But a key difference is exposed in these prepositions—"to" and "about"—and Sarra's prominence is more seeming than actual. The revelation of her name may not evoke Abraam's perspective, as in the MT; as Wevers notes, the passive construction of the Greek makes the announcement of her new name "a general statement of fact," not a correction of what Abraam calls her.[57] But this

---

57. Wevers, *Notes*, 236.

remains a statement, however general, that only Abraam is privileged to hear. Moreover, the blessing with which God pledges to favor Sarra is immediately restricted to her production of a child—for Abraam (v. 16).[58] Sarra's blessing is to be the initial conduit for Abraam's "seed" (σπέρμα), which is supposed to enjoy a "permanent covenant" (διαθήκη αἰώνιος) with the deity (v. 19). Given the primacy and endurance of Sarra's infertility, the reversal of this trait, even in pledge, is no small development; her name change, then, however phonetically meaningless, may help to represent this shift. But the promise of blessing and covenant only funnels through Sarra. As an instrument in the broader and more important web of relationships between Abraam, Isaac, and their God, Sarra has no more say in the deity's plan than did Masek in Abraam's, or Hagar in Sarra's own.

Volition and Restriction (Gen. 18:1-15 LXX)

Gen. 18:1 Now God appeared to him near the oak of Mambre, while he was sitting at the door of his tent at midday. 2 And looking up with his eyes he saw, and see, three men stood over him. And when he saw them, he ran forward from his tent door to meet them and did obeisance upon the ground 3 and said, "Lord, if perchance I have found favor before you, do not pass by your servant. 4 Do let water be taken, and let them wash your feet, and you cool off under the tree. 5 And I shall take bread, and you will eat, and after that you will pass by on your way—inasmuch as you have turned aside to your servant." And they said, "So do, as you have said." 6 And Abraam hurried over to the tent to Sarra and said to her, "Hurry, and mix three measures of fine flour, and make loaves baked in ashes." 7 And Abraam ran to the cows and took a little calf, tender and good, and gave it to the servant, and he hastened to prepare it. 8 Then he took butter and milk and the little calf that he had prepared and set it before them, and they ate, and he stood by them under the tree. 9 And he said to him, "Where is your wife Sarra?" And he said in reply, "There, in the tent." 10 And he said, "I will come to you, when I return, during this season next year, and Sarra your wife shall have a son." And Sarra, who was behind him, listened at the tent door. 11 Now Abraam and Sarra were old, advanced in days, and menstruation had ceased to happen to Sarra. 12 And Sarra laughed within herself, saying, "It has not yet happened to me up to the present, and my lord is rather old." 13 And the Lord said to Abraam, "Why is it that Sarra laughed within herself, saying, 'Shall I then indeed give birth? But I have grown old.' 14 Can it be that a matter is impossible with God? In this season

---

58. Compare ibid., 237.

I will come back to you next year, and Sarra shall have a son." 15 But Sarra denied, saying, "I did not laugh," for she was afraid. And he said, "No, but you did laugh." (NETS)

Though Sarra, at least as a device in the advancement of the divine plan, served as the absent object of Abraam and God's thought and discussion in Genesis 17, she has not played a bodily role in the narrative since her harming of Hagar in 16:6, many years ago in story time (v. 16; 17:1, 24). Instead her part in the story has been almost totally concealed from the reader's mental eye. As the episode of Hagar's surrogacy depicted Sarra's emerging (if always subordinate and often derivative) agency while hinting at subtle realignments in the power relations of the characters, Sarra's story activity in the interim might be supposed to exhibit continuations of these trends. This expectation is not entirely dashed by the details of the divine visit in Genesis 18; Sarra does show flashes of volition here, though some of these seem derivative, too, if not necessarily consciously imitative of Abraam. But other aspects of the narrative push back against any potential displays of initiative. The persistent scenic element of the "tent" (σκηνή, vv. 1-2, 6, 9-10), for instance, appears almost contrived to restrain Sarra's developing agency by keeping her from view. Even when the narrator describes her actions, in vv. 10, 12, and 15, the broader narrative perspective or focalization remains with the characters outside the tent; Sarra, insofar as she is shown, is exposed in glimpses, through a kind of cutaway, or cross-section of the tent that screens her. This confinement is reminiscent of her captivity in Egypt, where she is taken inside Pharaoh's house (12:15), and partly recalls her earlier attribution of her infertility to the Lord, who, she says, "closed me up," or "enclosed me" (συνέκλεισέν με, 16:2).

Several of these narrative aspects come together in connection with Sarra's first mention in this episode: "Abraam hurried to the tent, toward Sarra, and said to her, 'Hurry! …make hearthcakes!'" (18:6).[59] There is no explicit indication that Abraam enters the tent; his almost comical haste, in fact, makes it plausible that he simply blurts out his orders as he runs past on his way to the herd (v. 7). Sarra thus remains obscured from every eye, a point that is emphasized by the indeterminacy of her response to Abraam's command. As there is no hint that "hearthcakes" ever appear before the visitors (v. 8), it is reasonable to suspect that Sarra takes no action at all here. While this inaction calls to mind Sarra's inertia

---

59. ἔσπευσεν Ἀβραὰμ ἐπὶ τὴν σκηνὴν πρὸς Σάρραν καὶ εἶπεν αὐτῇ Σπεῦσον… ποίησον ἐγκρυφίας.

in the first parts of her narrative, it also, somewhat paradoxically, shows initiative, even defiance—a reading that may be bolstered by accounts of Sarra's deceptions to come.

A number of these motifs and tensions endure as the episode nears its climax. After one of the guests—apparently the Lord, on the evidence of 18:13—asks after Sarra's whereabouts and learns that she is "in the tent," the visitor predicts the reversal of her infertility (vv. 9-10). Pointedly directed to Abraam alone (v. 10), and couched in language that evokes his last divine interview (17:19, 21), this is a reminder rather than a revelation. But Sarra overhears: Σάρρα δὲ ἤκουσεν πρὸς τῇ θύρᾳ τῆς σκηνῆς, οὖσα ὄπισθεν αὐτοῦ (18:10). Questions come out at once here: does the speaker intend for Sarra to hear? She is not addressed, which may mean the question prefaces an attempt to communicate something not for her ears; however, the entire episode seems wanting in motivation if the purpose of the visit is simply to reiterate what Abraam knows already. And is Sarra "listening," that is, trying to follow the conversation, which implies initiative, or does she simply "hear"? The former possibility seems recommended by the fact that ἤκουσεν lacks an explicit object, while the likelihood of the latter may be bolstered by the verb's aspect. The epexegetical flavor of the trailing participial phrase, however, counts in favor of happenstance: "Sarra heard [his remark] near the door of the tent—seeing as she was behind him," or "behind him as she was."[60] Again, then, Sarra appears both hidden and inactive, her subjectivity merely receptive of the volition of another.

But this only makes the next development more startling. After a narratorial aside that underlines Abraam and Sarra's advanced age and even notes that "Sarra's menses had ceased" (18:11), Sarra reacts with a healthy skepticism that is entirely appropriate to the absurdity of overhearing a stranger make predictions about her reproductive chances: "Sarra laughed internally saying, 'Not yet has it happened to me, all the way until now—and my lord [or "husband"] is old!'" (v. 12).[61] The word order elegantly leaves open the question of the audibility of Sarra's laugh and comment: does ἐγέλασεν δὲ Σάρρα ἐν ἑαυτῇ λέγουσα mean that she laughed "in herself," spoke "in herself," or both? Sarra's sentiment, regardless, is wholly credible. Notably, she makes no comment about her own age or her menses—really, no remark about her personal condition at all. Sarra's first statement, apparently referring to the guest's prediction that "she will

---

60. Compare Brayford, "Taming and Shaming," 183–4.
61. ἐγέλασεν δὲ Σάρρα ἐν ἑαυτῇ λέγουσα Οὔπω μέν μοι γέγονεν ἕως τοῦ νῦν, ὁ δὲ κύριός μου πρεσβύτερος.

have a son" (ἕξει υἱόν, 18:10), is simply a sensible, factual observation, formulated impersonally: "it," she says, "hasn't happened to me yet" (v. 12).[62] Sarra gives no indication of thinking that she is too old. Abraam is old, though, and Sarra's lifelong experience recommends against credulity here—the thought of a child, now, is simply laughable.

So Sarra's laugh and soliloquy seem to point to a woman who is nobody's fool—someone who has the will and the mental freedom to form her own skeptical, private evaluation of events. However, this image begins to pale at the recognition that it is built, at least in part, of elements that have already been associated with Abraam. Sarra's laugh (ἐγέλασεν...Σάρρα) precisely recalls Abraam's initial reaction to the same news (Ἀβραάμ...ἐγέλασεν); her observation about Abraam's age likewise echoes part of his internally expressed doubts there (compare 18:12 and 17:17). Moreover, her position by the tent door resembles, to a degree, that of Abraam at the start of this episode. While the parallel is less exact than that of the MT, this is so in a way that actually serves to decrease Sarra's physical prominence in the scene. While the Hebrew describes Abraham's and Sarah's respective attitudes with a participle followed by a simple פתח האהל, unmodified by a preposition, here the expressions are formally distinct: Abraam is sitting "in the door" (ἐπὶ τῆς θύρας, 18:1), presented in the context of a genitive absolute, while Sarra, as the subject of a finite verb, hears the stranger's remark "near the door" (πρὸς τῇ θύρᾳ, v. 10).[63] The bodily senses associated with Abraam and Sarra also clarify their respective positions: Abraam need only glance up to see out (v. 2), while Sarra can only overhear (v. 10).

To call these echoes imitative would not be quite correct. Sarra's laugh is derivative to the reader, on a discourse level, much as her proposal of a child by a slave was; there is, however, no evidence in either case that she is aware of Abraam's earlier speech or conduct. But these similarities in presentation begin almost to look like a persistent narratorial tendency to hamstring Sarra's initiative, to strip her of opportunities to demonstrate color and vitality.[64] Other narrative elements may start to coalesce around this idea of curbing Sarra's originality, or combating her ability to surprise. Certainly other restrictions on Sarra's prominence here contribute to a broader, suppressing effect: the shrouding device of the tent—specified

---

62. Compare Wevers, *Notes*, 252.

63. Ibid., 244, 251, takes these expressions as equivalent, but the other prepositional phrase in v. 1 supports this understanding of πρός plus the dative here—unless God is perched up "in the oak" (πρὸς τῇ δρυΐ).

64. Contrast the findings of Tervanotko, *Denying Her Voice*, 209–10, on the treatment of Miriam in the Greek tradition.

in the Greek, notably, as belonging to Abraam (τῆς σκηνῆς αὐτοῦ, 18:1)—hiding her from view; the fact that this message about her reproductive biology is not addressed to her at all; or the deity's intimidating rebuke that aims at Sarra's silence (vv. 13-15).

This general paling of Sarra's character is bolstered by the plainest disparity between the MT and the LXX here, which is in her response to the stranger's prediction. Whereas Sarah reacts by thinking, sarcastically, "After my being worn out, there's pleasure for me!" (אחרי בלתי היתה־לי עדנה), Sarra says "Not yet has it happened to me, all the way until now" (Οὔπω μέν μοι γέγονεν ἕως τοῦ νῦν, 18:12). In the MT, her thought communicates exasperation at the idea of more fruitless sex with Abraham, and shows incredulity at the possibility of her pleasure in intercourse; in the LXX, however, she emphasizes the logical improbability of conception in the light of experience. Both responses are completely skeptical, to my reading, but the MT's earthy imagery—Sarah being "worn out" like a rag, rolling her eyes at her chances of finding moist "pleasure" in sex with the elderly Abraham—yields, in the LXX, to a cool and sober appraisal, formulated impersonally, of the merits of the proposition.

This disparity is the linchpin of Brayford's argument that the LXX casts Sarra as a "shameful" Hellenistic matron more appropriate to the sensibilities of the translators' Alexandrian milieu. The absence of notes that evoke the mechanics of intercourse, and the oblique reference to conception and childbirth, Brayford says, depict a woman who models a social ideal by avoiding "impure thoughts" while focusing on her sanctioned reproductive role.[65] While it seems too much to conclude that Sarra's remark means that she "reflects on her spousal duty of producing the required heir" for Abraam, Brayford's analysis here is essentially sound.[66] I would emphasize, though, that Sarra's literary character seems diminished in proportion to her alignment with these social norms, a process that Brayford argues is intended to "improve" Sarra's "moral character" in the eyes of the original audience of Greek Genesis.[67] Brayford also makes a significant broader point here about intentionality

---

65. See Brayford, "Taming and Shaming," 184–87; her arguments are also summarized in Brayford, "To Shame or not to Shame," 169–70, and Brayford, "Sarah Laughs Last," 324–5.

66. Brayford, *Genesis*, 313; compare Brayford, "Sarah Laughs Last," 324.

67. Brayford, to be clear, does not regard "the domesticated Sarah of the LXX" as an improvement (Brayford, "Taming and Shaming," 187). Her primary concern, however, is the relationship of Sarra's depiction to the compositional context of the LXX.

in translation.⁶⁸ Motive is ultimately irretrievable. But even if a rendering represents a simple misunderstanding, as Wevers convincingly argues is the case here, the resulting text still reflects its compositional environment.⁶⁹ I would only add that such details of the circumstances of a text's generation, insofar as they are recoverable, have no effect on the impact of an element in its literary context. The importance of Sarra's remark to her character's construction is weighed in the mind of the reader alongside innumerable other narrative data. Mistranslation or not, Sarra's logical response to the visitor's prediction becomes just one more narrative element that drains some of her color away.

The disputatious close of this scene can also be read as a short series of responses that undermine Sarra's agency in a variety of ways. Sarra's rational assertion of skepticism, whether overheard or supernaturally detected by the Lord, is twisted in reportage in both content and tone (18:13). Sarra's indirect reference to reproduction becomes explicit, and the whole is imbued with doubt about her own physical fitness—not Abraam's advanced age. The interrogative particle ἆρα, very infrequent in the LXX or OG, contributes a note of anxious concern to the misquotation: "Is there any way I can give birth? But *I* have grown old!" (Ἆρά γε ἀληθῶς τέξομαι; ἐγὼ δὲ γεγήρακα).⁷⁰ Sarra's laugh clashes somewhat with this attributed worry, which emphasizes the report's inaccuracy. Moreover, that the Lord disdains a direct address here, continuing to speak to Abraam alone, only strengthens the impression that Sarra's volition is something to be ignored or denied.

Sarra, interestingly, declines to be ignored, and asserts her initiative. Despite being a third party to the Lord's lecture of Abraam, Sarra interrupts with a flat denial of her earlier, frank response (18:14-15). In fact, the flow of the discourse teases the reader with the prospect of Sarra rejecting the deity's entire project: the Lord declares to Abraam, "'Sarra will have a son.' But Sarra denied it..." (ἔσται τῇ Σάρρα υἱός. ἠρνήσατο δὲ Σάρρα...). Immediately, however, Sarra's interjection is specified: "I

---

68. Brayford, *Genesis*, 313; Brayford, "Taming and Shaming," 185–6.

69. Brayford, "Taming and Shaming," 185–6; compare Brayford, *Genesis*, 26. See Wevers, *Notes*, 252, for his persuasive explanation of the misreading. In brief, he proposes that בלתי was read not as the first person of the verb בלה but as the particle of negation with the same consonants (BDB 115a versus 116b), hence οὔπω, "not yet"; the unusual עדנה was construed, Wevers suggests, as עד הנה, or ἕως τοῦ νῦν, "until now," or "up to this point." Compare Marguerite Harl, *La Genèse*, La Bible d'Alexandrie 1 (Paris: Cerf, 1986), 175.

70. LSJ 233a; compare *GELS* 89a.

didn't laugh" (Οὐκ ἐγέλασα, v. 15). Though small in scope, this claim, apparently aimed at deceiving one or more of the characters outside the tent, still shows a vigor foreign to the inert woman who floated through the early portions of this narrative. But the Lord has the final word: "No—not at all, but you laughed" (Οὐχί, ἀλλὰ ἐγέλασας).

In my analysis of the MT, I raised the knotty question of narratorial candor in the explanation of Sarah's attempt at deception. This direct attribution of motive, the only comment of its kind concerning her in the entire narrative, could hardly be clearer in either version: her denial of her laughter is offered, the narrator clarifies, "because she was afraid" (כי יראה; ἐφοβήθη γάρ). But why this should be so is left wholly to the reader's inference; contrast the relatively prolix explanation of Abraam's lie in Gerar (20:2), on which I will say more just below. Here, some menacing, undisclosed story-level event might be posited; otherwise, it seems that Sarra must somehow have intuited the alarming, divine power of the visitor, soon to be demonstrated down in Sodom. If so, her earlier laugh and present denial both point to a character with more sense than Abraam displays in 17:17. But Sarra's unexplained fear here leaves me uneasy; for one thing, as in the MT, it seems to jar with her character's activity in Genesis 16, when she last occupied the stage. In my discussion of the Hebrew narrative, I left this problem of narratorial honesty short of full resolution; in the LXX, though, I wonder if there isn't enough other evidence of a tendency to rob Sarra of initiative to tip the scales—and reject the narrator's explanation here.

For it is almost as if opportunities for Sarra's assertiveness and individuation are undermined before they can arise. Sarra's ill-treatment of a subordinate is prefigured in her own experience in Egypt; her idea of providing an heir by a slave, after Abraam's remarks about Masek, lacks the capacity to surprise; Sarra's laughter echoes Abraam's. Other aspects, such as the scenic device of the tent, or the deity's harsh response to Sarra where Abraam's identical reaction went unremarked, contribute to a general impression of restriction. Later, Sarra's collaborative action in Gerar is effectively merely a paraphrase of Abraam's script for her in 12:13, while Sarra's final act of initiative, where she urges Hagar and Ishmael's banishment, is followed by her own complete disappearance from the discourse until the note of her death. Many of these elements are familiar from the narrative of the MT. But a number of little tweaks in the LXX contribute to a persistent enervation and paling of Sarra's character: her somewhat more pronounced inertia in the opening chapters; the mention of Masek; Sarra's slightly more explicit shrouding in the tent; and her markedly less colorful remarks at hearing of her impending conception, which will find an analogue later in what might be described as her more conventional reaction to Isaac's birth. Finally, there is the matter of the narratorial explanation of Abraam's subsequent deception (20:2). Interestingly, this is also a note peculiar to the LXX; the fact that it was almost certainly copied from the similar passage in 26:7 has no bearing on its function in its context.[71] What seems significant is that there, too, the narrator names fear as the motive for a character's lying speech (ἐφοβήθη γάρ, 20:2). But the full explanation—"he said…'She is my sister' (because he was afraid to say 'She is my wife,' lest sometime the men of the city kill him on account of her)"—is patently incredible after the events of Egypt.[72] I am all the less inclined, therefore, to trust the narrator here, and for me the motive behind Sarra's denial of her laughter remains murky. But her attempt at deception can still be seen as an assertion of will and initiative, now restricted not only by the Lord's rebuttal, but also by the narrator's obfuscation.

The range of this discussion makes it useful to review Sarra's trajectory so far. When Sarra as an actor last appeared in the discourse, so long ago in story time, she surprised, a bit, by breaking free of the torpor that had previously kept her inert and free of agency. Her newfound volition was exercised in cruelty; but even this seemed to aid in the definition of Sarra as a human character in opposition to the "pretty-faced" object that occupied the earlier narrative. The edges on this development were blunted, however, by a recognition of the derivative nature of Sarra's proposal, and by an odd gender-blurring motif that softened the distinctions between her and Abraam.

Here, this oscillation between volition and restriction develops, not least under the influence of the scenic enclosure of the tent. While Sarra's burst of will in Genesis 16 apparently occurred in the open, here she is explicitly contained and hidden; yet she may still show defiance, even in inaction, over the matter of the bread for the visitors. Moreover, although Sarra betrays no ambition to overhear the conversation outside, she startles with a skeptical laugh—at least until it creeps in that here, too, Sarra's action merely echoes Abraam's. Indeed, looking across the tradition, Sarra's soliloquy in the LXX reflects a figure just a bit paler, a bit drained of vigor. In response to her laughing but sober reaction, the deity twists her words, declining to speak to her directly—until she

---

71. See the discussion of this verse in Wevers, *Notes*, 289.
72. εἶπεν…Ἀδελφή μού ἐστιν· ἐφοβήθη γὰρ εἰπεῖν ὅτι Γυνή μού ἐστιν, μήποτε ἀποκτείνωσιν αὐτὸν οἱ ἄνδρες τῆς πόλεως δι' αὐτήν.

again asserts herself, interrupting with a bold lie, and is rebuked back into silence. Sarra's utility to the fulfillment of the divine promises, which was first specified in her absence in Genesis 17, continues to be defined very narrowly: "Sarra will have a son" (ἕξει υἱὸν Σάρρα, 18:10). But Sarra will not, apparently, be invited to emerge from isolation in order to receive this remarkable news face to face, nor allowed to demonstrate any real initiative, nor permitted even to speak, let alone asked to offer an opinion on her appointed role. As elements accumulate that restrict Sarra, that show her actions to be derivative, that leave her wanting in originality and narrow her capacity to surprise, I, at least, begin to wonder about a suppression collaboratively effected by Abraam, God—and the narrator.

More Imitative Agency—and Questions of Consistency (Gen. 20:1-18 LXX)

Gen. 20:1 And from there Abraam moved to the land toward the southwest and lived between Kades and between Sour and resided in Gerara as an alien. 2 And Abraam said of his wife Sarra, "She is my sister," for he was afraid to say, "She is my wife," lest perhaps the men of the city kill him on her account. Then Abimelech king of Gerara sent and took Sarra. 3 And God came in to Abimelech in his sleep during the night and said, "Look, you are about to die by reason of the woman whom you have taken, whereas she is married to a man." 4 Now Abimelech had not touched her, and he said, "Lord, will you destroy an unwitting and righteous nation? 5 Did not he himself say to me, 'She is my sister'? And she herself said to me, 'He is my brother.' I did this with a pure heart and righteousness of hands." 6 Then God said to him during his sleep, "I too knew that you did this with a pure heart, and I was the one who spared you so that you did not sin in regard to me. Therefore I did not allow you to touch her. 7 And now return the woman to the man, for he is a prophet, and he will pray for you, and you will live. If, however, you do not restore her, know that you shall die, you and all that are yours." 8 And Abimelech rose early in the morning and called all his servants and spoke of all these matters in their hearing; then all the men were very much afraid. 9 And Abimelech called Abraam and said to him, "What is this you have done to us? Surely we have not committed some sin in regard to you, that you have brought great sin on me and on my kingdom? You have done a deed to me that no one shall do." 10 And Abimelech said to Abraam, "What did you observe that you did this?" 11 And Abraam said, "Because I said, It appears there is no piety in this place, and so they will kill me because of my wife. 12 For indeed, she is truly my sister by my father, but not by my mother, and she became a wife to me. 13 Now it came about when God brought me forth from my father's house, that then I said to her, 'This righteousness you shall do for me: in every place, there where we enter, say about me, He is my brother.'" 14 Then Abimelech took a thousand didrachmas, sheep and calves and male and female slaves and gave them to Abraam and restored his wife Sarra to him. 15 And Abimelech said to Abraam, "Look, my land is before you; settle where it may please you." 16 And to Sarra he said, "Look, I have given your brother a thousand didrachmas; these shall be to you for the honor of your person and to all those with you, and tell the whole truth." 17 Then Abraam prayed to God, and God healed Abimelech and his wife and his female slaves, and they gave birth. 18 For the Lord had, in shutting off, shut off from the outside every womb in the house of Abimelech because of Sarra, Abraam's wife. (NETS)

Much of the narrative data concerning Sarra in Gerar is familiar, not only from the similar scene in Egypt, but also from the MT. While the initial ties between Genesis 20 and 12:10-20 in the LXX are somewhat less marked, with παροικέω representing the only significant lexical link (20:1; 12:10), Abraam's first words here—"She is my sister," 20:2—instantly recall the Egyptian episode. Close parallels with the themes of Egypt, moreover, continue throughout: Sarra never speaks directly, but is taken bodily in a cynical exchange, partly aided by God, that sees the innocent harmed and those responsible enriched. Sarra's role in the central deception, however, is much different in Gerar. Although theirs is hardly an equal partnership, as Sarra remains subordinate to Abraam and absorbs nearly all of the plausible risk in this scheme, Sarra does help convince Abimelech that she is Abraam's sister: "She told me"—the king protests—"'He is my brother'!" (αὐτή μοι εἶπεν Ἀδελφός μού ἐστιν, 20:5). This claim of connivance is implicitly affirmed by God (v. 6). Abraam's explanation that Sarra is actually his non-uterine sister (v. 12), on the other hand, is not credible at all. Sarra has been ἡ γυνὴ Ἀβρά[ά]μ from the start; the false claim is introduced in this episode as being περὶ Σάρρας τῆς γυναικὸς αὐτοῦ (v. 2); and Abraam's first direct speech in the broader narrative (12:11-13), considered alongside subsequent events, established him as a deceiver on this very matter. Sarra's resemblance to Abraam here, then, is not based in a blood relationship, but in her continuing adoption of his callous lack of regard for others.

There are, however, a few interesting developments between the traditions; one of these stems from the plainest textual disparity between the MT and the LXX that pertains to Sarra. Abimelech, in the Hebrew, winds up his short speech to Sarah by merely explicating or reinforcing what he has already said. After speaking of his payment to Abraham as a "covering of eyes" (כסות עינים), he reassures Sarah: "you are justified before everyone" (את כל ונכחת, 20:16). As I indicated in my discussion of the MT, the simple fact that the king addresses Sarah marks a small distinction between the object of Egypt and the junior collaborator of Gerar. But here, in the LXX, Abimelech adds a startling remark to his mention of the money he has paid to Abraam, issuing what reads like a moral rebuke to Sarra: "just tell the truth in every respect!" (καὶ πάντα ἀλήθευσον).[73] This implicit accusation of deception underlines Sarra's active agency in the plot of the episode to this point, while the assumption that she has the power to make ethical decisions presumes moral initiative going forward. However, the king's chiding of Sarra here also recalls not only his own scolding of Abraam (vv. 9-10), but Pharaoh's upbraiding of Abraam, as well (12:18-19). Thus, once again, it seems as if part of the price of Sarra's agency is to play Abraam's role; in a small paradox, then, Sarra's actions sap her character of originality and initiative.

This same address also picks up the minor motif of Sarra's "face." The deceptive connotation of Abraam's description of Sarra as "pretty-faced" (εὐπρόσωπος, 12:11), which gained no traction in Egypt, is most apt here, where, in a similar situation, Sarra actively works to misrepresent her relationship with Abraam. Several relevant themes are raised as Abimelech turns to Sarra and says: "Look—I have given 1000 didrachmas to your 'brother'; this will be for you as a τιμὴν τοῦ προσώπου σου" (20:16; compare v. 14).[74] Under the circumstances, τιμή is a bit ambiguous at first. It is possible to construe this, as Wevers does, as "esteem," as in "honor" or "dignity," especially given the following clause, "and for all those with you" (καὶ πάσαις ταῖς μετὰ σοῦ, presumably referring to female slaves).[75] The payment is thus a restoration of honor for Sarra's "face" in the wake of her irregular relationship with the king. But the only other occurrence of τιμή in Genesis is in 44:2, where it refers to the "price" Joseph's brothers paid for grain (τὴν τιμὴν τοῦ σίτου).[76] Moreover, not only is the general context here one of frank exchange, just as in Egypt, but the referent of the subject pronoun in the clause in question can only be this sum of "1000 didrachmas": this is the "value," then, of Sarra's "face," or "person."[77] Attracting if inanimate before Pharaoh, repelling

---

73. For this καί in imperative clauses, see Smyth §2873; compare the example there, from Plato's *Apology* (25a): καί μοι ἀπόκριναι, "Just answer me!" Its force is disjunctive.

74. Ἰδοὺ δέδωκα χίλια δίδραχμα τῷ ἀδελφῷ σου· ταῦτα ἔσται σοι εἰς τιμὴν τοῦ προσώπου σου.

75. Wevers, *Notes*, 296–7, acknowledges the ambiguity referred to below, but finally favors "esteem" here.

76. Compare, among other examples, Exod. 34:20, or Lev. 27 throughout.

77. Compare Lancelot Charles Lee Brenton, *The Septuagint Version of the Old Testament with an English Translation and with Various Readings and Critical*

to Hagar, Sarra's face represents a commodity here. Once again, Sarra's more prominent role in the plot points to an agency more apparent than real; for all the years that have passed since Egypt, she is still an item rented to rulers by Abraam.

In my analysis of this episode in the MT, I argued that Sarah could not be as thorough a victim in Gerar as she was in Egypt. This is so not only due to the differences between the episodes, though these are significant— the question of Sarah's connivance in Egypt in the MT remains open, while her collaboration in Gerar is explicitly claimed by the king, for instance—but also because Sarah's broader narrative arc makes a precise reprise of her former role less than credible. Sarra's trajectory in the LXX, considered over the same span, traces a more extreme course. In keeping with her passive depiction in the introduction to the narrative, Sarra in Egypt was almost completely inert, her involvement in Abraam's scheme ordered and scripted. However, in the event, she did not demonstrate even a mechanical obedience, but remained silent and free of agency, almost as if she were inanimate. It was difficult, in fact, to posit any credible story-level action for Sarra at all. This alone would make her active role in the seemingly very similar situation of Gerar more pronounced, and Abimelech's rebuke in the LXX only underlines Sarra's participation, pushing these poles in her character even farther apart.

These swings may begin to intimate the kind of contradictions in Sarra's character that emerge in the episode to follow, where her behavior grows increasingly erratic. I do not believe, however, that these apparent inconsistencies strike at the basic coherence of Sarra's character, even when considered alongside the often derivative species of action that seems to be her specialty in the LXX. As a theoretical matter, it seems to me that a mimetic understanding of character can cede an assumption of integrity in personality only as a last resort. Moreover, I recognize on an experiential level that human capacities for vacillation and contradiction are vast. Most of us, I think, maintain a number of traits that are strictly incompatible; and this is not even to consider personalities that are so far from the mean as to be judged abnormal.

A consideration of Sarra's programmatic role in the broader narrative of God's promises to Abraam and his descendants, a narrative element only to be emphasized in the coming scenes, may also provide some insight here. There are several related, recurring factors that combat Sarra's individuation in the LXX. Sarra's early passivity and lack of

---

Notes (1844; repr., London: Samuel Bagster & Sons, 1870): "for the price of thy countenance." NETS, while rendering "honor" in the main text, as quoted above, also includes a note indicating that "price" is possible here. Compare LSJ 1793b–1794a.

agency eventually give way, but only to specially limited varieties of activity and agency, as her initiative is persistently undermined—most often by casting her actions as imitative of Abraam's—and her attempts at self-assertion are met with restriction. To my reading, part of the effect of this consistent counterpressure on Sarra's individuation is to underline firmly the primary perspective from which she is regarded by the narrator, by Abraam, and by God: Sarra is useful to the fulfillment of the divine pledges. As will be seen in the next episode, Sarra's utility forms a common thread that may help to explain the depictions of her seemingly incompatible actions.

Who Will "Rejoice with" Sarra? (Gen. 21:1-14 LXX)

Gen. 21:1 And the Lord visited Sarra as he had said, and the Lord did for Sarra as he had spoken, 2 and when Sarra had conceived, she bore Abraam a son in his old age at the appointed time, as the Lord had spoken to him. 3 And Abraam called the name of his son who was born to him, whom Sarra bore him, Isaak. 4 And Abraam circumcised Isaak on the eighth day, as God had commanded him. 5 Now Abraam was a hundred years of age when his son Isaak was born to him. 6 And Sarra said, "The Lord has made laughter for me, for anyone who hears will congratulate me." 7 And she said, "Who will report to Abraam that Sarra is nursing a child? For I have borne a son in my old age." 8 And the child grew and was weaned, and Abraam made a great banquet on the day his son Isaak was weaned. 9 But when Sarra saw the son of Hagar the Egyptian, who had been born to Abraam, playing with her son Isaak, 10 then she said to Abraam, "Cast out this slave-girl and her son; for the son of this slave-girl shall not inherit together with my son Isaak." 11 Now the matter seemed very hard in the sight of Abraam on account of his son. 12 But God said to Abraam, "Do not let the matter be hard in your sight on account of the child and on account of the slave-girl; whatever Sarra says to you, obey her voice, for in Isaak offspring shall be named for you. 13 And as for the son of the slave-girl, I will make him also into a great nation, because he is your offspring." 14 Then Abraam rose in the morning and took bread loaves and a skin of water and gave them to Hagar and put them on her shoulder, along with the child and sent her away. And when she departed she began wandering about the wilderness over against the well of the oath. (NETS)

At last, Sarra's most enduring trait is reversed completely, as she conceives and bears a son after a divine visitation (21:1-2). The Lord's presence and activity, as well as a reference to the advanced age of either Abraam or Sarra (NETS's rendering supplies the pronoun here), attest to supernatural influence on her pregnancy and birth; but there is no indication here of divine parentage. Sarra's bearing is "to" or "for Abraam" (τῷ Ἀβραάμ, v. 2), and that Isaac is "his son" is underlined repeatedly in the verses that follow. This tracks solidly with Sarra's concern for Abraam's posterity in 16:2. Indeed, Sarra has demonstrated virtually no interest in bearing a child for herself. Her scheme with Hagar was explicitly for Abraam (16:2), while her laughing response in the tent, as clarified by her soliloquy there, reflected skepticism, not delight at the possibility of bearing a child at ninety (18:12).

But this makes Sarra's response to Isaac's birth all the more unexpected. In distinction to the MT, where her comments appear to reflect deep ambivalence, partly rooted in a concern for her appearance before others, Sarra's remarks in 21:6-7 seem prompted by a genuine feeling of happiness, even joy. Their story context is almost completely undetermined, and it is impossible to tell whether Sarra is speaking to herself, perhaps in the presence of a cradled or nursing Isaac, or in a broader social venue. Her first statement, too, might initially seem to be of uncertain force: "the Lord," Sarra says, "made a laugh," or "an occasion of laughter for me" (Γέλωτά μοι ἐποίησεν κύριος, v. 6).[78] The syntax, unlike that of the Hebrew, precludes the idea that Sarra has herself been made into a "joke" here. But γέλως, as a prompt for laughter, is naturally not always positive; compare Jer. 20:7 or Job 17:6, where it evokes an object of scorn and ridicule. However, Sarra's following explanation excludes such an understanding entirely. The Lord has made laughter for her, she clarifies, "because anyone who hears will rejoice with me," or "congratulate me" (ὃς γὰρ ἂν ἀκούσῃ, συγχαρεῖταί μοι, Gen. 21:6).[79] The employment of σύν in composition, alongside the first-person pronoun, demands Sarra's own emotional involvement here; that this relative clause is inferentially bound to Sarra's first statement removes any lingering ambiguity. The Lord's visitation, her conception and birth of Isaac: all this is a "cause of [happy] laughter" that Sarra expects to share with others. In this context, the tone of Sarra's next rumination can hardly be other than one of wonder and quiet pride: "Who would have expected to tell Abraam, 'Sarra is nursing a child'? Because I bore a son in my old age!" (v. 7).[80]

The scene that follows on these joyful moments, however, raises a question of its own: who, precisely, "will rejoice with" Sarra? At first, the context seems wholly appropriate to this kind of shared emotion, as Abraam gives a "big reception" or "great banquet" (δοχὴν μεγάλην) on

---

78. LSJ 342b; compare GELS 126b, 570a.
79. LSJ 1668a; GELS 644a.
80. Τίς ἀναγγελεῖ τῷ Ἀβραὰμ ὅτι θηλάζει παιδίον Σάρρα; ὅτι ἔτεκον υἱὸν ἐν τῷ γήρει μου.

the occasion of Isaac's weaning-day (21:8). But Sarra herself puts an end to the only happiness that is implied here: "when Sarra saw the son of Hagar the Egyptian, who was born to Abraam, playing with Isaac her son, she said to Abraam, 'Cast out this slave and her son; because the son of this slave shall not inherit with my son Isaac'" (vv. 9-10).⁸¹ As in the MT, Ishmael's offense is ill-defined; παίζω can mean "to play," whether a game or an instrument, "to dance," or "to jest" in action or word.⁸² The term's possible sexual connotations are perhaps stronger here in the Greek, as the relevant clause, with its clarifying prepositional phrase added to the Hebrew's laconic מצחק, is precisely equivalent to the description of Isaac "toying with Rebekah his wife" in 26:8—conduct that leads Abimelech to deduce that the two are sexually involved.⁸³ Moreover, such connotations for παίζω are native to Greek.⁸⁴ However, this is still not the simplest reading of this scene here: the root meaning of παίζω—derived from παῖς, as is even clearer in its Doric orthography, παίσδω—is simply "to play as a child does," and Sarra makes no reference to sexual matters in her declaration about these two youngsters. Rather, the key element is that Ishmael is playing *with* Isaac; and the denotation of μετά, which is "participation" and "community of action," is what Sarra cannot abide.⁸⁵ Ishmael "shall not inherit...with" Isaac (οὐ...κληρονομήσει...μετά), a decree prompted by the sight of him "playing with" Isaac (παίζοντα μετά). The LXX's addition of "with Isaac her son" in 21:9, then, as Wevers contends, adroitly makes the best of a bad job in communicating the force of the untranslatable pun on Isaac's name contained in מצחק, and is sensibly informed by the context of v. 10.⁸⁶ In fact, I might go further than Wevers and suggest that it is possible to read παίζοντα as a truly inspired choice here: as the MT features Ishmael מצחק, or "Isaac-ing," perhaps the LXX sees Ishmael "kidding" around, "acting the child"—and as Sarra,

---

81. ἰδοῦσα δὲ Σάρρα τὸν υἱὸν Ἁγὰρ τῆς Αἰγυπτίας, ὃς ἐγένετο τῷ Ἀβραάμ, παίζοντα μετὰ Ἰσαὰκ τοῦ υἱοῦ αὐτῆς, καὶ εἶπεν τῷ Ἀβραάμ "Ἔκβαλε τὴν παιδίσκην ταύτην καὶ τὸν υἱὸν αὐτῆς· οὐ γὰρ κληρονομήσει ὁ υἱὸς τῆς παιδίσκης ταύτης μετὰ τοῦ υἱοῦ μου Ἰσαάκ.

82. LSJ 1288b.

83. In 26:8, Isaac is spotted παίζοντα μετὰ Ῥεβέκκας τῆς γυναικὸς αὐτοῦ; here, in 21:9, Ishmael is seen παίζοντα μετὰ Ἰσαὰκ τοῦ υἱοῦ αὐτῆς. These two verses contain the only instances of παίζω in LXX Genesis.

84. See παιξοῦνται πρὸς ἀλλήλους near the end of Xenophon's *Symposium* (9.2), cited in LSJ 1288b.

85. See Smyth §1691.

86. See Wevers, *Notes*, 302: the plus of μετὰ Ἰσαὰκ τοῦ υἱοῦ αὐτῆς is "not textual in origin but rather due to the translator's attempt not only to translate מצחק but also to interpret the point of the Hebrew word play."

supported by God, makes clear, there can be only one child to inherit. In any event, the implication of togetherness as Ishmael "kids with Isaac" only increases the sad irony of this scene in the broader episode, which pictures Sarra both anticipating communal rejoicing and advocating the fracture of her household.

Sarra, with her expression of joy at the conception and birth of Isaac, has finally generated true surprise. Her reaction is difficult to anticipate on the evidence of her actions in Genesis 16, seems unusual given her response in Genesis 18, and is flatly strange in the wake of her participation in the ruse of Gerar—which occurs, after all, sometime not long after Sarra overhears the prediction of the event that will bring her such happiness. Moreover, her emotional outcry here is an act that has not been prospectively robbed of its force by association with a previously related idea or action of Abraam's, as was the case with her provision of Hagar, her laugh, and her collaboration in the duping of Abimelech. But I confess that this "surprise" strikes me as rather unsatisfying in its conventionality—Sarra, so often derivative, at last demonstrates her originality by hewing closely to what seems to be a rather stereotyped and predictable script of the overjoyed new mother. This may be a mere value judgment on my part; but it is hard for me to see how her reaction here can be a significant step toward real individuation. In fact, the narrator's emphases here seem to reveal more about Sarra's role as an instrument than they illuminate her as a character. Sarra's production of the heir to the promises doesn't satisfy any deeply held desire of her own, if her narrative data to this point is any guide; rather, it completes a crucial link in the broader divine plan. Surely the woman who scoffs at her predicted pregnancy and goes on to collaborate in her own sale to Abimelech experiences a rather complex mix of emotions, both at once and over time, as radical developments in her postmenopausal body culminate in her delivery of a son at ninety. That the narrator relates only Sarra's simple joy at these events casts her as a cipher for a narratorial perspective that subordinates her completely to the fulfillment of God's promises to Abraam, Isaac, and their descendants. In this way, Sarra's image is washed out even as her oldest trait is transformed.

Similar considerations can help to explain Sarra's urging of the banishment of Hagar and Ishmael in the wake of her anticipated shared joy over Isaac, which at first seems not so much surprising as flatly contradictory, even incoherent. The hardening arc of her character in the MT, which was well expressed in her ambivalence, rooted in self-regard, over Isaac, and which culminated in the pursuit of her and her son's interests at Hagar and Ishmael's dismissal, is replaced here with a less credible wavering between joy and cold calculation. No one "will rejoice with" Sarra here; rather, at the same event's ostensible celebration, Abraam will find her order "cruel" (σκληρόν), and Hagar and Ishmael will meet harsh exile the following morning (21:11, 14). And while Sarra's demand may appear to show initiative, however callous, once again this impression is somewhat weakened—here by a recollection of whose interests are truly being served. Sarra is, first, a tool in the resolution of the divine pledges to the men in her family, and with this final act her utility, at least as a sentient actor, is at an end. The responsible speculation of a sympathetic reader might posit motives of jealousy here, or unresolved resentment, or any compound of a range of familiar human feelings. But the narrator's interests are far too narrow to encompass any complexity of emotion in Sarra; instead, what the narrator highlights is Sarra's function in the final establishment of the divinely ordained succession from Abraam to Isaac (vv. 10-12). In the end, in keeping with restrictive responses to her volition elsewhere, Sarra's advocating of Hagar and Ishmael's disappearance ironically seals her own permanent departure from the discourse as a living person. Now the narrator sends Sarra away, not into a tent but apparently to the "city of Arboch" (πόλει Ἀρβόκ), from which she will emerge only as a corpse (23:2).

The Death of Sarra (Gen. 23:1-20 LXX)

Little enough distinguishes the accounts of Sarra's death in the LXX and the MT. So thorough is her effacement from the intervening discourse that almost nothing can be said about the thirty-plus years that pass in the story between the banishment of Hagar and Ishmael and Abraam's now-familiar use of Sarra's body as a bargaining chip for gain in Genesis 23. Sarra remains hidden away, in the LXX, "in the hollow" (ἐν τῷ κοιλώματι, v. 2), a note that evokes one of the Greek words for "womb" (κοιλία) and recalls Sarra's other concealments or captivities, whether in the house of Pharaoh, in the "enclosure" of her fertility by the Lord, or in Abraam's tent. Abraam may be living elsewhere at the time of Sarra's death, as he must "come" (ἔρχομαι) to perform the rites of mourning; his emotional investment in these observances is indeterminate (v. 2).

Sarra's inertia and passivity, so marked in the beginning of the LXX narrative, is perfected here: once virtually inanimate and objectified, she is now a pure object, Abraam's corpse (τοῦ νεκροῦ αὐτοῦ, 23:3; and compare throughout, vv. 4, 6, 8, 11, 13, and 15). Though she is finally referred to as a human being here, this is only to note that she remains Abraam's woman, as in the very beginning (τὴν γυναῖκα αὐτοῦ, v. 19); and her burial is one last device in the accomplishment of God's pledges to Abraam. Sarra may be entombed in this cave, but it is "for Abraam as a possession" (τῷ Ἀβραὰμ εἰς κτῆσιν, vv. 18, 20).

Conclusion: Sarra in the LXX

In my treatment of Sarah in the MT, I argued that she is complex but coherent, invoking the metaphor of an arc to speak of her character's progress through the narrative. This relative stability, even in development, allowed me to frame my summary discussion largely in terms of Sarah's relationships. In the LXX, however, Sarra's image, while still complex, is drawn with strokes that at times seem erratic, and her trajectory describes a rather more jerky, halting line. Without losing focus on the relational aspects of her characterization, therefore, it seems better here to take a mostly linear view of Sarra's construction.

In the scenes that lead up to her family's descent into Egypt (11:26–12:9), Sarra in the LXX is almost wholly passive and defined in the negative. Her childlessness is described in terms that suggest an enduring condition, which both adds to the general impression of Sarra's inertia and increases the impact of this trait's eventual reversal. Sarra's powerlessness and lack of connections, familiar from the MT, combine with her slightly increased passivity and the meaninglessness of her name to form a character who appears somewhat muted in comparison. While nearly every character indicator here is relational, this, too, especially considered retrospectively, begins to look like just another aspect of this muting, as Sarra will go on to be repeatedly and derivatively defined in Abraam's image. When brought into Egypt (12:10-20), Sarra continues, inert, on a course predicted in part by her earlier trajectory. She needs no persuasion here; her role is ordered and scripted. But she displays no hint of agency, not even in mouthing the words Abraam forms for her, and remains completely passive, even inanimate: a medium of exchange, no more.

When Sarra, after the ascent from Egypt, disappears from the discourse for some time (13:2–15:21), she hovers, undeveloping in the background, for her passive portrayal to this point discourages much speculation as to her story activity. The introduction of Masek, Abraam's slave and, he supposes, mother of his heir (15:2), prospectively robs Sarra of some initiative in her coming offer of Hagar. This reinforces Sarra's lack of individuation and marks an occasion where Sarra's actions are undermined—echoed, as it were, before they can occur. Although Sarra does demonstrate a sudden break from the inertia that has held her fast up to this point, other elements work to tame the novelty of what she does in 16:1-6. A curious motif of gender ambiguities in the characters' speech blurs distinctions between Sarra and Abraam, helping to suggest subtle shifts in their balance of power but also smudging the edges of Sarra's character. This lack of clarity is only underscored by the derivative nature of Sarra's "taking" and disposal of a subordinate's sexuality (v. 3), which recalls her own treatment in Egypt; the stated aim of Sarra's scheme, moreover, in her first direct speech in the narrative (v. 2), is not her benefit, but Abraam's—precisely recalling his first discourse-level communication in 12:11-13. If Sarra does show glimpses of true agency here, its end is the exercise of cruelty, abetted by the deity who will employ and then discard Sarra as an instrument in the divine plan. The first clear intimations of this follow shortly in the discourse, as God symbolizes the predicted reversal of Sarra's enduring infertility by changing her name—just slightly, and without intrinsic meaning in the Greek—and specifying her role in the promises that have been given repeatedly to Abraam since Haran (17:15-21). But Sarra herself does not merit an audience here, and it is her son and his descendants who will truly enjoy the fruits of God's pledges. Sarra is a vital conduit, but only that; just as in Egypt, she is an object used toward an end.

In the following episode of Abraam's entertainment of the strangers (18:1-15), elements emerge that appear almost calculated to combat Sarra's volition. With Hagar, Sarra demonstrated some developing agency and relatively increased power; here, she may first show defiance in inaction, by refusing to prepare the bread (vv. 6, 8), but remains throughout shrouded from view, hidden in Abraam's tent. When she overhears the visitor's prediction, her laugh at first startles—but just as soon recalls the identical, earlier response of Abraam (v. 12; 17:17). When laid alongside developments such as the mention of Masek, this kind of echoing may start even to suggest a narratorial strategy that aims to preempt Sarra's initiative. Other aspects of the narrative contribute to this feeling of restriction, or paling of Sarra's character. Considered across the tradition, Sarra's logical reply in 18:12 drains her of some vitality. Moreover, as Sarra's words are twisted and she is spoken of in the third person, she attempts to assert herself with a plain lie (vv. 13, 15). This, however, earns her not only a divine rebuke, but the narrator's possibly untrustworthy evaluation of her motivation (v. 15).

A number of these themes continue in Gerar, where Sarra exercises agency—but only, in a fulfillment of the deceptive connotations of Abraam's earlier description of her as "pretty-faced," to help Abraam restage his Egyptian scheme (20:1-18). Here she receives another rebuke, this time from Abimelech, who urges her to tell the truth (v. 16). Once again, however, this merely casts Sarra in the mold of Abraam, whose scolding by rulers is by now a familiar motif. Sarra's active collaboration here, moreover, only highlights her character's dramatic shift away from the inert object that featured in the similar situation of Egypt. These erratic swings in activity, especially when set alongside the derivative nature of much of her behavior, may start to trouble a reader seeking a coherent image of Sarra's character. Here as elsewhere, however, contradiction or instability in her characterization might be, at least in part, an artifact of the narrator's basic interest in Sarra, which begins and ends in her utility to the divine promises.

The prominence of this theme of instrumentality endures in Sarra's final scenes as a living actor, where her persistent childlessness is reversed (21:1-10). As Sarra had never explicitly betrayed interest in a child of her own, her delight at Isaac's birth (vv. 6-7) is a true surprise, if a somewhat frustratingly conventional response, and Sarra's course seems increasingly erratic and difficult to understand as the episode continues. In the wake of her remark about "rejoicing with" others over Isaac, Sarra urges the "cruel" and final banishment of Hagar and Ishmael at a celebration—of Isaac (vv. 6, 8-14). However, the depictions of her puzzling joy and sudden vindictiveness are both at least partly explained by Sarra's programmatic role in the narrator's broader project: her seeming contradictions resolve in their contribution to the achievement of the purposes of the deity, as the provision of emotional motive nuance to Sarra's actions fails to engage the narrator's curiosity. As in Genesis 16 and 20, what agency Sarra exercises here is in the interest of the injury of others; and in what reads like a last underlining of the theme of restriction on Sarra's volition, and a penultimate confirmation of her identity as a narrative tool, this act precipitates her own disappearance—not that of Hagar and Ishmael—from the discourse. Hidden away in a "hollow," Sarra will reappear only as a corpse, representing the ideal of her passive, inert characterization in the opening of the narrative: as a true object at last, her body becomes a perfect pawn in the realization of part of Abraam and God's plans (23:1-20).

The elements I have drawn out in this summary do not exhaust the figure of Sarra in the LXX. Aspects of her characterization that were prominent in the MT, such as the theme of gain and loss, or possession and lack, are by no means absent here. But even this is a little weaker, robbed of elements such as the subtle play with her regal name, or her ostensible hope to be "built up" out of Hagar, or her ambiguous response to giving birth at last. Other familiar themes are also less prominent.

Sarra's character doesn't precisely describe a hardening arc here, but moves erratically, especially near the end, from collaboration in the sale of her body, to frank joy at Isaac's birth, to urging the callous ejection of Hagar and Ishmael. Sarra's sensitivity to her image in the eyes of others, to take another example, simply never achieves the traction that this motif obtains in the MT. A partial analogue might be sought in the notes about Sarra's "face" in the LXX, but this element primarily illuminates her external features and offers limited penetration into questions of motive.

What strikes me as most indelible about Sarra's image in the LXX, however, is this: when she is not passive or mute, a virtual or actual object, what she does is so frequently and unambiguously derivative of Abraam's actions that her individuation suffers. This is not an entirely new theme, and her resemblance to her husband is a significant facet of her characterization in both the Apocryphon and the *Antiquities*, too, though mostly in novel ways. But here, when notes such as the mention of Masek or Abimelech's rebuke of Sarra accumulate on top of familiar elements such as Sarra's laugh, or her treatment of Hagar, the effect is not merely additive but geometric. Moreover, when these derivative echoes are laid alongside Sarra's erratic swings in activity in the LXX, her character's definition can appear further blurred.

But I do not think that Sarra ends in incoherence; nor do I believe that her complexity makes her "psychotic," as Adele Berlin memorably claims of another erratic character, Saul.[87] Rather, Sarra in the LXX is dialed back from the beginning, prospectively washed out, subtly but insistently, by the narrator. Mimicry on the story level does not account for most of Sarra's derivative activity. Instead, her initiative is often stolen before she can exercise it, and her attempts at agency are met with restriction. The cumulative effect of the notes of passivity and narrowly limited subjectivity that work to compress Sarra's individuation is to emphasize her utility to the narrator's overriding interest in the fulfillment of the divine promises to Abraam. This is proven in the breach when Sarra finally and genuinely surprises, for her joy at Isaac's birth only sanctions the deity's plan by delight at its accomplishment. It seems unfair, given her struggles to individuate herself, that I should find Sarra here to be slightly less sympathetic than her incarnation in the MT; but sympathy requires knowledge and understanding, and the small but telling changes to Sarra in the LXX seem almost calculated to prevent the acquisition of these.

87. Berlin, *Poetics*, 40.

I noted earlier that Sarra's disappearance from the discourse after the banishing of Hagar and Ishmael makes it almost impossible to speculate about the final thirty-plus years of her life. But a final little surprise waits in 24:67, where Isaac is said to have "entered his mother's house," there to be "comforted"—apparently by his love for Rebekah, whom he takes as a wife—"about Sarra his mother."[88] This occurs a few years after Sarra's death, as Isaac is now forty (25:20). Sarra's relationship "with Isaac her son" endures, then, in some fashion, over the decades of story time in which Sarra is lost to view. Just why Isaac needs to be comforted is not immediately clear. While the MT's אחרי אמו is terse, its most likely meaning seems to be "after his mother['s death]," which implies grief; περὶ Σάρρας τῆς μητρὸς αὐτοῦ, however, is at once plainer and even less specific.[89] It is just possible, recalling Sarra's history of anger and cruelty, to wonder whether Isaac's new, loving relationship helps to heal scars from his mother's abuse. But there is no indication that Sarra's joy at Isaac's birth was feigned, even if this single feeling fails to encompass the full range of Sarra's likely emotional response, and the discourse contains no hint that Isaac had anything to fear from his mother—something that cannot be said about Abraam after Genesis 22. Moreover, the employment of παρακαλέω in 37:35 and, perhaps to a lesser degree, 38:12, suggests a context of bereavement here. Isaac, then, obtains comfort for his grief at the loss of his mother. Perhaps here, finally, there is a little something more "about Sarra" that is not derivative, not an echo from elsewhere. For while Isaac may fulfill his filial duty by entombing Abraam after his death (25:7-10), he betrays no sign of grief there; but in Isaac's long mourning of Sarra's passing, there is an implication of love.

---

88. εἰσῆλθεν δὲ Ἰσαὰκ εἰς τὸν οἶκον τῆς μητρὸς αὐτοῦ καὶ ἔλαβεν τὴν Ῥεβέκκαν, καὶ ἐγένετο αὐτοῦ γυνή, καὶ ἠγάπησεν αὐτήν· καὶ παρεκλήθη Ἰσαὰκ περὶ Σάρρας τῆς μητρὸς αὐτοῦ.

89. Compare Wevers, *Notes*, 376.

Chapter 4

Sarai in the Genesis Apocryphon

Introduction

Sarai (שרי) in the Genesis Apocryphon traces an unusual, mercurial trajectory. After a slow start, Sarai's depiction in my reading grows rapidly in definition and complexity, revealing an inquisitive, clever, vocal, and emotional woman whom Abram seems to value as a companion. Indeed, as Abram relates it—for he is not only a character in this tale, but also its narrator—the two are similar in a number of ways. Sarai demonstrates agency and initiative after Abram describes an unsettling, seemingly predictive dream, and subsequently somehow so impresses visiting Egyptian nobles that they return to court and regale Pharaoh with a lengthy poem devoted to her striking beauty, profound wisdom, and impressive manual skill. Inflamed, the king apparently abducts Sarai and attempts to kill Abram, who is saved by Sarai's opportune lie—"he is my brother"—but is nonetheless distraught at his loss. But here, just when Sarai's image has gathered fine color and detail, and just as her centrality to the plot is clearest, she is reduced abruptly and permanently to the status of a disputed object. Similarities and apparent mutuality notwithstanding, it becomes plain that Abram values only Sarai's sexual exclusivity; her liberty is of no concern by comparison. Moreover, Sarai's objectification—by Abram, Pharaoh, and God—coincides precisely with the disappearance of her subjectivity. After her timely words save Abram's life, Sarai is virtually drained of humanity, and her role from that point onward could as easily be played by a lovely treasure chest, locked up tight.

At least in the case of Sarai, then, Sidnie White Crawford's claim that the Apocryphon features "strong female characters," though common enough among scholars, needs significant qualification.[1] Sarai does seem

---

1. Sidnie White Crawford, "Genesis in the Dead Sea Scrolls," in Evans, Lohr, and Petersen, eds., *The Book of Genesis*, 364; compare Crawford, *Rewriting Scripture*,

to display genuine definition and an engaging roundness until she vanishes into Pharaoh's house; but then her image is so empty that story-level speculation seems positively idle. Her varied traits prove to have disappointingly little endurance, and her ultimate worth to the narrative, as to Abram, is almost entirely mechanical. Moreover, Sarai in the Apocryphon is curiously well-illuminated, yet hard to make out with full confidence, for she is only and ever filtered through Abram. This effacement is different in kind than that which confronts the reader of Sarra in the Septuagint, but it is no less serious: instead of an outside party, however prejudicial, describing all of the characters, here one, Abram, holds nearly complete power over his depictions of himself and Sarai. Relationality, always a vital component of characterization, becomes the point of departure for almost every observation about Sarai here.

Practical Preliminaries

I note a few preliminaries here, touching on my approach, the text and its challenges, its division into episodes, and the English translation that I have included as an aid to the reader. As before, my reading relies on the poetics of character and characterization developed in Chapter 1, and seeks to train a light on Sarai in her connections to a variety of other narrative elements. Central among these is the figure of Abram, whose role as narrator, unique among the works considered in this study, means that his perspective must be constantly engaged: everything is "according to Abram," and his reliability needs frequent scrutiny. I do not adopt the posture of a first-time reader, but draw observations from across the narrative as needed to illuminate my discussion. While there may be minor tension, some perhaps unconscious, between my knowledge of Genesis and the Apocryphon's recognizably analogous narrative components, this does not raise the kind of theoretical obstacles that complicated my analysis of the Septuagint. Instead, I try in the main "to read the Apocryphon on its own," as Moshe Bernstein has urged, in my pursuit of Sarai's image here.[2]

---

118. Nickelsburg, "Patriarchs Who Worry," 192, has been influential in this regard. Compare Daniel K. Falk, *The Parabiblical Texts: Strategies for Extending the Scriptures in the Dead Sea Scrolls*, LSTS 63, Companion to the Qumran Scrolls 8 (London: T&T Clark, 2007), 80, 93–4.

2. See Bernstein, "Unity," 133–4. Bernstein argues that this kind of reading better approximates the perspective of the narrative's ancient reader or auditor. However, his program is also congruent, it seems to me, with narrative-critical priorities.

There have been a number of editions of the Genesis Apocryphon since Naḥman Avigad and Yigael Yadin issued theirs in 1956; I primarily employ that of Daniel Machiela, though I have taken others into account, especially those of Joseph Fitzmyer and Klaus Beyer.[3] The Apocryphon poses no text-critical difficulties arising from divergent manuscript traditions, as the remains from Qumran's Cave 1 represent the only certain copy of this Aramaic composition.[4] However, perplexities resulting from the scroll's advanced state of deterioration more than make up for this. Although the columns relevant to Sarai (19–20) are coincidentally found among those best preserved, and successive editions have pushed what remains here very close to what Machiela calls a "final form" of the text, this is still badly damaged in places.[5] The poor condition of the manuscript adds a special layer of ambiguity: in addition to the conceptual gaps that are intrinsic to any narrative, the Apocryphon features material gaps, holes, wrinkles, disappearing ink, and entire sections dissolved into dust, which leads to scores of uncertainties. I openly admit, then, the contingency of my readings.

In this chapter I closely examine the Apocryphon from the beginnings of the remaining text in column 19 through the large *vacat* in 21.4, which finds Abram, Lot, and (presumably) Sarai back home in Bethel after a number of years spent at various points south, most notably Egypt. Often features of the manuscript provide fitting demarcations for episodes

---

3. It makes good sense to adopt the text of Daniel A. Machiela, *The Dead Sea Genesis Apocryphon: A New Text and Translation with Introduction and Special Treatment of Columns 13–17*, STDJ 79 (Leiden: Brill, 2009)—hereafter *DSGA*—as a working standard, as his textual notes function as a virtual apparatus of earlier readings. See also Naḥman Avigad and Yigael Yadin, *A Genesis Apocryphon: A Scroll from the Wilderness of Judaea* (Jerusalem: Magnes Press, 1956); Joseph A. Fitzmyer, *The Genesis Apocryphon of Qumran Cave 1 (1Q20): A Commentary*, 3rd ed. (Rome: Pontifical Biblical Institute, 2004)—hereafter *GA*; Klaus Beyer, *Die aramäischen Texte vom Toten Meer samt den Inschriften aus Palästina, dem Testament Levis aus der Kairoer Genisa, der Fastenrolle und den alten talmudischen Zitaten* (Göttingen: Vandenhoeck & Ruprecht, 1984)—hereafter *ATTM*, and comprising two additional volumes, cited below, issued in 1994 and 2004. See Machiela, *DSGA*, 21–6, for a history of the major editions.

4. See, however, Daniel A. Machiela, "The Aramaic Dead Sea Scrolls: Coherence and Context in the Library of Qumran," in *The Dead Sea Scrolls at Qumran and the Concept of a Library*, ed. Sidnie White Crawford and Cecilia Wassen, STDJ 116 (Leiden: Brill, 2016), 247, who suggests that 3Q14 frg. 8 may represent the remains of another copy. All there is to go on, though, are the words די סדום, and this orthography differs from that of 1Q20 (compare 21.33 and 22.18).

5. Machiela, *DSGA*, 26.

and scenes, though I divide the text otherwise when scenic, thematic, or temporal shifts justify this.⁶ I also unapologetically devote much more space to discussion of those parts of the narrative that illuminate Sarai most directly, namely 19.14-23 (Abram's dream and its immediate aftermath), 20.2-8 (the courtiers' praise of Sarai), and the lacunose and fragmentary scene in 19.23-31 (the courtiers' visit) that lies between these key episodes. Sarai's final exercise of subjectivity is her saving lie to Pharaoh in 20.9-10; after this, her reduction to an object is startlingly abrupt.

I provide an English translation at the head of each section of text under examination as an aid to the reader. Since critical texts vary in their particulars, my choice of Machiela's Aramaic transcription as a primary text means that it is sensible to use Machiela's English rendering here. Translations in the body of the discussion are mine, unless otherwise noted.

A Fragmentary Beginning (GenAp 19.7-10)

> GenAp 19.7 [ ]... ...I called there on the na[me of G]o[d], and I said, "You are 8 God... ...and King of Etern[i]ty." [And] he spoke with me in the night "...and take strength (?) to wander; up to now you have not reached the holy mountain." So I set out 9 to [g]o there. I was going to the south of Moreh..., I went until I reached Hebron—now I b[u]ilt Hebron for that region—and I lived 10 [the]re for [two] years.   *vacat* (Machiela, *DSGA*, 69–70)⁷

What remains of the narrative featuring Sarai in the Genesis Apocryphon stutters to life here, near the top of the relatively well-preserved column 19. The text as it stands begins *in medias res*, with an as-yet undefined

---

6. The most important instances are the following. I take 19.14-23 as one episode, despite the *vacat* in 19.17, due to chronological and thematic continuities; moreover, the five-year gap noted in 19.23 justifies treating the remainder of the column separately, although no *vacat* appears until line 31, at which point the text is almost completely destroyed. Further, I treat the poem in 20.2-8 as a self-evident unity, though there is no *vacat* until line 11. In addition, the relation of Abram's prayer (20.12-16) seems sensibly divided from his report of the prayer's aftermath, which covers a span of two years (20.16-21), though no manuscript feature suggests this. Finally, while there is a *vacat* at the beginning of 20.33, for my purposes there is little reason to devote a separate discussion to Abram's return to the land, as Sarai has, by this time, disappeared from the discourse for good.

7. I have not sought to render Machiela's varied spacing precisely in this or following block quotations.

narrator relating his or her own past actions and speech in an unspecified location. Later internal clues show, however, that the narrator is Abram himself—he repeatedly self-identifies as אנה אברם, "I, Abram" (19.14; twice in 20.10-11; 20.33; and 21.15)—and that the scene of his invocation of God's name is likely Bethel, to which he returns in 21.1. The beginning of Abram's account is unfortunately lost, likely somewhere within the almost completely illegible column 18. However, extant portions of these initial fragments coincidentally reveal *inclusios* with the close of Abram, Sarai, and Lot's time in Egypt, related in 20.33–21.4. Here, as there, Abram speaks of his "building" (בני) activities (19.9; compare 21.1); moreover, his mention of his calling upon the divine name neatly ties the two scenes together (וקרית תמן בשׁ[ם], 19.7; וקרית תמן בשם, 21.2).[8]

Little enough about Sarai—whose existence is not indisputably indicated until 19.17—can be deduced from these few broken lines.[9] There are, however, a couple of elements worth noting here. The first is the profundity of the filter through which the reader must infer the story: the entire discourse proceeds from the mouth—or even, perhaps, the pen, as it seems to be suggested in 19.25 that he can read and write—of the character of Abram himself. He is speaking from the very beginning of the relevant textual remains, both in his narration and in his own self-reported actions, calling (קרי) on the divine name and speaking (אמר) to God (19.7). This raises the issue, to be discussed at various points later, of the impact of Abram's perspective on his narration of the events in which he participates.

The second notable element—which cannot be entirely untangled from the first—is that Abram is here reputedly the beneficiary of direct divine revelation "in the night" (בליליא, 19.8).[10] This not only

---

8. Machiela, *DSGA*, 26, employs the diacritical conventions of the DJD series: dots indicate "relatively sure" reconstructions, while circlets mark "tentative" readings often best regarded as "educated guesses."

9. Beyer, *ATTM*, 171, transcribed a reference to Sarai in 19.7, a reading that gained little traction. While Beyer allowed the lines to stand in 1994's *Ergänzungsband*, by the issue of Klaus Beyer, *Die aramäischen Texte vom Toten Meer samt den Inschriften aus Palästina, dem Testament Levis aus der Kairoer Genisa, der Fastenrolle und den alten talmudischen Zitaten*, Band 2 (Göttingen: Vandenhoeck & Ruprecht, 2004), 101, he had revised Sarai out of his text.

10. Compare Daniel A. Machiela, "Genesis Revealed: The Apocalyptic Apocryphon from Qumran Cave 1," in *Qumran Cave 1 Revisited: Texts from Cave 1 Sixty Years after Their Discovery*, ed. Daniel K. Falk et al., STDJ 91 (Leiden: Brill, 2010), 217. This claim of divine revelation only holds if Machiela's transcription is correct; there is much debate over the best reading of 19.8.

implies that Abram enjoys God's special favor, an impression that Abram's narration will reinforce throughout his tale, but also helps to suggest a divine source for Abram's subsequent dream, which likewise comes בלילה (19.14, 17; compare 21.8, where Abram claims another night vision from God). Thus Abram's dream may be cast as a kind of divine warrant for his later suggestion that Sarai claim: "He is my brother" (אחי הוא, 19.20); indeed, most criticism of the Apocryphon assumes that the dream is a communication from God.[11] As my reading will show, however, the dream's message is curiously ambiguous and incomplete.

Famine and Entry into Egypt (GenAp 19.10-13)

> GenAp 19.10 *vacat* Now there was a famine in all of this land, but I heard that there wa[s] w[h]eat in Egypt. So I set out 11 to go…[ ]to the land that is in Egypt…[ ]…and there was [ ]I[reached] the Karmon River, one of 12 the heads of the River, [I] sai[d] "Enter (?) [ ]…[until] now we have been within our land." So I crossed over the seven heads of this river, which 13 af[terwards en]ters [int]o the Great Sea [o]f Salt. [After this I said], "Now we have left our land and entered the land of the sons of Ham, the land of Egypt." (Machiela, *DSGA*, 70)

Abram's reference to the "hunger" (כפנא) that arises "in this land" (בארעא דא), prompting his journey south, anticipates his eventual return "to this land"—this time, however, "in prosperity"—after some years in Egypt (לארעא דא בשלם, 21.4). The demonstrative, used with ארע in Abram's direct narration only in these two places (19.10 and 21.4), helps to emphasize the foreignness of "the land of the sons of Ham" (19.13).[12] The phrase also raises an interesting, if largely unanswerable, question about Abram's conception of his narratee: who is listening to or reading this tale, in Abram's perception? In any event—as Abram relates it—the rumor of abundance in Egypt, probably of some kind of grain crop, provides the proximate cause of Abram's departure and foreshadows his acquisition of wealth there. These elements also provide provocative intertextual links with the Joseph and Jacob cycle, as Bernstein and Michael Segal have noted: a report of grain prompts the descent to Egypt of the family of the patriarch, which will endure oppression but, with the

---

11. See, for instance, Falk, *Parabiblical Texts*, 80, 83, who also speaks of a "divine warrant," and Crawford, *Rewriting Scripture*, 118.

12. The instances in 21.10 and 12 are in the reported speech of God to Abram.

help of God, best its oppressors and emerge the richer for the ordeal (Gen. 42:1-2; Exod. 12:35-36).[13]

Questions of Abram's addressee(s) also arise in his two brief accounts of his direct speech in this episode; here, a first possible hint of the existence of Sarai in the narrative emerges. In 19.12 Machiela reads [אמ]רת, followed eventually by עד] כען אנחנא בגו אׄרׄעׄנׄאׄ], which might be rendered "I said, '…up till now we have been in the midst of our land.'" The plural pronouns offer a mild surprise, as nothing in Abram's first-person singular narration to this point has implied the presence of human traveling companions. Shortly thereafter in the discourse, moreover, the impression of plurality is reinforced, as Abram relates that he said: "Look—now we have gone out of our land and we have entered… Egypt" (מצרין…ועלנא ארענא הלכנא כען הׄא, 19.13). These brief explanatory speeches, whether their motive be admonition or simple courtesy, seem to imply a certain mutuality, and point to some level of respect for Abram's interlocutor(s). That Sarai alone is in view here may not be as certain as Beyer, who supplies "[…Und ich sagte zu Sarai:]" before both statements, assumes; it is possible that Lot, who appears suddenly in the discourse in 20.11, is also part of Abram's audience.[14] But Sarai's active presence, and importance to the plot, are established the very night of Abram's second utterance—which, with its reference to the "sons of Ham" (בני חם, 19.13), is thematically linked to Abram's dream (19.14-21), and to the later, central complication of Sarai's abduction—making her presence among Abram's listeners here highly probable. This provisional thread of mutuality between Sarai and Abram, a novelty in the tradition, will be drawn out as the narrative proceeds, but only to snap conclusively when Abram reveals what he truly values in Sarai: her sexual exclusivity.

Abram's Dream (GenAp 19.14-23)

GenAp 19.14 *vacat* Now I, Abram, dreamt a dream in the night of my entry into Egypt. I saw in my dream that there was a single cedar and a

---

13. Moshe J. Bernstein, "Re-Arrangement, Anticipation, and Harmonization as Exegetical Features in the Genesis Apocryphon," *DSD* 3 (1996): 48; Michael Segal, "The Literary Relationship between the Genesis Apocryphon and Jubilees: The Chronology of Abram and Sarai's Descent to Egypt," *AS* 8 (2010): 76–9; compare Zakovitch and Shinan, *Abram and Sarai in Egypt*, 7, who note that parallels between Gen. 12 and the exodus story are already present in the biblical materials (139–40).

14. Beyer, *ATTM*, 172; these restored lines stand in his two later volumes. Compare Machiela, "Genesis Revealed," 220.

single date 15 palm, having sprout[ed] together from [one] roo[t]. And m[e]n came seeking to cut down and uproot the [ce]dar, thereby leaving the date palm by itself. 16 But the date palm cried out and said, "Do not cut down the cedar, for the two of us are sp[rung] from o[ne] root!" So the cedar was left on account of the date palm, 17 and they did not cut me down. *vacat* Then I awoke in the night from my sleep, and I said to my wife Sarai, "I dreamt 18 a dream, (and) on acco[unt] of this dream I am afraid." She said to me, "Tell me your dream, so that I may know (about it)." So I began to tell her this dream, 19 and I said to [her], "…this dream… … that they will seek to kill me, but to spare you. Therefore, this is the entire kind deed 20 th[at you] must do for me: in all cities (?) that [we will ent]er s[a]y of me, 'He is my brother.' I will live under your protection, and my life will be spared because of you. 21 [{*significant lacuna*—JM} t]hey [will s]eek to take you away from me, and to kill me." Sarai wept because of my words that night 22 …when we en[ter]ed into the dist[ri]ct of E[gypt…] … And Pharaoh Zoa[n]…t[he]n…Sarai to turn toward Zoan 23 …[and] she worried herself [g]reatly that no man should see her (for) [fiv]e years. (Machiela, *DSGA*, 70–72)

The length of my discussion of this very significant section of the Apocryphon makes it sensible to outline it briefly here. After a consideration of the content of Abram's dream as he relates it, I note a number of problems with the dream's conceptual adequacy, which leads me to a brief but important excursus on Abram's narratorial reliability and perspectival limitations. Next, I treat Abram's interpretation or interpretations of his dream, consider Sarai's reactions to his explanations, and, finally, summarize my findings on Sarai and her story to that point.

The Dream and Its Conceptual Adequacy

References to dreams, and the relation of their content and interpretation, feature prominently in the remains of the Genesis Apocryphon.[15] The related, broader theme of sight, which first appears here in the narrative about Sarai and Abram, also provides a substantial thread that links much of the narrative action and motivation going forward. As a result, apparently, of what Abram sees in his dream (וחזית בחלמי, 19.14), Sarai is said

---

15. See, at least, columns 7 and 14–15 outside the Abram, Sarai, and Lot cycle; in 14.9 and following, which refers to a dream of Noah, the symbol of a cedar (ארז) also appears. Falk, *Parabiblical Texts*, suggests that some of the revelations in the early, poorly preserved columns of the scroll may also be dreams (77; compare 31), and that the relation and interpretation of Noah's dream may extend from the end of column 12 through 15.20 (32).

to live in fear of being seen by men for five years (לא יחזנה כול בר אֱנוֹשׁ[ן] חמ[שׁ] שְׁנִין, 19.23); when this nevertheless occurs, a lengthy, mostly visual description of Sarai (20.2-8) entices Pharaoh to lay eyes on her himself (וחזהא, 20.9), and he marries her immediately as a result; finally, Abram prays that God make God's hand "be seen" (ואחזי, 20.14) in punishment of Pharaoh, and the fulfillment of this request eventuates in the king's sight of Abram in his dream (בְּחֻלם חֻזְ[נִי, 20.22), which sets the resolution of the entire episode in motion. Thus the first and last references to "seeing" (חזי) in this Egyptian episode appear in the context of dreams: Abram's relaying of his own here, and the courtier Herqanosh's mention of Pharaoh's in 20.22. Both dreams have distinct impacts on the plot, even as both leave substantial doubts as to the adequacy of their communication.

The scene from 19.14-21, neatly bound by temporal references to the night on which Sarai and Abram enter Egypt (19.14; resumption after the *vacat* in 17; and near the end of 21), exhibits considerable literary appeal. Abram's initial description of his dream begins וחלמת...חלם בליליה ("I dreamed a dream in the night," 19.14); as he details his waking and informing Sarai of the dream, he reverses the word order: בליליא...חלם חֻלמת (19.17-18). A similar device is found in Abram's exposition of the scene in the dream and the date palm's protest: Abram notes the origin of the two trees, "sprouted from one root" ([צְמַחוּ[ן] מִן שֹׁרְ[שׁ חד], 19.15), while the date palm cries מן שרשׁ חֻ[ד] צֻ[מח]נָא (19.16). Alternating play on the concept of "sparing," or "leaving behind" (שבק), also weaves the episode together. The men in Abram's dream first seek to leave the date palm behind (וּלְמִשְׁבֹּק, 19.15), but the date palm's intervention results in the cedar being left behind (וּשְׁבִיק, 19.16); and compare 19.19, where Abram predicts that Sarai will be left behind in the absence of action (למשבק), with 20.10, where he notes the actual, eventual result: "I, Abram, was left behind" (ושביקת אנה אברם). Further lexical play may be suggested by the etymological links of בטלל to words for "shadow" in various Semitic languages, including the Hebrew צל: the cedar, perhaps, is spared "in the shade" cast by the date palm (ושביק ארזא בטלל תמרתא, 19.16).[16] Moreover, Abram as narrator displays a fine rhetorical sensibility, from my readerly perspective, as he first delays revelation of the dream's

---

16. See Fitzmyer, *GA*, 186–7, supported by Takamitsu Muraoka, "Notes on the Aramaic of the Genesis Apocryphon," *RevQ* 8 (1972–74): 40, commenting on the first edition (1966) of Fitzmyer's commentary (compare Muraoka, *Notes*, 43, "Postscriptum"). Muraoka's remarks reference a parallel Japanese expression that employs the word for "shadow" in an idiom meaning "by the protection of." Compare *HALOT* 1024b–1025a, 1884a–1885a.

interpretation, then refrains from reiterating the substance of the dream's plot even as he relates it to Sarai on the story level (19.18-19): "I began to tell her this dream. And I said to her"—then presumably beginning to unpack the dream's supposed significance somewhere in the lacunose remains of the first half of 19.19.

This scene also begins to reveal something of Abram's presentation of Sarai. His interpretation of his dream makes it clear that he conceives it, or at least characterizes it, as a prognostic and admonitory allegory, with himself represented by the cedar and Sarai by the date palm.[17] Noah is also depicted as a cedar in the context of a dream in the Apocryphon (14.9, 11, 14, and perhaps line 27, according to Machiela's text), and Esther Eshel points out that both of these dreams share notes of "prediction and warning," in addition to their employment of arboreal symbols.[18] However, the remains of the interpretation of Noah's dream in column 14 contain no mention of a date palm. And while this pairing of a cedar and a palm has some rough parallels in the wider tradition, these are only of partial help in explaining the dream's imagery. Psalm 92:13, which asserts that "the righteous one sprouts like the palm tree (כתמר), grows like a cedar (כארז) in Lebanon," is explicitly if tenuously linked by the rabbis to the biblical episode of Abram and Sarai in Egypt.[19] As Marianne Gevirtz points out, however, none of the relevant discussions maps the two species to Abram and Sarai, respectively; a somewhat better parallel in this regard might be that suggested by Eva Osswald, who notes the similar imagery in the Song of Songs, where the male's appearance is

---

17. If Machiela's proposal is correct, Abram's identity as the cedar is also explicitly noted in his relation of the dream (ולא קצצוני, "and they did not chop me down," 19.17). See Machiela, *DSGA*, 71, and Fitzmyer, *GA*, 187, for discussion of the reading here. The allegorical mapping of the cedar and the date palm is likewise encouraged by the respective genders of the nouns; compare also the potential fate of the date palm (ולמשבק, 19.15) with the predicted fate of Sarai (למשבק, 19.19).

18. Esther Eshel, "The Dream Visions in the Noah Story of the Genesis Apocryephon and Related Texts," in *Northern Lights on the Dead Sea Scrolls: Proceedings of the Nordic Qumran Network 2003–2006*, ed. Anders Klostergaard Petersen et al. (Leiden: Brill, 2009), 46–8, 51.

19. See *Gen. Rab.* 41.1; Tanḥ., *Lekh.* 5; and the Zohar to Genesis 12. Some of the relevant portions are printed in Marianne Luijken Gevirtz, "Abram's Dream in the Genesis Apocryphon: Its Motifs and Their Function," *Maarav* 8 (1992): 238. Fitzmyer, *GA*, 185, also mentions these. Eshel, "Dream Visions," 50–2, suggests that the Apocryphon "provides the missing link" in the rabbis' association of Gen. 12:17 and Ps. 92:13, but I think that her own presentation shows that the tradition's intricacy significantly complicates arguments about influence.

likened to cedars (5:15) and the female's attributes are compared to the features of a date palm (7:8-9).[20] Still, this sheds relatively limited light on the symbolism of Abram's dream, lacking as it does any hint of danger, or mention of a personified tree's speech. Both of these elements do appear in the tradition, as Gevirtz notes: felled trees function as metaphors for disaster and death, and speaking trees and plants feature in disputation proverbs common in the ancient Near East.[21] While all these may be common motifs, however, Abram's dream seems to aggregate them in a novel manner. Gevirtz contends merely that the differing human uses of cedars and date palms—cedars must be cut down to be of use, while a felled date palm's primary utility is at an end—prompt the choice of imagery in a natural, pragmatic way.[22] This may help to illuminate the action of the dream, though the metaphors in question mostly disintegrate in the plot to come, as shown below. What can be safely said about Sarai's figurative identity as the date palm, I think, draws on some of the rough parallels cited above and common human knowledge: a date palm possesses both beauty and utility.[23] This utility, moreover, is closely bound up with the tree's fertility. Likewise, the trait of Sarai's beauty dominates the poem delivered in praise of her in GenAp 20.2-8, while her usefulness, which is eventually narrowed to the question of her sexual availability, serves as a kind of shorthand for her ultimate value to the other characters in the narrative.

---

20. Gevirtz, "Abram's Dream," 238–9; Eva Osswald, "Beobachtungen zur Erzählung von Abrahams Aufenthalt in Ägypten im 'Genesis-Apocryphon'," ZAW 72 (1960): 21 n. 17. The suggestive image of the lover climbing the palm in Song 7:9 is reminiscent of *Gen. Rab.* 41.1, where Pharaoh's activity with Sarai is related to the danger of recklessly climbing to the top of a tree.

21. Gevirtz, "Abram's Dream," 234–7. For biblical examples, see Dan. 4:10-15; Judg. 9:8-15.

22. Gevirtz, "Abram's Dream," 232–3, 237, 239.

23. The aesthetic element is explicit in the proposal of Fitzmyer, *GA*, 98–9, 185: "a date palm, (which was) [very beauti]ful" (שׁ[גי]א י[אי] חדא ותמרא; 19.14-15; note that Fitzmyer uses only one kind of dot to indicate uncertain letters). This reading is rejected, however, by Machiela, *DSGA*, 71, as fitting "neither the available space nor the ink remains." The palm as evocative of female beauty is also a Greek trope, as in the late antique Peter Bing and Regina Höschele, eds., *Aristaenetus, Erotic Letters*, WGRW 32 (Atlanta: Society of Biblical Literature, 2014), 2–3, where the motion of the beloved's gait is likened to a "palm gently swaying" (φοίνιξ σειόμενος ἡσυχῇ, their translation; 1.1). The context is reminiscent of a descriptive poem such as that celebrating Sarai's beauty in GenAp 20.2-8.

Nevertheless, Abram's relation of his dream to his narratee raises serious questions about its explanatory power—or, on the other hand, about Abram's candor. A close consideration of the dream in its broader context makes it difficult to accept Crawford's contention that "there can be no doubt to the reader that [the dream] is sent by God and foretells future events."[24] Leaving aside for the moment the question of whether Abram's exposition asserts that the cedar and date palm are actually "sprouted from one root" (19.15), it is curious that the action of the dream as related maps rather poorly against the plot of the rest of his tale. When the three powerful men of Egypt seek Abram out, according to his later account, they are after his profound learning, not his death (19.24-26).[25] Moreover, by the time Pharaoh reportedly does seek to kill Abram, the king has already sent men and taken Sarai away (20.9)—an order of events that fits with Abram's second attempt at explicating the contents of the dream in 19.21, but not with his initial recounting here in 19.15. In the event, Sarai, the "date palm," not Abram, is the primary focus of the men. Even further, while the date palm is spontaneous in its defense of the cedar in the dream (19.16), Sarai's intervention on Abram's behalf was scripted years before (19.20; 20.10).

But the central difficulty with Abram's relation of his dream is that he wakes up entirely too soon.[26] The failure of the cedar tree to say anything in its own defense seems to track with Abram's later presentation of the scene in which he is "spared," or "left behind," due to Sarai's voicing of the script Abram sets for her in 19.20: Sarai says אחי הוא, "he is my brother," in 20.10, while Abram is apparently the silent beneficiary of her intervention. Yet Pharaoh's rebuke of Abram in 20.26-27, with its periphrastic הוי plus participle, implies Abram's active and ongoing participation in the ruse: "why did you keep saying to me that 'She is

---

24. Crawford, *Rewriting Scripture*, 118; see also Gevirtz, "Abram's Dream," 241. Compare Eshel, "Dream Visions," 52, and Andrew B. Perrin, *The Dynamics of Dream-Vision Revelation in the Aramaic Dead Sea Scrolls*, JAJSup 19 (Göttingen: Vandenhoeck & Ruprecht, 2015), 133–4.

25. On Fitzmyer's reading here—"and concerning my wife," ועל אנתתי, meaning that the men already know Sarai by reputation—see the discussion below.

26. It is interesting to consider whether the literal force of ואתעירת ("I was awakened," 19.17; Fitzmyer, *GA*, 187) could imply an untimely return to full consciousness. Compare the translation of Martin G. Abegg Jr. and Michael O. Wise, "1Q20 (1QapGen ar)," in *The Dead Sea Scrolls Reader*, Part 3: *Parabiblical Texts*, ed. Donald W. Parry and Emanuel Tov (Leiden: Brill, 2005), 25, "Then I started from my sleep while it was still night."

my sister'?" (בדיל [מא] הוֹית אמר לי די אחתי היא).²⁷ What is more, Abram and Sarai's encounter with the men of the land is not resolved with the sparing of Abram, the "cedar," as his relation of the dream suggests; instead, Sarai, the "date palm," is herself uprooted (compare 19.15) and taken away, where she will languish in captivity for two years (20.8-11, 17-18).

And what of the dream's implication, at least as transcribed in the editions of Beyer and Machiela, that Sarai and Abram are truly "sprouted from one root"? By this text, the men who seek to chop down and uproot the cedar are understandably fooled by above-ground appearances; the date palm's cry that the two are grown from the same root merely makes the hidden truth plain. But there are no other indications in the text as it stands that Abram and Sarai are actually brother and sister. Abram's first extant reference to her is as "Sarai my woman" or "wife" (שרי אנתתי, 19.17), an epithet that he repeats twice in his later speech to God (20.14-15), and a description of Sarai echoed by Lot (20.23), Herqanosh (20.25), and Pharaoh (20.27). Further, Abram's proposal for Sarai's speech doesn't assert that what she is to say is true, and in fact it makes more sense if it is a lie—by Abram's admission, it's a "kindness," or "favor" (טבו), after all, that she pronounce these words for him (19.19-20). Finally, and perhaps most tellingly, Abram does not report that he protests when he is upbraided by Pharaoh for lying about his and Sarai's relationship (20.26-28).²⁸

Does this mean, then, that the original, unrecoverable text of Abram's relation of his dream is unlikely to contain the first mention of "sprouted from one root" (19.15)? It might make more sense if Abram's initial exposition of the dream situation did not contain the claim, and that the date palm's cry is an innovative lie to help the cedar. Thus the date palm's conduct becomes practical if devious advice to Abram, the dream's interpreter, who, in an interesting twist, recommends to Sarai the course

---

27. See Takamitsu Muraoka, *A Grammar of Qumran Aramaic* (Leuven: Peeters, 2011), 175 (§55 f) on this "syntagm explicitly designed to indicate a durative, habitual, repetitive or iterative *Aktionsart*."

28. This is somewhat puzzling, given the influence of other motifs reflected in Genesis 20 on this account; see Bernstein, "Re-Arrangement, Anticipation, and Harmonization," 49–52, and various points in the discussion below. As Bernstein notes (51), the Apocryphon anticipates Abraham's report to Abimelech of the favor he supposedly had asked Sarah (Gen. 20:13) by working it into Abram's plea to Sarai in GenAp 19.19-20: "wherever we are, say regarding me that 'he is my brother'" (Bernstein's translation). But in the extant remains of the Apocryphon, Abram does not assert, as he does in Gen. 20:12, that he and Sarai are actually non-uterine siblings.

of action suggested to him by her dream analogue. But at least in this case, any textual argument based upon narrative logic must end inconclusively—for, as will be clear at a few places further along, too, Abram cannot be assumed to be consistent in his telling of this tale.

Abram's Reliability and Perspectival Limitations

The question of Abram's reliability as narrator dogs his entire presentation. The various inconsistencies already mentioned comprise only part of the problem here. A more basic issue is Abram's identity as a first-person narrator who claims to have been intimately involved in most of the events that he is relating: he is a "narrator-character" not as a theoretical construct, but in fact. I am prone here simply to disagree with the assertions of George Nickelsburg and Stephen A. Reed, who both say that the first-person narration of the Apocryphon lends it "reliability," or "credence."[29] Rather, as Rimmon-Kenan demonstrates, "personal involvement" in a story is one of the "main sources of unreliability" in a narrator, and narrators who "are also characters in the fictional world" are "on the whole more fallible."[30]

Besides Abram's personal involvement in most of the events he describes, he exhibits another, rather converse indicator of narratorial unreliability, as defined by Rimmon-Kenan, which is a "limited knowledge" of some affairs that he nonetheless undertakes to relate.[31] This is, in part, an artifact of the kind of restrictions that naturally operate on any person's perspective; but Abram's confidence in his telling raises questions of candor and credibility, as well. Reed hits upon this phenomenon, too, noting with reference to 20.16-21 that "no explanation is given about how [Abram] knows what is happening in the court and even the bedroom of Pharaoh."[32] I would think that the problem is more acute in, for instance, Abram's relaying of the lines of verse spoken by Herqanosh and his fellow courtiers in 20.2-8; most of the action at Pharaoh's household might plausibly have been related to Abram by Herqanosh, who clearly

---

29. Nickelsburg, "Patriarchs Who Worry," 197–8; Stephen A. Reed, "The Use of the First Person in the *Genesis Apocryphon*," in *Aramaic in Postbiblical Judaism and Early Christianity: Papers from the 2004 National Endowment for the Humanities Summer Seminar at Duke University*, ed. Eric M. Meyers and Paul V. M. Flesher (Winona Lake, IN: Eisenbrauns, 2010), 213. Perhaps, though, Nickelsburg and Reed intend their remarks to bear on ancient reception.
30. Rimmon-Kenan, *Narrative Fiction*, 100, 103.
31. Ibid., 100–103.
32. Reed, "First Person," 204–5.

gives a number of story-level details to Abram and Lot in 20.21-22, or, later, by Sarai. Alternatively, such a remarkable sequence of events might well have made its way into the common gossip of the realm over a span of two years (20.18). On the specific point of Abram's assertion that Pharaoh was never successful in having sex with Sarai (20.17), Abram could be extrapolating back from the king's oath to that effect in 20.30—or merely protesting too much. But this general line of questioning exposes what, at root, Abram is about here: in his every utterance, he is making claims. And Abram, as a human character within the tale he's telling, is at all times potentially subject to all of the limitations—of perspective, knowledge, and descriptive power, among others, not to mention a weakness for portraying oneself in a favorable light—common to humans telling stories about themselves.

The Dream's Interpretation(s)

After Abram wakes up, according to his account, he speaks to Sarai, who here starts to take on more flesh as a character. What Abram says first reads like a simple confidence, even a confession, whose halting repetitions nicely evoke the stammer of someone rudely awakened: "A dream I dreamed—from which I am afraid—from this dream" (חלם חלמת מן ח[ל]מא דן דחל א̇נ̇ה̇ [ד], 19.17-18). Sarai's response is to speak in return: "Tell me your dream, and I'll know it" (אשתעי לי חלמך ואנדע, 19.18), an innovation in the tradition that partly anticipates at least one later reading, a Christian Syriac homily in which Sarai and Abram converse before entering Egypt.[33] It is no small matter that Abram records Sarai's direct speech, especially here, in what is her first appearance in the discourse as the text stands. Their verbal interchange contributes to the development of a tone of mutuality in this sparely but credibly sketched scene: a person awakes, disturbed, a bit confused by an alarming dream—and it is still night. The person's partner seeks a remedy, perhaps aiming to explain away the fear, or at least to lessen its weight by sharing it: "Tell me about your dream, so that I'll know about it, too." Sarai's urging betrays no deference, merely concern; her engaged courtesy partly recalls Abram's informative travelogue notes of 19.12-13.

---

33. Brock and Hopkins, "Verse Homily," 106, 110, 112, 114. Note in particular Sarah's solicitous questioning of a distraught Abraham (108, 110). In their broader interaction, Sarah's initially servile response ("Let your will be done, for you are the head and I the heel…") gives way to frank disagreement with Abraham's plans. I owe van Rensburg, "Intellect and/or Beauty," 119, 122, for the reference.

Abram reports that he acquiesces immediately: "tell me your dream," Sarai says—"so I began to tell her this dream" (ושרית...חלמך לי אשתעי לאשתעיא לה חלמא דן, 19.18). He has seemingly recovered his wits very quickly, for after relating the dream's content, Abram offers an initial interpretation, recommends a response, and predicts its result in rapid succession. The dream signifies, says Abram,

> that they will seek to kill me, but you to leave behind. But this is the whole favor that you need to do for me: in every city that we come to, say about me that "He is my brother." And I will live with your help, and my life will be saved because of you. (19.19-20)[34]

The saving cry is scripted here, which lends it a kind of preemptive function, and there is no indication that Sarai and Abram are really from one family of origin. However, most of this explanation fits the rough outlines of the initial narration of Abram's dream reasonably well. Michael Becker goes too far, though, in maintaining that Abram's understanding of his dream "distinguishes him as a person of extraordinary and God-given wisdom"—for events to come will expose Abram's interpretation as completely inadequate, or at least shortsighted.[35] The phrase "the whole favor" or "kindness" (כול טבותא, 19.19), for example, implies something like "this is all you need to do"; and Abram's double expression of the expected benefit to him, coupled with the reader's knowledge of the content of the dream, suggests that the preservation of Abram's life will mark a happy end to the matter.[36] But Sarai's deceptive testimony to Pharaoh is only the beginning, for her, of a deeper stage of oppression, as

---

34. די יבעון למקטלני ולכי למשבק ברם דא כול טבותא ד[י ת]עׄבׄדׄיׄןׄ עׄמׄיׄ בכול עׄרׄוׄת די [נתה] לׄ[הן] אׄמׄ[ר]יׄ עלי די אחי הוא ואחׄהׄ בטליכי ותפלט נפשי בדיליכי.

35. Michael Becker, "Abraham in the Genesis Apocryphon," in *Rewritten Biblical Figures*, ed. Erkki Koskenniemi and Pekka Lindqvist, Studies in Rewritten Bible 3 (Winona Lake, IN: Eisenbrauns, 2010), 99. Becker partly draws on Gevirtz, "Abram's Dream," 231, 239–41, one of whose main contentions is that the Apocryphon burnishes Abram's reputation as a "wise man" in this dream scene. Compare John H. Choi, *Traditions at Odds: The Reception of the Pentateuch in Biblical and Second Temple Period Literature* (New York: T&T Clark, 2010), 148–9; and Beate Ego, "The Figure of Abraham in the Genesis Apocryphon's Re-Narration of Gen 12:10-20," in Donald W. Parry et al., eds., *Qumran Cave 1 Revisited*, 235, 242, who speaks of Abram's "mantic competence."

36. Compare B. Jongeling, C. J. Labuschagne, and A. S. van der Woude, *Aramaic Texts from Qumran*, SSS 4 (Leiden: Brill, 1976), 91: "This is the only favour…that you must do for me" (emphasis indicating reconstructed text removed).

she moves from living in fear to bodily captivity. Sarai will not be "left behind," but abducted with violence—according to Abram's later account, anyway (20.9-11). However this may be, Sarai's imprisonment will also serve as an analogical signal of her effacement from the narrative. And though Sarai eventually emerges from detention (20.27-32), she never comes out of this narrative obscurity, or regains the subjectivity or human definition that occasionally mark her character in these earlier episodes.

At the beginning of 19.21, there is a sizeable lacuna, extending at least a third of the line. It seems just possible that the missing text noted Sarai's initial reaction to Abram's interpretation. This could help explain why the surviving text after the lacuna represents a somewhat different reading of the content of Abram's dream than that offered in 19.19. It is almost as if he is having another go at it: "they will seek to take you away from me," he says—employing עדי, "to remove," instead of שבק, "to spare" or "leave behind"—and, only then, "to kill me."[37] Notably, in its verbal conception and in its order of events, this explanation fits the later plot, as Abram relates it, quite well (20.8-9); on the same two counts, however, it functions poorly as an interpretation of his dream as recounted in 19.14-17. The disparities between Abram's two readings could suggest that a remark about Sarai's reaction, now lost, once lay between them.

In any event, Abram's second attempt at explanation proves to be little more perspicacious than his first. Indeed, its significant flaw is similar in kind. The broader context leaves it somewhat unclear—and this is not helped by the lacuna—whether the force of Abram's final remarks here is "if you don't pronounce this lie, they'll try to take you away, and kill me," or "when they attempt these things, you can save me by saying this." The false statement seems to serve as a prophylactic in 19.20, while the content of the dream in 19.16 suggests that the lie be produced in an emergency. The complex of predictions implies, then—at least as the text stands now—either that the whole mess can be avoided by concealing the truth, or that Abram can be protected by Sarai's well-placed falsehood. The latter more closely forecasts the plot to come; but both options fail utterly to foretell the consequences for Sarai. "They" will still "seek to remove" her; they will, in fact, succeed; and, what is more—in a sharp irony—it is only the revelation of the truth that finally resolves the matter (20.8-9; 22–32). Once again, the adequacy of the dream's message, perhaps even its basic congruence with the truth, is in doubt.

---

37. יב]עׄוׄן לאעדיותכי מני ולמקטלני, 19.21.

Sarai's Reactions

Whether or not Sarai's initial impression of Abram's dream interpretation was noted in the now-lost opening of 19.21, the extant text for about two lines following Abram's final predictions is, remarkably, mostly absorbed with describing Sarai's reactions. First, Abram says, "Sarai wept because of my words that night" (ובכת שרי על מלי בליליא דן, 19.21). Abram attributes no precise emotional motive to Sarai here, though it seems that his fear, noted in 19.18, has been contagious. Her reluctance, or fear "to turn toward Zoan" may be referred to at the end of 19.22, though the text is uncertain; somewhat less ambiguously, Sarai is next said to have been "afraid, very much so, in her inner self, lest any man see her—for five years."[38] The basic mechanics of the plot for some time going forward will turn principally on Sarai, an outcome foreshadowed by her prominence in the discourse here: aside from Sarai's desire to evade notice, all significant story-level activity, for half a decade, remains a matter of conjecture.

The extraordinary acceleration of the narration here—the following words, with barely a discernible space on the leather between, read "and at the end of those five years," ולסוף חמש שניא אלן—may partly obscure several interesting revelations about Sarai and her characterization. Whereas Abram had urged her to lie "in every city" they enter, Sarai seems to avoid taking this advice for as long as she can, concealing herself from view instead (19.20, 23).[39] Why, though, does Sarai cloister herself? The dream as narrated can give no warrant for this, as the sight of the date palm is not a motivating force in the men's actions. And Abram doesn't tell Sarai to hide; in fact, he says that she should lie everywhere. Despite Daniel Falk's assertion to the contrary, the "only favor" requested by Abram must assume that Sarai will be seen, indeed, that she will be in a position to speak directly with those who wish Abram harm.[40]

---

38. On the text see Machiela, *DSGA*, 72; Fitzmyer, *GA*, 189; and Beyer, *ATTM*, 172–3.

39. The reading of "cities" (עָרוֹת) in Machiela, *DSGA*, 72, is conjectural, but fits the context. Compare Avigad and Yadin, *A Genesis Apocryphon*, unpaginated center section; Fitzmyer, *GA*, 98; and Beyer, *ATTM*, 172–3.

40. The broader point of Falk, *Parabiblical Texts*, 86—that the exegetical problem addressed by the Apocryphon here is that, in Genesis, Sarai's ready visibility suggests that she does not behave like a "virtuous woman" of antiquity—is persuasive, especially in the light of similar devices in other parts of the tradition, such as the box in which Sarai is concealed in the telling of this story in *Gen. Rab.* 40.5, or Sarah's attempt at disguising herself recorded in Brock and Hopkins, "Verse Homily," 114. But the rewriting here does not avoid the implication of Gen. 12:12 that "Abram expected the Egyptians to see her," as Falk suggests; rather, it shows that Sarai made every effort to conceal herself despite Abram's assumptions.

The original contents of the lacuna in 19.21 are open to broad conjecture; but an instruction to stay out of sight fits rather poorly with a request to engage in repeated verbal defense of another—and, again, such a sentiment hardly follows as an explication of the dream. Could it be, then, that Sarai intuits something of what proves to be the real danger: that the male gaze, coupled with the apparently limitless entitlement of its subjects, could easily result in her abduction and imprisonment? In this understanding, Sarai formulates an alternate plan, ignoring Abram's advice until an extreme situation arises.[41] The late tradition represented in the Syriac homily provides a potential parallel here, as Sarah balks at Abraham's scheme and attempts to hide her beauty beneath rags and dust instead.[42]

Any agency or independence that might be posited here, however, is undercut by a consideration of how thoroughly Sarai's life appears to have been dominated by the uncertain implications of a single dream of Abram, imperfectly interpreted: she staves off imprisonment by holding herself captive. But how long can one be ruled by fear of a vaguely defined event that fails to happen as predicted? Perhaps this question has some bearing on one of the story's central gaps, treated in the next section: how, after taking such successful care for years to avoid detection, is Sarai finally revealed to the courtiers who come calling in 19.24?

Sarai, and the Story So Far

Before moving on to this next scene, which is unfortunately very poorly preserved, it is worthwhile to gather some of the findings thus far about Sarai, about Abram and his dream, and about an incipient motif that connects some of the traits of these two main characters. Although Sarai's presence as Abram's "woman" or wife (19.17) may be assumed, retrospectively, from the first relevant textual remains in 19.7, the first discourse-level hint of her role in the story is in 19.12-13, where Abram apparently speaks to his travel partner(s), offering simple observations on their whereabouts that nonetheless imply at least a modicum of respect for his listener(s). Sarai comes to some prominence, though, in the relatively lengthy and complex scene constructed around Abram's dream (19.14-21). Here, she is represented as a lithe date palm whose timely verbal intervention saves Abram's cedar—supposedly rooted, somehow, with the

---

41. Compare Blake A. Jurgens, "A Wandering Aramean in Pharaoh's Court: The Literary Relationship between Abram's Sojourn in Egypt in 1QapGen 19–20 and Jewish Fictional Literature," *JSJ* 49 (2018): 364–5 n. 34, on Sarai's "initiative" and "degree of agency" here.

42. Brock and Hopkins, "Verse Homily," 114.

palm—from destruction. Sarai's relationship with Abram is thus depicted as close, and this feeling of mutuality is reinforced as she prompts him to share the burden of his alarming dream (19.18). That she exercises direct speech establishes Sarai as something of an agent; the mere fact that she speaks, as Abram speaks, contributes to the note of mutuality even as it suggests a similarity between their characters. That speech is Sarai's first act as a subject indicated on the discourse level, moreover, may lend credence to proposals of other potential acts of her speech obscured or lost in and around the text's lacunae. In Abram's response to Sarai's urging, his interpretation or interpretations suggest that both of them are in danger, to which Sarai responds by weeping, and by fearfully concealing herself for a number of years (19.19-23). This latter act suggests some agency, as well, as Sarai seems to resist Abram's direct recommendation that she lie about their relationship everywhere they go; but cowering behind doors for years on the force of an enigmatic dream erodes notions of strength or independence.

While this study pursues an image of Sarai in the Genesis Apocryphon, a consideration of Abram's role here is unavoidable. This is not due merely to factors of relationality that affect characterization in any fictional work, but because Abram's words here form the filter through which the story—and thus Sarai, who lives there—must be at least partly distilled. Abram as narrator is a talker from the start; in his speech he exhibits some courtesy to his interlocutors in the narrative, and some skill in his artful relation of the tale as apprehended by me, the reader. However, perhaps counter-intuitively, this ability does not contribute to Abram's credibility, which is thrown into question by a number of inconsistencies in his relation of his dream as compared to his interpretations, and as compared to the later plot as he recounts it; what is more, as a narrator-character Abram faces perspectival challenges to his reliability that are intrinsic to the role.

That the dream and its interpretations are so rife with problems raises difficult questions about its conceptual adequacy—questions that are particularly pointed if the dream's source is implied to be divine. Why, if God sends the dream, is it so poorly predictive of events to come? Is the dream's communication deliberately incomplete? Does Abram relay it faithfully, but bungle its interpretation? Gevirtz offers a nicely nuanced reading that suggests that the dream's indirect, allegorical style of communication mitigates Abram's responsibility for later events without explicitly shifting the onus to the deity.[43] Neither misjudgment nor being misled are precisely to blame, then; and indeed, in Abram's presentation, the ploy he suggests does not seem entirely cynical. There is no noted

---

43. Gevirtz, "Abram's Dream," 241; compare Becker, "Abraham," 99.

benefit to him, pecuniary or otherwise, beyond the preservation of his life; on the other hand, he mentions this twice, and any benefit to Sarai remains implied only in the threat that "they will seek to remove you" (19.20-21). In this, as in everything, however, a recollection of Abram's control of the discourse is instructive; and, as will emerge more fully later, the value of Sarai, to Abram and to God, is very narrowly defined.

Finally, especially in view of coming narrative developments, it is useful to note a few connections between Abram's depictions of himself and Sarai. If the text of Machiela, following Beyer, is correct, the initial portrayal of Sarai as her dream analogue suggests that her relationship with Abram approaches identity: "together, they sprouted from one root" (19.15). Sarai's first independent action, both in her allegorical representation and as a woman, is utterance, just as Abram's was, in the extant text (19.7, קרי and אמר; 19.16, 18, כלי and אמר); moreover, her cry as the date palm makes or reiterates the claim of partial identity. Sarai's tearful reaction to her discussion with Abram anticipates his own weeping, both over Sarai and over Lot (19.21; 20.10-11, 16; 22.5, all בכי; plus compare 20.12), while the fear that leads her to hide herself away recalls that of Abram in the wake of his dream (19.18, 23, both דחל, if the latter reading is correct).[44]

Abram and Sarai's Three Visitors (GenAp 19.23-31)

> GenAp 19.23 Now at the end of those five years 24 ... ...to me, and three men from the nobles of Egypt...his [ ]... by Phara[oh] Zoan because of my words and my wisdom, and they were giving 25 m[e many gifts They as]ked scribal knowledge and wisdom and truth for themselves, so I read before them the book of the words of Enoch 26 [ ] in the womb in which he had grown. They were not going to get up until I would clearly expound for them... ...the words of 27 [ ] ...with much eating and much drinking ...[ ]... the wine 28 ...[ ]...[ ] ...to you, I ...[ ]...[ ] 29 [he wa]s entering...and I said to ... I ... to Zoan, by ...[ ] a[l]l the words of Enoch 30 [ ]...[ ] 31 [ ] *vacat* (Machiela, *DSGA*, 72–3)[45]

The poor preservation of the text of this episode is especially regrettable for an investigation of the figure of Sarai, for the lost or garbled

---

44. The proposal of דחלת in 19.23 is that of Fitzmyer, followed, cautiously, by Machiela.

45. The text becomes very fragmentary toward the end of column 19; several lines at the bottom are missing completely. As elsewhere, I have made no attempt to reproduce the spacing of Machiela's edition here.

scene(s) here represent what is probably the key gap in the Apocryphon's Egyptian narrative—and she is right in the middle of it. Sarai has apparently been successful at evading the notice of men for the five years preceding the pilgrimage of the three courtiers (19.23), one of whom turns out to be Herqanosh; but after their visit, her body and talents are claimed as objects of their intimate knowledge (20.2-8). It is clear from what survives that this intervening episode functions in part as an opportunity for Abram to polish his credentials as a sage, and it is possible that this informs Herqanosh's later request that Abram heal Pharaoh in the wake of the failure of the native wise men to do so (20.19-22). However, the proximate motive for Herqanosh's appeal is a dream, not a sudden recollection, after a lapse of two years, of Abram's wisdom. Moreover, the broader plot demands that the central development of all the lacunose remains of 19.23 through the end of the column be that Sarai is encountered: nothing of the rest of the tale, until Abram, Sarai, and Lot depart Egypt in 20.32-33, is comprehensible otherwise. Despite the significance of this event, however, most commentators venture very little here. Any conclusions about this fragmentary section must remain tentative, but the task of reading Sarai in this narrative calls for the advancement of a few responsible hypotheses.

The entire episode reflects Abram's presentation and perspective, but two key elements seem relatively certain. First, Sarai has sought to keep out of sight for years on end—efforts that have not been in vain, as the stated motive of the nobles' visit shows. The three arrive not in search of a beautiful woman who has been the topic of rumors, but on a quest for sapiential knowledge: they come, Abram says, "on account of my speech and on account of my wisdom," asking for "scribal learning and wisdom and truth" (סָפְרָא וְחָכְמְתָא וְקוּשְׁטָא...חכמתי, ‎19.24-25‎). The nearly universal reading of the object of the second preposition was, until relatively recently, אנתתי: thus, the men call not only to hear Abram's "words," but also, he says, "on account of my wife." However, both Falk and Machiela, working independently, read חכמתי with a high degree of confidence.[46] The narrative logic probably supports this latter reading: Abram's note of Sarai's extreme apprehension at being seen would jar with a matter-of-fact statement, produced with virtually no intervening narrative data, that a few powerful men came partly on her account. It might be possible to postulate a curiosity piqued by Sarai's concealment, but there are no hints of this in the extant text. Moreover, "my [learned]

---

46. Falk, *Parabiblical Texts*, 87–8; Machiela, *DSGA*, 72. Compare Avigad and Yadin, *A Genesis Apocryphon*, unpaginated center section; Beyer, *ATTM*, 173; Fitzmyer, *GA*, 98.

words" and "my wisdom" are a conceptual doublet, a common rhetorical feature in the Genesis Apocryphon that is also found, in triplet form, in the men's request, quoted just above; "my words" and "my wife," on the other hand, have little notional coherence.[47]

Second, Herqanosh and his companions meet Sarai. More than this—unless they fashion their poem celebrating Sarai (20.2-8) solely out of the formal conventions of its hyperbolic genre—they must pass some meaningful time with her. In fact, the poem breaks its generic constraints, for its composers praise more than her physical beauty. Not only do the courtiers see Sarai's face and body, but somehow, too, they witness her "profound wisdom" (חכמא שגיא, 20.7). It seems that more than a fleeting, accidental glimpse of a heretofore hidden Sarai is implied here.

So despite years-long efforts to avoid just such an event, Sarai has a significant encounter with three strange, powerful men. Why does this happen, and how? Perhaps the long span of time elapsed, during which none of the dire predictions prompted by Abram's dream have occurred, has led to a relaxation of vigilance. That five years pass in a breath in the discourse, with no action specified beyond Sarai's fearful concealment, hardly hints at a stimulating existence (19.23); likely the dream's power over her and Abram's behavior has waned. Furthermore, the context of Abram's entertaining seems conducive to the suspension of caution. In what little is preserved here, there is a reasonably clear reference to immoderate imbibing (בֹּמאכל שגי ובמשתה שֹׁגי, "with a lot of food and a lot of drink," 19.27), and the plain word חמרא ("the wine") occupies the end of the line.[48]

The beginnings of another clue may be found in the apparent errand of the nobles, who are seeking "wisdom" and cognate skills (19.24-25). According to Abram, they find it in him—as he reads them "the book of the words of Enoch" (סֹפֹר מלי חֹנוֹך, 19.25; compare line 26, and possibly 29; but see just below). But they likewise claim, later, to find it in Sarai (20.7); somehow, it seems, she also demonstrates her sapiential qualities. Perhaps she, too, with inhibitions lowered, offers her own wisdom, even reciting "the words of Enoch," in response to the quest of Herqanosh and his companions?

---

47. Moshe J. Bernstein, "Stylistic Features in the Narrative of the Genesis Apocryphon," paper presented at the Annual Meeting of the Society of Biblical Literature, Baltimore, MD, 24 November 2013, cites dozens of these. See also Jonas C. Greenfield, "Early Aramaic Poetry," *JANES* 11 (1979): 48.

48. Note also the reading of Fitzmyer, *GA*, 98, in 19.30: אֹבֹל]. Machiela reads nothing in this part of the line, however.

This hypothesis need not float wholly in the gaps of the narrative. The final few lines in which Machiela transcribes anything in this column (19.28–30) are even sketchier than the translation printed above indicates; in fact, the only full word transcribed without any diacritical caveats is ואמרת, in the first third of line 29.[49] Machiela renders "I said" here, and with good reason: Abram is the narrator throughout; he introduced his own direct speech with just this form in his first appearance in the extant text (19.7); and the final occurrence of this form also precedes Abram's speech (20.12). But this is not the only acceptable construal of ואמרת, especially in such a murky context—for the first common singular form is consonantally indistinguishable from the third feminine singular.[50] Indeed, the same form introduces Sarai's first actions in these episodes, both as her dream analogue, the date palm, and as a human character (19.16, 18); moreover, her final act as subject in the narrative is the same, as she speaks to Pharaoh on Abram's behalf (20.9). Sarai's speech thus displays not only discourse-level primacy and frequency, but also story-level significance. That ואמרת here in 19.29, then, refers to an act of speech of Sarai—"and she said"—is both morphologically possible and narratively plausible. If this is accepted, it is even conceivable that the mention of "all the words of Enoch" (כֹּ[ו]ל מֹּלִי חֹנֹוֹךְ) at the end of the line points to Sarai's own exposition of Enochic wisdom, as opposed to Abram's reiteration of his recital in line 25.[51] Notably, the theme of Sarai possessing special

---

49. Neither Beyer nor Fitzmyer read anything here, and Machiela offers no express comment in his apparatus. Based upon his prefatory remarks in Machiela, *DSGA*, 26–7, however, it seems fair to assume that the lack of diacritical marks on ואמרת indicates a high degree of confidence in the reading.

50. The 2 msg is also the same: אמרת, as in 11Q10 (11QtgJob) VI, 7; XXII, 2; XXX, 8. But while the broader context of the Apocryphon contains several examples each of אמרת as 1 csg and 3 fsg—apart from the episodes featuring Sarai and Abram, discussed here, see Lamech and Bitenosh in 2.3, 9—there is no instance where it may be sensibly read as 2 msg. In Pharaoh's accusation of Abram the periphrastic הוי plus participle is used instead (בדיל [מא] הֹוִית אמר, "why have you been saying," 20.26), according to Beyer, Fitzmyer, and Machiela; Avigad and Yadin had read ותאמר, but the *vav* with the imperfect is hard to explain (Fitzmyer, *GA*, 210).

51. Such a proposal need not founder on the pronoun "I" (אֹנֹה), which Machiela reads in the middle of the line. The uncertainties of the readings cut both ways: my suggestions must remain tentative, but the text, as indicated by its diacritical marks, is an "educated guess" to begin with (Machiela, *DSGA*, 26). It seems that the construal of ואמרת as 1 csg would naturally inform the difficult guesswork that follows; perhaps a reading of 3 fsg would prompt a different reconstruction. Again, as far as I know, Machiela is the only critic who offers any reading at all for this line.

discernment is found in the later tradition, where her prophetic abilities are said to eclipse those of Abram.⁵² In the Apocryphon, this would provide yet another link between Abram's portrayals of himself and Sarai. Most importantly, however, Sarai's verbal engagement here would offer narrative justification for the pronouncement of the nobles in 20.7. How do they know about her "great wisdom"? Perhaps because she reveals it to them here, in speech, in reply to their questions.

One further line of responsible speculation might also be useful here. A curious feature of the text of the Apocryphon as it stands is that there seems to be no clear narrative function for all "three men" (תְּלֹתָא גֻּבְרִין, 19.24; compare 20.8) who come to visit. It is worth considering, I think, whether this section may contain allusive elements that recall the events of Gen. 18:1-16 (and compare v. 22, 19:1).⁵³ There, too, three men call on Abraham (18:2), enjoy his hospitality (vv. 2-8), and engage him in dialogue (vv. 9-14). Moreover, there is some numerical ambiguity, or uncertain role division, in the account of the MT, as when the three visitors speak as one in vv. 5 and 9. Compare this with GenAp 20.8, where Pharaoh hears "the report of Herqanosh and the report of his two friends—because the three of them were speaking with one mouth" (מלי חרקנוש ומלי תרין חברוהי די פם חד תלתהון ממללין). As for Sarai, it is interesting that she begins this fragmentary scene in hiding (19.23), while Sarah in the MT is likewise sequestered in the tent, or at least out of sight of the men (18:6, 9).

If any of this is plausible, it is worth noting that Sarah plays an essential role in the plot of the visit in Genesis. Although Abraham initially absorbs the limelight, the episode pivots on an encounter with Sarah, who eventually speaks after her presence is revealed (18:9, 12, 15). I claim nothing conclusive here, but the parallels, I think, are suggestive.

---

52. *Exod. Rab.* 1:1; compare *b. Meg.* 14a: Aaron Rothkoff, "Sarah," in *Encyclopaedia Judaica*, vol. 14, ed. Cecil Roth and Geoffrey Wigoder (Jerusalem: Keter, 1972), 868; van Rensburg, "Intellect and/or Beauty," 122. Note also her introductory epithet, "sagacious," in Brock and Hopkins, "Verse Homily," 106; and her implied direct communication with God in *Ant.* 1.187.

53. As far as I know, only Zakovitch and Shinan, *Abram and Sarai in Egypt*, 61, have proposed an allusion to Genesis 18 here, noting the number of visitors and the feasting motif. Abram's entertainment of three men may even be a theme particularly prominent in the tradition reflected in the Apocryphon: compare 21.21-22, where the Amorite brothers Mamre, Arnem, and Eshkol eat and drink with Abram. As noted by Avigad and Yadin, *A Genesis Apocryphon*, 33, in the English section, though the names stem from Gen. 14:13, this particular feast "is not mentioned in the other sources" (MT, SP, LXX, *Jubilees*, and so on). Machiela, "Genesis Revealed," 218, also connects GenAp 21.21-22 with the end of column 19.

Perhaps, then, this is another note that hints at Sarai's presence, even her verbal interaction, in the original exposition of this scene in the Genesis Apocryphon.

In Praise of Sarai (GenAp 20.2-8)

> GenAp 20.2 ...[ ]... ...[ ]...how irresistible and beautiful is the image of her face; how 3 lovely h[er] foreh[ead, and] soft the hair of her head! How graceful are her eyes, and how precious her nose; every feature 4 of her face is radiating beauty! How lovely is her breast, and how beautiful her white complexion! As for her arms, how beautiful they are! And her hands, how 5 perfect they are! Every view of her hands is stimulating! How graceful are her palms, and how long and thin all the fingers of her hands! Her legs 6 are of such beauty, and her thighs so perfectly apportioned! There is not a virgin or bride who enters the bridal chamber more beautiful than she. 7 Her beauty surpasses that of all women, since the height of her beauty soars above them all! And alongside all this beauty she possesses great wisdom. Everything about her 8 is lovely! (Machiela, *DSGA*, 74–5)

Sarai's reactions to Abram's dream and its interpretations dominated the narrative matter just before the visit of the three nobles, and their encounter with Sarai constituted the primary development of the fragmentary end of column 19. Here, in a unique and dramatic advance in the tradition, Sarai forms the sole focus of a relatively lengthy descriptive poem replete with a variety of adjectives and other evocative parts of speech. The sheer number of narrative adjectives and the amount of detail on display in 20.2-8 would seem a certain boon to a reading that seeks to collect and evaluate Sarai's traits; however, much of the poem, at least until its conclusion, operates in a very circumscribed semantic realm. The repetition—ten times by my count—of adjectives, nouns, and verbal forms derived from שפר, referring generally to "beauty," even grows monotonous to my ear toward the end of the poem, and many of the other adjectives are near synonyms: נִיצָה, "irresistible" (20.2); נָעִים, "pleasant" or "attractive" (20.3); יאי, "fair" or "graceful" (20.3, 4, 5 [and 8, though this may not describe Sarai herself]); רגג, "desirable" (20.3); בְּלִילן, "perfect" (20.5); and חָמִיד, "enticing" or "stimulating" (20.5).[54] In this context, other, slightly more definite adjectives or descriptive nouns

---

54. According to Machiela's text, derivatives of שפר appear in 20.2, 3× in 20.4, 2× in 20.6, and 4× in 20.7; compare 20.9. For renderings of the other words, see Michael Sokoloff, *A Dictionary of Jewish Palestinian Aramaic of the Byzantine Period*, 2nd ed. (Ramat-Gan, Israel: Bar Ilan University Press, 2002)—hereafter

lose some of their specificity, too: Sarai's hair may be "soft" (רְקִיק, 20.3), her skin unmarked in "whiteness" (לבנהא, 20.4), her fingers "long and dainty" (אריכן וקטינן, 20.5), and her thighs "full" (שְׁלמָא, 20.6), but none of this provides much additional definition of her character.[55] The lone metaphor—"the whole blossom of her face" (כול נץ אנפיהא, 20.3-4)—is evocative but does little to extend the poem's rather limited range.[56]

This is not to say that the revelation of Sarai's beauty is unimportant. This knowledge is a net gain in an investigation of her character in the Apocryphon, as her loveliness, interestingly enough, is not explicitly mentioned before this point—though her self-awareness of this quality and its potential effects could be implied in her concern to secret herself away from "every son of man" (19.23). Nor do I suggest that Sarai's beauty is an insignificant attribute, or that it is necessarily subordinate, in the terms of some vague moral calculus, to her traits of personality. Her physical allure is no less a feature of her character than her propensity for speech, both of which prove to be important engines of the plot to come. Moreover, as I discuss below, at least one scholar has proposed that Sarai's attractiveness also points to mental or moral qualities in rough accordance with Hellenistic physiognomic conventions. But to my reading, the superfluity of synonymous descriptors of bodily beauty in 20.2-7 adds relatively little material detail to Sarai's characterization here.

Despite the poem's embarrassment of traits, then, its sum seems to fall somewhat short of its parts. Yet the climax of this recitation is a surprise, by both internal and generic criteria. "Pulchritude is the sole concern of descriptive songs," as Shaye Cohen notes, and the poem to this point has dealt almost exclusively with attributes that are apprehended visually.[57] But here is a word of praise for what seems like an intellectual or spiritual property: "along with all this beauty, much wisdom is hers" (ועם כול שפרא דן חכמא שגיא עמהא, 20.7).[58] The text is clear thus far, though it has been argued that the particular force of חכמה here is influenced by the final

---

DJPA—204b, 233a, 260a, 354b, 523a; compare James C. VanderKam, "The Poetry of 1 Q Ap Gen, XX, 2-8a," *RevQ* 10 (1979–81): 62, and Peter Y. Lee, "Aramaic Poetry in Qumran" (PhD diss., The Catholic University of America, 2011), 365.

55. Sokoloff, *DJPA*, 74b, 487b, 524b, 554a.

56. See ibid., 358b. Compare Sara Japhet, "The 'Description Poems' in Ancient Jewish Sources and in the Jewish Exegesis of the Song of Songs," in *A Critical Engagement: Essays on the Hebrew Bible in Honour of J. Cheryl Exum*, ed. David J. A. Clines and Ellen van Wolde (Sheffield: Sheffield Phoenix Press, 2011), 218, on the dearth of metaphor in this poem.

57. Cohen, "Beauty," 47.

58. Compare van Rensburg, "Intellect and/or Beauty," 121; Fitzmyer, *GA*, 196–7.

clause of the poem, ודלידיהא יאא (20.7-8). The transcription of the letters ודלידיהא is agreed upon universally, but its meaning has been the focus of some debate; at primary issue is whether this is one word or two. If it is read ודלידיהא, it consists of the relative ד- followed by the preposition ל- and the noun יד, an unusual combination apparently meaning "whatever is in her hands": hence Machiela's paraphrase "Everything about her is lovely!" If, however, the end of line 7 is taken as two words, ודל ידיהא, as Avigad and Yadin transcribed it originally, דל can be construed as related to the Akkadian *dullu* ("labor," or "work"), a loan word found in the Babylonian Talmud in this same formulation: דויל ידיה, meaning "handiwork."[59] Neither reading is free of difficulties, and major commentators are divided here, but Semitic parallels and notes in the near context lead me to favor the latter.[60] As Peter Lee points out, the poem dwells at length on the qualities of Sarai's hands (20.4-5), which meshes well with a mention here of the fineness of her manual craft.[61]

But it does not necessarily follow, as Muraoka would have it, that a note about Sarai's accomplishments at weaving, spinning, or the like indicates that חכמה means "skill" here.[62] The word may well have a "practical" component, as the root does in Biblical Hebrew; but it hardly

---

59. See *b. Pesaḥ.* 28a (twice there); compare Wolfram von Soden, *Akkadisches Handwörterbuch* (Wiesbaden: Otto Harrassowitz, 1985), 175a–b (3f). My discussion here is a bit of a simplification, for דל has also been taken to mean "tip" (Avigad and Yadin, *A Genesis Apocryphon*, 43, English section) or "daintiness" ("die Kleinheit," Osswald, "Beobachtungen," 13). Beyer originally offered "die Zartheit" ("delicacy" or "tenderness") in Beyer, *ATTM*, 174, supplemented by "(oder: das Werk)" in Klaus Beyer, *Die aramäischen Texte vom Toten Meer samt den Inschriften aus Palästina, dem Testament Levis aus der Kairoer Genisa, der Fastenrolle und den alten talmudischen Zitaten*, Ergänzungsband (Göttingen: Vandenhoeck & Ruprecht, 1994), 70. See Fitzmyer, *GA*, 197, for a few others.

60. Fitzmyer, *GA*, 101, 197, following a tentative suggestion of Franz Rosenthal, "Review of Avigad and Yadin, *A Genesis Apocryphon*," *JNES* 18 (1959): 84, favored the former reading from his first edition; Machiela, *DSGA*, 74, concurs. Reading דל as a separate word meaning "work" is advocated by, among others, Muraoka, "Notes," 41 (though see Takamitsu Muraoka, "Further Notes on the Aramaic of the Genesis Apocryphon," *RevQ* 16 [1993]: 45, where he retains the meaning "handiwork" but transcribes the letters without spaces); Greenfield, "Poetry," 50; VanderKam, "Poetry," 61–2 n. 16; and Peter Y. Lee, "Poetry," 364–5, 378–9. Several of these discussions, and in particular that of Fitzmyer (197), also contain brief histories of the debate.

61. Peter Y. Lee, "Poetry," 377–9.

62. Muraoka, "Further Notes," 45: "with all this beauty she has plenty of skill and all her handiwork is pretty." Compare Greenfield, "Poetry," 50.

seems justified to regard Abram's חכמה (19.24-25) as the abstract quality of a sage while Sarai's חכמה (20.7) means that she is good at loomwork.[63] In fact, of the Apocryphon's characters said to have "wisdom" it may well be Sarai of whom the noun, in its intellectual sense, is most credibly predicated. While her first utterance as a human character, significantly, aims at the acquisition of knowledge—"Tell me your dream, and I'll know it" (19.18)—Abram's wisdom, like that of Noah earlier (6.4, 6), is mentioned only in self-evaluation, and his interpretation of his dream is no evidence of perspicuity. Alternatively, the pragmatic aspects of Abram's own "wisdom" might be emphasized: likely Abram's attraction for the courtiers involves some real-world advantage for them, and Abram's reading and writing have practical utility. Either way, it is notable that it is a report of Sarai's חכמה, not Abram's, that reaches the ears of the king. But the central question is perhaps best informed by a recollection of the various parallels already noted between Abram's depictions of himself and Sarai. These other similarities strongly suggest that the חכמה of Sarai roughly encompasses whatever intellectual or sapiential qualities are displayed by Abram earlier. If my earlier proposals about Sarai's speech to the nobles, perhaps even extending to a recitation of "the words of Enoch," are plausible, the point is doubly underlined: this would not only be another similarity to Abram, but a patent display of sapiential prowess. Thus Sarai's manual dexterity is unlikely to define Sarai's "great wisdom," but is an additional, if possibly related, skill. The poem's final stanza, by my reading, then, contains three reasonably distinct thoughts: "But along with all this beauty, much wisdom is hers, and her handiwork is fine."[64]

Some caution may be called for here. One issue, centered on the limitations of perspective, is narratorial. It is unclear how Abram, as a character in this tale, is apprised of the precise content—let alone the form—of this lengthy poetic composition spoken in Pharaoh's court. It is impossible to resolve this question completely, but it is significant, I think, that much of what is said about Sarai in this poem dovetails nicely with her narrative data elsewhere in Abram's first-person account. The questionable reliability of Abram provides the uncertain foundation for the whole; yet to craft a reading, claims must still be weighed, and hypotheses responsibly advanced. Another issue regards the substance and heft of what is revealed

---

63. Compare Muraoka, "Notes," 41. The reading of חֹכמתי in 19.24 had not yet been proposed.

64. Compare the translation of VanderKam, "Poetry," 62: "But with all this beauty [//] she possesses great wisdom, [//] and her handiwork is lovely." See also Peter Y. Lee, "Poetry," 364–5.

about Sarai here. In my interpretation, Sarai is said, by Herqanosh and his companions, to possess not only beauty but also "much wisdom" and dexterity. I think it is certain that they encounter Sarai in the story sketched by the lacunose discourse at the end of column 19, and I believe it makes good narrative sense to posit that ואמרת, and possibly even בְּ[וּ]כֹל מֹלִי חֹנֹוֹךְ, may represent the traces of Sarai's verbal offering of her wisdom (19.29). Moreover, I consider it methodologically justifiable to push, within reason, what evidence remains: nothing ventured is nothing gained, and it seems an "impoverishment of aesthetic experience," as Chatman says, not to make such suppositions when they may enrich the reading of a character.[65] But it must be admitted that these notes of her wisdom and fine handiwork come after an avalanche of almost purely physical descriptors; it could be argued that these represent something of an afterthought, rather than constituting the climax of this paean to Sarai. From this perspective, Herqanosh's citation of "wisdom" might be better described as a hyperbolic flourish indebted to a stereotypical ideal of a "worthy woman," such as that depicted in Proverbs 31; this might imply, in turn, that the encounter between the men and Sarai was merely visual.[66]

Elements of the broader tradition are of relatively limited help in untangling these issues. The description poems of the Song of Songs, frequently cited as clear parallels to, or even the inspiration of, GenAp 20.2-8, lack any clear mention of the beloved's wisdom.[67] Muraoka notes several links with Proverbs 31, including the emphasis on the woman's work with her hands (vv. 13, 19, 31); so, too, I would add, this ideal woman exhibits wisdom, and specifically in speech (פיה פתחה בחכמה, "she opens her

---

65. Chatman, *Story and Discourse*, 117; compare 120.

66. Compare Cohen, "Beauty," 47, who likewise mentions the texts treated just below; see also van Rensburg, "Intellect and/or Beauty," 122–3, and Muraoka, "Further Notes," 45–6.

67. See, for example, Hindy Najman, "Early Nonrabbinic Interpretation," in *The Jewish Study Bible*, ed. Adele Berlin and Marc Zvi Brettler (Oxford: Oxford University Press, 2004), 1838, who says that the "language of praise used here is from the Song of Songs." However, Cohen, "Beauty," 47, notes that the Song of Songs "says nothing" about the woman's "intelligence, skill, erudition, or piety." Japhet, "Description Poems," 218, cites Song 4:3, which refers to the woman's "speech" (מדבר), as a possible allusion to wisdom. But "speech" can be "lovely" (נאוה) without being wise, and the typical English rendering of the *hapax* מדבר here as "mouth" (NJPS, NRSV, and many others) makes good sense in the near context, which also mentions teeth, lips, and cheeks (vv. 2-3). In any case, Japhet names the most important difference between the poems of the Song and that of the Apocryphon, which is the latter's almost complete lack of metaphor (218).

mouth with wisdom," v. 26).⁶⁸ But here is a converse problem: while the Song graphically extols the attractions of the female form, Proverbs actually disparages feminine beauty, or at least subordinates it clearly to piety and good behavior as defined by the masculine circles that generated it (31:30; compare 11:22). Ben Sira praises the beauty and domestic ability of the good wife (26:13-18), but pointedly excludes speech, of any kind, from her desirable qualities: "a silent woman is a gift of the Lord" (δόσις κυρίου γυνὴ σιγηρά, v. 14). If the poem of GenAp 20.2-8 were considered in abstraction, as in the work of the commentators cited here, the comparison might seem more apt. However, Sarai's talkativeness in Egypt is one of her most salient characteristics in the Apocryphon, and an important development in the tradition. The prominent female figures of Hellenistic Jewish literature, such as Esther, Judith, and Susanna, also mentioned by Cohen, are perhaps a better fit.⁶⁹ While these characters exhibit beauty alongside positive mental or spiritual qualities, though, I struggle to relate their overt piety—in the case of Esther, referring particularly to her Greek incarnation—to the depiction of Sarai in the Apocryphon.

So while its elements, both formal and thematic, have clear parallels elsewhere, the poem as a whole seems to be something of an innovation. Muraoka and J. F. van Rensburg both tacitly admit this, but consider its notes of wisdom and skill to be corrective additions to an imbalanced and not quite decorous concentration on the physical: Sarai's mental qualities are an afterthought, then, even from a compositional perspective.⁷⁰ More appealing is the solution of Cohen, who argues that GenAp 20.2-8 is a Hellenization of the Near Eastern descriptive song, influenced by the physiognomic canons of the era, which assumed the interrelationship of physical and moral or intellectual attributes.⁷¹ These principles would here be rather simplified; it is too much to suppose that each attribute

---

68. Muraoka, "Further Notes," 45–6; compare Zakovitch and Shinan, *Abram and Sarai in Egypt*, 62.

69. Cohen, "Beauty," 47.

70. Muraoka, "Further Notes," 45, seems to picture the author of the Apocryphon guiltily bringing to mind the equivocal attitude of Proverbs 31, after having gone somewhat overboard in praise of Sarai's beauty. Van Rensburg, "Intellect and/or Beauty," 123, likewise detects a moralizing impulse as the author "adds a reference" to Sarai's metaphysical charms.

71. Cohen, "Beauty," 42, 48. Compare Mladen Popović, *Reading the Human Body: Physiognomics and Astrology in the Dead Sea Scrolls and Hellenistic-Early Roman Period Judaism*, STDJ 67 (Leiden: Brill, 2007), 287, who concludes that the

of Sarai's appearance points to some inner quality, as in the detailed *Physiognomonica* attributed to Aristotle.[72] But the basic connection could help build a more gestalt conception of Sarai's character: her extraordinary beauty is thus a symbol of her remarkable mental or moral gifts of wisdom and skill. This general line of thought could even be profitably related to the note in the Septuagint that Sarai is found by the Egyptian men to be καλή…σφόδρα (Gen. 12:14 LXX), as καλή often encompasses both physical and moral qualities. Philo's evaluation in *On the Life of Abraham*—that Abraham "had a wife distinguished greatly for her goodness of soul and beauty of body, in which she surpassed all the women of her time"—may also resonate with this particular trend; the element of surpassing all others, too, is reminiscent of GenAp 20.6-7.[73]

Yet to my reading the text of the Apocryphon does not sit completely comfortably with any of these options. Although the mention of Sarai's fine handicraft may complement the poem's partial focus on her hands, Sarai's "wisdom" does not seem to be deeply interrelated with her physical beauty. Herqanosh presents it precisely as a bonus, not as something that follows naturally: "yet," or "but along with (ועם) all this beauty, much wisdom is hers" (20.7). Sarai is depicted as not only beautiful, but also wise. The events that ensue firmly underline the separability of these qualities: the "wisdom" and "handiwork" of Sarai do not, apparently, provide much draw for Pharaoh (20.8-9), and it is not the potential loss of her wit and needlepoint that irk Abram (20.15). This points up, once again, the chief weakness of the analyses noted above: none considers the broader context of the Apocryphon. But it also pulls the discussion back to the question that lies beneath most of the issues considered earlier: how much can the reader trust what is proclaimed by Herqanosh, according to Abram?

"praise of her body is meant to imply Sarai's impeccable character as a wife." Tamar Kadari, "The Beauty of Sarah in Rabbinic Literature," in *Hebrew Texts in Jewish, Christian and Muslim Surroundings*, ed. Klaas Spronk and Eveline van Staalduine-Sulman, SSN 69 (Leiden: Brill, 2018), 80–1, suggests that Sarai's "long and thin" fingers may place her "among those sons of light chosen by God" in the astrological and physiognomic literature at Qumran, but the parallel cited is only partial.

72. Cohen, "Beauty," 42.

73. *Abr.* 93 (F. H. Colson, LCL); here the relevant terms are ἀρίστη and περικαλλεστάτη. Vermès, *Scripture and Tradition*, 113, also mentions Philo in connection with the Apocryphon here. Compare Muraoka, "Further Notes," 45, on the theme of an ideal woman surpassing all others, which he notes is also present in Prov. 31:29.

Although the abundant, even microscopic attention to her features may promise rather more than it delivers, that Sarai is physically beautiful seems assured, given the mere fact of the courtiers' report, the sheer weight of its relevant adjectives, and the confirmation of Pharaoh's subsequent, no doubt expert, appraisal (20.9). For Sarai's wisdom and fine handiwork, each mentioned only once, the evidence may at first seem more tenuous. The testimony here is at one remove from Abram's narration, and almost nothing in the narrative to come contributes to the further definition of these traits. Looking back, however, Sarai demonstrates curiosity, or desire for knowledge (19.18); correctly divines where the real risk to her and Abram lies, and keeps her own counsel as to the appropriate course of action (19.23; compare line 20); and evinces several other similarities to Abram's depiction of himself (19.18, 23; 19.21, and compare 20.10-11, for example), which suggests that her "wisdom" be taken no less seriously than his (19.24-25; 20.7). When these elements are considered alongside the certainty of Sarai's encounter with the courtiers at the bottom of column 19, the motive of their quest, the possibility of her speech—even exposition of Enochic lore—in 19.29, and their eventual praise of her sapiential qualities in 20.7, I think it is appropriate to conclude that the absence of any further mention of Sarai's intellect is owing to the values of the men through whom the story is filtered, not to her lack of wisdom and skill. In characterization, all claims must be weighed, and a consideration of the narrative data beyond that contained within the poem of 20.2-8 indicates that these notes are not mere nods to convention, but of a solid piece with the rest of Sarai's image in the Apocryphon.

Sarai Uprooted, Abram Spared (GenAp 20.8-11)

> GenAp 20.8 Now when the king heard the words of Herqanosh and his two companions—that the three of them spoke as one—he greatly desired her, and sent someone 9 to be quick in acquiring her. When he saw her he was dumbfounded at all of her beauty, and took her for himself as a wife. He also sought to kill me, but Sarai said 10 to the king, "He is my brother," so that I would benefit on account of her. Thus I, Abram, was spared because of her, and was not killed. I, 11 Abram, wept bitterly—I and Lot, my brother's son, with me—on the night when Sarai was taken from me by force. *vacat* (Machiela, *DSGA*, 75)

Here again a report "heard" is crucial to the trajectory of the plot: as Abram finds a remedy to his lack when he hears about Egypt's grain supply in 19.10, thus setting this entire chain of events in motion, so Pharaoh's desire for Sarai is kindled as he hears his courtiers' poem of praise. While it seems fair to assume that the king hears the entirety of Herqanosh and his companions' report (20.2-8), it appears that his attention has wandered near the end, for Sarai's great wisdom and fine handiwork do not exercise his imagination. Instead, he "wanted her badly and sent someone in haste to take her" (שגי רחמה ושלח לעובע דברהא, 20.8-9). Any lingering doubt as to Pharaoh's motive is dispelled as soon as Sarai is brought in: "he saw her and was stunned by all her beauty, and he married her himself, as a wife" (וחזהא ואתמה על כול שפרהא ונסבהא לה לאנתא, 20.9). The repetition here of כול שפרהא (compare 20.7) underlines which of the three qualities mentioned in the poem's peroration resonates with the king, while נסב, "to take" or "marry," seems, at least at first, to carry an explicitly sexual force, especially in this context.[74]

Much, however, is submerged, unclear, or confused in Abram's telling of these events. That Sarai is violently abducted is implied by Pharaoh's covetous "haste" to "take" her, an impression strengthened by Abram's later description of the event as having occurred "by force" or "under compulsion" (באונס, 20.11; compare 14).[75] Moreover, Pharaoh's alleged designs on Abram's life, apparently aligned with some of the implications of Abram's dream, punctuate the atmosphere with sudden violence (20.9). Yet the precise circumstances under which Pharaoh seeks to kill Abram, but is restrained by Sarai's production of the line Abram wrote for her so long ago—"He is my brother!" (אחי הוא, 20.10; compare 19.20)—are very fuzzy and shot through with ambiguously commercial undertones. Language evocative of transaction may begin with Abram's description of Pharaoh's "marriage" of Sarai, for the meaning of נסב can extend to acquisition by purchase.[76]

Likewise obscure is the meaning of Abram's statement immediately following Sarai's exclamation. Both Fitzmyer and Machiela, along with many others, take כדי הוית מתגר על דילהא as a kind of purpose or result clause: "so that I would benefit on account of her."[77] But this would be an unusual function for כדי, which routinely means "when," as it does elsewhere in the near context: "when the king heard" (20.8); "on the

---

74. Sokoloff, *DJPA*, 352b–353b; Marcus Jastrow, *A Dictionary of the Targumim, the Talmud Babli and Yerushalmi, and the Midrashic Literature* (1903; repr., New York: Judaica, 1996), 915a–b.

75. Sokoloff, *DJPA*, 40b; Jastrow, *Dictionary*, 29a–b.

76. See *y. Šeb.* 35b(23), cited in Sokoloff, *DJPA*, 353a.

77. Fitzmyer, *GA*, 101, 200; Machiela, *DSGA*, 75. Compare Avigad and Yadin, *A Genesis Apocryphon*, 43, English section; Géza Vermès, *The Dead Sea Scrolls in English*, 4th ed. (New York: Penguin, 1995), 295; Florentino García Martínez, *The Dead Sea Scrolls Translated: The Qumran Texts in English* (Leiden: Brill, 1994), 233.

night when Sarai was taken from me" (20.11).⁷⁸ Indeed, the durative periphrastic construction here, הוי plus the participle, would seem ideally suited to follow a temporal adverb.⁷⁹ The precise derivation of the participle (מתגר) is also a matter of debate, although the roots in question, תגר and אגר, occupy similar semantic territory: significantly, both are found elsewhere in contexts of trade or employment.⁸⁰ It seems to me, then, that the proposal of Muraoka, first advanced in 1972, is still the best: Sarai voices her saving lie, Abram says, "while I was negotiating about what concerned her."⁸¹

It might be objected that such a reading makes little sense in light of what follows, where Abram weeps with "strong weeping" (בכי תקיף, 20.11), characterizes Sarai's transfer to Pharaoh's house as having been achieved "by force" (20.11, 14), and maintains that he was given "gifts" only after his healing of the king (20.30). The order of the near context seems odd, as well: Pharaoh has Sarai taken, marries her, then tries to kill Abram, who is saved by Sarai's intervention—while Abram negotiates on her behalf.⁸² But just as the textual question in 19.15—"sprouted together

---

78. Muraoka, *Grammar*, 262 n. 151, flatly states that "no Aramaic idiom attests to such a usage." Of all the instances of כדי listed in the concordance of Machiela, *DSGA*, I can find no other example that does not clearly mean "when," which is also his gloss here (277). Neither Machiela nor Fitzmyer, *GA*, 200, explain their rendering here. Compare Sokoloff, *DJPA*, 250b, and Jastrow, *Dictionary*, 613a–b, neither of whom offer any examples of כדי in purpose clauses; nor does the usage here seem to be a Hebraism, judging from *HALOT* 219a–b; compare 98b, 1852a. For an example of a translation that may retain at least a quasi-temporal force for כדי, see Jongeling, Labuschagne, and van der Woude, *Texts*, 95: "whereupon I was benefitted because of her." On this and other elements of this clause, compare Andrew G. Daniel, "A New Reading of Genesis Apocryphon (1Q20) 20.10: Syntax, Semantics and Literary Function," *RevQ* 28 (2016): 279–85.

79. Muraoka, *Grammar*, 175–9, especially 177, §55 fa.

80. See Sokoloff, *DJPA*, 575b, for תגר as "to trade, do business"; Jastrow, *Dictionary*, 1646b, similarly offers "to travel about, trade." Daniel, "New Reading," 281–3, argues that מתגר is derived from a distinct root of the same radicals and means "to dispute, debate, quarrel" in a legal context. *DJPA* defines אגר, on the other hand, as "to hire, rent" (35a–b); Jastrow, again, is very similar: "hire, employ, rent" (14a).

81. Muraoka, "Notes," 42–3. Muraoka has held to this interpretation through the appearance of his *Grammar* in 2011; see 9, §5b; 177, §55 fa; 262, §88Bb and n. 151.

82. Daniel, "New Reading," 284, resolves this by reading back from the context of Abram's prayer in 20.12-16 to argue that Abram is "negotiating" or "disputing" with God, on Sarai's behalf, in 20.10. With no discourse-level clue that God is part of the transaction in 20.10, however, or external evidence that מתגר is used of human-divine disputes, it is simpler to assume that the human characters are in view.

from one root" versus "very beautiful"—proved difficult to resolve on the grounds of narrative logic, so too these quandaries cannot simply be explained away on the assumption that Abram is consistent. Abram's deeply personal implication in the events he relates necessarily raises doubts about his candor, and these little inconsistencies may suggest that his story-level motives are rather more complex than his narration implies.

What emerges most clearly about Sarai in this episode is her great value—and how narrowly this is defined. Although her production of her lie to the king may suggest some timely wit, no further mention will be made of her wisdom and craft. What Pharaoh values is Sarai's physical beauty, which is a transparent cipher for her sexuality, as his actions make plain. It will become clear that this is also her primary value to Abram. Although his "strong weeping" (20.11) recalls Sarai's tears of long ago, shed in prospect of the very events that have just now come to pass (19.21), his emotion proves to be generated not by empathy for his abducted and captive wife, companion of his journeys and partner in his fears (19.18, 23), but by much more practical, even mechanical, concerns.

Abram's Prayer (GenAp 20.12-16)

> GenAp 20.12 That night I prayed and entreated and asked for mercy. Through sorrow and streaming tears I said, "Blessed are you Most High God, my Lord, for all 13 ages; for you are Lord and Ruler over everything. You are sovereign over all the kings of the earth, having power to enact judgment on all of them. So now 14 I lodge my complaint before you, my Lord, concerning Pharaoh Zoan, king of Egypt, for my wife has been taken from me forcefully. Bring judgment against him on my behalf, and reveal your mighty hand 15 through him and all of his house, that he might not prevail this night in rendering my wife unclean for me! Thus, they will come to know you, my Lord, that you are Lord over all the kings 16 of the earth." So I wept and was deeply troubled. (Machiela, *DSGA*, 75)

Further tears bookend Abram's relation of his prayer, delivered in response to Sarai's abduction (20.12, 16).[83] It is hard for me to agree with Crawford, however, that "we find Abram weeping and praying to God on Sarai's behalf" here.[84] In fact, Abram directly solicits divine judgment "on my behalf" (20.14), as Machiela renders, and self-referentiality is one of the prayer's most salient characteristics: El Elyon is repeatedly

---

83. Compare Ego, "Figure of Abraham," 238.
84. Crawford, "Genesis in the Dead Sea Scrolls," 364; compare Vermès, *Scripture and Tradition*, 125.

"my Lord" (מרי, 20.12, 14-15), in Abram's formulation, and Sarai—only referred to as "my wife" (אנתתי, 20.14-15)—is not merely "taken," but, more importantly, taken "from me" (מני, 20.14). In fact, Abram's central demand involves Sarai only insofar as her objective state of "cleanness" affects him: "may [Pharaoh] not have power this night to make my wife unclean for me" (20.15).[85] The basic theology of his prayer only emphasizes Abram's self-interest. He invokes God as "master over all the kings of the earth" (בכול מלכי ארעא...שליט, 20.13), a king of kings who can force Pharaoh to the divine will on Abram's behalf (compare Ps. 2:10-12), not God as defender of the oppressed, such as his defenseless, imprisoned wife (compare Ps. 68:6-7).

The underlying conception of Abram's primary request—that Sarai not be defiled "for me," or "away from me"—is completely mechanical: if Pharaoh has sex with Sarai, she can no longer be sexually accessible to Abram.[86] The parties' roles in this dispute are clear. In explicitly legal language, God is invoked as judge in the plaintiff Abram's suit: "Now I am lodging a complaint with you, my Lord, against Pharaoh Zoan, king of Egypt, because my wife has been taken away from me" (20.13-14).[87] The king, named more fully here than in any extant portion of the Apocryphon, is the defendant, while Sarai, who is not called by name at all in this section, is the property under dispute. Strangely, however—though it may be implicit in his plea that she not be spoiled for him—Abram does not ask for Sarai's return. As will become plain, the initial divine response is apt.

This forensic reification of Sarai signals a deeper shift in her depiction in the Genesis Apocryphon. Just this abruptly, Sarai is no longer an actor in this narrative. After uttering her lie in 20.10, Sarai displays virtually no volition or subjectivity, playing only the part of an almost inanimate object, a valuable chest, perhaps, that rightfully belongs to Abram: as long as Pharaoh cannot spring the lock, all will be well. This is a puzzling and frankly dissatisfying outcome after Sarai's relative prominence earlier in

---

85. טמי ואל ישלט בליליא דן לטמיא אנתתי מני plus מן literally means something like "defile away from"; see Muraoka, "Further Notes," 47. Compare Sokoloff, *DJPA*, 226b.

86. Muraoka, "Further Notes," 47.

87. וכען קבלתך מרי על פרעו צען מלך מצרין די דברת אנתתי מני. According to Fitzmyer, *GA*, 202, קבל has a "definite legal meaning, known from various Elephantine and Egyptian Aramaic texts," and is here employed in syntax recognizable from these documents: קבל plus על plus the "object of complaint," here Pharaoh, with the "judicial authority," here God, represented by the direct object (verbal pronominal suffix). Compare Sokoloff, *DJPA*, 473b.

the narrative. Spoken to (19.12-13), looked to for comfort (19.17-18), a captivating presence who displays curiosity (19.18), presence of mind (19.23), "great wisdom" and skill in craft (20.7-8), a clever beauty whose speech has primacy, frequency, and outsize impact on the action (19.16, 18, 29[?]; 20.10), Sarai is henceforth a mute object of trade. Her female humanity is presumed in the narrative's principal element of suspense, which turns on the possibility of Pharaoh having sex with her, but Sarai's most significant subsequent reemergence from obscurity is arguably in the context of the king's gifts to her in 20.31-32. Barring Hagar, this reception of money and clothing evokes, for me at least, nothing so much as the image I just suggested: a fine chest or trunk to put things in.

Perhaps Sarai's bloodless depiction in the discourse from this point on need not mean that nothing can be hypothesized about her story-level existence while captive to Pharaoh; maybe her relatively multifaceted characterization to this point could feed some speculation about her feelings and actions over this span of two years. For me, however, what Abram as narrator offers about Sarai going forward is so bland, when it is not completely blank, that such an effort would resemble less an act of criticism than a further attempt at rewriting the tradition. The importance of what ensued after the literal gap in the text at the courtiers' visit positively demanded speculation: what they purport to know about the previously hidden Sarai is the fulcrum of the entire plot—how do they know it? As concerns Sarai, however, the gap here is so profound as to be unbridgeable, for all the manuscript's clarity, because what issues from her captivity (20.27-32) is an inert shadow, promptly to pass away completely, of what she was.

Response to Abram's Prayer (GenAp 20.16-21)

> GenAp 20.16 During that night the Most High God sent a pestilential spirit to afflict him, and to every person of his household an evil 17 spirit. It was an ongoing affliction for him and every person of his household, so that he was not able to approach her, nor did he have sexual relations with her. She was with him 18 for two years, and at the end of two years the afflictions and hardships grew heavier and more powerful over him and every person of his household. So he sent 19 a message to all the wise me[n] of Egypt, and to all the magicians, in addition to all the physicians of Egypt, (to see) if they could heal him and (every) person 20 of his household of this affliction. But all of the physicians and magicians and all of the wise men were not able to succeed in curing him, for the spirit began afflicting all of them (too), 21 so that they fled the scene! *vacat* (Machiela, *DSGA*, 75–76)

God proves to be particularly detail-oriented in response to Abram's tearful prayer. Abram's disproportionate request that the king's entire household (כול ביתה, 20.15) be punished is fulfilled extravagantly, for example: the sufferings of "every man of his house" (כול אנש ביתה) are described in nearly every line (20.16, 17, 18; compare lines 19-20), and even outsiders who come to help are afflicted (20.20). As Bernstein and others have pointed out, several details here recall biblical narratives that feature elect descendants of Abram besting ineffectual Egyptian savants.[88] In Gen. 41:8, another Pharaoh "sends for" (שלח) and "calls" (קרא) "all the magicians of Egypt and all its wise men" (compare 20.18-19, וישלח קרא), who fail to comprehend the dreams that Joseph will interpret in vv. 25-36. Likewise, in Exod. 7:11 yet another Pharaoh "calls" (קרא) "the wise men and the sorcerers," collectively referred to as "the magicians of Egypt," whose conjuring is shown to be inferior to that of Moses and Aaron; compare the failure of the magicians to "stand" (עמד) because of a plague of boils, facilitated by the Israelite brothers, that afflicts the magicians as well as the people (Exod. 9:11; קום in GenAp 20.20).[89] These intertextual links, along with Abram's eventual success at healing the king (20.28–29), firmly underline God's identity here as "Lord over all the kings of the earth," as Abram pronounced in his prayer (20.15-16; compare line 13). Disturbingly, this display of power does nothing to rescue Sarai from captivity—but, again, that isn't one of the requests of Abram, who merely wants to keep her from being sexually spoiled for him (20.15). That God permits Sarai to languish for two years (20.17-18) confirms the alignment of the deity's appraisal of her worth with that of Abram: the salient issue is her sexual inviolability, and the king's low-grade, chronic harassment by a "spirit of striking" (רוח מכדש, 20.16) is enough to ensure, Abram claims, that Pharaoh "wasn't able to touch her—and he didn't 'know' her, either" (20.17).[90]

---

88. Moshe J. Bernstein, "The Dead Sea Scrolls and Jewish Biblical Interpretation in Antiquity: A Multi-Generic Perspective," in *The Dead Sea Scrolls at 60: Scholarly Contributions by New York University Faculty and Alumni*, ed. L. H. Schiffman and S. L. Tzoref (Leiden: Brill, 2010), 75; Moshe J. Bernstein, "The *Genesis Apocryphon*: Compositional and Interpretive Perspectives," in *A Companion to Biblical Interpretation in Early Judaism*, ed. Matthias Henze (Grand Rapids: Eerdmans, 2012), 173–4. Compare Fitzmyer, *GA*, 206; Zakovitch and Shinan, *Abram and Sarai in Egypt*, 90.

89. Compare Vermès, *Scripture and Tradition*, 114. Fitzmyer, *GA*, 206, provides other examples of this "motif of the failure of the non-Jewish experts to aid the king," such as Daniel 2; 4; 5:7-8.

90. ולא יכל למקרֹב בהא ואף לא ידעהא. On קרב plus ב as "touch," see Sokoloff, *DJPA*, 502b; compare the examples in Muraoka, "Notes," 33.

Sarai here is practically inert and referred to only by pronouns. Except for the verbless clause that notes her physical presence "with" Pharaoh for two years, "she" is defined only by what cannot be done to her (20.17-18); again, an image akin to an uncrackable safe comes to mind. Two ironies arise here. The first is that Sarai, though unnamed, has emerged as the key figure in this entire drama, the middle term of the equation between Abram and Pharaoh; but just as her value is established most plainly, her character becomes an object, virtually drained of humanity. The second, which will be clearest in retrospect, is that the deception first spoken by Sarai (20.10) and perpetuated by Abram (20.26-27) in order to forestall disaster is, in fact, the chief obstacle to the quandary's ultimate resolution.

Herqanosh's Errand, and the Revelation of the Truth (GenAp 20.21-23)

> GenAp 20.21 *vacat* At this point Herqanosh came to me asking that I come pray over 22 the king and lay my hands upon him, so that he would live. This was because he had seen [me] in a dream…. But Lot said to him, "Abram, my uncle, cannot pray over 23 the king while his wife Sarai is with him! Now go and tell the king that he should send his wife away from himself to her husband; then he (Abram) will pray over him so that he might live." (Machiela, *DSGA*, 76)

The pronouns in the telling of this scene give rise to some interesting instability. Who "saw" Abram "in a dream" (בְּחֵלֶם חֲז[וֹנִי, 20.22)—Herqanosh, or Pharaoh? The pronominal elements immediately preceding suggest Pharaoh is the dreamer, a reading bolstered by external considerations such as the narrative's probable adoption of other motifs from Genesis 20, where King Abimelech sees God in a dream (v. 3).[91] The context of Gen. 41:1 may also have something to contribute to this question: there, too, the release of a captive from a two-year imprisonment

---

91. Abimelech does not "approach" (קרב) Sarah in Gen. 20:4, a detail missing in Genesis 12; compare ולא יכל למקרב בהא, "he was not able to approach her" (GenAp 20.17). For this and other examples from Genesis 20, see Bernstein, "Re-Arrangement, Anticipation, and Harmonization," 49–52; compare Bernstein, "Multi-Generic Perspective," 73–5; Fitzmyer, *GA*, 208; and Crawford, *Rewriting Scripture*, 122–3. That Genesis 12 and 20 are "intimately linked" in the Apocryphon's retelling was noted already by Vermès, *Scripture and Tradition*, 115.

is catalyzed by a dream of Pharaoh.[92] The ambiguity around whose "woman" or "wife" Sarai is, exactly, is somewhat deeper, and neatly captures the narrative's central tension.

But Sarai's function in the plot, however important, only reinforces the mechanical conception developed earlier. Here, it seems that her continued possession by Pharaoh would create a spiritual obstacle to Abram's prayer, jamming the transmission of his intercession: Abram, Lot says, simply "cannot pray over the king while Sarai" remains "with him" (לא יכול...לצליא על מלכא ושרי...עֹמה, 20.22-23). Lot's abrupt adoption of the role of intermediary does nothing to suggest that Abram has Sarai's interests in mind. That Lot understands the mechanics of the situation, and thus the elements of its solution, suggests that Abram does, too; that Lot is the one finally to reveal the truth, further, implies Abram's continued reluctance on this score (compare 20.26-27), and his decided willingness to allow Sarai's captivity to continue.

Report and Rebuke; Healing, Payment, and Return to the Land (GenAp 20.24–21.4)

GenAp 20.24 *vacat* Now when Herqanosh heard the words of Lot, he went (and) said to the king, "All these afflictions and hardships 25 that are afflicting and troubling my lord the king are due to Sarai, the wife of Abram. Just return Sarai to Abram her husband 26 and this affliction and the spirit of foulness will depart from you." So the [k]i[ng] called me and said to me, "What have you done to me?! Why were you saying 27 to me 'she is my sister' when she was your wife, so that I took her as a wife for myself?! Here is your wife. Take her, go and get yourself out of 28 every district of Egypt! But now pray over me and my household, that this evil spirit may be driven away from us." So I prayed over [hi]m, that I might heal 29 him, and I laid my hands upon his [h]ead. Thus, the affliction was removed from him, and the evil [spirit] driven away [from him]. The king recovered, rose up, and gave 30 to me on t[hat da]y many gift[s], and the king swore to me by an oath that he did not have sexual relations with her, [nor] did he [de]file her. Then he returned 31 Sarai to me, and the king gave to her [m]uch si[lver and g]old and much clothing of fine linen and purple, which... ...[ ] 32 before her, as well as Hagar. Thus he restored her to me,

---

92. *Jubilees* also indicates that Sarai was held captive for two years (compare *Jub.* 13:11 and v. 16), as Fitzmyer, *GA*, 206, and others have noted, but dreams play no part in that text's abbreviated version of Gen. 12:10-20, and the tradition behind Genesis 20 is omitted.

and appointed for me a man who would escort me [from Egyp]t to[ ]...to your people. To you [ ] 33 *vacat* Now I, Abram, grew tremendously in many flocks and also in silver and gold. I went up from Egy[p]t, [and] my brother's son 34 [Lot wen]t with me. Lot had also acquired for himself many flocks, and took a wife for himself from the daughters of Egy[p]t. I was encamping [with him] 21.1 (at) every place of my (former) encampments until I reached Bethel, the place where I had built the altar. I built it a second time, 2 ...and offered upon it burnt offerings and a meal offering to the Most High God, and I called there on the name of the Lord of the Ages. I praised the name of God, blessed 3 God, and gave thanks there before God because of all the flocks and good things that he had given to me, and because he had worked good on my behalf and returned me 4 to this land in peace. *vacat* (Machiela, *DSGA*, 76–8)

The mechanical effect of Sarai's physical position is even more simply conceived here, in Herqanosh's report to the king: "Just return Sarai to Abram her husband and this striking will depart from you" (יְתִיבוּ נה לשרי לאברם בעלה ויתוך מנכה מֹכתשא דֹן, 20.25-26). As Abram relates it, the actual procedure is slightly more complex. After Pharaoh rebukes Abram, revealing that Abram has himself persistently verbalized the lie about his relationship with Sarai, the king presents her to him: "Here is your wife! Take her, go, and get yourself out of any region of Egypt!" (הא אנתתך דבְּרֹהּ אזל ועדי לך מן כול מדינת מצרין, 20.27-28). Now, apparently, with Sarai back in hand, Abram can pray over Pharaoh, which seems to fit with Lot's earlier evaluation to Herqanosh (20.22-23, 28-29), and the king, at least, is healed—no mention is made of his household's health.

It is curious to note, however, that Abram narrates Sarai's return to him, her rightful owner (compare בעל, 20.23, 25), three times. Pharaoh seems to give her back in line 27—"Here is your wife!"—and the fact of Abram's successful intercessory prayer, in the light of Lot's statement in 20.22-23, implies that he has taken possession of her. But after the king's recovery, Abram accepts "many gifts" (מנתנ[ן] שֹּגיאָֹן, 20.30) and solemn assurances that his earlier request by prayer was met, as the king swears that "he did not make her impure" (ו[לא טֹמֹ]יהא, 20.30; compare 20.15)— and then, Abram says, Pharaoh "returned Sarai to me" (ואתיֹב לי לשֹרי, 20.30–31). Even now, though, the king gives precious metals, clothing, and at least one slave to Sarai (לה, 20.31), after which Abram remarks, "he handed her over to me" (ואשלמהא לי, 20.32).[93]

---

93. Machiela's temporal and modal-adverbial subordination of the second and third "returns" is a sensible attempt to impose some order on this repeated information, but one that is purely contextual.

This puzzling series of returns may betray a mercenary tendency in Abram, similar to that implied in Genesis 12, that is routinely viewed as rectified by the Apocryphon's temporal displacement of Pharaoh's largess: Crawford, for instance, expresses a common sentiment in her contention that the change in sequence means that "Abram does not benefit from Sarai's narrowly averted defilement."[94] But the picture is not so clear if this scene is read instead as a provisional, even reluctant acceptance of Sarai's return that unfolds in stages. She is presented to Abram, which frees him to heal the king; but Abram seems to hold out, while Pharaoh sweetens the deal with gifts and guarantees that Abram's property is undamaged, and attempts to give her back once again; finally, after a full line devoted to the king's substantial payment to Sarai, Abram relents and takes her back, ratifying the deal. I am not as sure as Fitzmyer that "Abram's wealth is independent of" these gifts to Sarai; in fact, it seems likely to me that at least some of these blandishments find their way into Abram's own coffers, as he soon notes—after the *vacat*, but before he leaves Egypt—how he has "grown" in "a great many possessions and, in addition, silver and gold" (וגבלת אנה אברם בנכסין שגיאין לחדא ואף בכסף ודהב, 20.33; compare Sarai's reception of כ]סף וד[הב שׁ]גיא] in line 31).[95] Suggestively, as Machiela notes, the verb גבל seems to be used elsewhere of "growth" only in describing the increase of a parasite.[96] When set alongside the ambiguously pecuniary undertones of Abram's description of the night of Sarai's abduction, these notes of acquisition at her restoration may suggest, again, that Abram is not entirely forthcoming about the complex of motives that drive his conduct in this self-related tale. The Apocryphon's project of "renovating the character of Abram," as Falk puts it, remains incomplete, and in this way anticipates the much more ambitious attempt at apologizing for Abraham in the *Antiquities*.[97] Although Abram, in the Apocryphon, presents himself in a light that is more positive than that cast by the biblical narrator on his analogue in Genesis, there may yet be bits of less savory traits peeking through the fabric of his self-justifying narration.

As for Sarai, she disappears without a sound from the discourse of the Apocryphon, at least as the text stands, for good. Her last action, only implied, is merely receptive, and her collection of Pharaoh's money

---

94. Crawford, *Rewriting Scripture*, 123.
95. Fitzmyer, *GA*, 214. The extant text features כסף and דהב outside of these two lines only in the context of a dream of Noah (13.9), and there in the reverse order.
96. See Jastrow, *Dictionary*, 207a, citing *b. Ḥul.* 67b.
97. Falk, *Parabiblical Texts*, 80–5.

and goods provides a final parallel with Abram's depiction of himself, recalling his own acquisition of gifts (19.24-25; 20.30) and anticipating his sudden possession of money just before his departure from Egypt. Against the background of the broader tradition, Sarai's reception of "Hagar," introduced with no further definition in 20.32, suggests that Sarai might still reemerge from her state of inert but inviolate receptacle. In a different way, too, Abram's concern to keep Sarai sexually "clean" for him may imply the divine promise of offspring, made explicit in 21.8-14 (and compare 22.33-34, after which the text breaks off at a cut made in antiquity), which makes it likely that other episodes familiar from their presentation in Genesis filled the columns that once stood to the left of those that remain. However—barring the welcome, chance discovery of another substantial manuscript of this highly engaging text—the historical accidents of the Apocryphon's preservation unfortunately admit nothing but vague speculation about Sarai's trajectory in the remainder of the narrative. Might her penchants for speech and independent action have returned in her response to her predicted pregnancy, or at Isaac's birth? Could her sapiential qualities have affected her later interaction with Hagar, or her relationship with Ishmael? Or do Sarai's relative prominence and definition in 19.14–20.11 express a short-lived, creative aberration that gives way permanently to the object-like Sarai classified as property in Abram's legal complaint in 20.12-16?

Conclusion: Sarai in the Genesis Apocryphon

Sarai in the Genesis Apocryphon is a complex and evolving character who grows in prominence and definition until she is abruptly reduced to an object in Abram and Pharaoh's dispute over her sexual availability. The state of the text consigns the course of her trajectory before and after Egypt to fragile guesswork, and what remains is filtered through Abram's narration, but a remarkably full and interesting image of Sarai can still be made out. Sarai's emergence takes some time: there is no certain mention of her existence until 19.17, though a reasonably sure hint is implicit in Abram's brief travelogue in lines 12-13. His remarks there assume and imply togetherness, at least, and even some respect and mutuality between the characters, an impression that is initially reinforced by their interaction after Abram's dream. Sarai and Abram's similarity, which even approaches metaphorical identity in their growth "from one root" in the imagery of his dream, is only strengthened by parallels that trace throughout the narrative: as Abram speaks and is defined by his speech, whether truth or lies, so is Sarai (19.7, 18, 24-29; and compare 20.9-10 and 26-27); as Sarai reacts to events with significant emotion, weeping and exhibiting fear, so does Abram (19.18, 21, 23; 20.10-12, 16); and Abram claims wisdom, while Sarai demonstrates forethought and is celebrated for her sapiential qualities (19.23-24; 20.7). Even Sarai's last, pale implied action in the narrative resonates with an activity Abram has associated with himself, as she receives gifts from Pharaoh (19.24-25; 20.29-32). Paradoxically, however, these important symmetries do not lead Abram to appraise Sarai's value in holistic, human terms; her worth is ultimately assessed very narrowly, even mechanically, as a sexual receptacle that must remain exclusive to Abram in order to retain its utility.

Sarai's representation as a date palm in Abram's dream presages this motif of utility at the same time as it suggests her beauty, subsequently so firmly underlined in the courtiers' poem of praise (19.14-17; 20.2-8; compare 19.23). Her usefulness is not only implicit in the image of a fruitful tree, but also distinctly expressed in the tree's verbal intervention on Abram's cedar's behalf, a first virtual action that anticipates Sarai's last real act as subject (19.16; 20.9-10). Speech, in fact, constitutes a vital expression of Sarai's subjectivity until this final utterance. Her first statement as a character aims at the acquisition of knowledge, which accords with the courtiers' later testimony to her wisdom (19.18; 20.7). Sarai seems to offer an illustration of this sagacity as she intuits the true threat to her person, avoiding Abram's advised course and implementing an alternate strategy that apparently keeps her safe for five years (19.20, 23). However, this seeming demonstration of agency is undermined not only by the fear that is its motive force, but also by its result, which is a captivity, if self-imposed, not so different in kind from that which awaits her in Pharaoh's house.

Sarai's relative prominence in the discourse before the poorly preserved episode with the three nobles (19.14-23) foreshadows her vital role in the plot to come. The primacy, frequency, and significance of her speech, moreover, coupled with the nature of the courtiers' quest in search of wisdom and their eventual, credible citation of her great wisdom and fine handiwork (19.16, 18, 20, 24-25; 20.7, 9-10), makes it narratively plausible that Sarai once offered wise speech in what is now the regrettably lacunose end of column 19. What remains of the text, further, admits formal evidence (ואמרת, and maybe even בֹּ[ו]ל מֹלי חֹנוֹךָ, 19.29) that can be construed in support of this hypothesis. However this may be, it seems certain that Sarai's encounter with Herqanosh and his companions is the crucial pivot of this entire complex of Egyptian scenes in the Apocryphon. The men return to court deeply impressed with her physical, intellectual, and manual charms, mentioning nothing of their dealings with Abram, and their report triggers the central crisis that had been vaguely intimated in at least one of Abram's interpretations of his dream, so long ago (19.21; 20.8-9).

But here the primary irony of Sarai's story in the Genesis Apocryphon comes suddenly into view. Just as her character reaches an intriguing fullness, the varied traits of this garrulous, resourceful, beautiful, wise, and dexterous woman are funneled down to one quality that is identified with her beauty (20.9), but, in reality, is even narrower: her mechanical sexual receptivity. And just when it becomes clearest that Sarai is the central entity in the conflict that drives the plot, her humanity seems to collapse, leaving in her place an object to which legitimate access is disputed. Abram's relation of his prayer crystallizes this transformation, as he names himself as the injured party and petitions not for his wife's rescue from captivity, but for her maintenance in a sexually clean state—for him (20.13-15). Though Sarai, by Abram's own testimony, has just saved Abram's life (20.9-10), any mutuality that was evident earlier in the narrative has disappeared, and the similarities that have emerged between Sarai and Abram do not urge his sympathies. From this point onward, Sarai is inert, primarily defined not even by what is done to her, but what cannot be done to her, or what cannot be done because of her physical presence (20.17, 22-23).

This sketch of Sarai's mercurial trajectory in the Genesis Apocryphon only adds to the doubts that have surrounded Abram's narratorial reliability throughout. Why is her relative complexity distilled into pure functionality? What can be believed about her earlier, fuller depiction when it becomes plain that Abram values her, above all else, as an inviolate object? Again, Abram as narrator is a talker from the beginning, and certain elements of his tale seem not to add up. He comes off well in his own telling: he can divine the meaning of dreams, for example, and is a sought-after sage. But Abram's relation of his dream and its interpretations, especially as compared with his description of later events, provides more questions than answers, and no one mentions his wisdom later. His staging of events seems calculated to allay any concern about his improperly benefitting from Sarai's imprisonment: five years pass before his predictions begin to be realized, however imperfectly, and his gifts from Pharaoh are implied to be given in gratitude for his healing powers. Yet Abram's dealings with Pharaoh, both at Sarai's abduction and at her release, may hint at mercenary motives. What is he "negotiating" about in 20.10? Why does he seem to narrate Sarai's return only in stages punctuated by the reception of wealth (20.27-32)? Set against the context of Abram's prayer, in which he exhibits no clear concern for Sarai as a human being, these notes of transaction make Abram's purposes seem murky indeed.

As mentioned at the outset of this chapter, it is something of a scholarly commonplace to remark upon the "strong" female characters in the Genesis Apocryphon. My study here has supported this contention to a degree, but also shown that, at least for Sarai, this representation needs considerable qualification. Sarai's crucial function in the plot should not be confused with an enduringly round and nuanced characterization, for any definition, agency, or self-determination deflate entirely after her abduction and production of the lie Abram scripted for her, and her role shrinks to that of a contested, valuable box. Sarai's value as a wise, beautiful, and skillful woman proves irrelevant to the other characters in the end, for her true worth to Abram, Pharaoh, and God is ultimately located in her attractive anatomy. And there is no redemption or return from this state for Sarai in the Apocryphon, now or in antiquity: after Abram takes her and her new wealth back, she sinks without a trace, and the text soon ends at a cut in the leather, mid-sentence.

Chapter 5

SARRA IN THE *JEWISH ANTIQUITIES*

Introduction

Nearly all treatments of Sarra (as she is named here) in the *Jewish Antiquities* of Flavius Josephus compare her point-by-point with her analogue in the MT. Most choose to highlight her more "positive" depiction, while a few underline her contracted and weakened role.[1] Both of these emphases capture a part of Sarra's image in the *Antiquities*, but neither can be consistently sustained without significant qualification. Her character is considerably more complex, with both greater moral ambiguity and more displays of agency, than these sketches allow.

---

1. Bailey, "Matriarchs," 161, argues for the "rather positive portrait" of Sarra in the *Antiquities*. He is joined in this evaluation by Feldman, *JA 1–4*, 71 n. 589, 81 n. 654, 82 n. 661, 83 n. 666; Reinhartz and Walfish, "Conflict and Coexistence," 102–3; Troy A. Miller, "Surrogate, Slave and Deviant? The Figure of Hagar in Jewish Tradition and Paul (Galatians 4.21-31)," in *Early Christian Literature and Intertextuality*, vol. 2, *Exegetical Studies*, ed. Craig A. Evans and H. Daniel Zacharias (London: T&T Clark, 2009), 146–7; and Birgit van der Lans, "Hagar, Ishmael, and Abraham's Household in Josephus' *Antiquitates Judaicae*," in *Abraham, the Nations, and the Hagarites: Jewish, Christian, and Islamic Perspectives on Kinship with Abraham*, ed. Martin Goodman, George H. van Kooten, and Jacques T. A. G. M. van Ruiten (Leiden: Brill, 2010), 187–8. Halpern-Amaru, "Portraits in Josephus," 145–8, emphasizes Sarra's diminishment, as does Niehoff, "Mother and Maiden," 416–18; compare the brief remarks of Heather A. McKay, "Eve's Sisters Re-Cycled: The Literary *Nachleben* of Old Testament Women," in *Recycling Biblical Figures: Papers Read at a NOSTER Colloquium in Amsterdam, 12–13 May 1997*, ed. Athalya Brenner and Jan Willem van Henten (Leiden: Deo, 1999), 176, and Christopher T. Begg, "The Flight of Hagar according to Josephus," *Hermenêutica* 8 (2008): 17.

In the *Antiquities*, Sarra's linear "biography" proceeds in fits and starts. My reading accordingly highlights three interrelated motifs that are, in my estimation, central to her characterization. First, and most simply, Sarra is often—but not always—diminished in the retelling of the *Antiquities*. This attenuation has already been observed in brief treatments by Betsy Halpern-Amaru and Maren Niehoff, who both point to departures from the MT in concluding that the narrator of the *Antiquities* limits Sarra's role and initiative.[2] My discussion also points to many instances of this dynamic that are perceptible within the narrative itself, while not ignoring the occasions where the Sarra of the *Antiquities* actually gains in prominence in comparison with other strands of the tradition.

Second, Sarra's image is often conformed to that of Abraham in the *Antiquities*. This has become a familiar motif in my readings in this study. However, the ways in which these resemblances are expressed are almost always unique to the *Antiquities*, considered across the tradition treated here, lending support to an emerging idea that Sarra's similarity to Abraham represents a kind of "deep trait" that demands expression in a variety of ways in the different narratives that tell her story.

Third, Sarra's portrayal in the *Antiquities* is complicated by the persistent desire of the narrator to show the main characters in a positive light. The Josephan narrator is notorious for "improving" the characters of the heroes of the biblical stories, eliminating or apologizing for compromising behavior and delivering panegyrics articulating their heretofore unknown merits. Louis Feldman has pointed to this with regard to several male figures in the *Antiquities*, including Abraham, while James Bailey has done the same for Sarra and the other matriarchs of Genesis.[3] What is not usually noticed, however, is how often these attempts at character-polishing stumble on their own lights, as the narrator's solutions spawn further problems. So Sarra is indeed made to look "better" in the *Antiquities*, at least on the surface; but the renovation is hasty, and some unflattering features still show through the new paint. Importantly, these incomplete cover-ups are detectable not only by synopsis with the rest of the tradition, but also, as here, through patient probing of the narrative itself.

2. Halpern-Amaru, "Portraits in Josephus," 145–8; Niehoff, "Mother and Maiden," 416–18.

3. Louis H. Feldman, "Abraham the Greek Philosopher in Josephus," *TAPA* 99 (1968): 143–56; Louis H. Feldman, "Hellenizations in Josephus' *Jewish Antiquities*: The Portrait of Abraham," in Feldman and Hata, eds., *Josephus, Judaism, and Christianity*, 133–53; see also, among others, Louis H. Feldman, "Josephus' Portrait of Saul," *HUCA* 53 (1982): 45–99; and Bailey, "Matriarchs."

Practical Preliminaries

A few preliminaries need to be mentioned, regarding my approach, the extent of the narrative under discussion, the identity of the narrator, and the text and translation. My poetics of characterization remains as outlined in Chapter 1, and I attempt throughout to shine a light on Sarra in her narrative context. Of necessity, this includes Abraham, whose status as the primary character in this narrative is plain from the earliest scenes, where the narrator employs a long excursus to extol his many fine qualities in detail (*Ant.* 1.154-160). As before, I have eschewed the pose of a first-time reader, preferring to call on the full range of the narrative when needed. Theoretical issues stemming from the relationship of the *Antiquities* to its source tradition are relatively few; despite its explicit claim to render the "precise" (ἀκριβῆ) details of the scriptures, "adding nothing nor taking anything away" (οὐδὲν προσθεὶς οὐδ' αὖ παραλιπών, 1.17; compare 10.218), the narrative here is decidedly distinct from that of the MT or the LXX.

When I make references to "the narrative," or "this narrative," I refer not to the sprawling entirety of the *Antiquities* but only to those sections of the first book that primarily concern the story of Sarra and Abraham, 1.148-256.[4] Sarra first appears in 1.151, while her death is recorded in 1.237; Abraham lives on until 1.256, though much of the intervening material is devoted to obtaining Rebekah as a wife for Isaac. I treat all of the relevant episodes within this span (*Ant.* 1.148-160; 1.161-168; 1.186-190; 1.194-206; 1.207-212; 1.213-221; 1.222-236; 1.237), plus connecting material as appropriate.

The anonymous nature of the other works analyzed in this study makes speculation about their author(s) mostly moot. In the case of the *Antiquities*, however, we know quite a lot about its composer, even though much of the information that he relays in, for example, *The Life*, is undoubtedly tendentious. But this does not mean that Josephus is the narrator of the compositions that bear his name. Most scholars make no

---

4. Sarra also appears in a speech delivered by the character Josephus in *J.W.* 5.379-381, where he urges the defenders of Jerusalem to capitulate to the besieging Romans. The passage is notable as it preserves a very different tradition of Sarra's abduction by Pharaoh, in which the king invades Canaan at the head of a massive army and kidnaps her; a day later, Pharaoh, "trembling from visions in the night," restores Sarra "undefiled" and flees after giving riches to the "Hebrews" (5.381). However, Sarra is barely defined beyond the titles of "queen" (Βασιλίδα, 5.379; βασίλισσα, 5.381) and "the mother of our race" (τὴν μητέρα τοῦ γένους ἡμῶν, 5.379), so I omit discussion of this episode here.

distinction here, but the voices speaking in the works of Josephus—even, or perhaps especially, when the character of "Josephus" speaks directly, as in *J.W.* 5.376-419 and elsewhere—are not identical to that of the man eventually named Flavius Josephus, their "real author." This is a basic tenet of most mainstream work on narrative poetics, and requires no detailed defense here.[5] When referring to the storytelling voice in the *Antiquities*, then, I use the word "narrator," reserving "Josephus" for references to that man's broader body of work.

In my discussion of Sarra in the *Antiquities*, I use the text of Benedict Niese and follow his numbering scheme in my citations (*Ant.* 1.154-157, for instance).[6] As an aid to the reader, I have provided the translation of Feldman for each major section of the *Antiquities* discussed.[7] Despite a few infelicities, its "determined literalness" and relatively wooden diction make it a good choice for this purpose.[8] Compared to the other narratives under consideration here, the *Antiquities* is positively verbose, making it somewhat cumbersome to reproduce a full translation of all the sections discussed. I have tried to provide as much text as is necessary, without overwhelming the chapter with block quotations. Occasionally I have provided summaries, enclosed in brackets and marked with my initials, instead of quoting Feldman's translation in full. Bracketed character names, supplied for clarity, are mostly original to Feldman's text, though I have silently added a few myself. All translations in the body of the discussion are my own, unless otherwise noted.

*Beginnings (*Ant. *1.148-160)*

Ant. 1.148 I shall speak about the Hebrews.... Therros...was the father of Habramos, who was the tenth from Nochos and was born in the 992nd year after the Flood. 149 For Therros begat Habramos in his seventieth year.... 150 [Further genealogical data.—JM] 151 Habramos had brothers, Nachores and Aranes. Of these Aranes, having left behind a son, Lotos, and daughters, Sarra and Melcha, died among the Chaldeans in a city called Oures of the Chaldeans, and his tomb is shown unto the present day. Nachores married a niece Melcha, and Habramos a niece Sarra. 152 Because Therros came to

---

5. See, for instance, Rimmon-Kenan, *Narrative Fiction*, 86–9.
6. Benedict Niese, *Flavii Josephi Opera* (Berlin: Weidmann, 1885–95).
7. Feldman, *JA 1–4*.
8. Ibid., x. I have also consulted the translation of Henry St. John Thackeray, trans., *Jewish Antiquities, Books 1–4*, vol. 4 of *Josephus*, LCL (London: Heinemann, 1930), and, on occasion, that of William Whiston, trans., D. S. Margoliouth, ed., *The Works of Flavius Josephus* (London: Routledge, 1906), first published in 1737.

> hate Chaldaia owing to his grief for Aranes, they all emigrated to Charran in Mesopotamia, where Therros also died and was buried after living 205 years.... 153 Nachores had eight...legitimate children.... 154 Habramos, lacking a legitimate son, adopted Lotos, the son of Aranes his brother and the brother of his wife Sarra; and at the age of seventy-five he left Chaldaia when God bade him to move to Chananaia, in that he dwelt and that he left to his descendants. He was clever in understanding all matters and persuasive to his listeners and not mistaken concerning matters about that he might conjecture. 155–156 [Habramos infers and declares the unity of the deity by observation of the heavenly bodies.—JM] 157 Since, for these reasons, the Chaldeans and the other Mesopotamians fell into discord against him, he, having decided to emigrate in accordance with the will and assistance of God, settled in the land of Chananaia.... 158–160 [Summary of records of Habramos in the works of historians.—JM] (Feldman, *JA 1–4*, 53–9)

Although Sarra's name does not appear in the *Antiquities* until 1.151, the narrator details what turns out to be her paternal family line, all the way back to Shem, son of Noah, in 1.148 (and see 1.143-147). Her father Haran is one of the brothers of Abraham (1.151), who is the clear focus of the narrator's interest in this section. This focus, and the general level of detail here, help to camouflage some potential loose ends in the narrator's account. Abraham, for instance, who is specified as "tenth after Noah" (δέκατος...ἐστιν ἀπὸ Νώχου), and whose birth is reckoned in years after the flood, seems to be the first son of Terah in terms of both importance and chronology (1.148). Yet his brother Haran must father Sarra when Abraham is ten years old (compare 1.198), and Haran is by far the first of the brothers to die (1.151).

Haran's death apparently makes Sarra an orphan, despite her lengthy lineage, the instant she enters the discourse: along with her siblings, she's "left behind" or "abandoned" by her father before her name is even mentioned (Ἀράνης...υἱὸν καταλιπὼν Λῶτον καὶ Σάρραν καὶ Μελχὰν θυγατέρας...ἀπέθανεν, 1.151). Seemingly straightaway, however, Abraham marries Sarra, an act that could carry implications of adoption, even rescue, in its context. Their brother only recently dead, then—if the depth of their father Terah's grief, mentioned next in the discourse, can be taken as a reliable indicator of the event's freshness—Abraham and his brother Nahor each take one of their "abandoned" nieces under his wing. Some time later, moreover, Abraham will formally "adopt" Sarra's brother, Lot (Ἅβραμος...Λῶτον...εἰσεποιήσατο, 1.154).

The stated reason for this last move, however, hints at another possible reading of Abraham's speedy marriage, this one rather more mercenary, perhaps even predatory. In clear distinction to Nahor's eventual generation of no fewer than eight "legitimate children" (παῖδες γνήσιοι, 1.153) with Milcah, Sarra's sister, Abraham adopts Lot as he "lacks a legitimate child" (γνησίου παιδὸς ἀπορῶν, 1.154). The sexual and reproductive aims of Abraham and Nahor are thus expressed, or clearly implied, in the narrative; a motive of care for their recently orphaned, younger female relatives would demand a good deal more inference. That the brothers so swiftly move to wed and bed their "abandoned" nieces—women or girls presumably at least as grieved by their father's passing as their brokenhearted grandfather is—may owe as much to sexual opportunism as it does to avuncular concern.

In any case, the genuine blood tie between Sarra and Abraham, the first note of such a relationship that is narratively credible in the tradition examined to this point, gives a first hint of an interesting facet of the *Antiquities*.[9] A salient feature of Sarra throughout the works surveyed is her resemblance to Abraham. The *Antiquities* also displays this feature; however, more often than not, the particular cases of likeness are confined to this narrative. This may suggest that the quality of Sarra's similarity to Abraham is a kind of deep trait, a characteristic that consistently emerges regardless of her story's varied narrative trappings.

Sarra soon moves along with the rest of the extended family to Haran in Mesopotamia—"since Terah had come to hate Chaldea because of grief for [his son] Haran" (Θέρρου δὲ μισήσαντος τὴν Χαλδαίαν διὰ τὸ Ἀράνου πένθος, 1.152). Questions of narratorial knowledge or candor continue to nettle here: who buries Terah, when he dies in Haran? Both Feldman and Henry St. John Thackeray obscure the problem by rendering θάπτουσιν as a passive; but the natural subject here is πάντες: driven by Terah's grief, they "all migrated to Haran...where they also buried Terah after he died" (μετοικίζονται πάντες εἰς Χαρράν...ὅπου καὶ Θέρρον τελευτήσαντα θάπτουσιν, 1.152). Yet Abraham, fathered by Terah when the latter was 70 (1.149), must be 135 when Terah dies at 205; and Abraham, apparently along with Sarra and Lot, leaves for Canaan, never to return, at 75 (1.154).

The narrator's various remarks about this departure, moreover, only add to a vague sense of confusion over the precise order and nature of events in the plot. In his family's migration to Canaan, Abraham "leaves behind" (καταλείπει) Chaldea, not Haran (1.154), though these

---

9. *Jubilees*, outside the scope of this study, specifies from the outset that the pair are non-uterine siblings (*Jub.* 12:9). Oddly, this note has no narrative traction, as the plot in Egypt (*Jub.* 13:10-15) does not turn on a (mis)representation of Sarai's identity, and the tradition in Gerar is almost entirely omitted (*Jub.* 16:10-11).

places are distinguished earlier (1.152).[10] Did he, Sarra, and Lot move back to Chaldea, temporarily? This vagueness with regard to character movements, especially as concerns Sarra, will develop into a minor motif as the narrative draws on. And what prompts this more dramatic migration? In the event's first mention, Abraham leaves Chaldea "because God ordered him to move to Canaan" (τοῦ θεοῦ κελεύσαντος εἰς τὴν Χαναναίαν μετελθεῖν, 1.154), a simple if cryptic motivation. Yet after an encomium on Abraham's scientific and scholarly prowess (1.154–156), the narrator claims that "the Chaldeans and the other Mesopotamians rose up against him" (Χαλδαίων τε καὶ τῶν ἄλλων Μεσοποταμιτῶν στασιασάντων πρὸς αὐτόν) due to Abraham's revolutionary theological conclusions, and that Abraham accordingly "thought it best to move"—albeit "in accordance with the will and help of God" (μετοικεῖν δοκιμάσας κατὰ βούλησιν καὶ βοήθειαν τοῦ θεοῦ, 1.157). Much later, God claims in an address to Jacob to have led Abraham to Canaan "when," or perhaps "because," "he was driven away by his relatives" (ἐλαυνόμενον ὑπὸ τῶν συγγενῶν, 1.281).[11]

These uncertainties add to the difficulty of resolving a clear or detailed image of Sarra in these early parts of the narrative. In marked contrast to Abraham, who is the subject of many lines—some, indeed, purportedly taken from the work of published historians—that characterize him directly (1.154-160), the narrator's method of characterizing Sarra is quite indirect. In a first in the tradition surveyed so far, Sarra's lineage can be easily inferred, though the reproduction of the family tree of the "Hebrews" obviously aims primarily at the definition of Abraham (1.148-150). That Sarra and Abraham are actually related marks a new riff on the familiar motif of Sarra's similarity to Abraham. Despite these familial ties, however, Sarra is introduced as a woman or a girl left behind, along with her two siblings, by her father's death (1.151). Almost immediately, though, she is married by Abraham, her near-contemporary paternal uncle, someone who is said to be a renowned figure of acute perception and, apparently, political or military power: that his fellow Chaldeans and Mesopotamians were revolting against him (στασιασάντων πρὸς αὐτόν, 1.157; compare the στάσις in Egypt in 1.164) suggests as much, as does the cited report of Nicolaus of Damascus that Abraham was an "outsider with an army" who "reigned" in that city before moving on to Canaan

---

10. Compare Thomas W. Franxman, *Genesis and the "Jewish Antiquities" of Flavius Josephus* (Rome: Biblical Institute Press, 1979), 120.

11. Feldman, *JA 1–4*, 55 n. 476, 58–9 n. 505. Nodet, *Hebrew Bible of Josephus*, 263, suggests that sources are at work here and elsewhere in the Abraham materials in Josephus. The reader, however, must still grapple with the inconsistencies.

(ἐβασίλευσεν ἔπηλυς σὺν στρατῷ, 1.159). Abraham's wedding of his niece Sarra may be prompted by motives of protection or predation. Either way, their sexual relationship fails to produce a "legitimate" child; interestingly, Sarra is ascribed no blame, at least at this point, for this lack.[12] But the situation leads Abraham to adopt Lot—making Sarra, it seems, her brother's stepmother (1.154). This attempt of Abraham to solve their problem of childlessness partly anticipates Sarra's later effort, through the means of Hagar's body, to address the same issue. Neither endeavor will ultimately succeed.

Sarra migrates, apparently, from her ancestral and now marital home in Ur of the Chaldeans to Haran of Mesopotamia, driven by her grandfather's grief; she may bury him there, or move back to Chaldea (1.152). She migrates again, apparently, from Chaldea to Canaan, driven by her uncle and husband's unquestioning obedience to God, or, perhaps, by his decision to avoid the civil strife caused by his theological innovations, or, maybe, because the rest of their family drove him away (1.154, 157, 281). Much of this must be simply inferred. Sarra is the subject, and that only partly, of μετοικίζονται, referring to her first move—and, only possibly, of θάπτουσιν, which confuses rather than clarifies in any case (1.152). Otherwise she is acted upon: left behind, married, but mostly just left out. Sarra never speaks, directly, indirectly, or by implication; that she even accompanies Abraham to Canaan is not confirmed until 1.162, when she leaves the place, "brought along" (ἐπαγόμενος) by Abraham to Egypt. In fact, on a first reading the only certain companion of Abraham's move to Canaan would seem to be Lot, just adopted and thus the most likely source of Abraham's future "descendants" (ἀπόγονοι, 1.154).

Egypt (Ant. 1.161-168)

Ant. 1.161 Some time later a famine having taken hold of Chananaia, Habramos, learning that the Egyptians were prosperous, was eager to betake himself to them in order both to participate in their abundance and to be a listener to what their priests say about gods. For he said that either he would become their disciple if they were found to be better or he would convert them to a better mind if his thoughts should be better. 162 And taking Sarra along with him and fearing the frenzy of the Egyptians, lest the king kill him because of the beauty of his wife, he devised the following scheme. He pretended that he was her brother and instructed her that she should feign this, for it was in their interest. 163 And when they arrived in Egypt, it turned out for Habramos just as he had suspected. For his wife's beauty

---

12. Compare Franxman, *Genesis and the Antiquities*, 117.

became well known, wherefore Pharaothes, the king of the Egyptians, not being content with what was said about her, but seized with zeal to behold her, was on the point of laying hands on Sarra. 164 But God thwarted his unjust desire with a disease and civil strife; and the priests revealed to him, when he sacrificed to find deliverance, that the calamity had come to him because of the wrath of God, since he had wished to outrage the wife of the stranger. 165 And he, frightened, asked Sarra who she was and who was this man whom she had brought with her. And when he had learned the truth he apologized to Habramos. For thinking that she was his sister, not his wife, he had coveted her, wishing to enter into a marital alliance with her but not to outrage her driven by lust. And he showered him with many treasures, and he [Abram] associated with the most erudite of the Egyptians, whereby it happened that his virtue and his reputation for it became more illustrious. 166-168 [Abraham confounds the views of the Egyptians, gains renown for his persuasive teaching, and exposes the Egyptians to arithmetic and astronomy, of which they had been ignorant.—JM] (Feldman, *JA 1–4*, 60–4)

A fair amount of time lapses, unnarrated, between Abraham's settling in Canaan (1.154, 157) and the famine that eventually grips that region. When Abraham learns that the Egyptians are, in contrast, "well-off" (εὐδαιμονεῖν), this seems to provide him with a pretext to engage in an investigation, rather on the Socratic model, into Egyptian religious beliefs. To be sure, he is "eager to depart to them in order to share in their plenty"—but also "to be a pupil of their priests, as to what they would say about the gods" (1.161).[13] The narrator is careful to note that Abraham will keep an open mind in these colloquies; however, in the event, unsurprisingly, it is the Egyptians who benefit from Abraham's tutelage (1.161, 166-168).

Perhaps in the pursuit of the first of his two goals, Abraham also "brings along" Sarra, whose presence presents both risk and opportunity. The theology of the Egyptians may require some investigation, but their libidinous nature, apparently, can be taken for granted:

Since he brought Sarra along, too, and feared the madness of the Egyptians for women—lest the king do away with him because of the shapeliness of his woman—he conceived the following stratagem: he pretended to be her brother, and he taught her, too, to act this out, for it was profitable to them (1.162).[14]

---

13. μεταίρειν πρὸς αὐτοὺς ἦν πρόθυμος τῆς τε ἀφθονίας τῆς ἐκείνων μεθέξων καὶ τῶν ἱερέων ἀκροατὴς ἐσόμενος ὧν λέγοιεν περὶ θεῶν.

14. ἐπαγόμενος δὲ καὶ τὴν Σάρραν καὶ φοβούμενος τὸ πρὸς τὰς γυναῖκας τῶν Αἰγυπτίων ἐπιμανές, μὴ διὰ τὴν εὐμορφίαν τῆς γυναικὸς ὁ Βασιλεὺς αὐτὸν ἀνέλῃ, τέχνην

The narrator's aversion to reproducing direct speech in this part of the *Antiquities* makes it unclear whether the phrase συμφέρειν γὰρ αὐτοῖς is a narratorial gloss, or part of Abraham's "teaching." Its position, prior to the verb, probably suggests the latter: Abraham's assurance that the scheme is beneficial or profitable to them is part of his argument for Sarra to "act this out," or "play the role" (ὑποκρίνασθαι).[15] This is only one instance of Abraham's persuasive personality in the *Antiquities*.[16] At the beginning of the excursus on Abraham's excellent qualities in 1.154-156, he is said to be πιθανὸς τοῖς ἀκροωμένοις, "plausible" or "persuasive to his hearers." The evidence for this is slim in Mesopotamia, where Abraham has little luck persuading anyone of his monotheistic doctrine (1.157).[17] In Egypt, though, Abraham proves to be remarkable to the learned Egyptians precisely for his "persuasive ability concerning whatever he chose to teach" (πεῖσαι λέγων περὶ ὧν ἂν ἐπιχειρήσειε διδάσκειν, 1.167). Here, too, on the edge of Egypt, it seems likely that Sarra is convinced by what Abraham "teaches" her: she need not even directly lie, merely "play along" with the fiction, and coming events suggest that she does so, at least for a time.

Abraham's fear for his life is supposedly founded in the "madness" or "passionate lust for women" (τὸ πρὸς τὰς γυναῖκας...ἐπιμανές) that is said to be characteristic of Egyptians in general. That Pharaoh forms the focus of his concern, however, is telling: once again, Abraham is presented as a kind of royal figure, a peer of kings whose entourage, including "his woman," can expect to be noticed in the highest quarters. Naturally, the appeal of this woman also contributes to the action. She has "beauty of form" or "shapeliness" (ἡ εὐμορφία), a quality that she shares in the *Antiquities* with handsome figures such as Joseph (2.41) and Moses (2.231); soon, this trait is described more generally as τὸ κάλλος, referring to bodily beauty (1.163).

Several ambiguities impact possibilities for Sarra's characterization here. The movement of the plot suggests that she is initially convinced to "play her role"; but does she share in Abraham's knowledge of the likely repercussions? For the narrator notes that "when they entered

---

ἐπενόησε τοιαύτην· ἀδελφὸς αὐτῆς εἶναι προσεποιήσατο κἀκείνην τοῦθ' ὑποκρίνασθαι, συμφέρειν γὰρ αὐτοῖς, ἐδίδαξεν. It is not clear to me why Feldman omits the modifying prepositional phrase πρὸς τὰς γυναῖκας from his translation.

15. Thackeray makes this explicit: "he pretended to be her brother and, telling her that their interest required it, instructed her to play her part accordingly."

16. Compare Feldman, "Abraham the Greek Philosopher," 153.

17. Note, too, Abraham's later failure to persuade God (or the angels?) to spare the people of Sodom, 1.199.

Egypt, *it turned out for Abraham just as he guessed it would"* (ὡς δ᾽ ἧκον εἰς τὴν Αἴγυπτον, ἀπέβαινε τῷ Ἀβράμῳ καθὼς ὑπενόησε, 1.163). It is even possible that ἀποβαίνω carries a basically positive force, as it often does: everything "turned out well," or "succeeded for Abraham."[18] But to what does the narrator refer? Abraham is only on record fearing that the king, being an Egyptian, will murder him out of lust for Sarra—and, if συμφέρειν γὰρ αὐτοῖς represents Abraham's speech at some remove, predicting that playing his trick will benefit the two of them. However, here is what actually happens, according to the narrator: Sarra's reputation for bodily beauty spreads, making Pharaoh eager to see her for himself; having apparently achieved this aim in a suitably private venue, he is "just about to grab," "attack," or "have sex with Sarra" (οἷός τε ἦν ἅψασθαι τῆς Σάρρας) when God "checks his unjust lust with plague and civil discord" (ἐμποδίζει δὲ αὐτοῦ ὁ θεὸς τὴν ἄδικον ἐπιθυμίαν νόσῳ τε καὶ στάσει τῶν πραγμάτων, 1.163-164). Did all this happen just as Abraham surmised? After the truth about Sarra is confirmed, further, the narrator reports that Pharaoh "presented [Abraham] with a lot of money" (δωρεῖταί τε αὐτὸν πολλοῖς χρήμασι), which fulfills Abraham's first goal of "sharing in the plenty" of the Egyptians; moreover, Abraham is able to begin his association with the learned Egyptians, thus achieving his second goal (1.165). Is this, too, just as he thought it would be? After all, this is a man "quick to understand about everything" (δεινὸς ὢν συνεῖναί τε περὶ πάντων), and, significantly in the present context, "not at all wrong about things he conjectures" or guesses about (περί τε ὧν εἰκάσειεν οὐ διαμαρτάνων, 1.154).

Here, it seems, there is a crack in the narrator's aim—widely noted by commentators—to lionize Abraham at every turn.[19] If he is so perspicacious and preternaturally accurate in his conjectures, surely Abraham can deduce what will occur in Egypt; indeed, this is implied by the report that all falls out "just as he guessed it would," and by the fact that both his goals are achieved as a result of his trick. But Abraham's remarkable insight, at least here in Egypt, can only be exercised at the expense of his moral standing: Abraham's role as a victim of circumstance depends on

18. LSJ 192b.

19. See Franxman, *Genesis and the* Antiquities, 131; Carl R. Holladay, Theios Aner *in Hellenistic Judaism: A Critique of the Use of This Category in New Testament Christology* (Missoula, MT: Scholars Press, 1977), 73–4; and Louis H. Feldman, "Hellenizations." As Harold W. Attridge, *The Interpretation of Biblical History in the* Antiquitates Judaicae *of Flavius Josephus* (Missoula, MT: Scholars Press, 1976), 109–19, shows, this treatment of Abraham is representative of a much broader trend in the *Antiquities*.

his ignorance of the actual results of his ploy. As it is, the events that "turn out" so well for Abraham—"just like he thought"—include the apparent abduction and near-rape of Sarra, in addition to divinely sponsored plague and political upheaval. This may color the reader's impression of the narrator's eulogy at Abraham's death, where he is lauded as a "man tops in every moral excellence" (ἀνὴρ πᾶσαν ἀρετὴν ἄκρος," 1.256). Sarra, on the other hand, has received no encomium praising her powers of inference; moreover, at least so far, one of the more prominent of her limited traits seems to be a certain tractability, as she migrates at the instigation of others and is taken along on journeys (1.152, [154], 162). It seems unlikely, then, that Abraham labors over the details in his persuasive coaching of Sarra; and it seems particularly improbable, if a modicum of self-interest can be assumed for Sarra, that his explanation of his ploy included the prospect of her threatened sexual assault.

At any rate, Sarra, now a famous beauty, must be taken somehow into the presence and power of the king, in order that he see the truth of the reports and be on the point of "touching" her (1.163). Her purported sibling relationship with Abraham must also be known to Pharaoh, whose later questioning of Sarra shows that he is aware of Abraham's existence, but not, apparently, his true identity (1.165). Sarra's stay in court seems unlikely to have been brief.[20] God's intervention on behalf of Abraham's true tie to Sarra—Pharaoh's crime being his desire "to outrage the woman of the stranger" (ὑβρίσαι τοῦ ξένου τὴν γυναῖκα, 1.164), not Sarra as an individual—may prevent Sarra from being "touched," but the divine remedies do not resolve the situation immediately. In particular, the στάσις, or political unrest, that God creates demands a substantial period in which to unfold; but the νόσος, too, even if it is isolated to the person of Pharaoh, taken alongside the rest of Pharaoh's fact-finding, must absorb some time. Pharaoh falls ill, and his capital is in an uproar; while giving orders to deal with the disturbance, Pharaoh summons priests, offers sacrifices to find a remedy, and waits for the signs to be interpreted; upon learning that his troubles are "owing to the wrath of God" (κατὰ μῆνιν θεοῦ) at his unwitting violation of the laws of hospitality, he cross-examines Sarra, learns the full truth, and soothes Abraham (1.164-165). Only at this point, it seems, might Sarra be released—though the reader can only guess at this, as the narrator has since lost interest in her.

The brief narration of Sarra's private time with Pharaoh contains a number of interesting elements as concerns her characterization. She must be under his power for a significant interval, and in his physical presence

---

20. Contrast Franxman, *Genesis and the* Antiquities, 129–30.

at least part of this time: he obviously does "take a look" at her, and is on the verge of taking a good deal more than that (1.163). Moreover, in what proves to be a notable feature of the narrator's storytelling, the physical movements of the characters are almost entirely submerged: after the ill omens are read, Pharaoh interviews Sarra by simply beginning to speak to her, as if she has never left his side (1.165). This sudden appearance of Sarra in a colloquy anticipates her surprising and undetailed emergence from "inside" in the episode of the angelic messengers (1.197-198). That Pharaoh explicitly speaks to Sarra at all is significant; that he asks her to confirm or elucidate the truth of what was revealed to him by his priests about these grave matters of health and state, even more so. Both elements represent novel developments in the tradition here.

But the content of what he says, reported indirectly, might be even more noteworthy, given Sarra's characterization thus far: Pharaoh, "out of fear, asked Sarra who she was, and who this was she had brought along" (ὁ δὲ φοβηθεὶς ἠρώτα τὴν Σάρραν, τίς τε εἴη καὶ τίνα τοῦτον ἐπάγοιτο, 1.165). Remarkably, Pharaoh, whose emotional state recalls Abraham's supposed fear at the outset of this episode (φοβούμενος, 1.162), neatly inverts the previous roles of Abraham and Sarra. Abraham, according to the narrator, brought Sarra along to Egypt (ἐπαγόμενος δὲ καὶ τὴν Σάρραν, 1.162); in Pharaoh's question here, Sarra assumes the dominant, subject position, having brought Abraham along, almost as if she is his chaperon. This constitutes another instance of an interesting phenomenon in the *Antiquities*, in which the theme of Sarra's resemblance to Abraham, so prominent in the broader tradition, is reinforced—but in a manner that has no precise parallel elsewhere.

In a continuing development in the tradition, it is plainly implied that Sarra more clearly explains the finding of Pharaoh's sacrifice, which only refers to his offense against "the woman of the stranger" (τοῦ ξένου τὴν γυναῖκα, 1.164); Sarra herself must be the source of his "learning the truth" in full (πυθόμενος...τὴν ἀλήθειαν, 1.165). Abraham, apparently, isn't the only one who can teach the Egyptians something they don't know (compare 1.166-168)—another minor, unique tie between the two characters. Sarra's speech here is buried deep in the discourse, though Pharaoh's questions suggest that she first reveals, remarkably, "who she is" (τίς...εἴη, 1.165). If only the narrator had detailed her response! What does she say? And, for that matter, just "who is this one she had brought along" (τίνα τοῦτον ἐπάγοιτο, 1.165)? Plainly the relationship of these two mysterious figures is part, but perhaps not all, of "the truth" that Pharaoh learns from Sarra; importantly, Pharaoh's response (1.165) shows that this particular truth is not that the pair are brother and sister, which helps to evaluate claims made later, in the similar episode in Gerar (1.211; compare 1.208). But the primary revelation of this scene for a reading of Sarra is her relative independence—not forgetting that her presence here owes to abduction and imprisonment that nearly leads to sexual violation—and importance to the action. Apparently alone with the king, Sarra seizes the initiative to speak the truth, revealing her identity by dropping "the part" assigned her by Abraham, and, in fact, catalyzing the achievement of Abraham's goals as laid out at the outset of this episode (1.165; compare 1.161).

This last note, however, clarifies whose interests are truly being served here, and the tale's denouement tends to reimpose the characters' previous roles. Pharaoh may have referred to Abraham as the man Sarra "had brought along," but he placates Abraham, not Sarra, with his apologies (1.165); and later, in Gerar, in an episode that echoes this one in many particulars, Abraham will once again "bring along" Sarra, this time with no subsequent swapping of roles (1.207). Pharaoh may have learned "the truth" from Sarra, but he responds with lies of his own: he claims to Abraham that he had never been "eager to outrage [his woman] owing to lust" (ἐνυβρίσαι κατ' ἐπιθυμίαν ὡρμημένος, 1.165), yet "unjust lust" (ἄδικον ἐπιθυμίαν) is exactly how the narrator has defined his motive, and the divine response to Pharaoh's sacrifice specifically referenced his desire "to outrage the woman of the stranger" (ὑβρίσαι τοῦ ξένου τὴν γυναῖκα, 1.164). In the end, Pharaoh gives Abraham "a lot of money" (πολλοῖς χρήμασι) and permission to engage the learned Egyptians in dialectic, just as he had wanted, and it is Abraham's "virtue" (ἀρετὴν αὐτῷ), not Sarra's, that increases in renown as a result of this adventure (1.165). Sarra's minor emergence into agency here, then, in her private interview with Pharaoh, is not sustained through the end of the episode. In fact, as with the first move to Canaan, Sarra's accompanying presence must be simply assumed at Abraham's grammatically solo return to that land (Ὡς δ' εἰς τὴν Χαναναίαν ἀφίκετο..., 1.169).

"Left behind" at her first appearance in the narrative, Sarra is "brought along" to Egypt, convinced by a persuasive Abraham to "play her part" in a scheme that is meant to be "profitable to them" (1.162). But Abraham receives all the profit here, while Sarra, despite Abraham's ostensible fear for his own safety, takes all of the risks (1.163, 165). Given the outcome of Abraham's plan, which includes Sarra's abduction, near-rape, and imprisonment at court, it seems unlikely that Sarra is apprised of all that may come of her play-acting. Abraham, however, must either be "not at all wrong about things he conjectures" (1.154), or innocent of placing Sarra's body and life at risk—but not both. Given that everything "turned out for Abraham just as he guessed it would" (1.163), it seems that innocence is unlikely. This is only the first instance of the narrator's penchant for creating narrative problems by attempting to apologize for the main characters, a phenomenon that will also affect the depiction of Sarra in scenes to come.

Sarra is portrayed here as a notable beauty; Abraham and the narrator seem to agree as to her εὐμορφία, while her κάλλος is instrumental to the plot, the likely subject of the "reports" (τοῖς...λεγομένοις) that stimulate the king to his predatory moves (1.162-163). This quality has little traction beyond this episode, though it may be assumed to fire the "lust" of King Abimelech later, just as it does Pharaoh's here (ἐπιθυμία, 1.163-164, 207-208). Sarra's period of captivity that results paradoxically gives her an opportunity to demonstrate a kind of independence. In a new development in the tradition, Sarra, seemingly alone with Pharaoh, advises the king on a matter vital to monarch and state, shedding the role that Abraham wrote for her and revealing "the truth" about "who she is" (1.165). She, from the king's perspective, is the one who "brought along" Abraham, and she proves as capable as Abraham of teaching an Egyptian something he didn't know (1.165-168). Yet her relative prominence is short-lived; as Abraham collects his riches, Sarra disappears from the discourse for nearly one hundred lines.

Separation and War (Ant. 1.169-182)

The reader, then, must simply assume that Abraham has "brought along" Sarra on his return to Canaan (1.169). There is no hint of her presence in this lengthy section of the *Antiquities*, which contains correspondingly little that enhances an understanding of her character. In a retelling of the traditions represented in Genesis 13, Abraham divides the land with Lot, who lives apart from him from now on (1.169-170). This separation seems relatively amicable, and Abraham will see Lot again, when, in a retelling of the story of Genesis 14, he rescues him and others from the clutches of the "Assyrians" (1.179). Abraham's martial prowess reinforces his image as a kind of potentate and military leader.[21] But the narrator has, it seems, completely forgotten Lot's supposed role as Abraham's son: Lot is only

---

21. Louis H. Feldman, "Abraham," in *Josephus's Interpretation of the Bible* (Berkeley: University of California Press, 1998), 235–6; Louis H. Feldman, "Abraham the General in Josephus," in *Nourished with Peace: Studies in Hellenistic Judaism in Memory of Samuel Sandmel*, ed. Frederick E. Greenspahn, Earle Hilgert, and Burton L. Mack (Chico, CA: Scholars Press, 1984), 43–9.

referred to somewhat vaguely as Abraham's συγγενής, or relative (1.176, 179), and in the next small section Abraham is disgruntled at his lack of an heir (1.183).

Child and Sacrifice (Ant. 1.183-185)

Sarra continues to inhabit the deep background of the narrative here, as Abraham, in a scene that corresponds generally to Genesis 15, receives a divine message and offers a large sacrifice. However, the note of Abraham's concern for his continued childlessness (1.183) lays the ground for Sarra's reemergence in the following episode, where she will make an attempt, at God's command, to remedy the situation. This anxiety, and God's promise of a great posterity for Abraham—the first such pledge in this narrative—also foreshadow Sarra's own birth of Isaac. This connection takes longer to rise to the surface, though, and for a time it seems that Sarra will play only a mediating role in the production of a child for Abraham.

Sarra, Hagar, Abraham, and Ishmael (Ant. 1.186-190)

> *Ant.* 1.186 Habramos was dwelling near the oak called Ogyges (it is a place in Chananaia not far from the city of the Hebronites), and being distressed at his wife's not becoming pregnant, he besought God to grant him offspring of a male child. 187 When God encouraged him to be confident, as in all other things he had been led from Mesopotamia for his wellbeing, so also he would have children, Sarra, at God's command, caused him to lie down[22] with one of her handmaidens, Agare by name, who was an Egyptian by race, so that he might procreate children by her. 188 And becoming pregnant, the maidservant dared to show insolence to Sarra, assuming queenly airs, as though the rule would pass over to her son about to be born from her. And when Habramos handed her over to Sarra for punishment, she planned flight, being unable to endure her hardships, and she besought God to take pity on her. 189 But as she went forth through the wilderness, an angel of God met her, bidding her to return to her masters. For she would attain a better life through being self-controlled (for, indeed, she was in these troubles because she had been thoughtless and stubborn toward her mistress): 190 he said if she disobeyed God and went further on her way she would perish whereas if she returned she would be the mother of a son who would be king of that

---

22. This rendering is misleading. The direct object of the verb translated "caused to lie down," ἐπικλίνει, can only be "one of her slaves, named Hagar" (my translation); there is no masculine pronoun in the near context. Sarra forces Hagar, not Abraham, to lie down.

land. She obeyed this and returning to her masters she obtained pardon. Not long afterwards she gave birth to Ismaelos; someone might render it "heard by God," because God had listened to her entreaty. (Feldman, *JA 1–4*, 70–2)

An uncertain amount of story time later, Abraham again vents his displeasure over his lack of an heir, this time imploring God "to provide him with offspring of a male child" (γονὴν αὐτῷ παιδὸς ἄρσενος παρασχεῖν). Here, however, Abraham is specifically "frustrated," "impatient," or "angry at his woman not conceiving" (δυσφορῶν...ἐπὶ γυναικὶ μὴ κυούσῃ), the first explicit mention of Sarra's role in their childlessness (1.186). At this point, a modest flurry of notes begins to lend Sarra color in the *Antiquities*. To start, God encourages Abraham on the matter of children, noting that everything else had worked out in his favor since "he was led from Mesopotamia" (ἀπὸ τῆς Μεσοποταμίας ἠγμένον, 1.187). This divine invocation of Abraham's journey to Canaan recalls the context of his departure, where Abraham's "lack of a legitimate child" (γνησίου παιδὸς ἀπορῶν) was also at issue; moreover, Abraham was there said to move from his ancestral homeland "having been ordered by God" (τοῦ θεοῦ κελεύσαντος, 1.154). Here, in a novel development in the tradition, it is Sarra who acts τοῦ θεοῦ κελεύσαντος: "Sarra, having been ordered by God, made one of her female slaves (an Egyptian named Hagar) lie down so that [Abraham] could father children by her" (1.187).[23]

These thematic and verbal similarities point to a small web of links between Sarra and Abraham. What Sarra does here is important; so much is plain from the immediate context, for Sarra's act is "ordered by God."[24] But this explicitly stated divine motive also invites the appraisal of her act in the light of what Abraham does earlier, which serves to underline its significance even further: in being "ordered by God," what Sarra does to Hagar is thus roughly equated, perhaps, with Abraham's migration—a signal narrative event indeed.

Some of Abraham and Sarra's character traits are also brought into alignment here. Sarra, just like Abraham, is favored by direct divine communication, a note that may anticipate her rabbinic portrayal as a prophet.[25] Moreover, Sarra is shown to be obedient to God's command, which not only further associates her response with that of Abraham,

---

23. Σάρρα τοῦ θεοῦ κελεύσαντος ἐπικλίνει μίαν τῶν θεραπαινίδων Ἀγάρην ὄνομα γένος οὖσαν Αἰγυπτίαν ὡς ἐξ αὐτῆς παιδοποιησομένῳ.

24. Compare Feldman, "Abraham," 225.

25. *Gen. Rab.* 45.2; *b. Meg.* 14a; for others, see Ginzberg, *Legends*, 178 with n. 38, 180 nn. 43, 44. Compare Franxman, *Genesis and the* Antiquities, 138–9 n. 12; Feldman, *JA 1–4*, 71 n. 587.

but also ties her to what is arguably one of Abraham's chief characteristics in the broader tradition. That the near contexts of these commands involve the key issue of childlessness is also suggestive. The specific force of the earlier command was that Abraham should move to Canaan, but it is closely bound in the discourse to Abraham's adoption of Lot ("Abraham adopted Lot...since he lacked a legitimate child, and left Chaldea behind...having been ordered by God to move to Canaan," 1.154); here, the command itself is aimed directly at the production of a child. Interestingly, too, the attempt of the character in each instance to solve this problem of childlessness ultimately fails despite apparent initial success: Lot is adopted, but moves further and further away as the narrative draws on, ending up living "miserably, due to his isolation from humanity and want of food" (ὑπό τε ἀνθρώπων ἐρημίας καὶ τροφῆς ἀπορίας ταλαιπώρως, 1.204; compare 1.154, 169-170, 202-204); Ishmael is conceived, but his life is in danger even here, before he is born, and he, too, is eventually sent away from the family of Sarra and Abraham (1.188-190, 215-221). Elements of this particular motif are reminiscent of the Masek–Hagar connection in the LXX. But this broader complex of links is particularly significant, it seems to me, because it is not only congruent with a major theme of the narratives featuring Sarra studied so far—that she often resembles Abraham—but also another example of this theme without exact parallel elsewhere.

Another new piece of intelligence here regards Sarra's status as a slaveowner. To this point, there have been a few clues as to the size of Abraham's household: he has shepherds who belong to him (1.169), and he owns 318 οἰκέται, or household slaves (1.178). Here it is explicit that Sarra also owns slaves; Hagar, in fact, is only "one of her female slaves" (μίαν τῶν θεραπαινίδων, 1.187). Against the renderings of both Thackeray and Feldman, who each offer two variants of some kind of "maid" or "servant" here—despite the lexical identity of θεραπαινίδων (1.187) and θεραπαινίς (1.188)—there is no question that Hagar is a slave. Even if she were not plainly referred to as Sarra's δούλη later (1.215), Sarra's power over Hagar's body here, and her violent response to her slave's insubordination in just a few lines, make their relationship plain.

The expression used here of Sarra's act apparently aims at euphemistic delicacy. Sarra merely "caused Hagar to incline" (ἐπικλίνει...Ἀγάρην), a verbal usage that does not seem to have had any currency as a circumlocution for "to make have sex."[26] Abraham's role, meanwhile, is almost

---

26. LSJ 636b, 639a. According to Karl Heinrich Rengstorf, ed., *A Complete Concordance to Flavius Josephus* (Leiden: Brill, 1973), 2:163a, this is the only occurrence of ἐπικλίνω in the *Antiquities*.

completely submerged: in the near context, his part in the transaction is only suggested by the implied pronoun in παιδοποιησομένῳ.²⁷ Thus Hagar is not even made to lie "with" Abraham, but simply made to recline, as if in anticipation of a much-deserved nap.²⁸ But all this indirection cannot entirely mask the brutality at the core of Sarra's action here, despite Heather McKay's assertion that Sarra is "completely innocent" in this scene.²⁹ Just how does Sarra make Hagar lie down? There is a kind of physical, even manual color to the clause that is emphasized by the stark power differentials between the characters: "Sarra, on God's orders, 'laid' one of her slaves," or perhaps even "held one of her slaves down"—"so that [Abraham] could make children out of her" (1.187).

The fundamental violence of Sarra's response to God's command will soon be underlined. First, however, the narrator begins to open one of the central holes in Sarra's characterization in the *Antiquities*. After "the slave"—she goes unnamed for the remainder of this section—becomes pregnant as a result of being "laid" by Sarra, the narrator sniffs that this slave "dared" (ἐτόλμησε) "to display insolence" (ἐξυβρίζειν) to her master, "playing the queen" (βασιλίζουσα, 1.188). In distinction to the role-playing of Sarra in Egypt (1.162), or that of Abraham in Gerar to come (1.207), the narrator disapproves strongly of Hagar's play-acting here, which is based on the patently false notion that her child might inherit Abraham's authority: Hagar is playing the queen "as if the rule would devolve upon the [male] one to be born from her" (ὡς τῆς ἡγεμονίας περιστησομένης εἰς τὸν ὑπ' αὐτῆς τεχθησόμενον, 1.188). The tone is almost scornful—"she dared," "playing the queen," "as if"—and such presumption will shortly get its due. But here there is the seed of a significant problem with the narrator's presentation. For Hagar's impudent idea is precisely what the narrator will claim had, in fact, been in store for Ishmael—"the one to be born" from Hagar—in the scene following the birth of Isaac. There, Sarra is said to have been "accustomed to show affection" (ἔστεργεν) to Ishmael, just like he were her very own child, and specifically "because he was being raised," or perhaps "groomed for succession to the rule" (ἐτρέφετο γὰρ ἐπὶ τῇ τῆς ἡγεμονίας διαδοχῇ, 1.215).³⁰

---

27. Feldman's translation obscures this by introducing Abraham, with no warrant in the Greek, as the direct object.

28. Contrary to the gloss of Rengstorf, *Concordance*, 2:163a, "to cause to lie down with." However, the case of the participle may hint at this; perhaps it is best understood as a dative of interest.

29. McKay, "Eve's Sisters Re-Cycled," 176.

30. A glance at a lexicon may lead a reader to wonder whether ὡς in 1.188 couldn't be rendered "inasmuch as" or "since" (a kind of factual causal force, LSJ

But here, while Ishmael is still in the womb, Sarra treats his mother with a complete lack of tenderness. It is hard to agree with Bailey that Sarra is "clearly pictured as the victim of severe abuse" here, and almost impossible to concur that she "does not deal harshly" with Hagar, for Sarra's implied action toward her pregnant slave is disturbingly violent.[31] Hagar, the narrator notes, "decided on flight after Abraham handed her over to Sarra πρὸς αἰκίαν" (1.188).[32] The term αἰκία is much stronger and more specific than Feldman's rendering of "punishment" implies, commonly referring in the *Antiquities* to an act of physical torture leading to death (7.52; 13.232-233; 15.289), or standing in parallel with βάσανος ("torture" or "torment": 10.115; 16.389); compare the lexis and syntax of *J.W.* 2.246, where Claudius orders a certain "Keler the chiliarch" to be "handed over to the Judeans for torture" (παραδοθῆναι Ἰουδαίοις πρὸς αἰκίαν), an ordeal that is to culminate in his being dragged bodily around Jerusalem and beheaded.[33] The context here, moreover, supports the

---

2039a, B. IV.), meaning that these two evaluations of Ishmael's prospects are, in fact, not in conflict: in 1.215 Sarra's behavior is explained by Ishmael's original destiny ("because [γάρ] he was being raised for succession to the rule"), while here in 1.188 Hagar's behavior is owing to the same reason ("since [ὡς] the rule would pass to the one to be born from her"). However, the syntax here—ὡς plus a participle, and a future participle in particular—points to a very specific but not uncommon usage where ὡς signals "the ground of belief on which the agent acts, and denotes the thought, assertion, real or presumed intention, in the mind of the subject of the principal verb or of some other person mentioned prominently in the sentence, without implicating the speaker or writer" (Smyth §2086; compare §§2240b, 2241, on causal clauses, in which ὡς carries a similar nuance). As Smyth explains, this "ground of belief" may be genuine or feigned—that is, Hagar may truly believe that her son will succeed, or she may be pretending as much—but this usage "implies nothing as to the opinion of the speaker or writer," here the narrator of the *Antiquities* (§2086). This narratorial opinion, however, is often clear from the broader context, as shown in Smyth's many examples, and here I think it is plain that the narrator does not regard the actions of "the slave," who "dared to act insolently, playing the queen," to be well-founded in fact; note, as well, that Hagar's conduct is described as "arrogant and stubborn" when the angel criticizes her lack of "self-control" (1.189). The three major English translations, then, are correct in their renderings: Hagar in 1.188 acts "as if" (Whiston) or "as though" (Thackeray and Feldman) her unborn son is to inherit the rule—an unwarranted assumption that leads to actions that result in severe punishment.

31. Bailey, "Matriarchs," 159. Compare McKay, "Eve's Sisters Re-Cycled," 176.
32. Ἀβράμου...αὐτὴν πρὸς αἰκίαν παραδιδόντος τῇ Σάρρᾳ δρασμὸν ἐπεβούλευσεν.
33. The verbal form αἰκίζω is also commonly used in these contexts: *Ant.* 7.161; 12.255-256; 13.4; 15.71. Compare 2 Macc. 7:42, where τάς...αἰκίας is used to summarize the treatment of the seven martyred brothers and their mother; the verb

reading of αἰκία as severe physical abuse. Sarra's willingness to fulfill her aims with force has been demonstrated already, when she "made Hagar lie down" (1.187); Hagar's response to Sarra's act is telling, too, as the slave, "unable to endure her sufferings" (οὐχ ὑπομένουσα τὰς ταλαιπωρίας), determines that running away, pregnant, to an uncertain fate, is preferable to remaining with her master (1.188). Whatever violence Sarra perpetrates, then, it must be very bad for Hagar; and it cannot be good, either, for "the one to be born from her"—the child that Sarra will supposedly treat as her own, for thirteen years or so, until her own son is finally born (compare 1.191-193, 215).

That Sarra now, for the first time, forms the focus of Abraham's frustration at their lack of a child (1.186) presages the relative wealth of information that can be gleaned about her character in this section. An important cluster of notes relate Sarra's portrayal to that of Abraham. That her act with Hagar is "ordered by God" (τοῦ θεοῦ κελεύσαντος, 1.187) likens its significance to Abraham's migration, precisely so "ordered" earlier (1.154). Sarra, like Abraham, receives direct divine communication; Sarra, like Abraham, is obedient to God's orders; Sarra, like Abraham, attempts to solve their problem of childlessness in the near context of God's command—an endeavor that will eventually fail, just as Abraham's did. These connections between Sarra and Abraham provide a thematic echo of the kind of tie that is prominent in the broader tradition surveyed in this study, while constituting, in themselves, unparalleled examples of this motif. This phenomenon, which was also seen in association with Sarra and Abraham's blood relationship, and with their role-swapping in Egypt, may suggest that the resemblance of Sarra to Abraham plays an almost archetypal role in their story as it finds expression in a variety of ancient narratives. That Sarra is like Abraham, it seems, is one fundamental aspect of her character—not the only, and not necessarily the most important aspect, but a fundamental one—something felt so deeply that it bubbles up, in different narratives, in ways that are themselves often singular and unpredictable.

Sarra's identity as a slaveholder is also revealed and cruelly underscored here, as Sarra treats Hagar with a brutality that is ill-disguised

---

αἰκίζω also appears in vv. 1, 13, and 15. *GELS* 14b offers only one definition for the OG materials: "act of torture." Compare Henry St. John Thackeray and Ralph Marcus, *A Lexicon to Josephus* (Paris: Geuthner, 1930–55), 12b, "outrage or usu. torture," and Rengstorf, *Concordance*, 1:33b, "ill-treatment, torture—defacement, disfigurement—humiliating treatment."

by the narrator's attempt at delicacy. Especially in the light of coming events, the description of Sarra "making Hagar recline" so that Abraham can make children out of her (1.187) fails miserably as a euphemism, suggesting nothing so much as Sarra holding Hagar down during her rape. Sarra's implied act after Abraham "hands over" an insolent and play-acting Hagar πρὸς αἰχίαν, moreover, is a disturbing and inhumane event that points to severe physical abuse of an underling who is pregnant at least partly by Sarra's own doing (1.188).

As I discussed in my readings of the MT and LXX, to look across the tradition, there seems to be some connection between Sarra's treatment in Egypt and her own subsequent treatment of Hagar. This tie is particularly tight in the MT, with its verbal correspondences that suggest reading the latter episode partly in the light of the former; and while the links are not as prominent in the LXX, their presence is still clear. For the *Antiquities*, I do not want to claim that Sarra's experiences in Egypt, which I suggested included abduction, near-rape, and imprisonment, have no bearing on what she does to Hagar here. But the association must depend mostly on psychological factors. However appropriate these may be in a mimetic reading, the connection can only be more tenuous in the absence of significant verbal parallels; that Hagar is "an Egyptian by race" (*Ant.* 1.187) seems to be the most substantial here. In distinction from some other cases, this situation does not seem to be caused by deliberate narratorial meddling; rather, the narrator's assiduous avoidance of direct character speech, to name one factor, eliminates the link between Abram's and Sarai's first speeches as recorded in the MT (Gen. 12:11-13; 16:2). But the end result for Sarra in the *Antiquities*, I think, is that she is somewhat less sympathetic in her exploitation of Hagar here, for even the conscientious reader's attention is drawn less readily to Sarra's own trials in Egypt.

Finally, the narrator has laid the ground for a vexing problem with Sarra's characterization, to be compounded later. Here the idea of her son succeeding to Abraham's rule is explained as Hagar's misguided motive for the way she acts toward Sarra (1.188). The narrator regards this slave's idea as fantasy, not fact: it would be difficult to understand describing Hagar as "daring to show insolence" and "playing the queen" if her grounds for confidence were considered sound. Hagar, then, acts, unjustifiably, "as if" (ὡς) her son were to inherit Abraham's authority (ἡγεμονία). But a key moment in the narrator's presentation of Sarra's character later, as it is perhaps the most direct characterization of Sarra in the entire narrative, claims that Sarra's initial if temporary affection for Ishmael is prompted by this very understanding: Hagar's son, now thirteen, has been groomed to claim Abraham's authority (ἡγεμονία, 1.215).

It seems to me that the best way to explain this contradiction, apart from positing poorly integrated sources, lies in the often-noted tendency of the narrator of the *Antiquities* to cast the story's heroes in the best possible light—though I would suggest that the narrator's efforts on this score are not always successful even in their own near contexts, as the example of the failed euphemism of ἐπικλίνει shows. The narrator's partiality emerges in the attempt to justify Sarra's actions here—she was pushed beyond all reasonable bounds!—by portraying Hagar's ridiculous presumption in assuming her child would inherit. The same partiality emerges in the attempt to justify Sarra's actions there—Ishmael's banishment had nothing to do with her personal feelings!—by explaining that the child was supposed to inherit. Abraham faced a similar quandary in Egypt, where the narrator's earlier attempts to extol Abraham's perspicacity and farsightedness undermined his potential for moral integrity in his scheme with Sarra. Nor does the character of God escape the fallout from this narratorial inclination; the divine prescription for Hagar's impregnation in the *Antiquities* makes a minor puzzle of God's motive, considered within the narrative and across the tradition. As Bailey and Feldman both note, the attribution of this plan to God helps shield Sarra from criticism for her unconventional, possibly immoral solution to the quandary.[34] However, this tinkering also vitiates the logic of God's actions. In the MT, Ishmael's conception in Genesis 16 is a human response to the problem of Abraham's childlessness, an ultimately defective initiative of Sarah that is corrected by the deity's action with Isaac. Here, God commands Ishmael's conception—but to what purpose? This move, after all, is eventually superseded by God's own initiative with Sarra and Isaac, in parallel with the rest of the tradition (1.191). Noticing this interplay, in turn, tends only to undermine an initial impression of the importance of Sarra's being "ordered by God" here (1.187). These complications lead to some frustration, as it makes it hard to know what to trust; better, however, to know that caution is advised, than simply to be duped unawares.

*Another Child, and Circumcision (*Ant. *1.191-193)*

This brief section of the *Antiquities* is a highly abridged account of parts of the tradition reflected in Genesis 17. Thirteen years after the events just described, God predicts Isaac's birth by Sarra in an appearance to Abraham, and institutes the command to circumcise Abraham's descendants. There is no mention of covenant, no name changes, no favorable predictions

---

34. Bailey, "Matriarchs," 159; Feldman, *JA 1–4*, 71 n. 587.

for Sarra, and no laughter, on Abraham's part, at the promise of Isaac. God's announcement comes out of nowhere, and appears somewhat illogical, as it would seem that the issue of Abraham's childlessness has been addressed, by God's own command, in the previous section; this revelation's narrative utility, moreover, proves to be uncertain, as visiting angels will make a very similar prediction in the episode that follows. The prescription to circumcise Abraham's stock on the eighth day (1.192) does set up a later scene that shows an interesting facet of Sarra in the *Antiquities* (1.214). Other than this very modest contribution, and despite the direct reference to Sarra in 1.191, this episode aids little in constructing a reading of her character.

*Angelic Visitation (*Ant. *1.194-206)*

Ant. 1.194-195 [The residents of Sodom behaved outrageously to humans—hating strangers especially—and acted impiously toward the deity. God therefore decided to destroy their city.—JM] 196 After God had issued this judgment concerning the Sodomites, Habramos, noticing three angels—and he was sitting near the oak of Mambre before the door of his courtyard—and thinking that they were strangers, stood up and welcomed them and leading them within his home[35] invited them to enjoy his hospitality. 197 And when they agreed, he ordered loaves of bread to be made immediately from finest wheaten flour, and, sacrificing a calf and cooking it, he brought it to them as they were lying down under the oak. And they presented to him the appearance of eating. Moreover, they inquired about his wife as to where Sarra was. And when he said that she was within, they said that they would come in the future and would find that she had already become a mother. 198 But when his wife smiled at this and said that child-bearing was impossible, since she was 90 years old and since her husband was 100, they no longer disguised themselves but revealed that they were messengers of God and that one of them had been sent to make a disclosure concerning the child, and the other two to destroy the Sodomites. 199-206 [Abraham's attempted intercession on behalf of Sodom fails, and God eventually destroys the city with a lightning bolt. Some of Lot's family escape, only to eke out a wretched and isolated existence.—JM] (Feldman, *JA 1–4*, 73–8)

---

35. The movements of the characters in this passage are vague, but not as confused as this rendering implies. The passive of κατάγω plus παρά τινι is an idiom meaning "to turn in and lodge" with someone (LSJ 888a). The visitors aren't physically "led inside"—note their subsequent position "under the oak," *Ant.* 1.197—but encouraged to stay: "he urged them to stay with him and share his hospitality" (παρ' αὐτῷ καταχθέντας παρεκάλει ξενίας μεταλαβεῖν, 1.196).

The narrator's description of Abraham's solicitous gestures toward these three angels, whom he takes to be strangers (νομίσας εἶναι ξένους), draws a wincingly obvious distinction between Abraham and the residents of Sodom, whose reputation as μισόξενοι, or xenophobes, has just been reported to contribute to God's decision to destroy their city (1.194-196). The sincerity of Abraham's hospitality is underlined by his personal efforts at entertaining his guests; except for the hint in his command that "loaves be made immediately" (ἄρτους...εὐθύς...γενέσθαι), Abraham might be home alone (1.197).

Abruptly, however, after Abraham serves the strangers as they are "reclining under the oak" (ὑπὸ τῇ δρυῒ κατακειμένοις), the narrator brings Sarra's name into the discourse in an almost comical non sequitur: "they gave him the impression of eating, and besides they also inquired about his woman, just where Sarra might have gotten off to" (1.197).[36] The fame of Abraham's cooking has not drawn these strangers here, clearly; but what, precisely, is their errand? For it seems at first that their question is aimed at ensuring that Sarra not hear their message, as it is when they hear that Sarra is "inside" (ἔνδον) that they announce that they will return at some point and "find that she has already become a mother" (εὑρήσειν αὐτὴν ἤδη μητέρα γεγενημένην, 1.197). Yet the basic thrust of this is not news to Abraham, to whom the deity has, and rather recently, personally relayed very similar information (1.191; compare 1.194, 198). Suddenly, however, in a puzzling development that recalls her unexpected appearance in the scene of her private interview with Pharaoh (1.165), it is clear that Sarra is not only within earshot, but even in plain view.[37] For "when the woman smiled at this and said that childbearing was impossible, she being ninety and her husband one hundred," the strangers seemingly react to her directly, dropping their pose and revealing both their angelic nature and their mission "to tell

---

36. οἱ δὲ δόξαν αὐτῷ παρέσχον ἐσθιόντων, ἔτι δὲ καὶ περὶ τῆς γυναικὸς ἐπυνθάνοντο, ποῖ ποτ' εἴη Σάρρα. Thackeray, 97 note "c," notes that this "docetic" conception of the incorporeality of the visiting angels is paralleled in Philo, *Abr.* 118 and the Palestinian Targum. The *Testament of Abraham* develops this notion into an extended comic subplot in which the archangel Michael feigns the need to urinate in order to consult privately with God about how to appear to eat Abraham's food (*T. Abr.* 4, Recension A). The general theme also appears in other Second Temple narrative contexts such as Tobit (12:19 in both versions). Compare, as well, the novel strategy of the angel fed by Manoah and his wife in *Ant.* 5.283-284, who lights his food on fire with a rod and rides the smoke to heaven.

37. Compare Franxman, *Genesis and the* Antiquities, 143.

about the child" (1.198).³⁸ Sarra's smile, at least, must be visually apprehended: μειδιάω, "to smile," is specifically distinguished from γελάω, "to laugh aloud."³⁹ But her startling, apparently physical translation from "inside"—the "courtyard" (αὐλή, 1.196), perhaps, or an assumed γυναικεία, or women's quarters—adds to the almost uncanny feeling first prompted by the offhand description of angels pretending to eat.

Sarra's undetailed, spectral motion, here something like the movement of a knight on a chessboard, also contributes to an impression of a story told in haste. The tale of Sodom's destruction provides a heavy frame for this brief scene (1.194-195, 199-206), casting the angelic visit to Abraham and Sarra as a kind of aside; even the proportions of the angelic assignments—one to proclaim Sarra's future child, but two to destroy Sodom (1.198)—add to a sense of the relative insignificance of this nativity announcement. That this detail is actually contradicted by the narrative, as angels, in the plural, have already pronounced the prediction (ἔφασαν, 1.197), only adds to the general sense of a tale evading the full control of its teller.⁴⁰ For Abraham, too, the message about Sarra's impending motherhood, which he allows to pass without comment, is less affecting than the news about Sodom's imminent destruction, as he grieves over the fate of its residents and attempts to intercede on their behalf (1.199). The pledge of the angels "to come in the future" (ἥξειν...εἰς τὸ μέλλον, 1.197), moreover, is never fulfilled. In fact, the narrator seems to forget that the angels ever came at all, claiming later that Abraham names his son Isaac "because Sarra smiled when *God* told her she would bear" (1.213).⁴¹ Sarra's response here also prepares the ground for confusion later, for Isaac "means laughter" (γέλωτα σημαίνει), as the narrator is careful to note (1.213)—not "a smile." This seems to be another example of a narrative difficulty created by the narrator's tendency to trim sharp edges from the personalities of the main characters.

The narrator, then, treats this scene as if it were rather insignificant; but there are a few details about Sarra that can still be picked up here. This is the first explicit mention of Sarra's advanced age; at ninety, she turns out to be a near-contemporary of her uncle and husband, Abraham. Her smile,

---

38. τῆς δὲ γυναικὸς ἐπὶ τούτῳ μειδιασάσης καὶ ἀδύνατον εἶναι τὴν τεκνοποιίαν εἰπούσης αὐτῆς μὲν ἐνενήκοντα ἔτη ἐχούσης τοῦ δ' ἀνδρὸς ἑκατόν...σημανῶν περὶ τοῦ παιδός.
39. LSJ 1092b; μειδιάω is a later form of μειδάω, under which it is listed.
40. Compare Franxman, *Genesis and the Antiquities*, 143–4.
41. Compare Feldman, *JA 1–4*, 80 n. 653; Franxman, *Genesis and the Antiquities*, 153.

formed in direct reaction (ἐπὶ τούτῳ) to the audacious claim that she will yet become a mother, seems in keeping with someone who has reached a sober and knowing old age; but here, too, the narrator's stubborn refusal to let the characters speak for themselves means that it is not entirely certain how far Sarra's reported thoughts extend. Surely she says that "childbearing is impossible" (ἀδύνατον εἶναι τὴν τεκνοποιίαν εἰπούσης). But is the note of their ages that follows—αὐτῆς μὲν ἐνενήκοντα ἔτη ἐχούσης τοῦ δ' ἀνδρὸς ἑκατόν—Sarra's own elucidation of her categorical declaration, or a narratorial gloss?

Sarra does appear to exercise a modicum of power here, in that she seems directly responsible for provoking the angels to drop their disguise. The description of Sarra's smile and remarks about childbearing is a long chain of clauses subordinate to the verbs detailing the angels' direct revelation, and could even be rendered causally: "Because the woman smiled...and said...they no longer continued incognito but made themselves known as angels of God" (1.198). These messengers showed no such consideration for Abraham, who might have held off on dinner had he been aware of his guests' incorporeality. Sarra's apparent emergence from "inside," too, might seem to carry some liberating force, read across the tradition: in contrast to the MT, Sarra is "brought out into the open," as Franxman notes.[42] Yet once this perspective is engaged, all that is stripped from Sarah of the MT in exchange for Sarra's tour of the yard in the *Antiquities* must also be brought out into the open. Bailey points out, with some justification, that the abridgement of Sarra's role here is mostly due to the omission of "apparently negative references to her" in the corresponding scene in Genesis 18.[43] But I disagree that such omissions mostly "enhance" Sarra in the *Antiquities*, as he later claims; from a narrative perspective that even flirts with a mimetic view, these kinds of textual minuses only subtract from the "concrete semblance" that is Sarra in this story.[44] If Sarra is subtly washed out in this scene in the LXX, she is a threadbare outline here. The flow of the narrative at hand, moreover, rather enervates the modest note of power that may be implied by the angels' capitulation, and the mild suggestion of freedom contained in Sarra's presence outside. The entire episode seems somewhat poorly integrated, a bit of an afterthought; and Sarra displays neither power nor freedom in the next scenes in which she figures, in Gerar.

---

42. Franxman, *Genesis and the* Antiquities, 143. The same seems to be true in Philo, *Abr.* 110–113.
43. Bailey, "Matriarchs," 159–60.
44. Ibid., 170–1.

"Just Like Before"—but Now in Gerar (Ant. 1.207-212)

Ant. 1.207 And Habramos migrated to Gerara in Palestine, taking with himself Sarra, in the guise of a sister, making a pretense similar to the previous one because of fear. For he had feared Abimelechos, the king of the inhabitants, who also himself having fallen passionately in love with Sarra, was capable of seducing her. 208 But he [Abimelechos] was prevented from his lust by a painful disease that befell him from God; and when the physicians had abandoned hope, he saw in his sleep a vision in a dream that he should do no violence to the wife of the stranger; and when he felt better, he pointed out to his friends that God had inflicted this disease upon him in retribution for the stranger to protect his wife from violence, for it was not his sister that he had brought but his lawfully married wife, and that He promised that He would show himself well disposed in the future if he [Habramos] would be secure with regard to his wife. 209 Having said this, he [Abimelechos] sent for Habramos, upon the counsel of his friends, and bade him to have no further fear with regard to his wife, that she would suffer something shameful, for God was looking after her,[45] and through His alliance that had remained standing, he would bring her home free from outrage, with both God and the conscience of the woman being witnesses. And he said that he would not have desired her in the beginning if he had known that she was a married woman, but since he had brought her as his sister he had not done wrong. 210 And he entreated him to be indulgent with him and to make God well-disposed, and [said] that if he wished to remain with him, he would grant him every abundance; but if he preferred to depart he would obtain an escort and all things such as he desired in coming to him. 211 When he said this, Habramos said that he had not lied about the relationship of his wife, for she was the child of his brother, and that without such dissimulation he would not have supposed that the visit would be safe. And to show that he was in no way responsible for his sickness but that he was zealously eager for his recovery, he kept asserting that he was ready to remain with him. 212 And Abimelechos apportioned him both land and riches, and they made a covenant that they would conduct themselves without guile, taking an oath over a certain well that they call Bersoubai, that is to say, "well of an oath." It is thus still even now named by the inhabitants. (Feldman, *JA 1–4*, 78–80)

This episode opens with a welter of implicit and explicit ties to earlier narrative events. Abraham is said to "move" again, using one of the terms used previously to describe his migration to Canaan (μετοικέω, 1.207; compare 157, 160). No reason is provided for this move, though the king's

---

45. This is a simple mistranslation; God is said to be looking after Abraham (αὐτοῦ), not Sarra.

later statements imply that Abraham had a definite agenda in mind: after assuring him that "every kind of plenty would accrue" to him (πᾶσαν ἀφθονίαν ὑπάρξειν) if he stayed in Gerar, the king also declares that Abraham would obtain at his departure "everything he had desired, too, in coming to him in the first place" (πάντων ὅσων καὶ χρήζων πρὸς αὐτὸν ἀφίκοιτο, 1.210). This note of "plenty" (ἀφθονία) directly recalls Abraham's first goal in visiting the Egyptians earlier (1.161), and many lexical and thematic links immediately bind this journey to Gerar to that of Egypt. Abraham is once again "bringing along" Sarra, just as he did in Egypt (ἐπαγόμενος, 1.207; compare 1.162), pointedly "in the role of sister" (ἐν ἀδελφῆς...σχήματι, 1.207). This is the language of drama: Sarra is "starring as the sister"—in the event, a rather limited role—an understanding bolstered by the report of the narrator that Abraham is "playing the part" or, perhaps better here, "staging the play" (ὑποκρινάμενος, 1.207).[46] This is yet another lexical tie between these two episodes, and another example of a similarity between these two characters: on the edge of Egypt, Abraham also taught Sarra "to play the part" (ὑποκρίνασθαι, 1.162).[47] And just in case the reader nodded off during the Egyptian adventure, the narrator makes it even more plain: all this playacting is done "just like before" (ὅμοια τοῖς πρίν), and, just like before, it is supposedly done "out of [Abraham's] fear" (διὰ τὸν φόβον, 1.207; compare 1.162). This fear is said to be justified straightaway, when the local king, Abimelech, "who himself likewise came to lust after Sarra," is "just about to destroy her" (ὃς καὶ αὐτὸς ἐρασθεὶς τῆς Σάρρας φθείρειν οἷός τε ἦν, 1.207). The καί here—"also," or "likewise"—seems aimed specifically at the recollection of Pharaoh's very similar conduct, and if the notion of a monarch being "just about to" (οἷός τε ἦν) ruin Sarra is not enough to cement the association, the frustration of the king's "lust by a nasty disease" (ἐπιθυμίας ὑπὸ νόσου χαλεπῆς) sent by God surely will be (1.207-208; compare 163-164).[48] Nor are these the last of the correspondences between these episodes; Abimelech's offense, to take one further example—intending "to outrage the woman of the stranger" (ὑβρίζειν τὴν τοῦ ξένου γυναῖκα, 1.208)—is the same as that of Pharaoh (ὑβρίσαι τοῦ ξένου τὴν γυναῖκα, 1.164).

But what is the effect of all these echoes? Feldman, from an author-centered perspective, suggests that Josephus "anticipates" the "objection" of the reader to the relation of such a similar incident "by stating quite

---

46. LSJ 1745a–b; 1885b–86a.

47. These are the only instances of ὑποκρίνομαι in the first six books of the *Antiquities*.

48. I am not sure why Thackeray and Feldman both choose to translate φθείρειν οἷός τε ἦν in 1.207 differently than the identical idiom (οἷός τε ἦν ἅψασθαι) in 1.163.

openly...that Abraham here practiced the same dissimulation as before, and from the same motive, namely fear."⁴⁹ How, though, can the narrator's declaration of Abraham's motive be credible? If the rationale is the same, then Abraham must be afraid that Abimelech will do away with him on account of his shapely wife, as he is supposed to have feared in Egypt (1.162). Yet Abraham, in distinction to Sarra, Pharaoh, and those Egyptians caught up in civic unrest, faced no apparent danger in Egypt, and certainly none that accrued due to the revelation of his marriage to Sarra. To the contrary: the resolution of the matter owed solely to the emergence of the truth, and—at least on the testimony of Pharaoh—the entire sequence of events was triggered by Abraham's scheme (1.165). Importantly, Abimelech makes this same claim: "he said, with God and the conscience of the woman as witness, that he would never have longed for her in the first place, if he had known she was married; but since [Abraham] had brought her as a sister, [Abimelech] had done no wrong" (1.209).⁵⁰ In the Egyptian episode, it was already difficult to reconcile Abraham's remarkable capacity for inference (1.154) with a presumption of his innocence in the matter of Sarra's abduction and near-rape; here, such harmonization seems simply impossible. How could a man so "quick to understand about everything" and "not at all wrong about things he conjectures" (1.154) fall prey to the same unfounded fear, or fail to conclude that the same ruse, deployed "just like before," would have the same outcome? Far from burnishing Abraham's character, the complex set of correspondences between these two episodes decreases his credibility even further. Abraham's high regard for hospitality (1.196), moreover, begins to look rather one-sided given his lack of regard for his own hosts.

In the *Antiquities*, Sarra is better defined in Egypt than she is here in Gerar, where Abimelech, at least judging by the extent of his indirectly related speech and his involvement in the plot, could fairly be called the main character. This is in puzzling contrast to the tradition as depicted in the MT and the LXX, where Gerar represents—to differing degrees, and not without significant cost in either case—something of an advancement in agency, or at least in action, for Sar(r)a(h). Here again, Abraham goes to the region "bringing Sarra along in the role of sister," language that probably implies at least a passive willingness on her part to "play along." Yet it is Abraham who is "putting on the drama" (ὑποκρινάμενος, 1.207), taking from Sarra one of her few opportunities for subjectivity,

---

49. Feldman, *JA 1–4*, 78 n. 638; Feldman, "Abraham," 287.

50. τοῦ δὲ θεοῦ μάρτυρος ὄντος καὶ τοῦ τῆς γυναικὸς συνειδότος ἔλεγε μηδ᾽ ἂν ὀρεχθῆναι τὴν ἀρχήν, εἰ γαμετὴν οὖσαν ἠπίστατο, ὡς ἀδελφὴν δὲ ἀγόμενον ἦν οὐκ ἠδίκουν. The syntax at the end appears to outrun the composer.

albeit prompted by Abraham himself, in the earlier episode, where "he taught her, too, to act this out" (κἀκείνην τοῦθ' ὑποκρίνασθαι...ἐδίδαξεν, 1.162). What Abimelech is "just about" to do here, especially as interpreted by both Thackeray and Feldman, might seem to leave open a very small gap in which to posit Sarra's involvement; translating φθείρειν as "to seduce" (1.207) suggests at least a measure of reciprocation, even if coerced or obtained under false pretenses. Some examples of the term in the *Antiquities* are equivocal, as in parts of the re-presentation of the Pentateuch's legal material, where it seems to be used of a "corrupter" of the willing as well as the unwilling (4.251-252). The basic force of φθείρω, however, is to "destroy," and the narrative sections of the *Antiquities* offer better parallels, such as that of Dinah, whom Shechem φθείρει δι' ἁρπαγῆς or "defiles by means of abduction" (1.337), and that of Tamar, whose rape by her brother Amnon is described by φθείρω and other terms of brute violence (βιάζομαι, ἡ βία, ἡ ὕβρις, 7.168-172).[51]

Sarra's experience here, then, as the parallels with Egypt also suggest, is not a brush with illicit romance but another near-rape: in the king's "lust after Sarra," he is "just about to destroy" or "ruin" her when God's regard for Abraham's marriage prompts another divine intervention (1.207-208). That Sarra's person is only incidental to God's primary concern is even clearer here in Gerar. The problem is first characterized in language nearly identical to that of Egypt: Abimelech is "not to outrage the woman of the stranger"—the possessive, once again, being the key to the offense. Then, however, Abimelech underlines the fundamental issue more than once, explaining to his friends "that God brought this sickness on him in the service of the satisfaction of his guest, by safeguarding his woman undefiled," and, moreover, that God would prove "kindly in the future given that [Abraham] remain free of anxiety concerning his woman" (1.208).[52] Although Feldman's mistranslation obscures this, the king's subsequent explanation to Abraham makes the point even more succinctly, as he reassures his guest that his woman will be maintained free of shame "because God cared for him," that is, Abraham (θεὸν γὰρ αὐτοῦ κήδεσθαι, 1.209).[53]

---

51. LSJ 1928a.
52. ὡς ὁ θεὸς ταύτην αὐτῷ ἐπάγει τὴν νόσον ὑπὲρ ἐκδικίας τοῦ ξένου φυλάσσων ἀνύβριστον αὐτῷ τὴν γυναῖκα...εὐμενῆ τὸ λοιπὸν ἀδεοῦς ἐκείνου περὶ τὴν γυναῖκα γενομένου.
53. According to Niese, αὐτοῦ (representing the usual genitive object of the middle/passive of κήδω, "to be concerned, care for") is the reading of all manuscripts here; Feldman's "for God was looking after her" must be a simple mistake.

Yet the most interesting notes about Sarra in the Egyptian episode are without echo here in Gerar, and these other correspondences merely serve to highlight their absence. There, for example, uniquely in the tradition as surveyed to this point, Sarra, clearly unaccompanied by Abraham, engages in an intimate verbal exchange with Pharaoh. Though her speech is deeply submerged, as usual in this narrative, she plainly must reveal or confirm "the truth" in this conversation: not only the truth about who Abraham is—"the one she'd brought along"—but also "who she is" (τίς… εἴη) herself (1.165). No such scene is in view at all here in Gerar, despite the fact that Sarra is, once again, resident with the local monarch for some time. Abimelech must have her in his power to be "just about to destroy" her, and, quite a bit later—after the king falls ill, is treated ineffectually by his physicians, receives a revelatory vision in his sleep, partly recovers, confers with his friends, and summons Abraham for an interview—he pledges that Abraham will, at some point, "get her back undamaged" (ἀνύβριστον κομίζεσθαι, 1.209). Franxman claims that Sarra "was never taken from Abraham to begin with" in this episode, and thus that her promised return is a "contradiction" and an oversight in the account.[54] This seems by far the harder way to resolve the issue. Instead, this is simply another instance of the now-familiar motif of the indeterminacy of Sarra's movements, providing yet another link between this episode and that of Egypt, as well as a tie to Sarra's ambiguous physical disposition in the scenes with the angelic visitors. Here, however, Sarra's stay with the king yields very little additional information about her. There is a bare hint, in Abimelech's invocation of "the woman's conscience" (τοῦ τῆς γυναικὸς συνειδότος, 1.209), that Sarra could testify about her time in the palace; but this, too, comes to nothing.

As for Sarra and Abraham's relationship, the account of Gerar in the *Antiquities*, in distinction to those in the MT and LXX, offers no new information. Once again, the narrator seems caught out by efforts to improve the moral standing of the main characters. As many have noted, the stated relationship between the two in the *Antiquities*, a marriage between uncle and niece, is licit under the laws of Moses, while the relationship claimed by Abraham in Gen. 20:12 of the MT and LXX—that the two are actually married, non-uterine siblings—is not.[55] In the tradition reflected in Genesis, there is no direct narratorial claim about their blood tie. While to my reading Abraham's contention is not credible, it remains just possible, then, that he is telling the truth in Gen. 20:12. But here in the *Antiquities*

---

54. Franxman, *Genesis and the* Antiquities, 148–50.
55. See, for instance, the lengthy note of Feldman, *JA 1–4*, 54 n. 475.

the narrator is painted into a corner by the earlier, precise specification of Sarra and Abraham's blood relationship: Sarra is in fact not Abraham's sister (ἀδελφή) at all, but his niece (ἀδελφιδῆ, *Ant.* 1.51). The story of the pair as siblings, moreover, was plainly introduced as a "trick" or "scheme" (τέχνη) in which Abraham "pretended to be her brother" (ἀδελφὸς αὐτῆς εἶναι προσεποιήσατο, 1.162). So Abraham's claim here in Gerar—that he did not, in fact, lie about their relationship—relies explicitly on verbal sleight of hand: ἀδελφιδῆ versus ἀδελφή. That "the latter can be used loosely" to mean "kinswoman," as Thackeray rightly notes, only underlines the fact that this is a gambit relying on a disingenuous use of language; even Abraham, by referring to his "pretense" (ὑπόκρισις), admits as much in the same context (1.211).[56] Abimelech thought, then, and quite reasonably, that ἀδελφή meant what it usually meant. In the king's reported speech to his friends, he declares after his admonitory dream that "she is not his sister" (μή...ἀδελφὴν οὖσαν...αὐτῷ, 1.208); that Abraham and Abimelech later agree to deal with each other "without guile" (ἀδόλως, 1.212) only underlines the trickery that has marked much of their interaction. The narrator's attempt to rectify the legally awkward possibility of Sarra and Abraham's half-sibling relationship in the broader tradition, then, only reinforces the reality of their deception: one moral "improvement" leads directly to an ethical failure.

The ties in the *Antiquities* between Gerar and Egypt include a few significant connections for Sarra. Again, Abraham "brings along" Sarra, which anticipates numerous explicit correspondences between the episodes (1.207; compare 1.162). In fact, things are said to be "just like before": Sarra, again, becomes a royal captive as a result of a lie about her relationship with Abraham, and is "just about to" be assaulted when God, ever protective of Abraham and his possessions, intervenes (1.207-208; compare 1.162-164).

Yet all is not actually the same. The carefully drawn similarities between the episodes, for example, paradoxically reveal that Abraham's motive of fear is incredible here. Sarra, for her part, is more sketchily drawn in Gerar, in a development that runs counter to the traditions reflected in MT and LXX. Abraham, instead of Sarra, "is playing the part" (ὑποκρινάμενος) here, another association of these characters that has no strict parallel in the tradition surveyed here; Abraham's adoption of Sarra's earlier implied act is just one example of her lack of definition in these scenes. Even the supposed revelation about Sarra and Abraham's blood relationship is

---

56. Thackeray, 104–5 note "a."

missing here, from the reader of the tradition's perspective, anyway, as the narrator has long ago anticipated its implicit moral quandary—while creating a new one in the process. Most importantly, however, Sarra in Gerar has no private, solo audience with Abimelech in which she is defined as the one who "brought along" Abraham, and thus engages in no truth-telling, no teaching, no implied speech at all (compare 1.165).

Birth and Banishment (Ant. 1.213-221)

Ant. 1.213 Not long afterwards a son was born to Habramos from Sarra, as had been foretold to him [Habramos] by God, whom he called Isakos. This signifies laughter. He was called thus because Sarra had smiled when God said that she would give birth, since she did not expect it, being too old for childbirth. For she was 90 years old, and Habramos was 100. 214 The child was born in the latest year for both. Immediately after the eighth day they circumcised him, and from that time on the Jews have a custom to perform circumcisions after so many days. And Arabs do so after the thirteenth year. For Ismaelos, the founder of their race, born of a concubine to Habramos, was circumcised at that time. Concerning this I shall expound the entire subject with much exactness.[57] 215 Sarra at first used to feel affection towards Ismaelos, who had been born from her servant Agare, showing no less affection than if it were her own son, for he was being nurtured for the succession to the rule; but when she herself gave birth to Isakos she did not deem it proper for Ismaelos, who was older and was able to cause him harm after his father had died, to be reared with him. 216 She, therefore, kept persuading Habramos to send him away with his mother and to settle elsewhere. He, at first, did not grant his consent to the proposals that she had pursued with zeal, considering it the most cruel of all things to send away a child and a woman destitute of the necessities of life. 217 But later, for God also approved of the things decreed by Sarra, having been persuaded, he handed over Ismaelos, who was not yet able to go by himself, to his mother, and bade her to carry water in a skin and bread and to depart using necessity as a guide. 218 And when the necessaries of life had been exhausted as she went away, she was in distress, and with the water being scarce she placed the child who was at his last gasp under a certain fir-tree and proceeded further on in order that he might not give up his soul while she was present. 219 But an angel of God met her and told her of a spring nearby and bade her to look after the nurture of the child, for great blessings awaited her

---

57. This apparently refers to the projected but never-written work *On Customs and Causes*, also referred to elsewhere (*Ant.* 1.25, 29, 192, and so on; the title seems to come from 4.198, τὴν περὶ ἐθῶν καὶ αἰτιῶν ἀπόδοσιν or "the explanation about customs and causes"). See Feldman, *JA 1–4*, 73 n. 599, 81 n. 659; Thackeray, 95 note "c."

through the preservation of Ismaelos. And she took courage through these promises, and meeting shepherds escaped her misfortunes because of their attention. 220–221 [Details about the descendants of Ishmael, the Arabs, and their territory.—JM] (Feldman, *JA 1–4*, 80–3)

After ending the previous section with another travelogue-style note, this one about the meaning and persistence of the name of a well in Abimelech's land, the narrator treats the meaning of the name of Abraham and Sarra's son, Isaac. The transition is very casual—"not much later" (μετ' οὐ πολύ, 1.213)—and there is no indication that the household has moved on from Gerar, where Abraham has only recently declared his readiness to remain (1.211). At first, Abraham is the focus of the discourse: "A child was born to Abraham (Ἀβράμῳ) by Sarra, as had been foretold to him (αὐτῷ) by God, whom he named (ὠνόμασε) Isaac" (1.213). The significance of this name, however, is supposedly due to the action of his mother: Isaac "means 'laughter'" (γέλωτα σημαίνει), and Abraham "called his son so because Sarra smiled when God told her she would give birth—not expecting pregnancy any longer due to old age" (1.213).[58] But this explanation makes little sense.[59] On the face of it, γέλως or "laughter" has only an associative semantic relationship, not a lexical tie, to the verb used of "smiling," μειδιάω. Moreover, the narrator has already revealed why Abraham should name his son "Isaac": a year or two ago, God simply commanded him to do so, without offering any kind of justification, etymological or otherwise (1.191). Even further, God is not the speaker of the prediction referred to here, while Sarra does not seem to be its intended addressee; and though she does respond to the claim, it is to call it flatly "impossible" (ἀδύνατον), not merely unexpected (1.197-198).[60] These inconsistencies, and especially the disparity between Sarra's reported action and the meaning of Isaac's name, do not strike me as symptomatic of a narrator who is simply, or only, careless. Rather, they hint at a narrator with something to hide. A reader with an awareness of the broader tradition knows that what is concealed is not only Sarra's skeptical laugh in the tent and its aftermath (Gen. 18:12-15),

---

58. διὰ μέντοι τὸ τὴν Σάρραν μειδιάσαι τέξεσθαι φήσαντος αὐτὴν τοῦ θεοῦ μὴ προσδοκῶσαν ἤδη τοκετοῦ πρεσβυτέραν οὖσαν τὸν υἱὸν οὕτως ἐκάλεσεν.

59. Compare Bailey, "Matriarchs," 160.

60. The narrator's lapse here—the visiting angels, not God, had relayed the prediction about Sarra's impending motherhood in 1.197—is frequently noted (Franxman, *Genesis and the* Antiquities, 153). I would only add that the ambiguity is also present in the earlier scene, where Abraham gets up from dinner with the angels, yet speaks to God directly about the imminent destruction of Sodom (1.199).

or her deeply ambiguous remarks about laughter after Isaac is born (MT Gen. 21:6), but also Abraham's own derisive laughter at the first prediction of Isaac's birth (Gen. 17:17).[61] This desire to smooth the edges of Sarra's character, in particular, will continue to shape the narrator's account in this episode.

Abraham's initial domination of the narrative matter does not continue here, and the narrator's attention soon shifts to Sarra. First, though, the language bridges this gap. Isaac's birth is reckoned with reference to both of his parents, though the precise meaning of τίκτεται δὲ παῖς ἑκατέρων τῷ ὑστάτῳ ἔτει (1.214) is not clear; its plain sense, "a child is born in the last year of both of them," as if Abraham and Sarra were both about to die, seems untenable even in the face of other examples of narratorial confusion. Thackeray's solution here, that ὕστατος is standing in for ὕστερος, as in other idiomatic late-Greek uses of temporal superlatives for comparatives, may offer the best hope of leaving the text unamended: something, then, like "a child is born of the both of them in the next year."[62] What seems significant, and a material shift from the language at the beginning of 1.213, is the mutuality implied in ἑκατέρων—Isaac is not only Abraham's child here, but Sarra's too—a concept that is remarkably reinforced in what follows, where "they circumcise" (περιτέμνουσι) the boy after eight days (1.214). The natural referent here is Sarra and Abraham, not some indefinite "they"; in this way, the narrator knits Sarra into the foundational myth of one of the fundamental markers of male Jewish identity, noting "and from that [time], the Jews have a custom to perform circumcision after so many [days]."[63] This is truly surprising, at least to this reader, and is certainly not inspired in full by Gen. 21:4, where it is simply said that "Abraham circumcised Isaac his son when he was eight days old" (וימל אברהם את־יצחק בנו בן־שמנת ימים). Sarra's participation in this rite anticipates her prominence in much of the remainder of this episode, where her feelings and actions will receive a sustained focus so far unparalleled in this narrative.

Indeed, after a few more ethnographic remarks, these on the circumcision practices of the Arabs, descended from Ishmael, the narrator reflects in some detail on Sarra's conduct and motives, even venturing to offer what might be called an internal view:

---

61. Feldman, *JA 1–4*, 73 n. 602, 81 n. 654.
62. Thackeray, 106–7 note "a." See also Feldman, *JA 1–4*, 81 n. 655; Franxman, *Genesis and the* Antiquities, 153.
63. κἀξ ἐκείνου μετὰ τοσαύτας ἔθος ἔχουσιν οἱ Ἰουδαῖοι ποιεῖσθαι τὰς περιτομάς.

> Now Sarra was accustomed to show affection to Ishmael after he had been born of her slave Hagar, at least at first, not lacking in the kind of goodwill she would have had for her own son, because he was being raised for succession to the rule; but after bearing Isaac herself she didn't think it right for Ishmael to be raised alongside him, [Ishmael] being older, and capable of hurting him after their father's death.[64] (1.215)

In another example of the narrator's ham-handed efforts to polish the portraits of the primary characters, Sarra's reason for supposedly showing affection for the son of her slave "at first"—"because he was being raised for succession to the rule" (1.215)—seems to fall somewhat short of admirable. If στέργω carries a stronger force than "affection," as it sometimes does, and refers to the "love" between parent and child, the dissonance between feeling and motive is even greater.[65] Perhaps other, less mercenary motives may also have been operative. But this is the only one mentioned; and the fact that Sarra's affection dries up so precipitously when she gives birth to a son of her own—there are no discourse clues, at least, to suggest that Isaac is much older than a week here—might throw the depth of her feeling into doubt.[66]

But the chief issue that affects the portrayal of Sarra here was raised earlier in the discussion of her treatment of Hagar. There, the idea of Ishmael inheriting Abraham's authority (ἡγεμονία) was Hagar's motive for "playing the queen," insolent behavior that seemed to justify, in the narrator's conception, Sarra's brutal treatment of her slave. The way Hagar acted was unwarranted, apparently, because her perception of the situation was not based in fact: with intolerable presumption, she played the queen "as if" her unborn son would succeed to the rule (1.188). Yet here this is precisely what is presented as fact, and, once again, as a kind of apology for Sarra's ethically dubious behavior. The result, I think, is a small jam in the works of Sarra's characterization. Does she, in fact, show "affection for Ishmael," "not lacking in the kind of goodwill she would have had for her own son"? If the narrator offered any other explanation here, or none at all, this might seem credible; but Sarra is said to do it explicitly on the grounds of Ishmael's role as presumed heir, an idea previously discredited

---

64. Σάρρα δὲ γεννηθέντα τὸν Ἰσμαῆλον ἐκ τῆς δούλης αὐτῆς Ἀγάρης τὸ μὲν πρῶτον ἔστεργεν οὐδὲν ἀπολείπουσα τῆς πρὸς ἴδιον υἱὸν εὐνοίας, ἐτρέφετο γὰρ ἐπὶ τῇ τῆς ἡγεμονίας διαδοχῇ, τεκοῦσα δ' αὐτὴ τὸν Ἴσακον οὐκ ἠξίου παρατρέφεσθαι τούτῳ τὸν Ἰσμαῆλον ὄντα πρεσβύτερον καὶ κακουργεῖν δυνάμενον τοῦ πατρὸς αὐτοῖς ἀποθανόντος.

65. LSJ 1639b.

66. Contrast the assumption of Feldman, *JA 1–4*, 82 n. 662, that Isaac's weaning still sets the timeline of Ishmael's expulsion, as in the account of the MT.

by the narrator. Or again, if Hagar had simply displayed her insolence having bested her master in the realm of fertility, Sarra's fondness for Ishmael, perhaps even prompted by an ulterior motive, might mellow her image here. As it is, however, the narrator's explanations seem to collide head-on, and the resolution of the matter isn't as easy as choosing one over the other, for these competing reports both serve the same function: to soften the sometimes violent and callous edges of Sarra's character. In any case, this portrayal of Sarra as acting against Ishmael despite her affectionate feelings toward him anticipates the depiction of Abraham's competing feelings and actions in the episode of Isaac's near-sacrifice—another interesting and singular tie between Sarra and Abraham in the *Antiquities*.

As for the stated reason for Sarra's apprehension over Isaac's safety, which Feldman finds "very plausible," the evidence, to my reading, is inconclusive.[67] If Ishmael has in fact been groomed his entire life "for succession to the rule," being summarily cast aside for an infant might understandably chafe. Yet the status of this claim is, I think, as uncertain as Ishmael's actual claim to Abraham's authority turns out to be. And the image of Ishmael as "capable of hurting" Isaac is difficult to square with the pathetic descriptions of this "infant child" (παῖδα νήπιον) who will soon lie abandoned by his mother under "some fir tree...gasping his last" (ὑπ' ἐλάτῃ τινί...ψυχορραγοῦν, 1.216, 218). Is Ishmael "able to hurt," or "act maliciously to" Isaac (κακουργεῖν δυνάμενον, 1.215), yet "not yet able to go by himself" (μήπω δι' αὐτοῦ χωρεῖν δυνάμενον, 1.217)?[68] Noting that Ishmael is supposed to be about fourteen at this point (1.193) contributes little to a resolution of the matter, as this merely raises further questions about the narrator's candor or level of knowledge. One thing, however, is certain: in this narrative, there is no suggestion that Ishmael has ever hurt anyone—something that cannot be said for Sarra (1.188).

After this, the narrator moves from claims about Sarra's interior motives to the action that they prompt. Sarra, supposedly, fears the future capability of Ishmael for violence; "therefore" (οὖν)—despite the deep maternal affection she'd long been accustomed to show him—"she kept after (ἔπειθεν) Abraham to send him away, along with his mother, εἰς ἀποικίαν" (1.216).[69] This brief sentence contains a relative wealth of

---

67. Feldman, *JA 1–4*, 81 n. 660; Feldman, "Abraham," 243. Compare Bailey, "Matriarchs," 160.

68. Reading δι' αὐτοῦ with Thackeray; Niese's text reads δι' αὑτοῦ, but see his apparatus.

69. ἔπειθεν οὖν τὸν Ἄβραμον εἰς ἀποικίαν ἐκπέμπειν αὐτὸν μετὰ τῆς μητρός.

material bearing on Sarra's character. Sarra's urging of this course goes on for a significant period of time; the description of Abraham's subsequent dithering ("at first...but later," 1.216-217) confirms the suggestion of duration in ἔπειθεν. That this ongoing process of persuasion apparently includes Hagar in its focus from the beginning may throw some doubt on the later justification for her to accompany the boy—simply that Ishmael is "not yet able to go by himself," as if otherwise Hagar would be welcome to stay. But the bare fact that Sarra eventually succeeds in her persuasion here forms yet another tie between her character's traits and those of Abraham, who has been significantly defined by his convincing rhetoric (1.154, 162, 166-167).

Just where Sarra persuades Abraham to send Ishmael and Hagar, or for what purpose, is far less clear, which is why I have left εἰς ἀποικίαν untranslated above. Feldman argues that Sarra's image is improved by this phrase, in comparison with the tradition reflected in the MT, as "she seeks here merely to have [Ishmael], in the fashion familiar from Greek history, found a colony (εἰς ἀποικίαν)."[70] This reading is lexically plausible. While the term is not used with great frequency in Josephus, ἀποικία is sensibly rendered "colony" in several other contexts, including, most tellingly, that of Isaac's marriage to Rebekah. Several parallel themes emerge there, where Isaac is said to have come into sole possession of Abraham's estate "because the sons of Keturah," likewise offspring of Abraham by a different woman, "had left for their colonies" (οἱ γὰρ ἐκ τῆς Κατούρας εἰς τὰς ἀποικίας ἐξεληλύθεισαν, 1.255). Moreover, Thucydides employs a very similar phrase to *Ant.* 1.215 (ἀποικίας ἐξέπεμψε, *Hist.* 1.12) to describe the initial colonizing activity of Greece.[71] Yet surely the founding of a "colony" entails the reasonable provision of the colonists, at least some hope of success, and an intended destination—all of which are lacking here. Abraham's scruples indicate that he suspects that this course of action amounts to a death sentence: "at first" (κατά...ἀρχάς), he refuses to consent, "considering it the most cruel thing of all to send away an infant child and a woman bereft of [life's] necessities" (*Ant.* 1.216).[72] Here, Abraham's celebrated quality of being "not at all wrong about things he conjectures" (1.154) happens to be confirmed by subsequent events, as Hagar, "using necessity as a guide" (ὁδηγῷ τῇ ἀνάγκῃ χρωμένην), nearly

---

70. Feldman, *JA 1–4*, 82 n. 661; compare van der Lans, "Hagar, Ishmael, and Abraham's Household," 194.

71. See this and other examples in LSJ 200a.

72. πάντων ὠμότατον ἡγούμενος εἶναι παῖδα νήπιον καὶ γυναῖκα ἄπορον τῶν ἀναγκαίων ἐκπέμπειν.

meets her end along with Ishmael in some deserted place (1.217-218). Looking further into the narrative, finally, it is worth noting that a "colony" is difficult to define apart from some kind of sustained relationship with its "mother city," or μητρόπολις.[73] From this point on, however, the only significant contact between the lines of Isaac and Ishmael, beyond the half-brothers' joint burial of Abraham (1.256), is Esau's third marriage, to a daughter of Ishmael (1.277).

It seems to me that there are two primary possibilities here. The first is that what Sarra "kept persuading" Abraham to do is simply to send Ishmael and Hagar away εἰς ἀποικίαν, "to settle elsewhere," as Thackeray, and Feldman's primary text, have it; the tone here could range from "send to look for a new place to live" to "send into forced exile," a usage supported by Nebuchadnezzar's reported practice of settling "captive Jews" (τοὺς αἰχμαλώτους Ἰουδαίων) and others in ἀποικίαι in Babylon (*Ant.* 10.222-223). The second, and perhaps more interesting option, probably supported by Birgit van der Lans's detailed investigation of this and related terms in the Abraham narrative of the *Antiquities*, is that the narrator is reporting that Sarra's repeated argument was in fact "to send [Ishmael] out to found a colony, along with his mother."[74] In this case, too, there are a range of possibilities. This could be a ploy, a piece of play-acting not so different from those perpetrated in Egypt (1.162) and Gerar (1.207): here, Abraham realizes, correctly, that the prospects for Ishmael and Hagar are less rosy than Sarra's repeated suggestion implies. Alternatively, this could be yet another attempt by the narrator to soften the main characters' edges, one that, as usual, proves to fit rather imperfectly with the rest of the narrative data. Sarra, the narrator claims, makes the best of a bad situation by finding a solution amenable to all: Ishmael and his mother could just found a colony elsewhere. But Abraham's doleful reaction, and the exiles' ill-provisioned, patternless wandering that almost ends in death, show that this is a narratorial cover-up, incompletely patched over a grimmer story. For a reader who casts an eye on the broader tradition, sympathy may even be in order for the overworked narrator of the *Antiquities*, for the tasks set are complex, and difficult to balance: improve Abraham's character, here by emphasizing his initial refusal to send Ishmael and Hagar away; improve Sarra's character, here by implying that her resolution is even contrary to her motherly affection

---

73. LSJ 200a; 1130b. See, though, van der Lans, "Hagar, Ishmael, and Abraham's Household," 194, who notes that the establishment of colonies in the *Antiquities* seems sometimes to be aimed at separating groups with the potential for conflict.

74. Van der Lans, "Hagar, Ishmael, and Abraham's Household," 192–8.

for Ishmael; yet manage, somehow, to avoid wholly eviscerating the story.[75] Complete success, here as elsewhere, proves elusive.

Whatever the details, it is clear that Franxman's claim that Sarra appears "both kindly and reasonable" in this scene needs to be revised significantly.[76] What does seem beyond dispute, and an important note for Sarra's characterization, is that this plan to send Ishmael and Hagar away is formed on Sarra's initiative alone. Sarra's earlier scheme involving Hagar was "ordered by God" (1.187); however, its issue proves to be impermanent, and ultimately not entirely successful, in large part due directly to Sarra's scheme here, which she launches on her own. In fact, Sarra's persistent persuasion of Abraham, described as "that which Sarra had so fervently pursued" (οἷς ἡ Σάρρα ἐσπουδάκει, 1.216), is ultimately convincing to Abraham because it is convincing to God: "but later—*for even God was pleased with what Sarra had commanded*—having been persuaded, [Abraham] handed over Ishmael to his mother…" (1.217).[77] There is even an outside chance, suggested not only by the capacity of the imperfect to express an "inchoative" or inceptive nuance, but also by the temporal adverb, that ἠρέσκετο refers to God's entrance into a state of approval. Just possibly, then, the narrator says "but later—for even God came to approve…" Either way, earlier God's command (τοῦ θεοῦ κελεύσαντος, 1.187) determined Hagar's fate; now, Sarra's command (τοῖς ὑπὸ τῆς Σάρρας προστattομένοις, 1.217) does, and for Ishmael, too. Abraham, on the other hand, perhaps, betrays Ishmael (παρεδίδου, 1.217) just as he did Ishmael's mother (παραδιδόντος, 1.188). It is possible, however, to find a positive here. Once, Hagar, "unable to endure her sufferings" (οὐχ ὑπομένουσα τὰς ταλαιπωρίας, 1.188), determined to run away from Sarra; now, finally, forced to leave by Sarra's resolve, Hagar "escapes" these sufferings (διαφεύγει τὰς ταλαιπωρίας, 1.219).

After a brief, initial concentration on Abraham, the focus of this episode begins to shift to Sarra. Isaac is not only Abraham's son, but Sarra's, too, and apparently named after her reaction to the prediction of his birth. Moreover, Sarra is involved, somehow, in Isaac's circumcision, which, as the narrator notes, serves as a founding myth for this important sign of male Jewish identity (1.213-214). Her emerging role here forecasts her

75. On the heightened compassion of Abraham, and the narrator's "defense" of Sarra, see Feldman, *JA 1–4*, 81–2 nn. 660–2; compare van der Lans, "Hagar, Ishmael, and Abraham's Household," 188.
76. Franxman, *Genesis and the* Antiquities, 154.
77. ὕστερον δέ, καὶ γὰρ ὁ θεὸς ἠρέσκετο τοῖς ὑπὸ τῆς Σάρρας προστattομένοις, πεισθεὶς παρεδίδου τὸν Ἰσμαῆλον τῇ μητρί.

central part in the scenes to come, as the narrator offers—for the first and only time—something that approaches direct definition and an internal view of Sarra, detailing her supposed affection for Ishmael and fear for Isaac (1.215). Despite this affection, the narrator implies, and prompted by this fear, Sarra moves into resolute and persistent action, repeatedly urging Abraham to send away Ishmael, her once-beloved adopted son, and Hagar, her slave, εἰς ἀποικίαν (1.216). Sarra is ultimately persuasive, a note that ties her depiction, once again, to that of Abraham. Yet this entire initiative is Sarra's alone, and she finally convinces Abraham to act when it becomes clear that God approves of her plan (1.217). Sarra's success here makes a partial failure of God's own initiative with Hagar, an enterprise that depended on Sarra's compliance, or at least reveals that earlier provision of "offspring of a male child" to have been a merely temporary fix (1.186).

Much of Sarra's relative prominence and power here, however, is systematically undercut by the narrator's increasingly obvious struggle to maintain a balance between the logic of the narrative and a kind of hagiographic imperative. The unsatisfying explanation of Isaac's name hints at characters' concealed impieties, while Sarra's depiction as a loving adoptive mother jars not only with her subsequent urging of Ishmael's exile, but also with her affection's seemingly Machiavellian motive. The narrator's note on this motive, moreover, leads to a jam in Sarra's depiction that appears insoluble. Something is hidden, somewhere, for Ishmael is either originally destined to be raised to the rule, or not. So is Sarra's violent behavior with the pregnant Hagar even more inexplicable, as she attacks or tortures the bearer of Abraham's heir? Or is Sarra's resolution to expel Ishmael even more simply conceived than it is said to be, as Sarra rids the family of a rival, slave-born son, for whom she perhaps naturally has little native affection? This quandary is of the narrator's own making: in both cases the issue of Ishmael's status is an amplification of the tradition, or at least employed in a novel way.[78] The same is true of Sarra's supposed reason for advocating Ishmael's banishment: her fear of his latent violence mitigates the apparent harshness of her move, yet the narrator's retention and even extension of the pathetic descriptions of Ishmael's plight in the tradition directly undermine the plausibility of her

---

78. The question of Ishmael's inheritance is raised, by Sarah, in Gen. 21:10. It seems plausible that this note has been read back into the scene in the *Antiquities* (1.186–190) that corresponds to Gen. 16:1-16. Yet the idea of Ishmael being groomed for the rule, or not, is still an extension of this note on inheritance that is inserted into *Ant.* 1.188, and used for a new purpose, namely the illustration of Sarra's once-tender feelings, in 1.215.

motive. Finally, yet another similar problem lies in the potential force of εἰς ἀποικίαν. If Feldman is correct that Sarra "is here depicted...as not so harsh in the penalty she recommends for Hagar and Ishmael," that is, in proposing they settle a colony elsewhere, or something similar, then the other narrative data shows that this depiction is a rather shabby front for a command that results in suffering and near-death.[79] It is unfortunate, if perhaps not surprising, that all of these narratorial issues come to a head just when a more dynamic Sarra has drawn the storyteller's focus.

Isaac's sacrifice (Ant. 1.222-236)

Ant. 1.222 His father Habramos exceedingly loved Isakos, who was his only child and who had been born to him on the threshold of old age, as a gift from God. And the child, practicing every virtue and showing attention to his ancestors and exhibiting zeal for the worship of God, won even more the affection and the love of his parents. 223-224 And Habramos put his own happiness solely on the hope that on departing from life he should leave behind his son unscathed. He attained this, to be sure, by the will of God, who, wishing to make trial of his piety toward Himself, appeared to him and...asked him himself to offer this one [Isakos]...as a burnt offering. For thus he would demonstrate his piety toward Himself if he valued what was pleasing to God above the preservation of his child. 225 Habramos, judging it just to disobey God under no circumstances...concealing from his wife the command of God and the resolution that he had concerning the slaughter of the child, and, on the contrary, revealing it not even to anyone of his household, for he would have been hindered from rendering service to God, took Isakos with two servants and loading a donkey with the things needed for the sacrificial rite departed to the mountain. 226-235 [Abraham leads Isaac to what later becomes the Temple Mount, sets up an altar, and explains to Isaac that it is better for him to die in this fashion than to suffer a more pedestrian fate; plus, it seems, Abraham will benefit from having Isaac as a heavenly intercessor. Isaac is overjoyed at the plan and rushes to the altar; but God steps in, halts the sacrifice, and predicts great things for the pair.—JM] 236 Having said these things, God brought forth a ram from obscurity for them for the sacrifice. And they, having borne themselves beyond their hopes and having heard promises of such blessings, embraced one another and, having sacrificed, returned home to Sarra and lived happily, with God supporting them in all that they wished. (Feldman, *JA 1–4*, 84–94)

---

79. Feldman, *JA 1–4*, 82 n. 661; Feldman, "Abraham," 244.

This is not the place for a full analysis of this lengthy episode, which Franxman calls the "most elaborate effort in the whole series of Abraham stories."[80] However, the narrator of the *Antiquities* seems to have felt the same dissatisfaction at the complete absence of Isaac's mother from this tale that some modern exegetes have.[81] Sarra plays only a small role here, limited mostly to potentialities, but the fact that she does not disappear entirely from the discourse between the expulsion of Ishmael and Hagar (*Ant.* 1.217) and the mention of her death (1.237) constitutes a new note in the tradition surveyed here. Indeed, although she is kept mostly in the background, small reminders of Sarra's continuing presence bookend the episode (1.222, 236).

In a pattern that recalls the opening of the episode featuring Isaac's birth, the narrator initially focuses on Abraham before shifting to language that acknowledges the roles of both parents:

> His father Abraham loved Isaac beyond measure, seeing as he was his only child and was born to him as a gift of God "on the threshold of old age." For his part, the boy attracted the goodwill and love of his parents all the more by his pursuit of every virtue, dedication to his forebears, and zeal in the worship of God. (1.222)[82]

Here, the "goodwill" (εὔνοια) that Sarra was once supposed to have exhibited to Ishmael (1.215) is directed at Isaac, provoked in her and in Abraham partly by Isaac's own dedication to them.[83] Against the background of the tradition, one item of interest here is the implied duration and consistency of Sarra's relationship with her son, now twenty-five years old (1.227). This might be inferred from Gen. 24:67, where Isaac is "consoled after his mother," a note omitted in the *Antiquities*, but here

---

80. Franxman, *Genesis and the* Antiquities, 156.

81. For example, Trible, "Sacrifice of Sarah"; Zierler, "Feminist Reading of the Akedah."

82. Ἴσακον δὲ ὁ πατὴρ Ἄβραμος ὑπερηγάπα μονογενῆ ὄντα καὶ ἐπὶ γήρως οὐδῷ κατὰ δωρεὰν αὐτῷ τοῦ θεοῦ γενόμενον. προεκαλεῖτο δὲ εἰς εὔνοιαν καὶ τὸ φιλεῖσθαι μᾶλλον ὑπὸ τῶν γονέων καὶ αὐτὸς ὁ παῖς ἐπιτηδεύων πᾶσαν ἀρετὴν καὶ τῆς τε τῶν πατέρων θεραπείας ἐχόμενος καὶ περὶ τὴν τοῦ θεοῦ θρησκείαν ἐσπουδακώς. The expression ἐπὶ γήρως οὐδῷ, "on the threshold of old age," is a stock phrase from Homer: Feldman, *JA 1–4*, 84 n. 677; Louis H. Feldman, "Josephus as a Biblical Interpreter: The *'Aqedah*," *JQR* 75 (1985): 215–17; Feldman, "Abraham," 267–9.

83. Assuming that style motivates the lexical variety, I take both τῶν γονέων and τῶν πατέρων as referring to Isaac's immediate "parents," Sarra and Abraham; contrast Feldman, *JA 1–4*, 85 n. 681.

their relative intimacy is placed in its logical narrative frame. But this "goodwill," too, provides a lexical tie to the episode of Ishmael's banishment that points to a further thematic link between Sarra and Abraham. Earlier Sarra, despite her sincere motherly feelings for Ishmael, did what had to be done, sending him to his death, but for mediated divine intervention, in some distant place (1.215-219). Here Abraham, despite his overwhelming fatherly feelings for Isaac, does what needs doing and leads him to his death, but for divine intervention, in another distant place (1.222-236). This is a curious instance of Sarra's resemblance to Abraham, for considered narratively it is she, unusually, who anticipates his portrayal and actions. However, considered as a development in the tradition, it is Sarra's supposed affection for Ishmael that is the new note; thus in the history of the tradition it is she, once again, who is conformed to Abraham's image.

After Abraham receives another command from God, this time to offer his beloved Isaac as a whole burnt offering (1.223-224), there is another engaging note that reflects on Sarra's depiction in the *Antiquities*. Abraham, after deciding that nothing could justify his disobedience, takes Isaac, two household slaves, and a donkey on a journey to the specified place of sacrifice (1.225). But the way Abraham packs for his trip suggests that someone might not approve of his plan: Abraham acts "having concealed from his woman both God's instructions and his own intentions regarding the slaughter of his boy" (1.225).[84] That Abraham is specifically noted to have felt the need to disguise his true purpose from Sarra hints at a good measure of power on her part, and a fair bit of reciprocal caution on his. It seems that more is in play here than a general notion of maternal protectiveness. This is still the same woman, albeit twenty-five years older, whose initiative and persistence won the day in the episode dealing with the aftermath of Isaac's birth. If she had found out, what would have happened? The narrator implies that the entire enterprise might have been scuttled: Abraham concealed his design from Sarra, and divulged it "not even to one of his household slaves" (μηδὲ τῶν οἰκετῶν τινι), "because he would have been prevented from serving God" in this undertaking (ἐκωλύετο γὰρ ἂν ὑπηρετῆσαι τῷ θεῷ, 1.225). There is a small range of options in understanding this last clause; κωλύω could mean "hinder," or the like, meaning that Abraham's aims would have been complicated, but not completely stymied, by knowledge of his plan getting out, while the force of ἄν could indicate mere potential, that is, what might have

---

84. ἐπικρυψάμενος πρὸς τὴν γυναῖκα τήν τε τοῦ θεοῦ πρόρρησιν καὶ ἣν εἶχεν αὐτὸς γνώμην περὶ τῆς τοῦ παιδὸς σφαγῆς.

happened had events taken a different path.⁸⁵ Then, too, Sarra is not the only one mentioned as a possible obstacle, as the household slaves, even the two who accompany Abraham on his errand, are also kept in the dark. Yet Sarra, the character from whom Abraham specifically "conceals" the truth, is Isaac's mother, whose at least ostensible concern for her son's safety has already affected the plot in a significant way (1.215-217). Moreover, as there is nothing to suggest how these slaves might have thwarted their master's will alone, it may be more reasonable to assume that Abraham's general silence is aimed at preventing the news from reaching Sarra's ears.

It is a provocative exercise to speculate on the possibilities here. Does the *Antiquities* suggest that Sarra could have prevented Abraham's ultimate success, if that is the right word, in the "experiment" (διάπειραν, 1.223) that God conducts on him here?⁸⁶ The "obedience" supposedly underlined so decisively by Abraham's attempted sacrifice of his son is one of his defining traits in the pious tradition that comments on his story. Would Abraham's devout willingness to do the deed (1.225) have been enough, had he been deprived, by Sarra, of the opportunity to actually lift the knife (Gen. 22:10)? But this last dramatic detail is, in fact, elided by the narrator of the *Antiquities*, whose decorousness sometimes borders on cowardice (1.233); and in the event, Sarra is kept from finding out about Abraham's plan, her potential acts left permanently in the realm of the theoretical. Sarra is not taken along this time; rather, as in her introduction in this narrative, she is left behind (compare 1.151; 1.162, 207).

In fact, the incredible continuation of events here suggests that the ventured sacrifice would still have gone forward, even in the face of Sarra's maternal objections. For after the altar is ready, Abraham reveals the necessity of Isaac's death to him, emphasizing the advantages that will accrue to the both of them from this act (1.228-231). Isaac's exemplary virtue (1.222) now swells fantastically, as he listens to Abraham's speech "with pleasure" (πρὸς ἡδονήν), pronounces himself ready to die even if it were only Abraham's whim that he do so, and rushes to the altar of his own accord (1.232).⁸⁷ It is hard to say why Feldman calls this a "glorious

---

85. LSJ 1017a–b; Smyth §§1784–87.

86. "Experiment" is the memorable rendering of Whiston; see also LSJ 406b.

87. Here the *Antiquities* offers an extreme instance of the widespread theme of Isaac's willingness to be sacrificed, found also in *LAB*, *4 Maccabees*, and *Genesis Rabbah*. See Isaac Kalimi, "The Binding of Isaac: Biblical Narrative in Late Second Temple and Rabbinic Exegesis and Thought," in *Fighting Over the Bible: Jewish Interpretation, Sectarianism and Polemic from Temple to Talmud and Beyond*, BRLJ 54 (Leiden: Brill, 2017), 170–3.

scene"; Franxman is only a bit closer in noting that Isaac's response is "unrealistic."⁸⁸ The biblical account, which is ethically troubling on a variety of levels, both human and divine, at least evokes the terrible gravity of its central conceit; here, the story of a father's divinely sanctioned murder of his son inspires a kind of humorless spoof.

The air of unwitting satire continues unabated through the end of the episode, which literally ends "happily ever after," God having intervened in the human sacrifice and pledged great rewards in return for obedience to "even such a command" (καὶ τοιαῦτα προστασσόμενος, 1.233): "And they—with [Isaac] having been restored beyond expectation, and with [both of them] having heard tidings of such good things—embraced each other and, having sacrificed, returned home to Sarra and lived happily," or "prosperously," "God coming to their aid in everything they wanted" (1.236).⁸⁹ One wonders, in vain, whether Abraham, Isaac, and God continued to "conceal" what had happened from Sarra; for in the narrator's next breath, over a decade of unreported time later, Sarra is dead.

Sarra's Death *(Ant. 1.237)*

> *Ant.* 1.237 And not long afterwards Sarra died after living 127 years. They buried her in Nebron, with the Chananaians granting her burial ground at public expense. But Habramos bought the place for 400 shekels from Ephraimos, someone from Nebron. And Habramos and his descendants built tombs in that place. (Feldman, *JA 1–4*, 94–5)

Strangely, Sarra's death is said to occur "not long after" (οὐ πολὺ ὕστερον) Abraham and Isaac's return to their shared life of bliss; however, some dozen years have passed (compare 1.213, 227, 237). Had the note of the family's happy reunion not immediately preceded, the effect might have been to tie her death more closely to the trauma of Isaac's near-sacrifice, as in a variety of rabbinic traditions.⁹⁰ The event itself is reported in cursory fashion, and Sarra is not favored with the kind of brief valedictory homage that Abraham receives at the mention of his death in 1.256. The circumstances of her interment, however, seem to reflect Sarra's

---

88. Feldman, *JA 1–4*, 92 n. 720; compare Feldman, "Abraham," 226; Franxman, *Genesis and the* Antiquities, 160.

89. I read αὐτοῦ κεκομισμένου with Niese's text: οἱ δὲ παρ' ἐλπίδας αὐτοῦ κεκομισμένου καὶ τοιούτων ἀγαθῶν ἐπαγγελίας ἀκηκοότες ἠσπάζοντό τε ἀλλήλους καὶ θύσαντες ἀπενόστησαν πρὸς τὴν Σάρραν καὶ διῆγον εὐδαιμόνως ἐφ' ἅπασιν οἷς ἐθελήσειαν τοῦ θεοῦ συλλαμβάνοντος αὐτοῖς.

90. See Franxman, *Genesis and the* Antiquities, 158 n. 9, for some of these.

importance, with "the Canaanites even conceding a plot for her tomb at the public expense" (συγχωρούντων...τῶν Χαναναίων καὶ δημοσίᾳ χοῦν αὐτῆς τὸν τάφον, 1.237). In the Greek materials, funerals δημοσίᾳ, an adverbial usage meaning "by public consent" or "at the public expense," are usually reserved for civil heroes, such as Tellus, the man Solon names "most fortunate of all humans" in his interview with Croesus in the *Histories* of Herodotus.[91] Yet this proposed honor for Sarra is immediately rejected, with no explanation: "but Abraham purchased the spot for 400 shekels" (Ἀβράμου δὲ ὠνησαμένου τὸ χωρίον σίκλων τετρακοσίων, *Ant.* 1.237). One more time, perhaps, the narrator is caught between competing demands, attempting to burnish the depictions of the main characters while maintaining some fidelity to the underlying traditions. In Gen. 23:6, the offer of free land for a burial site is meant as an honor for Abraham, the "mighty prince" (נשיא אלהים); his reasons for refusing it are not completely clear, though a sentiment similar to that shown in Gen. 14:21-24, where Abraham is wary of entering the debt of the king of Sodom, may be in play. Here, it is Sarra's importance that is emphasized by the willingness of the locals to give her a state funeral. But Abraham's rejection of this tribute in the *Antiquities*, transplanted almost free of context from its source, not only undermines the apparent aim of this development by implying that Abraham's own estimation of Sarra's worth does not match that of the Canaanites; by painting Abraham as somehow churlish and mean, it also further weakens the narrator's case for Abraham as a "man tops in every moral excellence" (1.256).

Conclusion: Sarra in the Antiquities

It is a challenge to make a linear account of Sarra's characterization in the *Antiquities* cohere, as her path is often hard to trace. Her image is fuzzy in the beginning, as she is acted upon—left behind, scooped up, protected or preyed upon—but only rarely acting, and mostly an object of inference. The lack of literary ties between the episode in Egypt and that of Hagar's forced pregnancy contributes to a sense of disconnection in the progression of Sarra's depiction; on the other hand, the intricate literary links between Egypt and Gerar illustrate almost nothing about her development. The visit of the angels, meanwhile, reads like a narrative afterthought, wedged between scenes the narrator is keener to relate. Suddenly, when Isaac is born, Sarra emerges as a figure of some power and initiative, and her expulsion of Hagar and Ishmael, unlike elsewhere

---

91. *Hist.* 1.30. See LSJ 387a; Feldman, *JA 1–4*, 94–5 n. 732.

in the tradition surveyed, does not spell her own dismissal from the discourse; yet she remains only as a figure of potential, not action, and Sarra's death comes just the same.

A tradition that could already be fairly described as fundamentally episodic thus atomizes even further in the telling of the narrator of the *Antiquities*, forming a series of short vignettes that feature some interconnections, of varying strength, between them. The trajectories of the "biographies" of the characters, however, offer only weak support to these links. In summarizing Sarra in this narrative, then, I will treat her character as revealed—or concealed—by three related, sometimes overlapping motifs that seem to me to be most significant to her depiction. First, Sarra is often, but not always, diminished in the telling of the *Antiquities*, whether considered in the context of the tradition or in the narrative itself. Second, Sarra's image is frequently conformed to that of Abraham, an element familiar from the tradition but expressed here in mostly novel ways. Third, Sarra's characterization is complicated by the narrator's urge to burnish the presentations of the main characters; again, this phenomenon is noticeable not only in comparisons with other tellings of this story, but also within the narrative itself.

Sarra's Diminishment

That Sarra in the *Antiquities* is somewhat shrunken, in comparison with her portrayal in the MT, has been observed in broad terms by scholars such as Halpern-Amaru and Niehoff.[92] Bailey, too, despite his insistence that Sarra's image is improved in the *Antiquities*, inadvertently highlights the relative poverty of her depiction by noting how often narrative data about her in the MT is "omitted" in the retelling here.[93] Sarra never speaks directly, for example, and her movements are of such little interest to the narrator that her presence sometimes comes as a surprise (1.165, 198). That these elements are typical of the narrator's rather dull presentation makes little difference to an evaluation of Sarra, whose characterization, laid alongside her images elsewhere, is still less vivid. There are moments that cut against the grain: her implied speech in Egypt, her background appearances in the episode of Isaac's near-sacrifice, and, most significantly, her relative dynamism as the object of the narrator's focus after Isaac's birth (1.165, 213-217, 222, 225, 236).

---

92. Halpern-Amaru, "Portraits in Josephus," 145; Niehoff, "Mother and Maiden," 416. Compare Begg, "Flight of Hagar," 17.

93. Bailey, "Matriarchs," 170–1.

Yet any advances that Sarra makes in the *Antiquities* are mostly undermined elsewhere, sometimes in comparison with other tellings of her story, but often simply in the course of the narrative itself. She demonstrates a little independence in Egypt, but the episode ends by reinforcing her insignificance relative to Abraham (1.165-168). Her agency regresses further, with respect to both tradition and narrative, in her mostly inert appearance in the similar tale in Gerar (1.207-212). Sarra's action with Hagar must be significant, as God directly tells her to do it; but in a number of small ways, including being commanded by God, what Sarra does is an echo of what Abraham has already done (1.154, 187). In her emergence from within during the angelic visit, Sarra may display just a little power (1.198). Her minor liberation here, though, is at the expense of much personal color, considered across the tradition. After Isaac is born, Sarra is vigorous at last, and the center of the action for just a little while: she participates in her son's circumcision, the mythic origin of an important cultural rite; her feelings are purportedly revealed; she is persistent and persuasive in action, perhaps convincing even the deity to support her initiative (1.213-217). But so much of this is thrown into doubt even as it unfolds by the collapse of various narratorial façades; and as Halpern-Amaru points out, Sarra's advocacy here is on Isaac's behalf, not her own.[94] Again, a bit of power may be suggested by Abraham's caution in concealing from Sarra his intent to kill his son; yet this comes to nothing, and, once more, this power, and her presence in this episode, are really still all about Isaac (1.225). At the end of her life, too, after Sarra's social significance seems to be underlined by the offer of a funeral at the public expense, Abraham's abrupt refusal of this honor cuts her reputation back down to size, and she disappears as a character for good (1.237).

Sarra's Resemblance to Abraham

Sarra resembles Abraham in the *Antiquities* in a number of ways. On the most basic level, the two are actually related by blood: Sarra is Abraham's niece (1.151, 211). But their traits and actions also display important correspondences. Abraham "brings along" (ἐπαγόμενος) Sarra to both Egypt and Gerar, which is suggestive of her mostly subordinate role in these episodes (1.162, 207); yet Pharaoh frames their relationship the other way around, asking Sarra "who this was she had brought along" (τίνα τοῦτον ἐπάγοιτο, 1.165). In this same scene, too, it is implied that Sarra teaches Pharaoh "the truth" (τὴν ἀλήθειαν), much as Abraham, after showing that the beliefs of the learned Egyptians

---

94. Halpern-Amaru, "Portraits in Josephus," 148.

"contained nothing true" (μηδὲν ἔχοντας ἀληθές), teaches them things of which they had previously been "ignorant" (ἀμαθῶς; 1.166-168). In their playacting, as well, Sarra and Abraham resemble each other: she is taught "to play her part" (ὑποκρίνασθαι) in Egypt, just as he "plays his part" (ὑποκρινάμενος), in a restaging of the same drama, in Gerar (1.162, 207). The plot shows that their acting is persuasive; indeed, this is another trait that the two share. Abraham is defined early as "persuasive to his hearers" (πιθανὸς τοῖς ἀκροωμένοις, 1.154), and his "persuasive ability" (πεῖσαι λέγων, 1.167) is also demonstrated among the Egyptians, while Sarra's persistent and successful persuasion on the topic of Ishmael and Hagar's banishment convinces Abraham, and perhaps even God, to yield to her initiative (ἔπειθεν...Ἄβραμον...πεισθεὶς [Ἄβραμος], 1.216-217). In this latter episode, moreover, Sarra is depicted as willing to send away Ishmael to an uncertain fate, despite her once-strong maternal feelings for him, described in part as "the kind of goodwill she would have had for her own son" (οὐδὲν ἀπολείπουσα τῆς πρὸς ἴδιον υἱὸν εὐνοίας, 1.215); Abraham, too, some years later, is willing to lead away Isaac to his death despite his deep love for him as his "only child" (μονογενῆ), and the "goodwill" (εὔνοιαν) that Isaac engenders (1.222). Perhaps most significantly, finally, there is a small but meaningful web of connections between Sarra and Abraham that centers on God's commands to them. Both act having been "ordered by God" (τοῦ θεοῦ κελεύσαντος), which emphasizes the importance of what they do; both are worthy of direct communication from the deity, and both show obedience to God's command (1.154, 187). Both, too, take steps to remedy their childlessness in the near context of these commands—and both efforts eventually fall short.

Strikingly, all of these correspondences, small and large, are essentially unique to the *Antiquities*, at least in the tradition as surveyed in this study. The tie between the moves of the characters to address the lack of a child may bear a passing thematic resemblance to the connection between the putative slave mothers of an heir for Abraham, Masek and Hagar, in the LXX (Gen. 15:2-3; 16:1-2), but the likeness is not very close. Instead, both links may represent different expressions of the same deep trait: Sarra resembles Abraham. To approach the question from the other side, there are many important links between these characters in the rest of the tradition that do not appear here at all, for one reason or another: in the MT, for example, Sarah's first speech partly mimics Abraham's first speech, as her subsequent action with Hagar echoes her own treatment by Abraham in Egypt (Gen. 12:10-20; 16:1-6); both are renamed, and laugh at the announcement of Isaac's predicted birth (17:5, 15, 17; 18:12); both appear, in this last episode, in identical positions in the opening of their tent (18:1, 10). These connections, and others from the rest of the tradition, are elided in the *Antiquities*, but new ones have risen to take their places.

So what do these correspondences say about Sarra's depiction in the *Antiquities*? Earlier, I showed that Sarra in the LXX is even more closely conformed to the figure of Abraam than is the case in the MT, and argued that this is symptomatic of the narrator's broader penchant to compress her individuation. This process, in turn, helps to highlight Sarra's true value to the narrator in the LXX, which is her utility to the fulfillment of the divine promises to Abraam. Here, the question is more complicated, not least because so many of the relevant instances of Sarra's conforming to Abraham in the wider tradition are left out; the new examples of resemblance do not accumulate on top of the old, but simply replace them. Abraham himself, moreover, is depicted quite differently in the *Antiquities*. The narrator's encomiastic descriptions of Abraham are not all credible; yet, as nearly all agree, the narrative clearly aims at "improving" Abraham's image and casting him as a great man.[95] This tendency is also seen, to a lesser degree, in the depiction of Sarra, whose questionable acts in the tradition are the object of attempted cover-ups by the narrator of the *Antiquities*. So does Sarra's resemblance to Abraham here merely hollow her out, as seemed to be the case in the LXX—or does it honor her by association? Abraham is claimed to be a "man tops in every moral excellence" (1.256), deserving of divine and human accolades; if Sarra is like him, perhaps this only shows her in a positive light. Moreover, at least one example of their resemblance, their willingness to sacrifice children despite their personal feelings, seems to cast Sarra as the type, and Abraham as the imitator. Yet the issue of Abraham's glorious reputation cuts both ways. He is clearly the hero of this part of the *Antiquities*, and Sarra's own supposed virtues, and her resemblance to him, may simply contribute to his stature: such a great man must "bring along" a worthy woman.[96] And an important objection to this line of thinking has already been raised: the narrator's repeated attempts to polish the images of both Abraham and Sarra buckle so frequently under their own weight as to throw the entire project into doubt.

95. See, among others, Feldman, "Abraham the Greek Philosopher"; Feldman, "Hellenizations."
96. Compare the evaluation, reached by different means, of Halpern-Amaru, "Portraits in Josephus," 145, 148. See also van der Lans, "Hagar, Ishmael, and Abraham's Household," 188, and the remark of Feldman, "Abraham," 225: "Abraham benefits…from the aggrandizement of his wife"; compare 238, 243, 288.

"Improvements" to Sarra and Others

One of the most distinctive features of this narrative, finally, is the narrator's stubborn desire to cast the main characters in a flattering pose—and the inadvertent narrative fallout that results from this ambition, which often creates as many problems as it attempts to solve. At points, the narrator's inclination leads even to minor crises in characterization. The phenomenon appears in the presentations of both Abraham and God; most of these instances also touch on the portrayal of Sarra. Abraham's moral standing is jeopardized in Egypt by the narrator's prior insistence on his perceptive intelligence (1.154, 163): how could such a perspicacious man have failed to foresee the danger Sarra would face? The question is yet more pointed in Gerar, where things happen "just like before," and Abraham only looks worse due to the narrator's initial apologetic definition of his and Sarra's true blood relationship (1.151, 207-211). Sarra's honor at her death, too, ends up being of no interest to the supremely virtuous Abraham (1.237, 256). God's initiatives regarding Abraham's heir(s), meanwhile, are hard to understand, as the narrator apparently protects Sarra from a spontaneous, indecorous suggestion in the matter of Hagar, which makes God's later motive with Isaac a puzzle (1.187, 191).

But it is a similar effort to burnish Sarra's character that leads to one of the most complex problems with her characterization in the *Antiquities*. Sarra's action with Hagar is partly justified by emphasizing Hagar's insolence, which is motivated by her presumptuous, seemingly flatly wrong expectation that Ishmael will inherit Abraham's rule (1.188). Yet Sarra's action with Ishmael and Hagar later is partly softened by underlining Sarra's affection for Ishmael, which is said to be prompted by his original destiny as heir to Abraham's rule (1.215). The narrator's credibility, here specifically with reference to the image of Sarra in the story, is thus strained: what can be trusted? Which one of these apologies is really a cover-up? Picking at this knot only loosens other threads in the near contexts of these two incompatible moves to soften Sarra's edges. That she "makes one of her slaves lie down" aims at euphemism, but ends up hinting at a brutality that only seems confirmed by her implied torture of Hagar (1.187-188). And more: did Sarra really show affection for Ishmael "at first"? Did she genuinely fear for Isaac's life? Did she actually recommend a humane solution to the quandary posed by competing heirs (1.215-216)? It is important, in the broader context of this study, that the generation of these questions does not depend on synoptic comparison alone. Such comparison may draw out significant elements of Sarra's character here; but much distinct data can also be collected from deliberate, careful prodding of the narrative itself.

That the episode after Isaac's birth is where these narratorial problems bite hardest may serve to bind the major points of this digest of Sarra in the *Antiquities*. The dynamics of her diminishment are amply illustrated by these scenes, which feature Sarra at her most prominent, yet most dramatically undercut by this persistent narratorial tendency to polish her depiction. The narrator's desire to apologize for Sarra, moreover, combined with the troubling relics left behind by this strategy, form yet another unparalleled way in which she resembles Abraham. Sarra's portrait in the *Antiquities* has indeed been "recolored in favorable tones," as Bailey claims of Sarra, Rebekah, Rachel, and Leah.[97] But the job was left undone, at least in Sarra's case, partly obscuring her image in some areas, while leaving a few old flaws to show through.

---

97. Bailey, "Matriarchs," 175.

Chapter 6

CONCLUSIONS, CONTRIBUTIONS, AND PROSPECTS

In this brief final chapter, I collect and synthesize the findings of my readings of Sarah, then consider some of this study's contributions and prospects for future work.

Sarah in the Hebrew Bible, the Septuagint, the Genesis Apocryphon, and the Antiquities

The following sections look both inward and outward, into each narrative and across the tradition. I refer throughout to "Sarah" due to the synthetic nature of the discussion.

Sarah in the Masoretic Text

My reading of Sarah in the MT demonstrates her complexity and coherence, even as it emphasizes her utility to Abraham and the deity, who both use her for their purposes and then discard her. Abraham's abuse and sale of Sarah in Egypt catalyzes her own abuse and disposal of Hagar, which is only the first example of Sarah's resemblance to Abraham, a feature that both illustrates and contributes to a gradual hardening of her personality. Throughout, Sarah is characterized by a motif of gain and loss, or possession and lack, a theme that is finally underlined after the birth of Isaac, where her reaction to the reversal of her childlessness is one of deep ambiguity and sensitivity to her image in the eyes of others.

This sketch of Sarah in what seems to be the earliest source that has come down to us contains themes, features, and traits that endure in the tradition, as well as others that wane in significance, or simply disappear. All of the readings that make up this study attest to her complexity, for example. Perhaps surprisingly, this feature coexists with Sarah's utility to others throughout most of the tradition surveyed. If Sarah is "chosen" in the MT, she is chosen as an instrument, and her instrumentality in the realization of the divine promises, at least as a focus of the narrator, only grows in the LXX. The Apocryphon also makes utility her ultimate value, despite the relative richness of her characterization before her abduction. Here, however, it is her sexual use that is emphasized; the regrettable state of preservation of the Apocryphon's single manuscript means that her utility to the promises must remain mostly an open question.

Sarah's hardening trajectory in the MT seems to contribute to her instrumentality: she is sharpened by abuse and the divine encouragement of her worst impulses, the better to obtain wealth by the deception and harm of others, or to banish competing heirs. Yet this hardening arc itself does not perceptibly endure in the tradition. Sarah's abuse of Hagar in the LXX is less well-linked to her own experiences in Egypt, while Sarah's remarks at Isaac's birth are uncomplicated and conventional in their joy; in the *Antiquities*, Sarah is barely a character in Gerar, and cannot credibly play the kind of junior collaborator role she fills elsewhere. However, Sarah's resemblance to Abraham in the MT grows as her hardness does, and this particular trait gets significant and compelling traction, often in novel ways, everywhere in the tradition surveyed. A brief list of Sarah's similarities to Abraham in the MT includes her learning from Abraham how to scheme, and how to dispose of the sexuality of subordinates; their similar language of blessing (for Sarah, specifically as a conduit for Isaac) and their renaming; their identical positions in the tent door; their laughing responses to the prediction of Isaac's birth; and their cooperation in the restaging of the Egyptian episode in Gerar, which shows, in further detail, Sarah's adoption of Abraham's willingness to hurt others in the pursuit of gain.

A similar pattern, where part of a complex of motifs falls away, while another part remains in the tradition, appears in connection with Sarah's sensitivity to her appearance in the eyes of others in the MT. Sarah's being worthy of notice in Egypt makes a complex and subtle contribution to a series of developments in the plot that center on the perspectives of others: Sarah's dramatic reaction to Hagar's "overlooking" of her after Hagar conceives; Sarah's ambiguous reaction to Isaac's birth, which seems to acknowledge and rue the absurdity of the situation; and perhaps even Abimelech's "covering of eyes" that he pays to Abraham on Sarah's behalf. This theme essentially vanishes in the rest of the tradition; but one of its constituent and complicating factors, Sarah's beauty, exhibits profound staying power. The broader point is expressed in a curious way in the Apocryphon, where her beauty provides the primary inspiration for a lengthy descriptive poem, but Sarah herself is afraid to be gazed upon, and hides out of sight for years on end.

The motif of possession and lack, finally, which has both heuristic and explanatory power in a reading of Sarah's development in the MT, also fades as the tradition progresses. Vestiges remain in the LXX, but the absence of notes such as the delicate play with Sarah's name in the Hebrew, her urging of Hagar's impregnation for her own "building up," and her ambivalence at Isaac's birth weaken this motif. In the other retellings, it does not contribute to her depiction in a meaningful way.

Sarah in the Septuagint

My reading of Sarah in the LXX reveals a complex character whose path is more extreme and, at times, erratic, as compared to her smoother, perhaps more plausible and sympathetic arc in the MT. When she is not more inert than her MT counterpart, Sarah in the LXX is more derivative of the figure of Abraham. Thus her agency is often bought at the price of imitative action, as in her vaguely familiar scheme with Hagar, which recalls Abraham's ideas about his household slave Masek, or in her slightly expanded but more emulative role in Gerar. These elements point to narrative pressures on her individuation that help to emphasize her programmatic function in the fulfillment of the divine promises. The scene in Genesis 21 again expresses a central theme of this narrative. As her oldest malleable trait, infertility, is revised, she finally surprises with an uncomplicated joy that is not derivative of an emotion of Abraham; yet to my reading her reaction is not entirely credible, alongside other narrative data, but serves as a simplistic reinforcement of the purposes of the deity. In this way Sarah is shown to be partly a cipher for a narratorial perspective that emphasizes her utility to Abraham, and to God's plans for Abraham. In the LXX it is not Sarah's hardening but her general effacement and paling—shown for example in her colorless reaction to the Lord's prediction of Isaac's birth in Genesis 18—and her conformity to the deity's purposes, that contribute to her utility. A general diminishment of Sarah's character is also on view in the *Antiquities*, but with less plain effect on her instrumentality, partly because issues of covenant are often elided there.

Sarah's beauty remains a salient feature of her character in the LXX, but instead of sharing in a complex of plot points that revolve around her appearance in the eyes of others, it contributes to a minor motif tied to her "face." While Sarah's face is attractive in Egypt, it leads Hagar to flee.

Abraham's initial description of Sarah as "pretty-faced" (εὐπρόσωπος), moreover, which can imply concealed deceptive intent, proves apt in her contribution to the deception and injury of Abimelech and his household, as is underlined by the king's scolding of Sarah.

Sarah, on balance, actually resembles Abraham more in the LXX than in the MT. Material familiar from the MT is mostly retained: Sarah's disposition of Hagar is still similar to her own disposal in Egypt; Sarah and Abraham's names are both changed, if to even more uncertain effect than is the case in the MT; both characters laugh and remark on Abraham's age when hearing about Isaac's advent; and Sarah embraces Abraham's disregard for others in Gerar. To these notes, however, are added Abraham's thematic undermining of Sarah's initiative with Hagar by his mention of the potential motherhood of Masek; the way in which both Abraham and Sarah's first speeches aim at the benefit of Abraham; the blurring in speech of the pair's gendered depictions in the episode with Hagar; and the way Sarah is chided by Abimelech, which recalls both the king's own and Pharaoh's prior criticisms of Abraham. In yet another case, actions of both Sarah and Abraham are explained by the narrator, less than credibly, with reference to their fear: Sarah's lie in the tent, familiar from the MT, is interpreted in this way, but so is the attempted justification for Abraham's restaging of the wife-as-sister scheme in Gerar. This may partially anticipate some of the notes of emotion in the Apocryphon, where both characters also show fear.

Given the other narrative operations that combine to restrict Sarah's individuality in the LXX, her increased resemblance to Abraham here contributes to an undermining of her agency, which in turn, again, emphasizes her utility to the achievement of the divine promises. This may be partly contrasted with the operation of these characters' similarities in the *Antiquities*, where Sarah's resemblance to Abraham seems to be just one more way in which his reputation is burnished, at least in attempt, by the narrator. A worthy man must "bring along" a worthy woman—and what worthier woman than one whose traits are, in part, refractions of those of the man?

Sarah in the Genesis Apocryphon

The Genesis Apocryphon is something of an outlier in this study, due not only to the sole surviving manuscript's unfortunate truncation and state of decay, but also to Abraham's unique role as narrator. Yet it offers a highly engaging image of Sarah that displays both continuities and developments alongside other parts of the tradition. Here, my reading sketches a woman who grows swiftly in complexity, evolving over a brief and mercurial trajectory. Sarah in the Apocryphon is inquisitive, vocal, emotional, and shows agency and initiative, as when she initially ignores Abraham's advice to lie about their relationship. Her beauty, familiar from the tradition, is the object of extended meditation in Herqanosh and the other courtiers' verses of praise, but new traits such as her great wisdom and dexterity are also revealed in the same context. It is plausible that Sarah displays her wisdom in a sapiential exposition to the visiting nobles, and it is possible that this extends to the exhibition of Enochic lore. In any event, although the nobles seek out Abraham due to reports of his sagacity, it is a report of Sarah's wisdom alone that is relayed to the king in the manuscript remains. But all Sarah's richness here is abruptly and unsatisfyingly distilled into a very limited species of utility: her mechanical sexual receptivity. The central plot development in this section of the Apocryphon is the lacunose encounter between Sarah and the courtiers, but after she voices her lie to save Abraham, Sarah becomes a disputed object whose worth, as agreed by Abraham, God, and Pharaoh, is coterminous with her sexual inviolability.

Before her reduction to inanimacy, the Apocryphon—curiously, again, in the voice of Abraham—presents what is perhaps the most appealing portrayal of Sarah among the works surveyed. Yet this image is still drawn at least partly with elements that also characterize Abraham himself. The primacy, frequency, and significance of Sarah's speech recalls that of Abraham, and may partly evoke these characters' tie in the MT that stems from the similarities between their first discourse-level addresses (Gen. 12; 16). But much is new, or at least expressed in fresh ways. The metaphoric image of Sarah and Abraham springing from "one root" is a new formulation of an old idea, though their relationship as brother and sister is still not credible here. The characters' displays of emotion extend the idea of Abraham and Sarah both showing fear, first expressed in the LXX, and add weeping to their list of shared reactions. Yet another extension in similarity is Sarah's own reception of gifts in the aftermath of her lengthy stay in Pharaoh's house. But most important is the novel idea of Sarah's great wisdom, a striking advance in the tradition that is also a unique link between Sarah and Abraham here.

Sarah in the Antiquities

In the *Antiquities*, Sarah's character, while still complex and developing, endures some familiar indignities. Her general diminishment recalls the action of the LXX, but this is not uniformly expressed. In fact, her important implied speech and relative independence in Egypt, her participation in Isaac's circumcision, and her background presence in the episode of Isaac's near-sacrifice, where it is hinted that she could have forced matters to take a different course, are all examples of advances in her character's agency and color.

Her conformity to Abraham, clearly expressed here, has also become an almost routine observation. In the *Antiquities*, however, most of the characters' similarities are new twists on this old theme, lending credence to a growing suspicion that Sarah's resemblance to Abraham is something of a deep trait, a story-level archetypal quality that demands expression in narratives as varied as the ones discussed here. In the *Antiquities*, the characters' similarities are first suggested in their genuine blood tie, the only credible narratorial assertion of such a relationship in the tradition surveyed in this study. Lexical play hints at Sarah and Abraham's role-swapping, literally in Egypt, where Sarah is taught to "play her role," as compared to Gerar, where Abraham does the same; likewise in Egypt, Abraham and Sarah are both said to have brought the other along, while Sarah's informing Pharaoh of the truth suggests connections with Abraham's teaching role among the Egyptian savants. This last note emphasizes Abraham's persuasive power, a motif perhaps developed from Gen. 18:16-33 that is heavily emphasized in the *Antiquities*, and persuasiveness is also a novel addition to Sarah's traits—or at least a significant, explicit extension of something implicit in the accounts of the MT and LXX—in the episode of Ishmael and Hagar's banishment. That the couple share in Isaac's circumcision may also suggest some similarity in purpose; just afterward, too, Sarah is shown to be willing to put Ishmael, a boy she had supposedly treated as her own, at risk, while Abraham counters later with his willingness to kill his son, Isaac, for whom he has special affection. Again, this may be read into the gaps of the MT-LXX tradition, but here it lies much closer to the surface. Most significantly, Sarah is ordered by God, just as Abraham was; both receive direct divine communication, both are obedient to God's command, and both are shown in the near context of these revelations to be initiating or catalyzing doomed schemes to rectify their childlessness.

A final kind of similarity may be implied in the narrator's treatment of the reputations of Sarah and Abraham, who are both the object of attempts at polishing their qualities, or apologizing for their shortcomings. Many of these endeavors stumble over themselves as they create further narrative problems, or somehow undermine their goal by inadvertently revealing different flaws. For Sarah, two of these narratorial efforts result in a plain dilemma in her characterization, as her behavior with Hagar and her treatment of Ishmael are both justified by appeals to Ishmael's purposed role in the family—appeals that seem to be factually contradictory. These apologies, however unconvincing, combine with other narrative elements, such as the repeated lionization of Abraham, to suggest a narratorial strategy that aims at bolstering Abraham's profile by means that include the retouching of the picture of "his woman."

Searching for Sarah

My finding that one of Sarah's deep or archetypal traits is a kind of similarity to Abraham is a discovery that is not entirely welcome to me—a fact that likely contributes to the probability of its genuine presence in the tradition.[1] Does this mean, then, that Sarah is reducible to a shadow of Abraham, even a figment composed as an afterthought for the Abraham narratives, as Noth suggested with reference to the traditions underlying the text of the MT?[2] I think that the answer, as borne out by the intricacy of the narrative features that contribute to her characterization, is certainly not. This deep trait is an important, trans-narrative link among these shifting perspectives on Sarah, but to name it as her ultimate distillation would be an act of reductionism at least as blameworthy as those perpetrated by some of the narrative voices engaged in this investigation. It is curious, too, that the phenomenon of Sarah's resemblance to Abraham serves different functions in some of the narratives considered. In the LXX, this feature helps to reveal her worth to the narrator, which is her utility to the promises; in the *Antiquities*, it helps to buttress Abraham's stature. The trait's role in the Apocryphon is less clear, but this is also likely the most vital, if sadly broken, retelling of Sarah's story among these narratives.

Another global finding of my study of Sarah is that she is everywhere a complex character, filled with evolving, competing, and sometimes contradictory traits, both within the individual narratives and in their synthetic contribution to her enduring image. In the same way, while her utility to Abraham and to the deity's promises is an undeniable feature of Sarah's depiction in the tradition, she cannot with justice be simply flattened to fit this function. Her individuality in complexity, I think, still sometimes succeeds in escaping the strictures of her narrators' service of an androcentric and patriarchal tradition. Sarah does not mimic Abraham in her rage at being overlooked, and her bold speech and initiatives in the episodes dealing with Hagar and Ishmael show Sarah and Abraham

---

1. Compare the suggestive notes on the "substantive correspondences" between Sarah and Abraham in Philo's *On the Life of Abraham* in Livneh, "Jewish Traditions," 538 n. 10; 543. See also Niehoff, "Mother and Maiden," 419–23.

2. Noth, *History*, 151.

at partial cross-purposes. Sarah's skeptical reaction in the tent, though laced with elements that recall Abraham's own responses and disposition, also exhibits her independence by its critique of Abraham and its frank reflection on her unlikelihood of achieving sexual pleasure. Sarah's birth and nurture of Isaac, while events that ultimately serve patriarchal ends, are acts that could never be anticipated by the doings of Abraham; and her responses to these happenings, whether shame, joy, or some combination of these, are not derived from Abraham's reactions. In the Apocryphon, Sarah's initial rejection of Abraham's proposed strategy shows that she is not merely his dim reflection; and though her wisdom is something that identifies her with Abraham, it is a report of her sagacity, not his, that reaches the ears of the king. Even in the *Antiquities* Sarah surprises as a confidant and revealer of truth to Pharaoh, and possesses enough latent power and self-will that Abraham is careful to conceal his murderous resolution from her.

Some Contributions and Prospects of This Study

I have tried here to acknowledge and rediscover Sarah as she is revealed, to me, in Genesis and its ancient retellings. Similar investigations of female characters in this literature, especially those of significant length, remain uncommon, and I hope my work may prompt ventures with broadly congruent goals. My reading of Sarah in the MT joins an ongoing conversation, though, I think, in a narratological register that has not received much play recently. My readings of the retellings of Sarah's story may help begin new conversations.

I have also tried to construct and employ a theoretically informed, character-driven poetics that is capable of drawing marginal or neglected characters into the light. For the retold narratives, this has enabled me to perform a kind of reading that can fairly be said to be in its infancy. Especially for the Apocryphon (not to mention other Dead Sea narrative materials) and the *Antiquities*, and despite occasional calls for a broadening of methodological perspectives in inquiries into these bodies of literature, there are very few, if any, relevant studies that engage narratological points of view. I will be gratified if my work suggests some potential rewards of taking a different, or at least complementary, approach toward these texts.

Finally, I have tried to find a way to read rewritten scriptural narratives without constant deference and comparison to their literary inspirations. Narrative criticism enables a perspective that highlights the internal operations of a narrative: structural, thematic, rhetorical, and other ties and movements that contribute to a narrative's aesthetics and its effects on its readers. These are some of the primary reasons that human beings value narratives in the first place, and my analysis has shown that regarding these retellings—even a translation—as works with their own integrity is an approach that can pay interpretive dividends. In my investigation of the LXX, for example, I demonstrate that careful attention to the horizontal interplay of narrative elements reveals a vitiated Sarah, a reading that challenges the findings of commentators who select a few disparities in the tradition as the basis of their interpretations. In my work on the Apocryphon, I show that questions about the degree of influence of gender conventions in other ancient verse on the descriptive poem celebrating Sarah's beauty, wisdom, and skill are better answered when the broader depiction of Sarah in the Apocryphon is considered. In my reading of the *Antiquities*, I establish that the narrator's desire to paint the primary characters in a positive light often founders precisely on the unintended effects of these tweaks to the tradition—a finding due not to interpretive acumen, but to a simple desire to read the narrative, start to finish, as a narrative, and not only as a deviation from its scriptural precursor.

Much text-critical work remains to be done on the literature of the Second Temple period, and "higher-level" critique can only be as good as its textual foundations allow. But our texts are certainly the best that they have ever been in the modern era, and they should be explored with all of the methodological tools available to biblical studies, and to the humanities more broadly. Moshe Bernstein has called for reading the Apocryphon as a composition in its own right.[3] George Brooke has advocated bringing approaches that are well-established outside Qumran studies to bear on the Scrolls.[4] Jan Willem van Henten has signaled the possibilities of reading Josephus narrative-critically.[5] In other venues, I have argued for a recognition of the Septuagint's narrative worth on its

---

3. Bernstein, "Unity," 133–4.

4. George J. Brooke, "From Bible to Midrash: Approaches to Biblical Interpretation in the Dead Sea Scrolls by Modern Interpreters," in Petersen et al., eds., *Northern Lights on the Dead Sea Scrolls*, 18–19, speaking here of "post-colonialism, spatial approaches, reader-response analysis, etc." See also Pieter B. Hartog, Alison Schofield, and Samuel I. Thomas, eds., *The Dead Sea Scrolls and the Study of the Humanities: Method, Theory, Meaning*, STDJ 125 (Leiden: Brill, 2018).

5. Jan Willem van Henten, "Characterization in Josephus," paper presented at the Annual Meeting of the Society of Biblical Literature, San Diego, CA, 22 November 2014.

own terms.[6] I add the contributions of this study to these efforts, and urge further serious and sustained narratological (and other) forays into the vast array of early Jewish and Christian literature that eventually found itself outside the canon.

---

6. For example, Joseph McDonald, "Rewriting the Matriarch: Reading Sarra in the LXX," paper presented at the Annual Meeting of the International Organization for Septuagint and Cognate Studies, San Diego, CA, 22 November 2014. Compare Benjamin J. M. Johnson, *Reading David and Goliath in Greek and Hebrew*, FAT 2/82 (Tübingen: Mohr Siebeck, 2015).

Bibliography

Abegg, Martin G. Jr., and Michael O. Wise. "1Q20 (1QapGen ar)." In *The Dead Sea Scrolls Reader*. Part 3: *Parabiblical Texts*, edited by Donald W. Parry and Emanuel Tov, 2–35. Leiden: Brill, 2005.
Alter, Robert. *The Art of Biblical Narrative*. Rev. ed. New York: Basic Books, 2011.
Alter, Robert. *Genesis: Translation and Commentary*. New York: Norton, 1996.
Alter, Robert. *The Pleasures of Reading in an Ideological Age*. New York: Simon & Schuster, 1989.
Amit, Yairah. *Reading Biblical Narratives: Literary Criticism and the Hebrew Bible*. Translated by Yael Lotan. Minneapolis: Fortress Press, 2001.
Aristophanes. *Birds; Lysistrata; Assembly-Women; Wealth*. Translated by Stephen Halliwell. Oxford: Clarendon Press, 1997.
Aristophanes. *Four Comedies*. Translated by Douglass Parker. Ann Arbor: University of Michigan Press, 1969.
Arnold, Elizabeth Mayfield, J. Chris Stewart, and C. Aaron McNeece. "Perpetrators as Victims: Understanding Violence by Female Street-Walking Prostitutes." *Violence and Victims* 16 (2001): 145–59.
Attridge, Harold W. *The Interpretation of Biblical History in the* Antiquitates Judaicae *of Flavius Josephus*. Missoula, MT: Scholars Press, 1976.
Avigad, Naḥman, and Yigael Yadin. *A Genesis Apocryphon: A Scroll from the Wilderness of Judaea*. Jerusalem: Magnes Press, 1956.
Bach, Alice. "Signs of the Flesh: Observations on Characterization in the Bible." In *Women in the Hebrew Bible: A Reader*, edited by Alice Bach, 351–65. New York: Routledge, 1999.
Bach, Alice. *Women, Seduction, and Betrayal in Biblical Narrative*. Cambridge: Cambridge University Press, 1997.
Bailey, James L. "Josephus' Portrayal of the Matriarchs." In *Josephus, Judaism, and Christianity*, edited by Louis H. Feldman and Gohei Hata, 154–79. Detroit: Wayne State University Press, 1987.
Bal, Mieke. *Narratology: Introduction to the Theory of Narrative*. 3rd ed. Toronto: University of Toronto Press, 2009.
Bar-Efrat, Shimon. *Narrative Art in the Bible*. BLS 17. Sheffield: Almond Press, 1989.
Becker, Michael. "Abraham in the Genesis Apocryphon." In *Rewritten Biblical Figures*, edited by Erkki Koskenniemi and Pekka Lindqvist, 89–108. Studies in Rewritten Bible 3. Winona Lake, IN: Eisenbrauns, 2010.
Begg, Christopher T. "The Flight of Hagar according to Josephus." *Hermenêutica* 8 (2008): 3–19.

Begg, Christopher T. "Genesis in Josephus." In *The Book of Genesis: Composition, Reception, and Interpretation*, edited by Craig A. Evans, Joel N. Lohr, and David L. Petersen, 303–29. VTSup 152. Leiden: Brill, 2014.

Bellis, Alice Ogden. "Feminist Biblical Scholarship." In *Women in Scripture: A Dictionary of Named and Unnamed Women in the Hebrew Bible, the Apocryphal/ Deuterocanonical Books, and the New Testament*, edited by Carol Meyers, Toni Craven, and Ross S. Kraemer, 24–32. Grand Rapids: Eerdmans, 2000.

Berlin, Adele. *Poetics and Interpretation of Biblical Narrative*. BLS 9. Sheffield: Almond Press, 1983.

Bernstein, Moshe J. "The Dead Sea Scrolls and Jewish Biblical Interpretation in Antiquity: A Multi-Generic Perspective." In *The Dead Sea Scrolls at 60: Scholarly Contributions by New York University Faculty and Alumni*, edited by L. H. Schiffman and S. L. Tzoref, 55–90. Leiden: Brill, 2010.

Bernstein, Moshe J. "The *Genesis Apocryphon*: Compositional and Interpretive Perspectives." In *A Companion to Biblical Interpretation in Early Judaism*, edited by Matthias Henze, 157–79. Grand Rapids: Eerdmans, 2012.

Bernstein, Moshe J. "Is the Genesis Apocryphon a Unity? What Sort of Unity Were You Looking For?" *AS* 8 (2010): 107–34.

Bernstein, Moshe J. "Re-Arrangement, Anticipation, and Harmonization as Exegetical Features in the Genesis Apocryphon." *DSD* 3 (1996): 37–57.

Bernstein, Moshe J. "'Rewritten Bible': A Generic Category Which Has Outlived Its Usefulness?" *Text* 22 (2005): 169–96.

Bernstein, Moshe J. "Stylistic Features in the Narrative of the Genesis Apocryphon." Paper presented at the Annual Meeting of the Society of Biblical Literature. Baltimore, MD, 24 November 2013.

Beyer, Klaus. *Die aramäischen Texte vom Toten Meer samt den Inschriften aus Palästina, dem Testament Levis aus der Kairoer Genisa, der Fastenrolle und den alten talmudischen Zitaten*. Göttingen: Vandenhoeck & Ruprecht, 1984.

Beyer, Klaus. *Die aramäischen Texte vom Toten Meer samt den Inschriften aus Palästina, dem Testament Levis aus der Kairoer Genisa, der Fastenrolle und den alten talmudischen Zitaten*. Ergänzungsband. Göttingen: Vandenhoeck & Ruprecht, 1994.

Beyer, Klaus. *Die aramäischen Texte vom Toten Meer samt den Inschriften aus Palästina, dem Testament Levis aus der Kairoer Genisa, der Fastenrolle und den alten talmudischen Zitaten*. Band 2. Göttingen: Vandenhoeck & Ruprecht, 2004.

Bing, Peter, and Regina Höschele, eds. *Aristaenetus, Erotic Letters*. WGRW 32. Atlanta: Society of Biblical Literature, 2014.

Bird, Phyllis. "Images of Women in the Old Testament." In *Religion and Sexism: Images of Woman in the Jewish and Christian Traditions*, edited by Rosemary Radford Ruether, 41–88. New York: Simon & Schuster, 1974.

"Blood, Sweat and Tears." *The Economist*, 27 September 2014, 42.

Brayford, Susan Ann. "Feminist Criticism: Sarah Laughs Last." In *Method Matters: Essays on the Interpretation of the Hebrew Bible in Honor of David L. Petersen*, edited by Joel M. LeMon and Kent Harold Richards, 311–31. Atlanta: Society of Biblical Literature, 2009.

Brayford, Susan Ann. *Genesis*. Septuagint Commentary Series. Leiden: Brill, 2007.

Brayford, Susan Ann. "The Taming and Shaming of Sarah in the Septuagint of Genesis." PhD diss., Iliff School of Theology; The University of Denver / Colorado Seminary, 1998.

Brayford, Susan Ann. "To Shame or not to Shame: Sexuality in the Mediterranean Diaspora." *Semeia* 87 (1999): 163–76.

Brenton, Lancelot Charles Lee. *The Septuagint Version of the Old Testament with an English Translation and with Various Readings and Critical Notes*. 1844. Repr. London: Samuel Bagster & Sons, 1870.

Brock, Sebastian P., and Simon Hopkins. "A Verse Homily on Abraham and Sarah in Egypt: Syriac Original with Early Arabic Translation." *Le Muséon* 105 (1992): 87–145.

Brooke, George J. "From Bible to Midrash: Approaches to Biblical Interpretation in the Dead Sea Scrolls by Modern Interpreters." In *Northern Lights on the Dead Sea Scrolls: Proceedings of the Nordic Qumran Network 2003–2006*, edited by Anders Klostergaard Petersen, Torleif Elgvin, Cecilia Wassen, Hanne von Weissenberg, Mikael Winninge, and Martin Ehrensvärd, 1–19. Leiden: Brill, 2009.

Campbell, Jonathan G. "Rewritten Bible: A Terminological Reassessment." In *Rewritten Bible after Fifty Years: Texts, Terms, or Techniques? A Last Dialogue with Géza Vermès*, edited by József Zsengellér, 49–81. JSJSup 166. Leiden: Brill, 2014.

Chatman, Seymour. *Story and Discourse: Narrative Structure in Fiction and Film*. Ithaca, NY: Cornell University Press, 1978.

Choi, John H. *Traditions at Odds: The Reception of the Pentateuch in Biblical and Second Temple Period Literature*. New York: T&T Clark, 2010.

Cohen, Shaye J. D. "The Beauty of Flora and the Beauty of Sarai." *Helios* 8 (1981): 41–53.

Conway, Colleen M. *Men and Women in the Fourth Gospel: Gender and Johannine Characterization*. SBLDS 167. Atlanta: Society of Biblical Literature, 1999.

Conybeare, Catherine. *The Laughter of Sarah: Biblical Exegesis, Feminist Theory, and the Concept of Delight*. New York: Palgrave Macmillan, 2013.

Cook, Joan E. *Hannah's Desire, God's Design: Early Interpretations of the Story of Hannah*. JSOTSup 282. Sheffield: Sheffield Academic Press, 1999.

Cotter, David W. *Genesis*. Berit Olam. Collegeville, MN: Liturgical Press, 2003.

Crawford, Sidnie White. "Genesis in the Dead Sea Scrolls." In *The Book of Genesis: Composition, Reception, and Interpretation*, edited by Craig A. Evans, Joel N. Lohr, and David L. Petersen, 353–73. Leiden: Brill, 2012.

Crawford, Sidnie White. *Rewriting Scripture in Second Temple Times*. Grand Rapids: Eerdmans, 2008.

Daniel, Andrew G. "A New Reading of Genesis Apocryphon (1Q20) 20.10: Syntax, Semantics and Literary Function." *RevQ* 28 (2016): 279–85.

Darr, John A. *On Character Building: The Reader and the Rhetoric of Characterization in Luke-Acts*. Louisville: Westminster John Knox Press, 1992.

Day, Linda. *Three Faces of a Queen: Characterization in the Books of Esther*. JSOTSup 186. Sheffield: Sheffield Academic Press, 1995.

Dijk-Hemmes, Fokkelien van. "Sarai in Exile: A Gender-Specific Reading of Genesis 12:10–13:2." In *The Double Voice of Her Desire*, edited by J. Bekkenkamp and F. Dröes, 136–45. Translated by David E. Orton. Leiden: Deo, 2004.

Dines, Jennifer M. "What If the Reader Is a She? Biblical Women and Their Translators." In *The Reception of the Hebrew Bible in the Septuagint and the New Testament: Essays in Memory of Aileen Guilding*, edited by David J. A. Clines and J. Cheryl Exum, 56–82. Sheffield: Sheffield Phoenix Press, 2013.

DiTommaso, Lorenzo. "Pseudepigrapha Notes I: 1. *Lunationes Danielis*; 2. Biblical Figures Outside the Bible." *JSP* 15 (2006): 116–44.

Driver, G. R. "Hebrew mothers (Exodus i 19)." *ZAW* 67 (1955): 246–8.

Ego, Beate. "The Figure of Abraham in the Genesis Apocryphon's Re-Narration of Gen 12:10-20." In *Qumran Cave 1 Revisited: Texts from Cave 1 Sixty Years after Their Discovery: Proceedings of the Sixth Meeting of the IOQS in Ljubljana*, edited by Donald W. Parry, Daniel K. Falk, Sarianna Metso, and Eibert J. C. Tigchelaar, 233–43. Leiden: Brill, 2010.

Eichler, Barry L. "On Reading Genesis 12:10-20." In *Tehillah le-Moshe: Biblical and Judaic Studies in Honor of Moshe Greenberg*, edited by Mordechai Cogan, Barry L. Eichler, and Jeffrey H. Tigay, 23–38. Winona Lake, IN: Eisenbrauns, 1997.

Eshel, Esther. "The Dream Visions in the Noah Story of the Genesis Apocryphon and Related Texts." In *Northern Lights on the Dead Sea Scrolls: Proceedings of the Nordic Qumran Network 2003–2006*, edited by Anders Klostergaard Petersen, Torleif Elgvin, Cecilia Wassen, Hanne von Weissenberg, Mikael Winninge, and Martin Ehrensvärd, 41–61. Leiden: Brill, 2009.

Exum, J. Cheryl. "Who's Afraid of 'The Endangered Ancestress'?" In *The New Literary Criticism and the Hebrew Bible*, edited by J. Cheryl Exum and David J. A. Clines, 91–113. Valley Forge, PA: Trinity Press International, 1993.

Falk, Daniel K. *The Parabiblical Texts: Strategies for Extending the Scriptures in the Dead Sea Scrolls*. LSTS 63; Companion to the Qumran Scrolls 8. London: T&T Clark, 2007.

Feldman, Louis H. "Abraham." In *Josephus's Interpretation of the Bible*, 223–89. Berkeley: University of California Press, 1998.

Feldman, Louis H. "Abraham the General in Josephus." In *Nourished with Peace: Studies in Hellenistic Judaism in Memory of Samuel Sandmel*, edited by Frederick E. Greenspahn, Earle Hilgert, and Burton L. Mack, 43–9. Chico, CA: Scholars Press, 1984.

Feldman, Louis H. "Abraham the Greek Philosopher in Josephus." *TAPA* 99 (1968): 143–56.

Feldman, Louis H. "Hellenizations in Josephus' *Jewish Antiquities*: The Portrait of Abraham." In *Josephus, Judaism, and Christianity*, edited by Louis H. Feldman and Gohei Hata, 133–53. Detroit: Wayne State University Press, 1987.

Feldman, Louis H. "Josephus as a Biblical Interpreter: The *'Aqedah*." *JQR* 75 (1985): 212–52.

Feldman, Louis H. "Josephus' Portrait of Saul." *HUCA* 53 (1982): 45–99.

Feldman, Louis H. Translation and Commentary. *Judean Antiquities 1–4*, edited by Steve Mason. FJTC 3. Leiden: Brill, 2000.

Feldman, Louis H., James L. Kugel, and Lawrence H. Schiffman, eds. *Outside the Bible: Ancient Jewish Writings Related to Scripture*. Philadelphia: Jewish Publication Society of America, 2013.

Fewell, Danna Nolan, and David M. Gunn. *Gender, Power, and Promise: The Subject of the Bible's First Story*. Nashville: Abingdon Press, 1993.

Fischer, Irmtraud. *Die Erzeltern Israels: Feministisch-theologische Studien zu Genesis 12–36*. BZAW 222. Berlin: de Gruyter, 1994.

Fischer, Irmtraud. *Women Who Wrestled with God: Biblical Stories of Israel's Beginnings*. Translated by Linda M. Maloney. Collegeville, MN: Liturgical Press, 2005.

Fitzmyer, Joseph A. *The Genesis Apocryphon of Qumran Cave 1 (1Q20): A Commentary*. 3rd ed. Rome: Pontifical Biblical Institute, 2004.

Fokkelman, J. P. *Reading Biblical Narrative: An Introductory Guide*. Translated by Ineke Smit. Louisville: Westminster John Knox Press, 1999.

Fox, Everett. *Genesis and Exodus: A New English Rendition*. New York: Schocken Books, 1991.

Franxman, Thomas W. *Genesis and the "Jewish Antiquities" of Flavius Josephus*. Rome: Biblical Institute Press, 1979.

Fuchs, Esther. "The Literary Characterization of Mothers and Sexual Politics in the Hebrew Bible." In *Feminist Perspectives on Biblical Scholarship*, edited by Adela Yarbro Collins, 117–36. Chico, CA: Scholars Press, 1985.

García Martínez, Florentino. *The Dead Sea Scrolls Translated: The Qumran Texts in English*. Leiden: Brill, 1994.

Gevirtz, Marianne Luijken. "Abram's Dream in the Genesis Apocryphon: Its Motifs and Their Function." *Maarav* 8 (1992): 229–43.

Ginzberg, Louis. *Legends of the Jews*. 2nd ed. Translated by Henrietta Szold and Paul Radin. 1909–38. Repr. Philadelphia: Johns Hopkins University Press, 2003.

Greenfield, Jonas C. "Early Aramaic Poetry." *JANES* 11 (1979): 45–51.

Gunn, David M., and Danna Nolan Fewell. *Narrative in the Hebrew Bible*. Oxford Bible Series. Oxford: Oxford University Press, 1993.

Halpern-Amaru, Betsy. *The Empowerment of Women in the Book of Jubilees*. Leiden: Brill, 1999.

Halpern-Amaru, Betsy. "The Portrait of Sarah in Jubilees." In *Jewish Studies in a New Europe*, edited by Ulf Haxen, Hanne Traudner-Kromann, and Karen Lisa Goldschmidt Salamon, 336–48. Copenhagen: C. A. Reitzel, 1998.

Halpern-Amaru, Betsy. "Portraits of Biblical Women in Josephus' Antiquities." *JJS* 39 (1988): 143–70.

Halpern-Amaru, Betsy. "Portraits of Women in Pseudo-Philo's Biblical Antiquities." In *"Women Like This": New Perspectives on Jewish Women in the Greco-Roman World*, edited by Amy-Jill Levine, 83–106. EJL 1. Atlanta: Scholars Press, 1991.

Harl, Marguerite. *La Genèse*. La Bible d'Alexandrie 1. Paris: Cerf, 1986.

Hartog, Pieter B., Alison Schofield, and Samuel I. Thomas, eds. *The Dead Sea Scrolls and the Study of the Humanities: Method, Theory, Meaning*. STDJ 125. Leiden: Brill, 2018.

Harvey, W. J. *Character and the Novel*. Ithaca, NY: Cornell University Press, 1965.

Hassan, Riffat. "Islamic Hagar and Her Family." In *Hagar, Sarah, and Their Children: Jewish, Christian, and Muslim Perspectives*, edited by Phyllis Trible and Letty M. Russell, 149–67. Louisville: Westminster John Knox Press, 2006.

Hens-Piazza, Gina. *Nameless, Blameless, and Without Shame: Two Cannibal Mothers Before a King*. Interfaces. Collegeville, MN: Liturgical Press, 2003.

Hens-Piazza, Gina. "New Historicism." In *New Meanings for Ancient Texts: Recent Approaches to Biblical Criticisms and Their Applications*, edited by Steven L. McKenzie and John Kaltner, 59–76. Louisville: Westminster John Knox Press, 2013.

Henten, Jan Willem van. "Characterization in Josephus." Paper presented at the Annual Meeting of the Society of Biblical Literature. San Diego, CA, 22 November 2014.

Herman, David, James Phelan, Peter J. Rabinowitz, Brian Richardson, and Robyn Warhol. *Narrative Theory: Core Concepts and Critical Debates*. Columbus: The Ohio State University Press, 2012.

Hochman, Baruch. *Character in Literature*. Ithaca, NY: Cornell University Press, 1985.

Holladay, Carl R. Theios Aner *in Hellenistic Judaism: A Critique of the Use of This Category in New Testament Christology*. Missoula, MT: Scholars Press, 1977.

Humphreys, W. Lee. *The Character of God in the Book of Genesis: A Narrative Appraisal*. Louisville: Westminster John Knox Press, 2001.

Iser, Wolfgang. *The Act of Reading: A Theory of Aesthetic Response*. Baltimore: Johns Hopkins University Press, 1978.

Iser, Wolfgang. "Indeterminacy and the Reader's Response in Prose Fiction." In *Aspects of Narrative: Selected Papers from the English Institute*, edited by J. Harris Miller, 1–45. New York: Columbia University Press, 1971.

Iser, Wolfgang. "The Reading Process: A Phenomenological Approach." In *New Directions in Literary History*, edited by Ralph Cohen, 125–45. Baltimore: Johns Hopkins University Press, 1974.

Jacobs, Mignon R. *Gender, Power, and Persuasion: The Genesis Narratives and Contemporary Portraits*. Grand Rapids: Baker Academic, 2007.

James, Elaine. "Sarah, Hagar, and Their Interpreters." In *Women's Bible Commentary*, 3rd ed, edited by Carol A. Newsom, Sharon H. Ringe, and Jacqueline E. Lapsley, 51–5. Louisville: Westminster John Knox Press, 2012.

James, Henry. "The Art of Fiction." In *The Art of Fiction and Other Essays*. With an introduction by Morris Roberts, 3–23. New York: Oxford University Press, 1948.

Japhet, Sara. "The 'Description Poems' in Ancient Jewish Sources and in the Jewish Exegesis of the Song of Songs." In *A Critical Engagement: Essays on the Hebrew Bible in Honour of J. Cheryl Exum*, edited by David J. A. Clines and Ellen van Wolde, 216–29. Sheffield: Sheffield Phoenix Press, 2011.

Jastrow, Marcus. *A Dictionary of the Targumim, the Talmud Babli and Yerushalmi, and the Midrashic Literature*. 1903. Repr. New York: Judaica, 1996.

Jeansonne, Sharon Pace. *The Women of Genesis: From Sarah to Potiphar's Wife*. Minneapolis: Fortress Press, 1990.

Johnson, Benjamin J. M. *Reading David and Goliath in Greek and Hebrew*. FAT 2/82. Tübingen: Mohr Siebeck, 2015.

Jongeling, B., C. J. Labuschagne, and A. S. van der Woude. *Aramaic Texts from Qumran*. SSS 4. Leiden: Brill, 1976.

Joosten, Jan. "Abram et Saraï en Égypte: Composition et message de Genèse 12, 10-20." In *La sœur-épouse (Genèse 12, 10-20)*, edited by Matthieu Arnold, Gilbert Dahan, and Annie Noblesse-Rocher, 11–25. Paris: Cerf, 2010.

Jurgens, Blake A. "A Wandering Aramean in Pharaoh's Court: The Literary Relationship between Abram's Sojourn in Egypt in 1QapGen 19–20 and Jewish Fictional Literature." *JSJ* 49 (2018): 356–89.

Kadari, Tamar. "The Beauty of Sarah in Rabbinic Literature." In *Hebrew Texts in Jewish, Christian and Muslim Surroundings*, edited by Klaas Spronk and Eveline van Staalduine-Sulman, 65–82. SSN 69. Leiden: Brill, 2018.

Kalimi, Isaac. "The Binding of Isaac: Biblical Narrative in Late Second Temple and Rabbinic Exegesis and Thought." In *Fighting Over the Bible: Jewish Interpretation, Sectarianism and Polemic from Temple to Talmud and Beyond*, 149–83. BRLJ 54. Leiden: Brill, 2017.

Keshet, Shula. *"Say You Are My Sister": Danger, Seduction and the Foreign in Biblical Literature and Beyond*. Translated by Anthony Berris. The Bible in the Modern World 53. Sheffield: Sheffield Phoenix Press, 2013.

Kirsch, Jonathan. "What Did Sarah See?" In *Abraham and Family: New Insights into the Patriarchal Narratives*, edited by Hershel Shanks, 107–10. Washington, DC: Biblical Archaeology Society, 2000.

Koenig, Sara M. *Isn't This Bathsheba? A Study in Characterization*. Princeton Theological Monograph Series. Eugene, OR: Pickwick Press, 2011.

Koskenniemi, Erkki, and Pekka Lindqvist. "Rewritten Bible, Rewritten Stories: Methodological Aspects." In *Rewritten Bible Reconsidered*, edited by Antti Laato and Jacques T. A. G. M. van Ruiten, 11–39. Studies in Rewritten Bible 1. Winona Lake, IN: Eisenbrauns, 2008.

Lans, Birgit van der. "Hagar, Ishmael, and Abraham's Household in Josephus' *Antiquitates Judaicae*." In *Abraham, the Nations, and the Hagarites: Jewish, Christian, and Islamic Perspectives on Kinship with Abraham*, edited by Martin Goodman, George H. van Kooten, and Jacques T. A. G. M. van Ruiten, 185–99. Leiden: Brill, 2010.

Lee, J. A. L. *A Lexical Study of the Septuagint Version of the Pentateuch*. SCS 14. Chico, CA: Scholars Press, 1983.

Lee, J. A. L. "A Note on Septuagint Material in the Supplement to Liddell and Scott." *Glotta* 47 (1969): 234–42.

Lee, Peter Y. "Aramaic Poetry in Qumran." PhD diss., The Catholic University of America, 2011.

Lefkovitz, Lori Hope. "Eavesdropping on Angels and Laughing at God: Theorizing a Subversive Matriarchy." In *Gender and Judaism: The Transformation of Tradition*, edited by Tamar Rudavsky, 157–67. New York: New York University Press, 1995.

Lefkovitz, Lori Hope. *In Scripture: The First Stories of Jewish Sexual Identities*. Lanham, MD: Rowman & Littlefield, 2010.

Livneh, Atar. "Jewish Traditions and Familial Roman Values in Philo's *De Abrahamo* 245–254." *HTR* 109 (2016): 536–49.

Machiela, Daniel A. "The Aramaic Dead Sea Scrolls: Coherence and Context in the Library of Qumran." In *The Dead Sea Scrolls at Qumran and the Concept of a Library*, edited by Sidnie White Crawford and Cecilia Wassen, 244–58. STDJ 116. Leiden: Brill, 2016.

Machiela, Daniel A. *The Dead Sea Genesis Apocryphon: A New Text and Translation with Introduction and Special Treatment of Columns 13–17*. STDJ 79. Leiden: Brill, 2009.

Machiela, Daniel A. "Genesis Revealed: The Apocalyptic Apocryphon from Qumran Cave 1." In *Qumran Cave 1 Revisited: Texts from Cave 1 Sixty Years after Their Discovery*, edited by Daniel K. Falk, Sarianna Metso, Donald W. Parry, and Eibert J. C. Tigchelaar, 206–21. STDJ 91. Leiden: Brill, 2010.

McDonald, Joseph. "Rewriting the Matriarch: Reading Sarra in the LXX." Paper presented at the Annual Meeting of the International Organization for Septuagint and Cognate Studies. San Diego, CA, 22 November 2014.

McDonald, Joseph. "Searching for Sarah in the Second Temple Era: Portraits in the Hebrew Bible and Second Temple Narratives." PhD diss., Brite Divinity School, 2015.

McKay, Heather A. "Eve's Sisters Re-Cycled: The Literary *Nachleben* of Old Testament Women." In *Recycling Biblical Figures: Papers Read at a NOSTER Colloquium in Amsterdam, 12–13 May 1997*, edited by Athalya Brenner and Jan Willem van Henten, 169–91. Leiden: Deo, 1999.

Miller, Laura. "A Study in Sherlock: How the Detective Escaped His Creator." *Harper's Magazine*, May 2014, 89–94.

Miller, Troy A. "Surrogate, Slave and Deviant? The Figure of Hagar in Jewish Tradition and Paul (Galatians 4.21-31)." In *Early Christian Literature and Intertextuality*, vol. 2: *Exegetical Studies*, edited by Craig A. Evans and H. Daniel Zacharias, 138–54. London: T&T Clark, 2009.

Mitchell, Stephen. *Genesis: A New Translation of the Classic Biblical Stories*. New York: HarperCollins, 1996.

Mudrick, Marvin. "Character and Event in Fiction." In *On Culture and Literature*, 141–59. New York: Horizon, 1970.

Muraoka, Takamitsu. "Further Notes on the Aramaic of the Genesis Apocryphon." *RevQ* 16 (1993): 39–48.

Muraoka, Takamitsu. *A Grammar of Qumran Aramaic*. Leuven: Peeters, 2011.

Muraoka, Takamitsu. "Notes on the Aramaic of the Genesis Apocryphon." *RevQ* 8 (1972–74): 7–51.

Najman, Hindy. "Early Nonrabbinic Interpretation." In *The Jewish Study Bible*, edited by Adele Berlin and Marc Zvi Brettler, 1835–44. Oxford: Oxford University Press, 2004.

Neusner, Jacob, trans. *The Mishnah: A New Translation*. New Haven: Yale University Press, 1988.

Nickelsburg, George W. E. "Patriarchs Who Worry About Their Wives: A Haggadic Tendency in the Genesis Apocryphon." In *George W. E. Nickelsburg in Perspective: An Ongoing Dialogue of Learning*, vol. 1, edited by Jacob Neusner and Alan J. Avery-Peck, 177–99. Leiden: Brill, 2003.

Niditch, Susan. "Genesis." In *Women's Bible Commentary*, 3rd ed, edited by Carol A. Newsom, Sharon H. Ringe, and Jacqueline E. Lapsley, 27–45. Louisville: Westminster John Knox Press, 2012.

Niditch, Susan. *Underdogs and Tricksters: A Prelude to Biblical Folklore*. San Francisco: Harper & Row, 1987.

Niehoff, Maren. "Mother and Maiden, Sister and Spouse: Sarah in Philonic Midrash." *HTR* 97 (2004): 413–44.

Niese, Benedict. *Flavii Josephi Opera*. Berlin: Weidmann, 1885–95.

Nodet, Étienne. *The Hebrew Bible of Josephus: Main Features*. CahRB 92. Leuven: Peeters, 2018.

Noth, Martin. *A History of Pentateuchal Traditions*. Scholars Press Reprint Series. Translated by Bernhard W. Anderson. Atlanta: Scholars Press, 1981.

Osswald, Eva. "Beobachtungen zur Erzählung von Abrahams Aufenthalt in Ägypten im 'Genesis-Apocryphon'." *ZAW* 72 (1960): 7–25.

Perrin, Andrew B. *The Dynamics of Dream-Vision Revelation in the Aramaic Dead Sea Scrolls*. JAJSup 19. Göttingen: Vandenhoeck & Ruprecht, 2015.

Perry, Menakhem. "Literary Dynamics: How the Order of a Text Creates Its Meanings (with an Analysis of Faulkner's 'A Rose for Emily')." *Poetics Today* 1 (1979): 35–64; 311–61.

Phillips, Elaine A. "Incredulity, Faith, and Textual Purposes: Post-Biblical Responses to the Laughter of Abraham and Sarah." In *The Function of Scripture in Early Jewish and Christian Tradition*, edited by Craig A. Evans and James A. Sanders, 22–33. JSNTSup 154; SSEJC 6. Sheffield: Sheffield Academic Press, 1998.

Popović, Mladen. *Reading the Human Body: Physiognomics and Astrology in the Dead Sea Scrolls and Hellenistic-Early Roman Period Judaism*. STDJ 67. Leiden: Brill, 2007.

Rad, Gerhard von. *Genesis: A Commentary*. Rev. ed. OTL. Philadelphia: Westminster Press, 1972.

Rahlfs, Alfred. *Septuaginta*. Stuttgart: Deutsche Bibelgesellschaft, 1935.

Reed, Stephen A. "The Use of the First Person in the *Genesis Apocryphon*." In *Aramaic in Postbiblical Judaism and Early Christianity: Papers from the 2004 National Endowment for the Humanities Summer Seminar at Duke University*, edited by Eric M. Meyers and Paul V. M. Flesher, 193–215. Winona Lake, IN: Eisenbrauns, 2010.

Reinhartz, Adele, and Miriam-Simma Walfish. "Conflict and Coexistence in Jewish Interpretation." In *Hagar, Sarah, and Their Children: Jewish, Christian, and Muslim Perspectives*, edited by Phyllis Trible and Letty M. Russell, 101–25. Louisville: Westminster John Knox Press, 2006.

Reis, Pamela Tamarkin. "Hagar Requited." *JSOT* 87 (2000): 75–109.

Rengstorf, Karl Heinrich, ed. *A Complete Concordance to Flavius Josephus*. Leiden: Brill, 1973.

Rensburg, J. F. van. "Intellect and/or Beauty: A Portrait of Women in the Old Testament and Extra Biblical Literature." *Journal for Semitics* 11 (2002): 112–25.

Rimmon-Kenan, Shlomith. *Narrative Fiction: Contemporary Poetics*. London: Methuen, 1983.

Roncace, Mark. "Josephus' (Real) Portraits of Deborah and Gideon: A Reading of *Antiquities* 5.198-232." *JSJ* 31 (2000): 247–74.

Rosenthal, Franz. "Review of Avigad and Yadin, *A Genesis Apocryphon*." *JNES* 18 (1959): 82–4.

Rothkoff, Aaron. "Sarah." In *Encyclopaedia Judaica*, vol. 14, edited by Cecil Roth and Geoffrey Wigoder, 866–9. Jerusalem: Keter, 1972.

Schneider, Tammi J. *Mothers of Promise: Women in the Book of Genesis*. Grand Rapids: Baker Academic, 2008.

Schneider, Tammi J. *Sarah: Mother of Nations*. New York: Continuum, 2004.

Scholz, Susanne. *Sacred Witness: Rape in the Hebrew Bible*. Minneapolis: Fortress Press, 2010.

Schorch, Stefan. "Hellenizing Women in the Biblical Tradition: The Case of LXX Genesis." *BIOSCS* 41 (2008): 3–16.

Schuller, Eileen. "Response to 'Patriarchs Who Worry about Their Wives: A Haggadic Tendency in the Genesis Apocryphon'." In *George W. E. Nickelsburg in Perspective: An Ongoing Dialogue of Learning*, edited by Jacob Neusner and Alan J. Avery-Peck, 200–212. Leiden: Brill, 2003.

Segal, Michael. "The Literary Relationship between the Genesis Apocryphon and Jubilees: The Chronology of Abram and Sarai's Descent to Egypt." *AS* 8 (2010): 71–88.
Shectman, Sarah. *Women in the Pentateuch: A Feminist and Source-Critical Analysis*. Sheffield: Sheffield Phoenix Press, 2009.
Sly, Dorothy. *Philo's Perception of Women*. BJS 209. Atlanta: Scholars Press, 1990.
Soden, Wolfram von. *Akkadisches Handwörterbuch*. Wiesbaden: Otto Harrassowitz, 1985.
Sokoloff, Michael. *A Dictionary of Jewish Palestinian Aramaic of the Byzantine Period*. 2nd ed. Ramat-Gan, Israel: Bar Ilan University Press, 2002.
Speiser, E. A. *Genesis: A New Translation with Introduction and Commentary*. 3rd ed. AB 1. Garden City, NY: Doubleday, 1982.
Sternberg, Meir. *The Poetics of Biblical Narrative: Ideological Literature and the Drama of Reading*. Bloomington: Indiana University Press, 1985.
Stone, Michael E., and Theodore A. Bergren, eds. *Biblical Figures Outside the Bible*. Harrisburg, PA: Trinity Press International, 1998.
Tervanotko, Hanna. *Denying Her Voice: The Figure of Miriam in Ancient Jewish Literature*. JAJSup 23. Göttingen: Vandenhoeck & Ruprecht, 2016.
Teubal, Savina J. *Sarah the Priestess: The First Matriarch of Genesis*. Athens, OH: Swallow Press, 1984.
Thackeray, Henry St. John, trans. *Jewish Antiquities, Books 1–4*. Vol. 4 of *Josephus*. LCL. London: Heinemann, 1930.
Thackeray, Henry St. John, and Ralph Marcus. *A Lexicon to Josephus*. Paris: Geuthner, 1930–55.
Tov, Emanuel. "Textual Harmonization in the Five Books of the Torah: A Summary." In *The Bible, Qumran, and the Samaritans*, edited by Magnar Kartveit and Gary N. Knoppers, 31–56. SJ 104; StSam 10. Berlin: de Gruyter, 2018.
Trible, Phyllis. "Depatriarchalizing in Biblical Interpretation." *JAAR* 41 (1973): 30–48.
Trible, Phyllis. "Genesis 22: The Sacrifice of Sarah." In *"Not in Heaven": Coherence and Complexity in Biblical Narrative*, edited by Jason P. Rosenblatt and Joseph C. Sitterson Jr., 170–91. Bloomington: Indiana University Press, 1991.
Trible, Phyllis. "Hagar: The Desolation of Rejection." In *Texts of Terror: Literary-Feminist Readings of Biblical Narratives*, 8–35. Philadelphia: Fortress Press, 1984.
Trible, Phyllis. "Ominous Beginnings for a Promise of Blessing." In *Hagar, Sarah, and Their Children: Jewish, Christian, and Muslim Perspectives*, edited by Phyllis Trible and Letty M. Russell, 33–69. Louisville: Westminster John Knox Press, 2006.
Vander Stichele, Caroline. "The Head of John and Its Reception or How to Conceptualize 'Reception History'." In *Reception History and Biblical Studies: Theory and Practice*, edited by Emma England and William John Lyons, 79–93. LHBOTS 615. Scriptural Traces 6. London: Bloomsbury T&T Clark, 2015.
VanderKam, James C. "The Poetry of 1 Q Ap Gen, XX, 2–8a." *RevQ* 10 (1979–81): 57–66.
Vermès, Géza. *The Dead Sea Scrolls in English*. 4th ed. New York: Penguin, 1995.
Vermès, Géza. "The Genesis of the Concept of 'Rewritten Bible'." In *Rewritten Bible after Fifty Years: Texts, Terms, or Techniques? A Last Dialogue with Géza Vermès*, edited by József Zsengellér, 3–9. JSJSup 166. Leiden: Brill, 2014.

Vermès, Géza. *Scripture and Tradition in Judaism*. StPB 4. Leiden: Brill, 1961.
Visotzky, Burton L. *The Genesis of Ethics*. New York: Three Rivers Press, 1996.
Wallace, Howard. "On Account of Sarai: Gen 12:10–13:1." *ABR* 44 (1996): 32–41.
Weems, Renita J. "A Mistress, a Maid, and No Mercy." In *Just a Sister Away: A Womanist Vision of Women's Relationships in the Bible*, 1–21. San Diego: LuraMedia, 1988.
Wegner, Judith Romney. "The Image of Woman in Philo." In *Society of Biblical Literature 1982 Seminar Papers*, 551–63. SBLSPS 21. Chico, CA: Scholars Press, 1982.
Weissman, Gary. *The Writer in the Well: On Misreading and Rewriting Literature*. Theory and Interpretation of Narrative Series. Columbus: The Ohio State University Press, 2016.
Wénin, André. "Abram et Saraï en Égypte (Gn 12, 10-20) ou la place de Saraï dans l'élection." *RTL* 29 (1998): 433–56.
Wénin, André. "Saraï, Hagar et Abram: Une approche narrative et contextuelle de Gn 16, 1-6." *RTL* 32 (2001): 24–54.
Wevers, John William. *Genesis*. Septuaginta: Vetus Testamentum Graecum auctoritate Academiae Scientiarum Gottingensis editum 1. Göttingen: Vandenhoeck & Ruprecht, 1974.
Wevers, John William. *Notes on the Greek Text of Genesis*. SCS 35. Atlanta: Scholars Press, 1993.
Whiston, William, trans., D. S. Margoliouth, ed. *The Works of Flavius Josephus*. London: Routledge, 1906.
Wilson, Rawdon. "The Bright Chimera: Character as a Literary Term." *Critical Inquiry* 5 (1979): 725–49.
Zakovitch, Yair, and Avigdor Shinan. *Abram and Sarai in Egypt: Gen 12:10-20 in the Bible, the Old Versions and the Ancient Jewish Literature*. [In Hebrew.] Research Projects of the Institute of Jewish Studies Monograph Series 2. Jerusalem: Hebrew University, 1983.
Zierler, Wendy. "In Search of a Feminist Reading of the Akedah." *Nashim* 9 (2005): 10–26.
Zucker, David J. "Sarah: The View of the Classical Rabbis." In *Perspectives on Our Father Abraham: Essays in Honor of Marvin R. Wilson*, edited by Stephen A. Hunt, 221–52. Grand Rapids: Eerdmans, 2010.

Index of References

Hebrew Bible/Old Testament

Genesis

Reference	Pages
3:24	81
4:5	28
4:14	81
6:11	56
6:13	56
8:6	44
11:10-29 LXX	94
11:10-28	37
11:10-26	36
11:26–12:9 LXX	93, 95, 134
11:26–12:9	34, 35
11:26-32 LXX	94
11:26-32	35
11:26-27	47
11:27-25:10	6
11:27-31	47
11:29	36, 37, 54, 75, 84
11:29 LXX	94, 109
11:30	36, 38, 62, 86
11:30 LXX	94–6, 104–6, 108, 110
11:30–16:1	53
11:31	37, 39, 47, 54
11:31 LXX	95, 109
11:32	37
11:32 LXX	95
12	55, 145, 148, 181
12 LXX	90, 94, 244
12:1-4	75
12:1-3 LXX	95
12:1-3	37, 39, 48
12:1	38
12:2	38, 61
12:2 LXX	96, 116
12:2-3	38, 61
12:3	71
12:4	47, 49, 60
12:4 LXX	96
12:4-5 LXX	96, 104
12:4-5	38
12:5	38, 39, 46, 47, 52, 54, 59, 85
12:5 LXX	96, 102, 109
12:6-9 LXX	96
12:6-8	39
12:7	39, 63
12:7 LXX	96
12:7-8 LXX	104
12:7-8	39
12:9 LXX	98
12:9-11	39
12:9-10	72
12:10	40
12:10 LXX	98, 126
12:10–13:2 LXX	93, 97
12:10–13:2	34, 40
12:10-20 LXX	126, 134
12:10-20	7, 84, 86, 179, 236
12:11	41, 52, 86
12:11 LXX	94, 98, 107, 115, 127
12:11-13 LXX	98, 109, 126, 135
12:11-13	40, 41, 45, 75, 207
12:11-12	43
12:12	40, 42, 43, 55
12:12 LXX	100
12:13	44, 52
12:13 LXX	94, 100, 101, 108, 123
12:14	39, 41
12:14 LXX	94, 99, 102
12:14 LXX	170
12:14-15 LXX	101, 115
12:14-15	43, 55, 86
12:15	41, 43, 46, 54, 59, 72
12:15 LXX	99, 118
12:16	44, 46, 73
12:16 LXX	101, 102
12:17	43, 72, 148
12:17 LXX	101, 102
12:17-20	43, 85
12:17-19	58
12:17-18	45
12:18-19 LXX	99, 127
12:18-19	43
12:19	43, 45, 46, 54, 57

Genesis (cont.)

Reference	Pages
12:19 LXX	101, 102, 109
12:20	40, 43, 46
12:20 LXX	98, 102
12:20–13:1	46
13	48, 200
13:1	43
13:1 LXX	102, 103
13:1-2	46
13:2	40, 47
13:2 LXX	102
13:2–15:21 LXX	103, 134
13:2–15:21	46
13:2-13	47
13:3-4	49
13:5	47
13:5 LXX	103
13:6	47
13:6 LXX	103
13:10	40
13:11	47
13:12	49
13:13	40
13:14–14:24	48
13:14-18 LXX	104
13:14-17	48
13:15-16	48
13:17-18	49
13:18	48, 75, 83
13:18 LXX	104
14	48, 200
14:1-24 LXX	104
14:11-21	49
14:13	48, 75, 163
14:14	48
14:18-20	61
14:21-24	233
14:22	61
14:24	48, 75
15	51, 201
15 LXX	104, 105
15:1	49
15:1 LXX	106
15:1-21	49
15:1-2	49
15:2	61
15:2 LXX	104, 134
15:2-5	50
15:2-4 LXX	107
15:2-4	49
15:2-3 LXX	106–8
15:2-3	53, 236
15:3	49
15:3 LXX	104
15:4	50
15:5 LXX	104
15:6	50
15:7-8	49, 50
15:8	61
15:8 LXX	104
15:10-11 LXX	104
15:13	57
15:13 LXX	112
15:13-14	50
15:14	49
15:16	50
15:17 LXX	104
15:18	49, 51
15:18 LXX	105
15:18-21	50
16	50, 54, 60, 74, 80, 81, 208
16 LXX	94, 97, 105, 118, 123, 124, 132, 136, 244
16:1	51, 54
16:1 LXX	103–6, 112, 113
16:1-16 LXX	93, 104
16:1-16	34, 51, 227
16:1-15	85
16:1-6 LXX	135
16:1-6	46, 84, 86, 236
16:1-3 LXX	113, 114
16:1-2 LXX	113
16:1-2	236
16:2	52–4, 57, 73, 78, 207
16:2 LXX	90, 101, 106–9, 112, 113, 116, 118, 130, 135
16:2-4 LXX	113
16:2-3	52
16:3	47, 54, 55, 74
16:3 LXX	109, 110, 112, 113, 135
16:3-4	56
16:4	45, 55
16:4 LXX	112–14
16:4-6	86
16:4-5	42, 55, 78
16:5	52, 55–8, 69
16:5 LXX	110–14
16:5-6 LXX	112, 114
16:5-6	60, 65
16:6	52, 53, 57, 58, 70, 71, 81, 83
16:6 LXX	111, 112, 114, 115
16:7-9 LXX	114
16:7	58
16:8	58
16:8 LXX	114, 115
16:9	52, 58, 68, 85
16:9 LXX	111, 114
16:10	58
16:13-14	58
16:13	61
16:15	60
16:15	92
16:15 LXX	91, 92
16:15-16 LXX	116
16:15-16	86
16:16	47, 74, 81
16:16 LXX	116, 118
17	60, 65, 70, 208

17 LXX	116, 118, 125	18 LXX	118, 132, 242	18:13-15 LXX	121
17:1	47, 61, 63, 81	18:1	63, 64, 66, 70, 237	18:13-14	65, 67, 70
				18:14-15 LXX	122
17:1 LXX	116, 118	18:1 LXX	120, 121	18:14	65, 67, 77
17:1-27 LXX	116	18:1-16	64, 163	18:15	65, 67, 68, 78, 163
17:1-27	60	18:1-15 LXX	93, 117, 135	18:15 LXX	118, 123, 135
17:2 LXX	116				
17:3	61	18:1-15	34, 63, 84	18:16–19:38	71
17:4-15 LXX	116	18:1-8	71	18:16-33	71, 245
17:5	38, 61, 236	18:1-2 LXX	118	18:16-17	68
17:5 LXX	116	18:1-2	63	18:22-33	81
17:6	61	18:2	163	18:22	163
17:6 LXX	116	18:2 LXX	120	18:25	81
17:7	61	18:2-8	63, 163	19	47
17:7 LXX	116	18:3	71	19:1-29	71
17:8	61, 84	18:5	65, 163	19:1-11	40
17:10-14	61	18:6	48, 64, 70, 163	19:1-3	71
17:14	61			19:1	163
17:15	7, 35, 62, 236	18:6 LXX	118, 135	19:3	79
		18:6-7	71	19:4-11	58
17:15 LXX	94	18:7	65	19:5	58
17:15-22	84, 85	18:7 LXX	118	19:8	57, 71
17:15-21 LXX	88, 107, 135	18:8	65	19:8 LXX	111
		18:8 LXX	118, 135	19:9 LXX	112
17:16	32, 61, 62, 64, 65	18:9-15	85	19:14	80
		18:9-14	163	19:19	71
17:16 LXX	116, 117	18:9-10 LXX	118, 119	19:22	71
17:16-21	86	18:9	65, 66, 163	19:30-38	71, 79
17:17	47, 61, 70, 78, 81, 221, 236	18:10	64–7, 70, 77, 237	20	44, 45, 74, 178, 179
		18:10 LXX	118–20, 125	20 LXX	90, 126, 136
17:17 LXX	120, 123, 135				
		18:11	66	20:1	72
17:17-18 LXX	116	18:11 LXX	119	20:1 LXX	126
17:18-21	86	18:11-12	70	20:1-18 LXX	93, 125, 135
17:18	61, 81	18:12	10, 13, 53, 66, 69, 70, 78, 163, 236		
17:19	62, 64, 65, 68			20:1-18	7, 34, 71, 85
17:19 LXX	116, 117, 119			20:2	75
		18:12 LXX	90, 118–21, 130, 135	20:2 LXX	123, 124, 126
17:21	62, 64, 65, 67				
				20:2-3	72
17:21 LXX	119	18:12-15	220	20:3	72, 75, 178
17:24 LXX	118	18:13	67–9, 78	20:3 LXX	90
18	8, 69, 212	18:13 LXX	119, 122, 135	20:3-10	73
				20:3-7	85

Genesis (cont.)

20:4	178	21:8	79	23:9	84		
20:5	73, 74	21:8 LXX	131	23:11 LXX	133		
20:5 LXX	126	21:8-21	85	23:13 LXX	133		
20:5-6	73	21:8-14 LXX	136	23:15 LXX	133		
20:6 LXX	126	21:8-14	85	23:18 LXX	134		
20:7	75	21:8-10	86	23:19	84		
20:9-10 LXX	127	21:9	79, 80	23:19 LXX	134		
20:9-10	75	21:9 LXX	131	23:20	84		
20:9	73	21:9-10 LXX	131	23:20 LXX	134		
20:11-13	75	21:9-10	86	24:36	34		
20:11	43, 75	21:10	53, 55, 69, 80, 83, 227	24:67	87, 229		
20:12	8, 74, 75, 151, 217	21:10 LXX	107, 113, 131	24:67 LXX	138		
				25:7-18	85		
20:12 LXX	126	21:10-12 LXX	133	25:7-10 LXX	138		
20:13	75, 76, 151	21:11	80	25:10	34		
20:14	73, 75	21:11 LXX	133	25:12	34		
20:14 LXX	127	21:11-12	80	25:20 LXX	138		
20:14-18	73, 85	21:12	68, 80	26:1-16	7		
20:14-16	49	21:12 LXX	107	26:7 LXX	124		
20:16	73, 78	21:14	81, 83	26:8 LXX	131		
20:16 LXX	126, 127, 136	21:14 LXX	133	27:11	27		
		21:22-34	83	30:3 LXX	110		
20:17-18	73, 76	21:31-34	83	31:18 LXX	100		
20:18	43, 75, 76	22	82, 87	34:2	57		
20:18 LXX	108	22 LXX	138	34:2 LXX	111, 112		
20:18-19	75	22:1-19	83	34:25-26	56		
21 LXX	242	22:2-3	81	34:31 LXX	111		
21:1-14 LXX	93, 129	22:10	231	36:6 LXX	100		
21:1-14	34, 76, 85	22:19	83	37:35 LXX	138		
21:1-10 LXX	136	22:20-23	36	38:12 LXX	138		
21:1-2 LXX	129	23 LXX	133	41:1	178		
21:1-2	77, 81, 86	23:1–25:18	82	41:8	177		
21:1	77	23:1-20 LXX	133, 136	41:25-36	177		
21:2 LXX	130	23:1-20	82, 85, 86	42:1-2	145		
21:4	81, 221	23:1	81	44:2 LXX	127		
21:5	47, 74, 81	23:2	83	49:5	56		
21:6	42, 53, 67, 77, 78, 80, 81, 86	23:2 LXX	133	49:31	34		
		23:3	83				
		23:3 LXX	133	*Exodus*			
21:6	221	23:4	83, 84	1:11-12	57		
21:6 LXX	130, 136	23:4 LXX	133	1:11 LXX	112		
21:6-7 LXX	130, 136	23:4-20	49	1:16 LXX	100		
21:6-7	86	23:6	84, 233	7:11	177		
21:7	78	23:6 LXX	133	9:11	177		
21:7 LXX	90, 130	23:8 LXX	133	12:35-36	145		
21:7-8	77	23:8-9	84	22:21-22	57		
				34:20 LXX	127		

Index of References

Leviticus
27 LXX	127

Numbers
22:33 LXX	100

Deuteronomy
8:4	67
21:14 LXX	111
22:24 LXX	111
22:29 LXX	111
29:4	67

Joshua
9:4-5	67
9:13	67

Judges
9:8-15	149
19:4 LXX	112
19:24 LXX	111
19:24	57, 112
20:5 LXX	111
20:5	57

1 Samuel
17:14	27
17:33	27
17:42	27
25:36	79

2 Samuel
13:12	57
13:12 LXX	111, 112
13:14	57
13:14 LXX	111
13:22	57
13:22 LXX	111
13:32	57
13:32 LXX	111

Ezra
9:3	28

Nehemiah
9:21	67

Esther
7:2	79

Job
1:1	27
1:4-5	79
13:28	67
17:6 LXX	130

Psalms
2:10-12	175
68:6-7	175
92:13	148
102:27	67

Proverbs
11:22	169
26:13-18	169
26:14	169
31	168, 169
31:13	168
31:19	168
31:26	169
31:29	170
31:30	169
31:31	168

Song of Songs
4:2-3	168
4:3	168
5:15	149
7:8-9	149
7:9	149

Isaiah
3:17 LXX	112
5:12	79
5:23 LXX	100
50:9	67
51:1	34
51:2	34
51:3	34
51:6	67
65:23 LXX	110

Jeremiah
12:2 LXX	110
20:7 LXX	130
36:6 LXX	110
38:8 LXX	110
51:34	56
51:39	79

Lamentations
2:5	112
5:11	57, 112

Ezekiel
22:10-11 LXX	112

Daniel
2	177
4	177
4:10-15	149
5:7-8	177

Amos
2:6 LXX	100
2:6	44

NEW TESTAMENT

Matthew
19:29	100

Mark
10:29-30	100

Luke
18:29-30	100

Romans
4:19	6
9:9	6

Galatians
4:21–5:1	6

Hebrews
11:11	6

1 Peter
3:6	6

Apocrypha

Tobit
12:19	210

Ecclesiasticus
26:22	111

2 Maccabees
7:1	206
7:13	206
7:15	206
7:42	205

Pseudepigrapha

Jubilees
12:9	191
13:10-15	191
13:11	179
13:16	179
14:2	106
14:21	50
16:10-11	191

Testament of Abraham
2 Recen. A	106
4 Recen. A	210
12 Recen. B	5

Dead Sea Scrolls

Genesis Apocryphon
6.4	167
6.6	167
7	146
12	146
12.12	156
13.9	181
14–15	146
14	148
14.9	146, 148
14.11	148
14.14	148
14.27	148
15.20	146
18	143
19–20	141
19	141, 142, 159, 163, 164, 168, 171
19.7-10	142
19.7	143, 157, 159, 162, 182
19.8	143
19.9	143
19.10-13	144
19.10	144, 171
19.12-13	153, 157, 176, 182
19.12	145
19.13	144, 145
19.14–20.11	182
19.14-23	142, 145, 183
19.14-21	145, 147, 157
19.14-17	155, 183
19.14-15	149
19.14	143, 144, 146, 147
19.15	147, 148, 150, 151, 159, 173
19.16	147, 150, 159, 162, 176, 183
19.17-18	147, 153, 176
19.17	142–4, 148, 151, 157, 182
19.18-19	148
19.18	153, 154, 156, 158, 159, 162, 167, 171, 174, 176, 182, 183
19.19-23	158
19.19-20	151, 154
19.19	147, 148, 154, 155
19.20-21	159
19.20	144, 150, 155, 156, 171, 172, 183
19.21	150, 155–7, 159, 171, 174, 183, 184
19.22	156
19.23-31	142, 159
19.23-24	183
19.23	142, 147, 156, 159–61, 163, 165, 171, 174, 176, 183
19.24-29	182
19.24-26	150
19.24-25	160, 161, 167, 171, 182, 183
19.24	157, 163, 167
19.25	143, 161, 162
19.26	161
19.27	161
19.28-30	162
19.29	161, 162, 168, 171, 176
19.30	161
19.31	142
20	28
20.2-8	11, 99, 142, 147, 149, 152, 160, 161, 164, 168, 169, 172, 183
20.2-7	165
20.2	164
20.3-4	165
20.3	164, 165
20.4-5	166

20.4	164, 165	20.18-19	177	22.18	141
20.5	164, 165	20.18	153, 177	22.33-34	182
20.6-7	170	20.19-22	160		
20.6	164, 165	20.19-20	177	*3Q14*	
20.7-8	166, 176	20.20	177	fr. 8	141
20.7	161, 163–7, 170–2, 183	20.21-23	178		
		20.21-22	153	*11Q10*	
		20.22-23	179, 180, 184	VI, 7	162
20.8-11	151, 171			XXII, 2	162
20.8-9	155, 170, 172, 184	20.22	147, 178	XXX, 8	162
		20.23	151, 180		
20.8	163, 172	20.24–21.4	179	MISHNAH	
20.9-11	155	20.25-26	180	*Nedarim*	
20.9-10	142, 182–4	20.25	151, 180	3.11	61
20.9	147, 150, 162, 164, 171, 172, 184	20.26-28	151		
		20.26-27	150, 178, 179, 183	BABYLONIAN TALMUD	
				Ḥullin	
		20.26	162	67b	181
20.10-12	183	20.27-32	155, 176, 184		
20.10-11	143, 159, 171			*Megillah*	
		20.27-28	180	14a	163, 202
20.10	147, 150, 172, 173, 175, 176, 178, 184	20.27	151, 180		
		20.28-29	177, 180	*Pesaḥim*	
		20.29-32	183	28a	166
		20.29	183		
20.11	142, 145, 172–4	20.30-31	180	MIDRASH	
		20.30	153, 173, 180, 182	*Genesis Rabbah*	
20.12-16	142, 173, 174, 182			40.5	156
		20.31-32	176	41.1	148, 149
20.12	159, 162, 174, 175	20.31	180, 181	41.2	43
		20.32-33	160	45.2	202
20.13-15	184	20.32	180, 182		
20.13-14	175	20.33–21.4	143	*Exodus Rabbah*	
20.13	175, 177	20.33	142, 143, 181	1.1	163
20.14-15	151, 175				
20.14	147, 172–5	21.1	143	Philo	
20.15-16	177	21.2	143	*On Abraham*	
20.15	170, 175, 177, 180	21.4	141, 144	93	170
		21.8-14	182	110-113	212
20.16-21	142, 152, 176	21.8	144	118	210
		21.10	144		
20.16	159, 174, 177, 183	21.12	144	Josephus	
		21.15	143	*Jewish Antiquities*	
20.17-18	151, 177, 178	21.21-22	163	1.17	188
		21.33	141	1.25	219
20.17	153, 177, 178, 184	22–32	155	1.29	219
		22.5	159	1.51	218

Josephus, *Ant.* (cont.)		1.165-168	200, 235	1.198	190, 210–
1.122-236	228	1.165	196–200,		12, 234,
1.143-147	190		210, 215,		235
1.148-256	188		217, 219,	1.199-206	211
1.148-160	188, 189		234, 235	1.199	195, 211,
1.148-150	192	1.166-168	194, 198,		220
1.148	190		236	1.202-204	203
1.149	191	1.166-167	224	1.204	203
1.151	47, 188,	1.167	195	1.207-212	188, 213,
	190, 192,	1.169-182	200		235
	231, 235,	1.169-170	200, 203	1.207-211	238
	238	1.169	199, 200,	1.207-208	200, 214,
1.152	191–3, 197		203		216, 218
1.153	191	1.176	201	1.207	199, 204,
1.154-160	188, 192	1.178	203		213–16,
1.154-157	189	1.179	200, 201		218, 225,
1.154-156	192, 195	1.183-185	201		231, 235,
1.154	47, 190–4,	1.183	201		236
	196, 197,	1.186-190	188, 201,	1.208	214, 216
	199, 202,		227	1.209	215–17
	203, 206,	1.186	202, 206,	1.210	214
	215, 224,		227	1.211	199, 218,
	235, 236,	1.187-188	238		220, 235
	238	1.187	163, 202–	1.212	218
1.157	192–5		4, 206–8,	1.213-221	188, 219
1.159	193		226, 235,	1.213-217	234, 235
1.160	213		236, 238	1.213-214	226
1.161-168	188, 193	1.188-190	203	1.213	211, 220,
1.161	194, 199,	1.188	203–7,		221, 232
	214		222, 223,	1.214	221
1.162-164	218		226, 227,	1.215-221	203
1.162-163	200		238	1.215-219	230
1.162	193, 194,	1.189	205	1.215-217	231
	197, 198,	1.191-193	206	1.215-216	238
	204, 214–	1.191	208, 209,	1.215	82, 203–7,
	16, 218,		220, 238		222, 223,
	224, 225,	1.192	209, 219		227, 236,
	231, 235,	1.193	223		238
	236	1.194-206	188, 209	1.216-217	224, 236
1.163-164	196, 200,	1.194-196	210	1.216	223, 224,
	214	1.194-195	211		226, 227
1.163	195–200,	1.194	210	1.217-218	225
	214, 238	1.196	209, 211	1.217	226, 227,
1.164-165	197	1.197-198	198, 220		229
1.164	192, 197–	1.197	209–11,	1.218	223
	9, 214		220	1.219	226

1.222-236	188, 230	10.218	188	Euripides	
1.222	229, 231,	10.222-223	225	*Helen*	
	234, 236	12.255-256	205	1145-46	110
1.223-224	230	13.4	205		
1.223	231	13.232-233	205	Herodotus	
1.225	230, 231,	15.71	205	*Histories*	
	234, 235	15.289	205	1.30	233
1.227	229, 232	16.389	205	2.181	111
1.228-231	231			7.168	99
1.232	231	*Jewish War*			
1.233	231, 232	2.246	205	Menander	
1.236	229, 232,	5.376-419	189	*Georgos*	
	234	5.379-381	188	29–30	112
1.237	188, 229,	5.379	188		
	232, 233,	5.381	188	Plato	
	235, 238			*Apology*	
1.255	224	CLASSICAL AND ANCIENT		25a	127
1.256	188, 197,	CHRISTIAN LITERATURE			
	225, 232,	Aristophanes		Soranus	
	233, 237,	*Lysistrata*		*Gynecology*	
	238	1162-74	110	1.16-18	110
1.277	225	1169-70	110	1.16	110
1.281	192, 193				
1.337	216	Aristotle		Strabo	
2.41	195	*Poetics*		*Geography*	
2.157	213	6 §§1450a–b	16	10.2	110
2.231	195				
4.198	219	Demosthenes		Thucydides	
4.251-252	216	*Against Neaera*		*Histories*	
5.283-284	210	59.67	111	1.12	224
7.52	205				
7.161	205	Diodorus Siculus		Xenophon	
7.168-172	216	*Bibliotheca Historica*		*Symposium*	
10.115	205	1.73	110	9.2	131

Index of Authors

Abegg, M. G., Jr. 150
Alter, R. 14, 16, 17, 25, 47, 56, 78, 80
Amit, Y. 17
Arnold, E. M. 59
Attridge, H. W. 196
Avigad, N. 141, 156, 160, 163, 166, 172

Bach, A. 3, 26, 29
Bailey, J. L. 11, 186, 187, 205, 208, 212, 220, 223, 234, 239
Bal, M. 3
Bar-Efrat, S. 17, 27, 28
Becker, M. 154, 158
Begg, C. T. 21, 186, 234
Bellis, A. O. 1
Bergren, T. A. 2
Berlin, A. 17, 27, 29, 30, 137
Bernstein, M. J. 4, 10, 140, 145, 151, 161, 177, 178, 248
Beyer, K. 141, 143, 145, 156, 160, 166
Bing, P. 149
Bird, P. 2
Brayford, S. A. 9, 10, 13, 90–2, 95, 100, 106, 114, 115, 119, 121, 122
Brenton, L. C. L. 127, 128
Brock, S. P. 11, 153, 156, 157, 163
Brooke, G. J. 248

Campbell, J. G. 1
Chatman, S. 14–16, 24, 27, 30, 34, 47, 168
Choi, J. H. 154
Cohen, S. J. D. 11, 165, 168–70
Conway, C. M. 29
Conybeare, C. 78
Cook, J. E. 2
Cotter, D. W. 30, 58
Crawford, S. W. 21, 139, 144, 150, 174, 178, 181

Daniel, A. G. 173
Darr, J. A. 20, 23
Day, L. 2
DiTommasso, L. 2
Dijk-Hemmes, F. van 7, 33, 43–5, 103
Dines, J. M. 89, 90
Driver, G. R. 38

Ego, B. 154, 174
Eichler, B. L. 13
Eshel, E. 148, 150
Exum, J. C. 7

Falk, D. K. 140, 144, 146, 156, 160, 181
Feldman, L. H. 3, 12, 186, 187, 189, 192, 195, 196, 200, 202, 208, 211, 215, 217, 219, 221–4, 226, 228, 229, 232, 233, 237
Fewell, D. N. 19, 20, 26, 27, 29, 44, 49, 54, 64, 72
Fischer, I. 8, 12, 32, 77, 84
Fitzmyer, J. A. 21, 141, 147-50, 156, 160–2, 165, 166, 172, 173, 177–9, 181
Fokkelman, J. P. 20
Fox, E. 79
Franxman, T. W. 192, 193, 196, 197, 202, 210–12, 217, 220, 221, 226, 229, 232
Fuchs, E. 8, 33

Garcia Martinez, F. 172
Gevirtz, M. L. 148-50, 154, 158
Ginzberg, L. 5, 202
Greenfield, J. C. 161, 166
Gunn, D. M. 19, 20, 26, 27, 29, 44, 49, 64, 72

Halpern-Amaru, B. 5, 6, 11, 186, 187, 234, 235, 237
Harl, M. 122

Index of Authors

Hartog, P. B. 248
Harvey, W. J. 14, 29, 46
Hassan, R. 5
Hens-Piazza, G. 3, 63–5
Henten, J. W. van 248
Herman, D. 23
Hochman, B. 14, 15, 17, 24, 25, 29, 30, 47
Holladay, C. R. 196
Hopkins, S. 11, 153, 156, 157, 163
Höschele, R. 149
Humphreys, W. L. 20

Iser, W. 18, 19, 30, 31

Jacobs, M. R. 29, 54, 74, 87
James, E. 13
James, H. 16
Japhet, S. 165, 168
Jastrow, M. 172, 173, 181
Jeansonne, S. P. 8, 42, 60, 75, 77, 84
Johnson, B. J. M. 249
Jongeling, B. 154, 173
Joosten, J. 13
Jurgens, B. A. 157

Kadari, T. 170
Kalimi, I. 231
Keshet, S. 44, 72
Kirsch, J. 79
Koenig, S. M. 2, 29, 34
Koskenniemi, E. 4
Kugel, J. L. 3

Labuschange, C. J. 154, 173
Lans, B. van der 186, 224–6, 237
Lee, J. A. L. 91, 96, 111, 114
Lee, P. Y. 165–7
Lefkovitz, L. H. 8, 66
Lindqvist, P. 4
Livneh, A. 6, 246

Machiela, D. A. 141, 143, 145, 148, 149, 156, 160, 162, 163, 166, 172, 173
Marcus, R. 206
McDonald, J. 6, 249
McKay, H. A. 186, 204, 205
McNeece, C. A. 59
Miller, L. 1

Miller, T. A. 186
Mitchell, S. 65
Mudrick, M. 14
Muraoka, T. 147, 151, 166–70, 173, 175, 177

Najman, H. 168
Neusner, J. 61
Nickelsburg, G. W. E. 11, 140, 152
Niditch, S. 42
Niehoff, M. 5, 6, 11, 13, 186, 187, 234, 246
Niese, B. 189
Nodet, E. 21, 192
Noth, M. 33, 246

Osswald, E. 149, 166

Perrin, A. B. 150
Perry, M. 30
Phillips, E. A. 13
Popović, M. 169

Rad, G. von 78, 79
Rahlfs, A. 93
Reed, S. A. 152
Reinhartz, A. 13, 186
Reis, P. T. 79
Rengstorf, K. H. 203, 204, 206
Rensburg, J. F. van 11, 163, 165, 168, 169
Rimmon-Kenan, S. 14–16, 18, 23–5, 27, 30, 31, 86, 152, 189
Roncace, M. 12
Rosenthal, F. 166
Rothkoff, A. 163

Schiffman, L. H. 3
Schneider, T. J. 8, 9, 32, 35, 44, 46, 54, 55, 57, 62, 66, 68, 77, 82, 83, 87
Schofield, A. 248
Scholz, S. 7, 54, 57, 58
Schorch, S. 89, 90
Schuller, E. 11
Segal, M. 145
Shectman, S. 62
Shinan, A. 13, 99, 163, 169, 177
Sly, D. 6
Soden, W. von 166

Sokoloff, M. 164, 165, 172, 173, 175, 177
Speiser, E. A. 56, 79
Sternberg, M. 25
Stewart, J. C. 59
Stone, M. E. 2

Tervanotko, H. 2, 21, 120
Teubal, S. J. 8, 36, 77
Thackeray, H. St. J. 189, 206, 210, 218, 219, 221
Thomas, S. I. 248
Tov, E. 21
Trible, P. 2, 7, 33, 44, 51, 54, 58, 73, 80, 229

Vander Stichele, C. 22
VanderKam, J. C. 165–7
Vermès, G. 2, 10, 170, 172, 174, 177, 178
Visotzky, B. L. 53

Walfish, M.-S. 13, 186
Wallace, H. 41
Weems, R. J. 7, 33, 58
Wegner, J. R. 6
Weissman, G. 23
Wénin, A. 42, 52
Wevers, J. W. 21, 91–3, 106, 109, 112, 113, 116, 117, 120, 122, 124, 127, 131, 138
Whiston, W. 189
Wilson, R. 14
Wise, M. O. 150
Woude, A. S. van der 154, 173

Yadin, Y. 141, 156, 160, 163, 166, 172

Zakovitch, Y. 13, 99, 145, 163, 169, 177
Zierler, W. 7, 229
Zucker, D. J. 5

www.ingramcontent.com/pod-product-compliance
Lightning Source LLC
Chambersburg PA
CBHW070021010526
44117CB00011B/1659